Does Time Heal All?

Exploring Mental Health in the First 3 Years

Miri Keren, Doreet Hopp, and Sam Tyano

Translated by Lahad Lazar

ZERO TO THREE
Early connections last a lifetime

Washington, DC

Published by

ZERO TO THREE
1255 23rd St., NW., Ste. 350
Washington, DC 20037
(202) 638-1144
Toll-free orders (800) 899-4301
Fax: (202) 638-0851
Web: http://www.zerotothree.org

These materials are intended for education and training to help promote a high standard of care by professionals. Use of these materials is voluntary and their use does not confer any professional credentials or qualification to take any registration, certification, board or licensure examination, and neither confers nor infers competency to perform any related professional functions.

None of the information provided is intended as medical or other professional advice for individual conditions or treatment nor does it replace the need for services provided by medical or other professionals, or independent determinations, made by professionals in individual situations.

The user of these materials is solely responsible for compliance with all local, state or federal rules, regulations or licensing requirements. Despite efforts to ensure that these materials are consistent with acceptable practices, they are not intended to be used as a compliance guide and are not intended to supplant or to be used as a substitute for or in contravention of any applicable local, state or federal rules, regulations or licensing requirements. ZERO TO THREE expressly disclaims any liability arising from use of these materials.

The views expressed in these materials represent the opinions of the respective authors. Publication of these materials does not constitute an endorsement by ZERO TO THREE of any view expressed herein, and ZERO TO THREE expressly disclaims any liability arising from any inaccuracy or misstatement.

References to other third party material and links to other websites does not mean that ZERO TO THREE endorses the materials or linked websites and, ZERO TO THREE is not responsible for any content that appears in these materials or on these linked websites.

Care has been taken to protect individual privacy. Names, descriptions and other biographical facts may have been changed to protect individual privacy.

Originally published 2013 by Modan Publishing House, Ben Shemen (Israel). Translated and published with permission. Additional reprint permissions appear on pp. 367–368.

Copyedited by Tyler Krupa

Cover and text design by K Art and Design, Inc.

CIP Data on file.

Printed in the United States of America

10 9 8 7 6 5 4 3 2 1

Suggested citation:
Keren, M., Hopp, D., & Tyano, S. (2017). *Does time heal all?: Exploring mental health in the first 3 years* (L. Lazar, Trans.). Washington, DC: ZERO TO THREE.

This book is dedicated
to the babies we were...
and the babies to come...

TABLE OF CONTENTS

FOREWORD

Professor Yoram Yovell

What does a baby experience, what does she want? Can mental issues exist in infancy? If so, what is their nature, what causes them, and how can they be treated? These questions, which lie at the heart of the present book, *Does Time Heal All?*, have gained tremendous importance in recent years. Why? Maybe because these past years have seen a revolution take place in two disciplines related to the infant's mental world.

First, neurobiology started taking an interest in the development processes occurring in the human brain from Day 1. It has shown the decisive influence of the environment—that is, those adults closest to the baby, and the quality of the baby's relations with them—on biological processes of brain maturation and the child's development. It is a two-way, dynamic interplay: Even biologically rooted developmental problems will manifest themselves within the delicate and complex fabric of relationships taking shape between the infant and the significant adults in his life.

Second, a concurrent research thrust has been underway in recent years to observe the kind of bond formed between the baby and her caregivers using objective scientific tools. These observations revalidate certain psychoanalytic theories pertaining to the baby–parent relationship while contradicting others and, more important, laying the factual groundwork necessary for the formulation of new, more accurate theories.

Miri Keren, Doreet Hopp, and Sam Tyano have undertaken a much-needed yet difficult task: to make the new knowledge on the mental world of infants and the problems that might arise within it readily and reliably accessible to the public at large. Their success has made *Does Time Heal All?* a ground-breaking book. Mental health practitioners will find this book fascinating and enriching, as will parents, educators, scientists, and—for that matter—anyone interested in the psyche and well-being of infants.

Professor Yoram Yovell, MD-PhD, is a psychiatrist, psychoanalyst, and brain researcher. He heads the Institute for the Study of Affective Neuroscience (ISAN) at the University of Haifa, Israel.

INTRODUCTION

Miri Keren, Doreet Hopp, and Sam Tyano

Writing about psychiatry, and more so infant psychiatry, is a challenge. Psychiatry is a branch of medicine that suffers from harsh social stigma. Despite the scientific and clinical knowledge built up on the subject and the establishment in Israel (the authors' country of origin) of seven infant and toddler mental health clinics between 1996 and 2005, the notion that a baby might develop symptoms of psychological distress and that these can be diagnosed and treated is still not sufficiently widespread among practitioners in Israel, and even less so among the general public. In this book, we seek to describe affective and behavioral disorders typical of infancy (from birth to 3 years old). We believe that, as with any other disease, these symptoms should also be treated early, and the sooner the better.

This book seeks to refute the view that babies are dependent, immature creatures devoid of any understanding—to debunk the idea that any abnormal behavior they exhibit will surely "pass with time." We believe that failure to attempt diagnosis and immediate treatment of such abnormal behaviors is a mistake. Why? Because, with time, problems might become exacerbated, often translating into more complex, lengthier treatment down the line. We believe in the importance of early intervention to treat abnormal behaviors in infancy while the brain is still flexible and malleable.

The understanding of pathological conditions in general, and in infants in particular, largely depends on the conceptualization of normative development. The multifactorial model underlying our current work, which we propose adopting in this book, is predicated on the new theories of Antonio Damasio and Nobel medicine laureate Eric Kandel, who have shown the extent to which the biological, emotional, and environmental factors are intertwined. This intricacy calls for adopting more complex thinking during diagnosis and treatment. The transactional model, developed by Sameroff and Chandler (1975), determines that the child's affective–cognitive–social state depends on the interplay between genetic, biological, psychological, and cultural variables present in both the child and her immediate environment. These variables generate parallel forces that map out the infant's course of development. Every event that a person experiences throughout his life can change his development path—all the more so with traumatic occurrences (e.g., war, violence, loss, and family crises). People can never know how their lives will unfold and what hurdles they will encounter down the road. When assessing an infant's mental health, clinicians must therefore take into account resilience variables as well as vulnerability variables. It is these variables that will determine the baby's present and future functioning levels as well as her ability to adapt to new situations and cope with unexpected stressful ones. Will it be like wheat, bowing in strong winds only to stand upright again after the storm has subsided? Will it be flexible enough to survive, or rather snap? We base our work on the knowledge—supported by ample studies—that the infant feels and assimilates all of his experiences, both good and bad. Symptoms that appear in infancy always signal distress, and distress is always accompanied by pain; the accumulation of pain can leave a scar. It is best to address the distress and the pain as soon as they emerge.

This book is intended for all those interested in the infant's psychological development, whether normative or abnormal; for all those wishing to learn how to diagnose disorders that might appear as early as the first year of life; and, particularly, for all parents who rightly want to be able to trace the thin line between normative behavior, even if extreme at times, and abnormal behavior caused by some psychological disorder requiring therapeutic intervention.

We have tried to cover the majority of disorders recorded in infants during their first 3 years of life, to describe how these disorders manifest themselves, and to suggest the most effective treatment methods. However, one must bear in mind that the knowledge is constantly changing, with more and more studies on the questions we discuss coming out all the time.

The structure of this book was the object of much deliberation. We asked ourselves how to provide readers with scientific, clinical, and therapeutic knowledge in sufficiently clear terms and in such a way as to serve the purpose for which the book was written; we also wanted to describe abnormal behaviors that we believe should be dealt with as soon as possible. We decided to weave clinical examples taken from our clinical work into each of the chapters. The case and treatment descriptions are wholly reliable, with the exception of details that compromise confidentiality. Also, to keep the chapters light, we chose to condense the basic knowledge in infant psychiatry into the first three chapters. These chapters serve as a kind of guide for those of you who are not clinicians, to help you understand the professional jargon and the up-to-date theoretical background that we build on in each chapter.

We have tried to share our knowledge with you and, more particularly, the experiences we have as clinicians and researchers when talking to babies and eliciting responses from them. Yes, even babies respond, and theirs are often more straightforward reactions than those of adults. Alongside the theoretical knowledge and case studies, we chose to have each chapter include a poem or a children's story bearing on its subject. The reason for choosing to integrate these into the book was that they express something that everyone carries inside. It is that thing we call the "inner baby," the one that reawakens when people become parents themselves. Furthermore, we thought it was important to show that many abnormal behaviors are not so rare and that a lot could be learned about them from the manner in which writers describe them, in poetic, experiential terms that both children and parents can understand, using special language that helps them sense that they are not the only ones to feel pain, sadness, or fear.

Literary texts verbalize vague and nagging sensations, indirectly and subtly articulate nameless problems, and thus reassure the readers, allowing them to let go of their internal tensions. The painful explicit or implied contents in the text allow every child to respond to them to the extent of her emotional capacity. The encounter of parents and infants with a literary text opens up an introspective space through identification with others—the protagonist of the poem or story—and allows the infant to meet with his authentic self. We hope that these literary texts will help parents find new ways to deal with the issues troubling them.

In our search for texts that could illuminate the issues with which this book is concerned, we have found that children's literature steers clear of many problems, such as autism, posttraumatic reactions, and parental mental disorders. We have found that although numerous books touch on one facet or another of serious disorders, no work of fiction, as opposed to didactic literature, approaches them as a whole. We have noticed that even when stories and poems relate emotional difficulties, these are mostly transient situations that invariably turn out well. The "happy ending" is one of the stronger conventions in children's literature. The promise that any difficulty will be resolved, and that every struggle—as hard and wearisome as it might be—will bear fruit, lies at the core of this literature. The "narrative envelope" is supposed to deliver the expected relief: "And they lived happily ever after." Safe in the knowledge that "all's well that ends well," even if it takes a while, and expecting the suffering to end and happiness to take its place, the child listening to the story is able to sit through the pain involved in the process itself. The mature understanding that not all obstacles are surmountable, and that we must learn to live with certain difficulties, is reserved for the more grown-up readers.

This book is not a guide or an ordinary textbook, and it lists only the most important and most recent scientific sources on which it rests. This is the story of babies and infants trying to express their distress through various symptoms. Hence, the chapters are titled as if they were spoken on behalf of the small child.

Note from the translator: All literary excerpts in this book have been rendered by the translator, unless otherwise mentioned.

References

Sameroff, A. J., & Chandler, M. J. (1975). Reproductive risk and the continuum of caretaking casualty. In E. D. Horowitz, H. Hetherington, S. Scarr-Salapatek, & G. Siegel (Eds.), *Review of child development research* (Vol. 4, pp. 187–244). Chicago, IL: University of Chicago Press.

CHAPTER 1
Speaking the Baby

"A couple wants to bring forth a child." This would once have been a classic opening line for a book on the world of babies. Today, many roads lead to parenthood, each different in terms of its impact on the baby's development. Any would-be parent expects to fulfill some desire. From a very young age, individuals play "mother and father," stuffing a pillow under a dress to look pregnant, like mom. From a very young age, people know their place in the family hierarchy and prepare themselves for the role of parent, usually by imitation. When two people making up a couple wish to become parents, two desires, two expectations, and two imaginations intermix to form a basis for a third person. The conjugal relationship turns triangular; the dyad becomes a triad. A single-parent family is a different story. Here, one person's desire ends up producing a dyad. The present book shows the extent to which these early processes shape infant development.

During the 9 months of pregnancy, a new being progressively forms and evolves. The sooner parents come to recognize this being's existence and give this being its due place, the better they will understand the secrets of this being's development. Parents each begin their dialogue with the fetus at a different stage of the pregnancy. The fetus is nourished by the substances received through the umbilical cord, but not exclusively. The fetus also feeds on the parents' desires, which likewise influence the development of the fetus.

The interaction among biological, psychological, and social factors can already be seen to influence the baby's development in the fetal stage: Every cell added to the mix contains the genetic matter of both parents. Their desires, as well as the mother's experiences during pregnancy, influence the fetus and fuse with the genetic heritage of the fetus; this complex interplay of factors will determine the child's development from birth onward.

The baby emerges into the world loaded with her experiences from the womb. From this moment on, she is subject to the rules of the society into which she was born. Upon birth, the baby is given a name, which serves as her entry card into human society. This name—rooted in her parents' fantasies, experiences, hopes, and passions—will accompany the child throughout life.

Since the publication of Damasio's (1994) *Descartes's Error*, the Cartesian distinction between body and soul prevalent for 400 years prior is no longer accepted. Today, it is known that every emotional experience is expressed physically, in the body and especially in the brain, just like any bodily occurrence is accompanied by an emotional component. This synthesis persists throughout life. The baby, for his part, will develop a relationship with each of the many adult figures surrounding him from birth. He will experience these relationships in both body and soul.

Only in the last 4 decades have health professionals started to understand the emotional needs of infants and toddlers and the connection between their emotional universe and their development; thus, the existence of emotional disorders appearing as early as the first 3 years of life has only started to gain recognition in the past 40 years. This lateness, not necessarily accidental, might reflect the change that has taken place—throughout history and across different cultures—in society's view of the family cell in general and babies in particular.

The Baby's Place Throughout History

Babies have seen their status change considerably throughout history. A baby's chances of survival have always depended on society's values and beliefs. Just one century ago, many healthy babies were still being left on church doorsteps for pecuniary reasons, whereas today efforts are made to save premature babies weighing as little as even 500 grams (1 pound). What has changed, then?

In the history of childhood, up until the middle of the 18th century, infant mortality was very high, and babies were considered to be transient creatures. They were perceived as full members of the family only when they reached 7 years old. This approach significantly changed in 1760. It was during that period that texts began to appear advocating the "protection" of children from infancy. These publications—among them *Emile* by Jean-Jacques Rousseau (1762)—were the first to emphasize the importance of providing moral and physical education to very young children. The authors of these publications were usually physicians, philosophers, and clerics, and their writings gradually became invaluable social assets embraced by people from all walks of life.

It was also around this period that, for the first time in history, a call was heard to train midwives and nannies and to provide guidelines for breastfeeding. For the first time ever, babies were seen as assets requiring protection and possessing social value from birth, and educational principles were established to be implemented from infancy. This was also the first time that parents stopped treating babies like adjuncts and accorded them a significant place in the family. Young children's education became important, and adults began to take them into account along with the other family members in considering the allocation of resources in the family. Parents started to match their progeny to the means available to the family. Although infant mortality did not yet drop significantly, each death was now deemed a tragedy. From this point on, the child would be perceived as having her own capacities and weaknesses, which would determine her vocational future in society. Some were apt for studies, others better suited for manual labor. Some were gifted, others were mentally disabled. Each group would be taken charge of by society's institutions according to its characteristics and needs. Notwithstanding this substantial change, however, the child's status retrograded with the advent of the industrial revolution in the 19th century. Children were seen as a source of cheap labor from a very young age.

Starting from the mid-20th century, researchers put together knowledge contributed by psychoanalysis regarding the importance of childhood experiences and knowledge gained from observations conducted by psychoanalyst René Spitz in English orphanages after World War II. This combined theoretical and practical knowledge led to the recognition that the child's personality was shaped very early on and was largely influenced by the experiences he had and the stimuli he was exposed to in childhood. The works of Anna Freud, Margaret Mahler, Melanie Klein, and Donald Winnicott also appeared during that period. Some 40 years later, possibly thanks to these publications, society's perception of children changed, and the concept of "children's rights" took shape. According to the United Nations Convention signed in 1989, the institutions of society must protect children and recognize their rights to have their physical, developmental, and emotional needs met from their time of birth. Also established on that occasion was the right of adopted children to know the identity of their biological parents when they come of age. In addition, family tribunals were set up, with a view to protect children whenever their parents do not have their best interests at heart. Society (at least, Western society) has thus taken upon itself to guarantee that children are afforded the minimal conditions for their development, be it by their parents, by members of their extended family, or by society's institutions in cases of parental incompetence. Among other things, children are entitled to assessment and guidance to allow them to make the best use of their natural aptitudes.

Nowadays, in the 21st century, the general public is exposed to a lot of information predominantly based on results of empirical studies. This information gives one the impression that a child's stages of development can be easily controlled and guided following a predefined plan. Reality is more complex than that. One should not forget the powerful, influential current that flows underneath the surface, in the social subconscious, that might be called "cultural heritage." Attempts are often made to criticize and belittle the role of this heritage in the name of new discoveries. Moreover, intergenerational transmission preserves cultural values from one generation to the next.

What Is Infant Psychiatry?

This historical review of infants' place in society helps to understand why this branch of medicine, child psychiatry, developed relatively late compared with the other medical disciplines. Pediatrics in general developed greatly during the 20th century but practically devoid of the affective component. The only psychiatric diseases recognized in the previous century were congenital ones, such as retardation and—from the 1950s—autism.

Even though awareness of babies' abilities has increased tenfold today, and people constantly read how important it is to provide babies with stimuli and to talk to them in their first years of life, babies remain insufficiently understood. Many still see them as creatures incapable of understanding or remembering and, therefore, incapable of feeling and expressing emotional distress. Although getting more attention today than before, babies are still treated as incomplete beings who will take more time to mature and turn into entities in their own right.

It is the recognition of the infant's ability to experience psychic pain that underlies infant psychiatry. This recognition gradually drove physicians to address the affective component of the symptoms that appear in babies as well, even if they appear to be exclusively somatic at first sight. Slowly, professionals started to understand the body language of infants, realizing that a baby, any baby, talks with her voice, eyes, crying, and gestures. This understanding contributed greatly to researchers' ability to tell apart normative and abnormal behaviors. In 1994, the first diagnostic classification of psychiatric disorders in infancy—the *Diagnostic Classification of Mental Health and Developmental Disorders of Infancy and Early Childhood* (DC:0–3; ZERO TO THREE, 1994)—appeared. This was later followed by the *Diagnostic Classification of Mental Health and Developmental Disorders of Infancy and Early Childhood, Revised Edition* (DC:0–3R; ZERO TO THREE, 2005). In an effort to update and expand previous versions of a nosology of infancy/early childhood disorders, the *DC:0–5*™: *Diagnostic Classification of Mental Health and Developmental Disorders of Infancy and Early Childhood* (DC:0–5; ZERO TO THREE, 2016) was released. These manuals have greatly contributed to the assimilation of this new field into child and adolescent psychiatry.

As clinical experience grew, the study of the brain greatly developed, considerably contributing in turn to the understanding of developmental processes in babies and, in particular, to the way in which these were influenced by the baby's interaction with his environment. The discovery of mirror neurons, for example (see chapter 3), has helped researchers to understand why a baby will return a smile but recoil from someone who manifests anger toward her. It also became clear that the limbic system in the brain played a key role in identifying facial expressions, in creating experiential and verbal memory, and in regulating positive and negative feelings. Izard and Malatesta's (1987) seminal studies showed that by 2 months old, a baby is able to express and recognize three basic emotions: interest, satisfaction, and distress. By the end of the first year, a baby can identify and express a range of eight human emotions—joy, anger, aversion, surprise, and sadness (in addition to the first three).

With infant psychiatry well-established as a branch of medicine, clinicians started to elaborate techniques for treating babies and their families and to test their effectiveness. Bringing the baby into the clinic was no easy task. Many claimed that guiding the parents was all that was needed. In the chapter on treating disorders in infancy (chapter 17), we show (a) how important it is to communicate verbally with the baby and to do so directly, without the parents' mediation; (b) how important it is to learn to read the baby's body language; and (c) the great value and power of words in therapy. For example, if a person speaks to a baby who is crying for boredom, pain, or distress and shows him how sensitive she is to his predicament, the baby is likely to stop crying and look at her. The baby might even smile and respond with a murmur.

The parent's inner world intertwines with the baby's. It is reflected in the way the parent communicates with the baby, and it influences the development of the latter's inner world. The baby unconsciously identifies with the content projected onto him by the parent. This process, called *projective identification*, is more commonly known as a "self-fulfilling prophecy." According to Stern (1995), a baby who develops symptoms of an emotional problem as a result of this process is called "the clinical baby." Here are a few examples of this phenomenon:

- A 2-year-old toddler exhibits severe violence toward his mother, younger brother, and peers in nursery school. His mother, as it turns out in a conversation with her, had hoped for a daughter. She believed that his kicks as a fetus were directed at her. Further still, she had expected that he would grow up to become an abusive man, like all the men she had known in her life (including the baby's father). The prophecy fulfilled itself: The baby identified, unconsciously, with the mother's negative perception, growing up to become a violent toddler rejected by those around him.

- An 18-month-old girl does not ask others for help when she experiences difficulty, not even her mother. In talking with her mother, it turns out that the mother is teaching her to be "independent" to learn how to deal with life's hardships, and that she is convinced that her daughter is "doomed" to a life just as hard as hers.

- A mother does not hear her 1-month-old baby when he cries. In talking with her, it turns out that, having experienced severe emotional deprivation in her childhood, she grew accustomed to not being seen or heard, even when crying.

Cramer and Palacio-Espasa (1993) identified three types of projections—that is, three ways in which parents project their internal images onto the actual baby—as specified in chapter 3: libidinal projections, conflictual projections, and narcissistic projections (defined as pathological). The three clinical examples provided earlier demonstrate narcissistic projections. In fact, babies who come in for treatment most commonly display symptoms of the second and third type of projection. Parent–baby therapy seeks to identify the set of projections involved but also those traits in the baby that may have triggered them (e.g., a bad temperament).

These pathological projections originate in what Fraiberg, Adelson, and Shapiro (1975) dubbed "the ghosts in the nursery." This refers to painful experiences from a parent's past, which continue to affect the way in which the parent perceives her baby in the present. Parents who practice healthy parenting are able to blot out past experiences and see their baby as she is. They allow their child to follow her own development path, even if on rare occasions, mostly hard existential or traumatic circumstances, these "ghosts" might emerge in the parents and affect their behavior toward the child. In other cases, the "ghosts" take over the relationship between parent and baby, blinding the parents to their child's true nature. These situations sometimes replicate the parents' childhood experiences, in a way, such that they end up treating their baby exactly as their parents had treated them. During therapy, the parents recall and work through these painful experiences, and this often allows them to understand their behavior and to identify with the baby rather than with the aggressive parent.

Treating the parent–child relationship helps parents recognize within them recurring patterns of interpersonal relationships that had been ingrained in the past and that continue to dictate their current behavior. These patterns have been firmly fixed in nonverbal memory, located in the right hemisphere of the brain, and have become part and parcel of the parent's personality. This part—the childlike part within people—is primarily unconscious and is what underlies their relationships with others. These traces of infancy and early childhood, present in every adult, are revived by the transition into parenthood. At the same time, the parent within adults also awakens—that is, the whole set of images pertaining to parental behavior patterns that they have internalized in their childhood. The complex interaction between these two parts—the childlike and parental components within individuals—is often related to the baby's symptoms. At times, the childlike part in the parent tries to push aside the parental side. This is very typically the case with parents who have internalized their parents in a negative way and consequently have a hard time assuming the role of educators and setting boundaries for their baby. In other cases, parents identify only with their parental side, incapable of listening to their "inner baby," and therefore they find it difficult to demonstrate empathy toward the baby. Situations also occur in which the arrival of a new baby into the family triggers one parent's internal images associated with the relationship he had with his siblings. A toddler's tantrum, for example, might remind his father how, during his own childhood, his stubborn brother was able to grab most of their parents' attention with severe tantrums; therefore, the father may react to his own child's tantrum inadequately, as if his child was his annoying brother.

Understanding these processes is important and requires professional skills; failure to address these processes will result in the parental projections becoming part of the baby's personality, and the symptoms will continue to exist as a kind of self-fulfilling prophecy. Below is an example of what Fraiberg et al. (1975) called "the ghosts in the nursery":

CASE STUDY

A., a 2 ½-month-old baby, was urgently referred to our clinic by a Well-Baby nurse. The nurse suspected that the mother was suffering from postpartum depression and observed the mother having trouble breastfeeding the baby. The mother did not show up for the meeting at the clinic at the appointed time. In view of the urgency expressed in the reference letter, the child psychiatrist went out to the family's home, a small caravan parked in the backyard of the paternal grandparents' house. The father was absent. The mother, dressed in a nightgown despite the late afternoon hours, opened the door with the baby in her arms.

The cluttered and messy caravan space made it hard for us to find a place to sit. A. was crying, and the mother took out her breast, but A. kept crying while suckling. "You see, she knows I'm a bad mother," said the mother. "She is already judging you at the age of two and a half months?" asked the child psychiatrist. "Yes," answered the mother, "I am transparent to her, she has this special power . . . Do you believe in reincarnation? I do"; to which she then added: "I never wanted to be a mother because I knew I'd suck at it like my mom . . . I also don't like sleeping with my husband . . . All men are the same . . . Only when my late sister appeared in my dream and told me she couldn't wait any longer and had to get me to have a daughter like her did I get pregnant, and I gave A. my sister's name, except for one letter . . . It's a bit confusing to me, but . . . ."

The conversation further turned up that when the mother was an adolescent, her 9-year-old sister died in a car accident. According to the mother, she and her sister had had a highly dependent, ambivalent relationship, and they were even bickering in the minutes leading up to the accident. Following the accident, A.'s mother went into pathological grief, adding to the affective and behavioral disorders she had suffered from previously. A.'s crying was strongly evocative of her late sister in the mother's mind, which is why she responded to it with considerable unrest, anger, and anxiety.

The mother turned out to have good intellectual abilities and some resilience, and the clinician believed she could persevere through treatment. Her husband also grew up in an abusive family but, unlike her, resisted treatment. Their relationship appeared to be on the rocks. "After all, he is just like any man . . . He can't be trusted all the way," said A.'s mother in one of the sessions. Further along the treatment, it transpired that underlying this statement lay a fear that the father would one day come and abuse their child sexually, as the mother's stepfather had done to her. Because of this secret concern, the mother agreed to have A. sleep with her in bed.

The dyadic treatment of A. and her mother lasted 2 years. By the end of this period, A.'s behavior had improved, and the mother was able, for the first time in her life, to trust others. A. grew up to be a functioning girl, but she was left with a certain vulnerability, which mainly manifests itself in stressful situations.

Despite these insights regarding the crucial role of intergenerational processes in the emotional development of the very young child, some of our colleagues still think that infant psychotherapy means treating only the parents. True, the baby does not yet talk and is entirely dependent on her parents, yet she is aware of the things going on around her; she listens to them and to the therapist, attuned to the emotional tone of the conversation. The baby's presence in therapy creates a sort of transitional space where baby and parent (and therapist, to some extent) meet at the unconscious level. This meeting allows the therapist to note problems in the relationship between the parent and the baby. For example, the therapist might discover that they are physically close yet emotionally detached from each other. Situations such as these sometimes come about when the mother is depressed: She holds the crying baby in her arms, even offering it the breast, but in fact remains emotionally aloof from it. Sensing this, the baby will not settle down. He will often avert his gaze sideways. The mother, who takes this behavior as proof of her failure, grows even more depressed, and the cycle goes on. In therapy, this closed vicious circle will be identified, addressing both the mother and the baby, jointly and separately.

This book is based on the premise that a baby's normative or abnormal behavior often reflects the way in which he is perceived by his parents, their projections onto him, but also his own constitutional attributes as well as the risk factors and protective factors present in his surroundings. This is not about "blaming" the parents but about taking a multidimensional look at the meaning of the symptom developed by the baby. This theoretical approach is reflected in both diagnosis and treatment: Neither the parent nor the child is treated alone, but their relationship is treated as a whole.

References

Cramer, B., & Palacio-Espasa, F. (1993). *La pratique des psychotherapies mères-bébés* [The practice of mother–baby psychotherapies]. Paris, France: Presses Universitaires de France.

Damasio, A. R. (1994). *Descartes's error. Emotion and human brain.* New York, NY: Grosset/Putnam.

Fraiberg, S., Adelson, E., & Shapiro, V. (1975). Ghosts in the nursery: A psychoanalytic approach to the problem of impaired infant–mother relationships. *Journal of the American Academy of Child and Adolescent Psychiatry, 14,* 387–421.

Izard, C. E., & Malatesta, C. Z. (1987). Perspectives on emotional development: I. Differential emotions theory of early emotional development. In J. D. Osofsky (Ed.), *Handbook of infant development* (2nd ed., pp. 494–554). New York, NY: Wiley.

Rousseau J. J. (1762). *Emile ou de l'Education,* Livre I. Electronic version by Jean Marie Tremblay, 2002, Chicoutimi, Québec, Canada.

Stern, D. (1995). *The motherhood constellation: A unified view of parent-infant psychotherapy.* New York, NY: Basic Books.

ZERO TO THREE. (1994). *Diagnostic classification of mental health and developmental disorders of infancy and early childhood.* Washington, DC: Author.

ZERO TO THREE. (2005). *Diagnostic classification of mental health and developmental disorders of infancy and early childhood* (Rev. ed.). Washington, DC: Author.

ZERO TO THREE. (2016). *DC:0–5™: Diagnostic classification of mental health and developmental disorders of infancy and early childhood* (DC:0–5). Washington, DC: Author.

Recommended Reading

Chuvin, P. (2006). Quand l'abandon n'était pas un crime. In *L'enfant et la famille.* Les collections de l'Histoire, Number 32, 8–13. Sainte-Geneviève Cédex.

Luthar, S. S. (2003). *Resilience and vulnerability: Adaptation in the context of childhood adversities.* New York, NY: Cambridge University Press.

Sameroff, A. J., & Fiese, B. (2000). Models of development and developmental risk. In C. H. Zeanah, Jr. (Ed.), *Handbook of infant mental health* (2nd ed., pp. 3–19). New York, NY: Guilford Press.

CHAPTER 2

They Think Me, Conceive Me, and Become My Parents

Introduction: The Notion of Parenthood in Historical Perspective

Parenthood is multidimensional and highly personal. The bible stories already reflect variation in parenting patterns. Abraham, Isaac, and Jacob differ in their parenting style, and Sarah is a different type of mother compared with Rebecca or Rachel. Furthermore, the stories of Cain and Abel as well as Jacob and Esau say something about the interaction between babies and their parents and the impact on parents of the temperament that the child brings with her into the world.

What is parenthood? Its definition varies across different periods and cultures. One of the more interesting definitions is this integrative one: "The totality of one's representations, feelings and behaviors vis-à-vis one's son or daughter, whether the child has already been born or is still in the womb or even not yet conceived" (Stoleru, Morales Huet, & Grinschpoun, 1985, p. 447). This definition suggests that parenthood comes about after the future parent starts to contemplate or picture it. As a matter of fact, people are all potential parents from birth, as already evidenced in childhood games. From a very young age, children play father and mother: They place a pillow under their shirt to mimic pregnancy, walk a doll around in a stroller, and imitate diverse parental behaviors.

Parenting has biological, psychological, and sociocultural dimensions. Papoušek and Papoušek (1987) were the first to define the biological basis of parenting. They coined the term "intuitive parenting." This term describes all those automatic behaviors that allow parents to adjust themselves to the baby's needs: holding the baby in the arms at the right distance in terms of his ability to focus, turning the gaze to where the baby is looking, and so forth. Moreover, the role played by the hormone oxytocin in strengthening the sense of parenthood and activating parenting behaviors in both mother and father has been proven in various studies, among others the one conducted by Feldman et al. (2009) from Bar Ilan University.

Winnicott, an English psychoanalyst and pediatrician, devoted considerable thought to understanding the psychological aspects of parenting. He introduced the term "good enough parenting." Good enough parents have unbounded love for their children; they gratify but also frustrate them. These two elements, gratification and frustration, must coexist because this is the only way that the baby can strike a balance between the pleasure principle and the reality principle.

Parenting also has an important sociocultural aspect, which passes on from one generation to the next. All cultures share the notion that parenting plays a major role in generational continuity. All cultures consider infertility to be an aberration. However, a new phenomenon is being witnessed: couples who positively refuse to have children, as a matter of principle, on various ideological grounds.

Who, then, deserves the title of "good enough parent"? The answer to this question varied greatly down the ages along with the status of the baby. A baby in Sparta was customarily entrusted to the care of a nanny, to be raised by her, fed when hungry, and taught not to fear the dark or being alone, but also not to shout excessively or lose his temper. This role persisted through many generations before society gradually started changing its view of babies. In the 13th century, for example, they were seen as fragile creatures in need of protection, and "good enough parents" were those who wrapped the baby's limbs and held them snug against their own bodies, those who kept their baby in semidark surroundings to shield him and his sensitive eyes from the light of day. A "good enough parent" would not dare give a baby medications. These were ingested by a wet nurse and administered to the baby via her milk. Later on, the higher strata of society came to realize that the educational figure and the interpersonal bond between a baby and his caregiver were highly significant very early on in his life, from birth in fact. This notion was apparent in the criteria laid down for choosing a nanny, such as not being too stupid or too sad, having a good breath and good-enough sized breasts (Chuvin, 2006). Moreover, what about fathers? Medieval fathers were expected to show their children some affection despite being only slightly involved in their upbringing. In the late Middle Ages, Joseph of Bethlehem was deemed the epitome of ideal fatherhood. From 1450 on, Mary and Joseph are represented together in paintings, kneeling before the Child Jesus.

The obligation imposed on parents to see to their children's education emerged during the 19th century, when, for the first time, several countries established elementary schools and enacted compulsory education laws. In the same vein, the law even stated parents' responsibility to care for their children's needs. In 1849, 10 years after passing a compulsory education law, France was the first country in the world to enact a law against parental maltreatment.

Family size and structure likewise underwent many changes throughout history. Up until the 18th century, parents hardly had a say in determining family size; these matters lay in the hands of the community and, more particularly, the church. Gradually, as a better understanding was gained of a child's early skills and how important it was to nurture them, parents started to plan their number of offspring while taking into account the investment required in raising each child. Family life started revolving around the children's needs. Obviously, these changes first took place within the upper social classes of the population, and only later trickled down to the lower strata. Financial considerations largely influenced the conduct of poor families in the 19th century, following the industrial revolution: Parents needed their children's wages to support the family. Mothers worked long hours in factories, sending their babies to nannies in the countryside or to day care with a childless female neighbor. In 1884, the first European public day nursery for children less than 2 years old was inaugurated in Paris, to which mothers could bring their children while they were at work. The idea gradually spread to other countries in Europe. Needless to say, the level of care in these institutions was very poor. This resulted in a high incidence of baby mortality: 50% of the babies who attended them died.

The close interplay between social processes on the one hand and parenting and family structure on the other hand can be seen to continue to this very day. Alongside the changes in the concept of family—the social devaluation of marriage, the higher incidence of divorce, the emergence of new forms of family, and the sharp percentage increase in single-parent families—medical technologies are being developed that are changing the nature of parenthood, for the most part in Western society. Women, for example, can conceive at an older age. Furthermore, these social processes are also changing the way in which mothers perceive their role: Nowadays, more mothers aspire to fulfill themselves, whereas fathers are becoming increasingly involved in their children's care. The traditional definition of parental roles is thus constantly shifting.

The Perception of Parenting in Israeli Society: From the Kibbutz's Communal Children's House to the Continuum Concept

The definition of good parenting has changed radically in Israeli society during the country's existence. When the State of Israel was established, its founding fathers were engaged in a fight for survival; work and collectivism were a paramount value, and the psychological aspects of raising kids were hardly a top priority. In the kibbutz, children did not live at home with their parents but in the children's house, where a caretaker would watch over them at night. Another expression of poor psychologically oriented parenting was the lack of attention among Holocaust survivors to the way their children interpreted their behavior. Expressing feelings about their past was hard for these survivors, and so they preferred to keep silent, often leaving their children to fill in the blanks.

> Momik,[1] *a novella by David Grossman, describes the mark left by the Neumans [new man], a couple of Holocaust survivors, on their only son Momik. In fact, most of Momik's acquaintances in Kiryat Yovel, the Jerusalem neighborhood in which he grew up, survived the Holocaust, which must not be talked about too much and can only be mentioned with a deep sigh. The daytime silences on the one hand and the nighttime cries on the other hand send Momik on a mission from which there can be no escape—a redemptive mission to which he devotes all his time, until he loses touch with reality. For him, it is an all-out war that is mostly his to wage, with very few clues, for the sake of his parents and their fellow survivors, in order to give them some peace of mind, some respite from their ongoing suffering. At one point, he makes up his mind to get himself one such animal (the "Nazi beast") and tame it into goodness so that it may stop with its torture.*

Gradually, with the improved standard of living in Israel and the changed nature of the family cell came the recognition of each child's unique needs and singularity. One sign of this transformation was the objection of mothers born and raised on a kibbutz to hand over their babies to the children's house at night. The pendulum seems to have swung the other way these days, perhaps even excessively so: Many parents believe that a baby should not be allowed to cry, should not be frustrated, and should be granted his every request. This is the so-called Continuum Concept approach. In our opinion, the transition from a stoic approach to an overly permissive one is not necessarily good. In our clinical work, we see behavioral problems in children who are bombarded with stimuli and gratifications, extracurricular activities, and material presents; behavioral problems also exist among children whose parents fail to set clear and coherent boundaries for them at home. This highly permissive stance might be due to the desire to make up for the long hours spent by both parents away from home and the meager "together time." After all, social reality has created a situation in which both parents work long hours and the child is under the care of caregivers for the better part of the day, whether at home or at day care centers. Movies, television, and computer games have become key ingredients in children's daily routine already in infancy. The child is often overstimulated. The problem with this is not necessarily related to the quality of the stimuli but to the fact that they are not mediated by a responsible adult.

---

[1] David Grossman. (2005). *Momik* (pp. 40–44). Published by Hakibbutz Hameuchad.

In our humble opinion, a new conception of family has formed within Israeli society whereby the child is at the center, the child is "king," and parents are obligated to give her whatever she wants, whatever it takes to spare her from frustration. This parental stance is based on what is called the Continuum Concept, which is at the opposite end of the education dispensed in Israel 60 years ago. Ever since the family has become a democratic group, negotiation has replaced discipline. Should everything really be negotiable? Does this centric status accorded to children at such a young age not reinforce the sense of omnipotence typical of infancy, thus preventing its mitigation, a mitigation so much needed for the normal development of their self-worth and personality?

The authority we are talking about is in fact the conduit that makes intergenerational transmission of values possible. Moreover, authority does not equal hegemony. Parents do not make up the rules. They get them from their parents and hand them down to future generations. It is true that society undergoes changes from time to time—research moves forward, the economy develops, morality changes—and as knowledge advances, changes also take place in family values and structure. These changes are incorporated into the legacy transmitted from one generation to the next.

In addition to these social changes in the role of parents and the approach to children, divorce and remarriage have become very common, leading to intrafamilial complexity: Young children more commonly grow up with half-siblings; frequently share their experiences with more than one set of parents; nest in more than one home; and might come to see love as a temporary, fleeting thing.

Technological revolutions such as those that have allowed in vitro fertilization could gradually effect a transformation in the very character of the family cell. For instance, in Israel, the percentage of single-parent families within the general population is constantly on the rise. A conjugal relationship is no longer a necessary building block in creating a family cell. Will the nature of intergenerational transmission change under the charge of a single parent?

Finally, in the last decade, the number of same-sex couples seeking to become parents has markedly increased, following a change in Israeli society's approach to LGBT individuals. The naysayers have argued that same-sex parenting is detrimental to the development of a child's sexual identity. This argument has been refuted by numerous studies, contrary to what the classic theories of development would have predicted.

In this chapter, we address the various aspects and stages of parenthood and parenting, from the moment the decision to become parents is reached to the moment parenthood actually starts. We also look at the normative sides of parenting while trying to understand pathological situations.

The Beginnings of Parenthood: The Desire, Pregnancy, and Childbirth

A poor peasant sat by the fireside, while his wife sat opposite him, spin-ning. In his bitterness, the farmer complained about his solitude, with no children to fill the house with their noise. Upon hearing him, the woman cried out to ask for a child, be it even a tiny one no larger than a thumb; a child who would fill their hearts with the joy of giving ("Tom Thumb," Grimm Brother Tales).

Every evening, the king and queen would sit side by side and converse about their longing to be blessed with a child of their own. Their plea went unanswered. Once, when the queen was in the bath-house, a frog leaped out of the water and promised her that this time her wish would be granted and exactly a year hence she would give birth to a daughter ("Briar Rose").

On a snowy winter night, the queen sat by a black-framed wooden window, sewing. While she was at it, she pricked her finger on a needle, and three drops of blood fell down onto the pure snow. Dazzled by the red blood against the white snow, the queen wished for a baby who would be white as snow, red like blood, and dark like the window frame ("Snow White").

A man and a woman, a poor peasant and his weaver wife, as well as a king and queen all share the desire for offspring. Some seek to assert their manliness, some their femininity; some want continuity, some see children as life's purpose. A few parents are willing to accept any child that destiny might deal them—a thumb-sized boy, a hedgehog-like child, even a small donkey, as long as their prayer is answered.

The overly eager willingness of these would-be parents to have just any child could be taken as either a sign of desperation—to the point of being willing to put up with defects—or a paradoxical expression of the parental fear of begetting abnormal children. It could also signify a hope that the very utterance of the wish—to have even a porcupine or a donkey for a child—would break the jinx. Standing out of the crowd is Snow White's mother, who wants no less than a beautiful boy or girl, a baby girl or boy whose beauty would lie in the correct combination of three colors: white, red, and black.

The Desire

The opening sentences of the fairy tales listed previously attest to the impor-tance that the storytellers attribute to the wishes of parents who are looking to bring a child into the world and to the impact that these wishes have on the life of the tale's hero. It is the desire for a succeeding generation, a desire that will shine bright or loom large over the infants about to be born, that will guide the character's life story.

Desire is an important, basic concept in understanding human development. According to the French psychoanalyst Jacques Lacan, it is a vital force that directs the passion in every human being and can manifest itself in different areas of one's emotional life. It is also the emotional driving force for bringing a child into the world.

According to Jewish belief, God made man, then Eve, and the two lived in paradise without a care in the world until they ate from the tree of knowledge. A new dimension, knowledge, was now added to the life instinct. After knowledge was present, they became conscious of their desires and passions. Only then did sexual intercourse become institutionalized within the framework of a meaningful emotional bond aimed at ensuring generational continuity.

The desire to bring forth a child can stem from various sources: the wish for intergenerational transmission, which occupies an important place in people's perceived identity; the need of both woman and man to prove their fertility; and the desire for a common creation that will express the love for the male or female partner.

The Pregnancy

Pregnancy is commonly divided into three terms that differ both biologically and psychologically:

During the first trimester of pregnancy (the first 12 weeks), the fetus develops meteorically, and nondescript cells morph into distinct tissues and organs. This is also the most vulnerable period: One in four pregnancies is miscarried between weeks 10 and 12.

During the second trimester of pregnancy (from the 13th week to 4–5 months), the fetus is already kicking (in fact, the fetus starts moving by the seventh or eighth week, but these motions go undetected by the mother). This is the period when the preparation for motherhood becomes more tangible.

During the third trimester, both the physiological and psychological systems get ready for labor.

Surprisingly for some, fathers also undergo physical changes during pregnancy. In fact, studies (Gordon, Zagoory-Sharon, Leckman, & Feldman, 2010a, 2010b) showed that the same hormonal changes—an increase in prolactin and estradiol as well as a drop in testosterone—occurred during pregnancy in both women and men. The only difference was quantitative.

Psychologically, too, pregnancy is a unique time in the male and female lifecycles. This period has been called a time of "psychic transparency" (Golse & Bydlowski, 2001). The transition into motherhood, so they claimed, reawakens the woman's internalized representations of her relationships with her own mother and therefore triggers emotional processes during pregnancy. This is, for example, an opportunity for the pregnant woman to mend her relationship with her mother or else re-engage in an internal dialogue from an autonomous stance. An emotional bond also develops between the mother and the fetus, alongside an awareness of her separateness from it. Reflective functioning (see chapter 3) allows the mother to imagine the baby as having a consciousness of his own, both during pregnancy and after childbirth. The mother's type of attachment to her own parents partly predicts the nature of her bonding to the fetus and, later on, the baby's type of attachment to her. Studies on the emotional state of fathers have found that 50% of them developed various psychological symptoms during pregnancy, including fear of castration, ambivalence, anxieties, and helplessness. These symptoms are, thus, not an exclusive maternal preserve. Raphael-Leff (2005) described three main styles of psychological response to pregnancy characterizing women and men within the general population:

- *Facilitator*: Parents who have this approach make pregnancy their top priority, putting aside all their other needs. Parents like this would typically say, "We want everyone to know we are pregnant, even if it still doesn't show that much . . . We feel proud, full, and happy."

- *Regulator*: These parents do not allow the pregnancy to take top priority and constantly feel a need to be in control of things. A regulator mother might say, "We haven't changed our habits . . . I still wear the same clothes; we haven't told anyone about the pregnancy, we don't want special attention."

- *Reciprocator*: These parents take into account their new situation but also leave room for their other needs. The reciprocating mother might say, "I find it hard to keep on working and pursuing my many occupations as if nothing has changed. I need to rest but must also invest in my work before giving birth."

Raphael-Leff (2005) and other researchers found a correlation between these different psychological positions adopted by parents with regard to pregnancy and the relationship they form with the baby after birth. In the following example, a mother experienced her pregnancy as a threat to her independence and ability to be in control, which led to a very tense relationship between her and her baby girl after birth.

CASE STUDY

A 4-month-old baby girl was referred to our clinic by the emergency room of a pediatric hospital because of "inconsolable crying and parental exhaustion." During our first session, the mother produced a photo from her handbag and said, "See, this is how I once was . . . This was my dance group; we appeared all over the globe . . . Now I can't do a thing, because this baby won't let me."

The intake interview showed the mother to be a Regulator. She had hoped that she would be able to regulate her baby after birth, like she regulated her pregnancy and any other event in her life. Among other things, she took the baby on all the dance group's tours and tried to breastfeed her between shows. The baby responded to this routine with incessant crying fits, which led the mother to seek professional help.

The relatively new awareness of the complexity of interactions between biological and psychological processes during pregnancy requires that all professionals who accompany pregnancies—physicians and all paramedical practitioners—detect those situations that might give rise to abnormal initial parent–baby relations and refer the parents to professional help. Following are the risk factors for the emergence of an early disorder in the mother–baby relationship:

- *Abnormal maternal mental state*: Postpartum depression, in its varying degrees of severity, is the most common problem, but anxiety and psychotic conditions are not rare.

- *Lack of partner support*: This risk factor is especially prevalent in those instances in which the mother suffers from emotional disorders rooted in traumatic events she experienced in childhood, such as physical or sexual abuse.

- *Maternal age*: This risk factor is most prevalent in adolescent pregnancy, in particular when coupled with other risk factors such as low intelligence, previous abuse, depression, posttraumatic stress disorder, and poverty.

- *Obstetric antecedents involving miscarriage or induced abortion*: Most women who undergo induced abortion or natural miscarriage recover emotionally, but 10%–15% of them develop a posttraumatic emotional state later on. These are usually women who did not benefit from social support immediately after the loss, or certain mothers who had held the stillborn baby in their arms. In fact, professionals used to encourage grieving parents to hold their dead baby to complete the farewell process. It turns out today that the experience itself is so hard that it may be detrimental to the grieving process. The experience of losing the fetus, through either spontaneous or induced abortion, can cause great sorrow and is not so quickly forgotten. Contrary to the common recommendation of some gynecologists, a period of mourning is advised before attempting a new pregnancy. It is important to allow parents to grieve the loss of their fetus and to respect the psychological process they are going through so that they recover the biological and emotional strengths necessary for a new, normal pregnancy.

Clinically, what the risk factors described above mean is that early detection of psychologically high-risk pregnancies is necessary because it makes it possible to treat families who are detected and to eventually nip serious problems in the bud. Olds et al. (1998) examined the effect of regular visits by community nurses to the homes of families at risk to provide support and developmental guidance to pregnant mothers. Ten years after this intervention, Olds et al. compared the intervention group with the control group and found that the therapeutic visits prevented the appearance of disorders in the mother–child relationship. Awareness of the need to locate pregnant mothers presenting high psychosocial risk also exists in Israel, and the prevention programs offered to parents who are in these situations seem to be proving themselves.

Childbirth

Childbirth confronts the mother with the limitations of her bodily control and the prospect of her own death. Most cultures have established behaviors and rituals meant to attenuate the fear surrounding childbirth. The presence of a supportive figure during labor makes things easier for the mother, and it improves the physical and emotional well-being of both mother and baby. Notwithstanding the relatively wide array of anesthetic and other analgesic methods, many women opt for a natural delivery, viewing the actual labor pangs as a sensory process embodying the separation from the fetus. More and more women choose to have a cesarean section (or "C-section") to ensure the "integrity" of the fetus, even if there is no medical justification to do this. This kind of decision might have an adverse effect on the early bond between mother and baby. It has been found that the secretion of oxytocin—the "attachment hormone"—is reduced in C-sections compared with ordinary deliveries and that breastfeeding, which is also accompanied by oxytocin secretion, provides only partial compensation.

An interesting conceptualization of the psychological process attending labor can be found in the work of French psychoanalyst Françoise Dolto (1999). Dolto called birth the "umbilical castration" or the first stage in the series of frustrations (named "symbolic castrations"; see chapter 3) required if the child's personality is to develop normally. "Umbilical castration," the cutting of the umbilical cord, symbolizes the transition from the warm, quiet uterine environment to the cold, noisy environment outside. According to Dolto, on the occasion of the first "castration," the baby is given her name and becomes part of human society.

Childbirth in developed countries is no longer as dangerous today as it once was. This is not to mean that physical and psychological complications cannot appear during and following birth. Although this book will not focus on perinatal physical complications, it is important to recall the link shown by many studies between these complications and the emergence of neuro-developmental disorders and psychiatric diseases such as schizophrenia.

One of the lesser known psychological complications is postdelivery traumatic stress reaction. This relatively rare condition seriously jeopardizes the mother–baby relationship. It has been lately described as a syndrome that appears after birth prevalently in mothers who had undergone physical or sexual abuse. These are cases in which the mother experiences childbirth as a repetition of the trauma, even if no traumatic event was objectively recorded during birth. Incapable of detaching emotionally from the trauma, these mothers are unable to bond emotionally with the baby. The delivery seems to reawaken feelings of loss of control and helplessness in the mother. It is as if labor unconsciously recreates traumatic physical sensations experienced by the mother in the past together with the emotion that went along with them. Put differently, labor is experienced as rape. Maternity ward teams are still insufficiently aware of this syndrome, and as a result, most cases are diagnosed retrospectively, after signs of a disorder in the mother–baby relationship have appeared.

Parenting After Birth

Parenting starts at birth, and it has interwoven biological and psychological aspects.

Biological Aspects of Parenting

Gynecologists call the first 6 weeks following childbirth the *puerperium period*. This is, in fact, a period in which the parturient is highly vulnerable because of her physiological and hormonal instability.

The endocrine system, which had played an important role during pregnancy, remains a key factor in the early phase of parenting. One of the hormones playing an important role in maternal behavior in mammals in general and humans in particular is oxytocin. Its secretion rises as pregnancy begins, and even more so during breastfeeding. It thus contributes a lot to the mother's initial bonding with the baby (bonding is further addressed in chapter 3). Oxytocin influences many systems in the body: It plays a role in quieting anxiety, allays fear and aggressiveness, brings down blood pressure, raises the pain threshold, and even promotes sociability. In fact, it acts as an antagonist to cortisol, a hormone secreted in stressful situations. Not only breastfeeding triggers secretion of oxytocin but also physical contact—hence, the beneficial effect of physical contact in the bonding process between parent and baby. The soothing effect of oxytocin has also been observed in hospital nurseries. Babies exposed to maternal contact from birth on cry less than those deprived of this contact. In the first minutes following birth, after the baby is placed on the mother's stomach, her body also secretes oxytocin.

It is important to note that the effect of physical contact on oxytocin secretion applies regardless of whether the baby suckles or drinks from a bottle. It is the actual bodily contact between the mother and the baby during feeding that triggers secretion of the hormone. The father's body secretes it as well following contact with the baby. Furthermore, it is known today that oxytocin influences not only the relationship between parent and baby but also the relationship between the parents. It influences the level of trust created between the spouses, their ability to deal with conflicts arising between them, and so forth.

The last decades have seen the status of men change in the couple in general and in parenting in particular. This change has given rise to a re-examination of the bonding process between fathers and babies at the biological level as well. Contrary to conventional thinking that only the mother's blood oxytocin levels go up, Feldman and Leckman (e.g., Gordon et al., 2010a, 2010b) found similar levels of the hormone in fathers as well, immediately after birth and 6 months later. The very parenting process is thus accompanied by an equal increase in the hormone's level in both parents. Its secretion rises in both parents during positive emotional interaction with the baby. Feldman and Leckman found that mothers saw their oxytocin level increase when looking at the baby was accompanied by a positive emotion and physical contact. In fathers, however, the hormone level rose when playing with the baby, in particular physical games. The baby, for his part, tends to choose the father for play and the mother for relaxation.

Psychological Aspects of Parenting

Most parents recall the first months following birth as a "crazy period," a period in which all daily habits change, and everything revolves around the baby's needs. Winnicott (1956, 1960) called this unique state of consciousness "primary maternal preoccupation," describing it as almost an illness that a mother must experience and recover from in order to create and sustain an environment and space that can meet the physical and psychological needs of her infant. This special state of heightened sensitivity comes close in magnitude to a dissociative state. Parents need it for them to learn their baby fast and sense her needs. Winnicott described these special circumstances characterizing the first 2 months following birth long before their biological basis was discovered. Feldman and Leckman (e.g., Gordon et al., 2010a, 2010b) showed that fathers also exhibited primary-preoccupation behaviors very similar in content to the maternal ones but different in emotional magnitude. This is further proof that parenthood constitutes an innate ability in both women and men. The lesser magnitude of these behaviors in fathers in the first months after delivery allows them to go to work and provide for the physical needs of the family, whereas mothers remain fully in preoccupation mode. This may be seen as an example of how biology-based behaviors serve survival.

Daniel Stern (1985, 1995) carried on Winnicott's work on primary maternal preoccupation, defining its content. He called the internal psychological change taking place in a woman upon becoming a mother "maternal constellation" (see chapter 3), which he characterized by four major themes: preserving the baby's life, creating a meaningful relationship with the baby, creating a beneficial environment for the baby, and integrating a new component into her identity—being a mother.

In cases in which a mother is unable to enter the state of primary preoccupation, a partial inability to fulfill her baby's emotional needs during his first year can be witnessed. This problematic state of affairs might be caused by psychiatric disorders—such as postpartum depression, psychosis, and obsessive-compulsive disorder—or when the mother experiences birth as a narcissistic injury to her own integrity.

CASE STUDY

L., a 3-month-old baby, the first child born to a very young couple, was brought to hospital because of refusal to eat, apathy, and failure to gain weight. A physical checkup in the pediatric ward did not yield any physical cause, but the medical team noticed that the mother was irritable for no apparent reason. The psychiatric consultant was called in to see the family. During the first assessment, the mother was asked to recount her pregnancy and childbirth. She reported that the pregnancy was desired and normal, but the delivery extended for a very long time, much more than she had expected. She went through a long bout of pain and experienced giving birth as a severe trauma. She felt as if her body had been damaged, for which she unconsciously blamed the baby. "He tore me up," she said. She also decided not to breastfeed the baby "so as not to damage her breasts." Her personal needs, mainly those related to her body image, were in conflict with her maternal tasks. She strived to regain her previous figure immediately after birth and could not bear the idea of "being dressed up casually." She adamantly refused to "be all about the baby." Because of the difficulty she experienced going into primary maternal preoccupation, she failed to learn how to read the baby's signals. Thus, for example, she failed to grasp the difference between hunger-related and fatigue-related crying, and she did not feed him properly. This was the sole cause of his eating disorder.

In the opposite situation, in which a mother is unable to let go of her preoccupied state even after 2 months have elapsed since birth, an anxious or symbiotic relationship might form between her and the baby, which will also affect her relationship with her spouse and the rest of the family.

CASE STUDY

B., a toddler 2 years and 10 months old, was referred to our clinic after starting to pull out his hair during his mother's second pregnancy. In our first assessment with him, we noticed that he was standing very close to her, pulling at her hair, pressing it between his fingers as if it were his own. The mother said, "From the very first day of his life, he can't do without my hair." We started to inquire about the nature of the relationship between the child and his mother since his birth and were under the impression that theirs was an almost symbiotic system most probably disrupted when his little sister was born. In our therapy sessions, it turned out that the mother's pregnancy with B. was preceded by a miscarriage at 4 months of gestational age. This was experienced as a traumatic loss, one that the mother dealt with—contrary to what she was advised—by getting pregnant right away. Her anguish over miscarrying and losing the baby continued even after childbirth, as manifest in her persistence in the state of "primary preoccupation" far longer than expected. She could not separate from the baby, breastfed him for hours, and allowed him to fondle her hair when breastfeeding. His breastfeeding was stopped when the mother started her second pregnancy, and B. seemed to have compensated himself for being "torn away" from his mother's breast by starting to rip out his own hair. This was his way of expressing his anger at her.

Coparenting

When a couple becomes parents, their interrelationship changes as a third player joins in the dance. This change can unite a couple but also can produce tensions between them. The more gratifying the relationship between them and the more welcome the father feels, the more he will be involved in pregnancy, childbirth, and raising the children. The relationship between the partners influences the father–child relationship much more than it does the mother–child relationship. It is important to note that the couple's relationship with their respective extended families sometimes changes after they become parents. This might give rise to conflicts between the spouses around loyalty to the family of origin. These difficulties are particularly evident when each partner's capacity for differentiation and individuation is weak, and are among the most common causes of divorce in the first 2 years after birth.

As parenting research has moved forward, it has been shown how caught up researchers were in associating the concept of parental relationship with the mother alone. It is in this light that the work of Fivaz-Depeursinge and Corboz-Warnery (1999) should be considered, because they were the first researchers to point out the baby's innate ability to respond to two significant figures simultaneously, which matures by 3 months old. The research world is slowly abandoning the primarily dyadic developmental view in favor of a triadic one involving two parents and a baby at its center. McHale (1997) pointed out the relationship between the baby's normal development and her parents' ability to establish coparenting—that is, march down a clear common path together and raise their child in an atmosphere of support and mutual respect. This has nothing to do with the division of technical housekeeping chores but with the emotional messages communicated by both parents to their baby.

Fathers therefore have an important role to play in their children's development, all the more so when the mother is keen to go back to work after her maternity leave. These changes in the father's place in raising his children stood at the center of the debate surrounding the amendment of Israel's so-called Tender Years Presumption Law, which automatically left custody of children 6 years old or younger to the mother.

Structure of the Single-Parent Family

The social change that has taken place worldwide in the definition of the concept of family stemmed, among others, from the 1978 scientific innovation that made in vitro fertilization of the ovule possible for the first time. This cleared a path for redefining the family cell. The couple theretofore required to create the embryo was no longer necessary, and a new option offered itself—a family of only one progenitor. Indeed, the incidence of single-parent families—headed by only one parent, either a mother or a father—climbed steeply in the world as in Israel.

Single parents can be divided into three groups: women who make a principled decision to bring forth a child alone without wishing to live as part of a couple (single mothers by choice), women who have not found a life partner and have decided to have a child on their own, and women and men who have divorced. Each group has its own psychological profile.

Single-Father Versus Single-Mother Families

Sufficient valid research on single fathers is still lacking, mainly because of the stereotypical assumption that only women establish single-parent families. Hence, the data available on this subject are mainly based on studies carried out among select groups of volunteer fathers and not—as one might expect in empirical research—among randomly sampled groups from the general population. Single fathers are generally better off financially than single mothers but worse off than married fathers.

Single Parenting Following Divorce

Divorced parents are still the largest group of single parents and the most financially successful. More often than not, custody of the children is awarded to the mother in most countries. However, the rising rate of divorce within the population and the increasing involvement of fathers in raising their children mean that there is a growing number of fathers who are claiming custody of their children and prepared to take the matter to court. A custodial parent (a divorced parent who has custody of the child) goes through several crises in the immediate wake of divorce. Recovering from the emotional experiences engendered by breakup and divorce usually takes long—months, even years. It is no surprise that this is a period when parents tend to be irritable and less patient and understanding toward their children. The first 2 years following divorce are the hardest; after that, most custodial parents function better than they did before the divorce, and they even feel happier.

The divorce process in fact requires custodial parents to adapt to another role that they did not necessarily fill when they were married. Besides their roles as homemakers, mothers must ensure an additional source of income, whereas fathers must keep shouldering the financial burden while also managing the household. A study among 626 custodial divorced single mothers and 100 such fathers found that in both groups the degree of satisfaction with the new role predicted the emergence of depression following divorce.

Single Mothers by Choice

An example of a clinical case involving a single mother by choice is provided below:

CASE STUDY

A 35-year-old single mother of a 2½-year-old girl, 6 months into her second pregnancy, was referred to the infant mental health clinic by a community nurse because of anxiety attacks. During the evaluation session, the mother—an educated, energetic, and independent woman—said that "psychology is for the weak." The mother had no notion of the source of the attacks, and when asked how she came to be a single mother, she replied, "My older daughter has a father, but I want nothing to do with him; he doesn't even know she exists. It was a short, insignificant relationship. I keep asking myself what attracted me to him . . . I prefer to do without men, and this pregnancy was courtesy of the sperm bank." During that session, it turned out that a fierce bout of the influenza contracted by the mother accelerated the onset of her anxiety attacks: "It suddenly dawned on me that I was about to become responsible for two kids . . . what if something were to happen to me?" She suddenly realized that her decision to be a single mom came at a price, and it was this realization that led to the appearance of uncontrollable anxiety attacks.

As previously mentioned, a distinction has to be made between two groups of single mothers: those who have willingly chosen to become single parents and those plunged therein for lack of choice or various other reasons. Those who opt for single parenthood to begin with usually attribute little significance to the father's role in the child's development. However, those who had no choice in becoming single parents would have likely preferred to conceive and raise a child within the framework of a romantic relationship. Contrary to other groups, the demographic profile of single mothers by choice is relatively homogenous. Most are between 35 and 40 years old, their socioeconomic status is middle-high, they are well-educated women of means, and most of them occupy a senior position in their workplace. They are usually egged on by their biological clock, and their decision to become single moms is usually reached after a long process of deliberation. Mothers who become single mothers by choice are for the most part independent, enjoy social support, and make a deliberate decision "not to mess with men." "Nonchoice" single mothers, however, often suffer from social and interpersonal difficulties, tend to seclude themselves, and experience economic hardship; such women might form an inseparable relationship with their baby.

Single Parenting as a High-Risk Situation

The child's socioemotional development and degree of resilience depend on the complex interplay between protective factors and risk factors in her life. This becomes an extremely complex situation when significant risk factors are present in both the baby and the parent. Clinicians are responsible for spotting these factors as soon as possible and trying to intervene before the child gets hurt.

When the risk factors in single-parent families are examined, any risk factor originating in the baby that might hinder the parent–child relationship should be considered. Parenting a child born with a chronic disease, to take one example, is challenging enough. Add that disease into a single-parenting context, with its already inherent difficulty, and the combined effect of the two might prove detrimental to the parent's mental state and, by extension, the child's development. This also holds true in the case of a baby with a difficult temperament.

Risk factors originating in the parent might also affect the parent–baby relationship. Mental disorders—such as anxiety, depression, and drug addiction—are significantly more widespread among single mothers than mothers who have a partner. In a review of the topic of single parenting (Tyano & Keren, 2010), we looked at mothers who came to the infant mental health clinic with their children. We found that of the total number of single mothers who sought the clinic's help, 45% had suffered from a common mental disorder within the preceding 12-month period, compared with only 23.6% of mothers living with a partner. In a longitudinal study conducted for 2 years among women who turned to the mental health clinic, single mothers were found to be 2 times more likely to succumb to an outburst of postpartum depression than married mothers. The above review also noted that statistical analysis summing up 84 studies found that single motherhood was one of 13 predictors of postpartum depression.

Moreover, young age takes first place among the factors upping the risk of a mental disorder appearing in single mothers. Seventy-nine percent of teenage girls who get pregnant become single moms. Combining several risk factors, these mothers have the highest probability of developing mental disorders within the single mothers group. Their level of education is usually poor, as are their achievements in school; they tend to be socially outcast and have a hard time earning a living. Financial distress, especially when coupled with lack of social support, is yet another risk factor in the single adolescent–mother population. The teen mother's social isolation increases with childbirth, and her chances of functioning independently as a mother diminish. Furthermore, single mothers, and even more so single teen moms, are at a high risk for giving birth to premature babies. For all these reasons, single parenthood presents a challenge to "good enough parenting."

Single-parent families can take on many characteristics. Consequently, the term "single-parent family" is somewhat vague and unpredictive of the development of any given child. It is important to emphasize that most single parents function well and provide a sufficiently good environment for their baby. Still, mental health clinicians need to catch the high-risk babies as early as possible. The risk factors we have listed in this chapter are the ones that should guide clinicians in the early detection of at-risk pregnant women and in the planning and implementation of psychosocial intervention programs already during pregnancy. Nurses and pediatricians in the community are key players in early detection: They are the ones who meet the single parent during the baby's first year of life on a routine basis.

Psychiatric Disorders During Pregnancy and After Childbirth

The most prevalent disorder during pregnancy and at childbirth or thereafter is depression. Depression is an affective disorder—that is, a mood disorder— whose key characteristics are prolonged sadness and inability to experience pleasure. That being said, at least three or more symptoms must be present to confirm this diagnosis: physical symptoms (sleep problems, eating problems, fatigue), cognitive symptoms (difficulties with concentration and memory, distorted perceptions), or psychological symptoms (guilt feelings, despair, low self-esteem, loss of interest in the surroundings, suicidal tendencies). Psychotic depression is a rarer, more severe form of depression, accompanied by delusions of a depressive and sometimes suicidal nature. Depression can also appear as part of a bipolar affective disease characterized by swings between states of depression and mania.

Maternal Depression During Pregnancy

Depression is quite a common disorder during pregnancy (10%–25% of all mental disorders). For some women, it actually starts before conception, and it becomes overt when the pregnancy-induced hormonal changes and changes in the marital relationship trigger the onset of the disorder. Depression tends to rear its head in the second or third trimester of pregnancy. It is important to note that sadness and depression come in different magnitudes that call for different kinds of treatment. Supportive psychotherapy will suffice in some cases, whereas others will require drug treatment.

Medical literature describes a possible link between depression during pregnancy and the appearance of physical complications inherent to pregnancy (preterm birth, pre-eclampsia, hyperemesis gravidarum, placental insufficiency, intrauterine growth retardation, and miscarriage). Newborn babies whose mother was depressed during pregnancy score poorly on Brazelton's Neurobehavioral Behavioral Assessment Scale (Brazelton & Nugent, 2011). Furthermore, hormonal tests conducted on both mother and child in these cases indicate low levels of dopamine in their blood and high levels of cortisone and norepinephrine. In short, these results suggest the importance of identifying mothers who suffer from depression during pregnancy as early as possible—for example, by using the Edinburgh Postnatal Depression Scale (EPDS) questionnaire (Cox, Holden, & Sagovsky, 1987).

Postpartum Depression

Postpartum depression is found at varying degrees of severity among 8%–13% of women in their reproductive years. It is the most common of all postpartum psychiatric disorders. The extent of damage caused by a mother's depression to her baby's development depends on three main factors: the father's mental health, emotional negativity (sadness, flat affect, and irritability) exhibited by the mother, as well as the magnitude and duration of the depression.

CASE STUDY

A young couple had a healthy first baby following a much desired and normal pregnancy. The delivery, however, was very long, and the baby ended up being extracted by vacuum. For the mother, this was torture, unlike anything she could have expected following her childbirth preparation course. During childbirth, as the mother later reported, she had felt lonely and had a hard time coping with the pain and anxiety that something bad might happen to the fetus. Despite the husband's presence by her bedside and the fact that the baby was born healthy, the mother was unable to recover from the delivery experience, following which she immediately felt distanced from those around her, including the baby. When they got back home, she managed to take care of the baby, but he gave her no joy. She could not explain what she was going through to her husband, and he never asked. They grew increasingly estranged. The mother became ever more sad and distanced. However, because she functioned well and the baby seemed normal, her immediate circle did not worry too much. That was before the day when she gave her baby a bath and felt a sudden urge to drown him. In a superhuman effort, she was able to resist the urge and called her husband, terrified. She decided to consult a psychiatrist, and she began to be treated with medications. The Well-Baby nurse was the one to notice abnormal behavior in the baby; he was not looking at his mother, preferred being with himself, and was losing weight. The parents and baby were referred to our clinic for clinical assessment and treatment. We diagnosed a disorder in the early relationship between the mother and the baby and suggested triadic treatment involving both parents and the baby to try to rebuild the baby's trust in his mother and to bring the father closer to the mother—that is, establish coparenting. The treatment lasted approximately 4 months.

This case illustrates how the mother's depression affects the baby and the parent–baby relationship. This influence does not necessarily disappear with the improvement in the mother's clinical condition. It is therefore not enough to treat just the mother; at the same time, one has to treat the mother–baby relationship and include the partner.

Postpartum Psychotic Depression

Postpartum psychotic depression is much rarer, affecting one or two in every thousand women who had given birth. It is a seriously acute disorder that significantly impairs a mother's ability to function as such, and sometimes requires keeping the baby away from her.

In a study that compared mothers who had suffered from postpartum depression with mothers who had developed postpartum psychosis (Weinberg & Tronick, 1998), a difference was found between these groups in terms of how the mothers experienced their relationship with the baby. Contrary to expectations, it was the mothers who suffered from depression, a milder disorder than psychosis, who tended to view this relationship in negative terms. The difference might lie in the fact that postpartum psychotic disorder lasts a shorter period of time than postpartum depression, which could go on for about 6 months on average.

Paternal Depression

A father also might fall into depression following the birth of a baby. Studies published in different countries show the incidence of paternal depression within the baby's first year of life: 3%–6% of fathers have it (compared with 8%–13% of mothers), and the figure is higher when the female partner also suffers from postpartum depression. Depression in fathers presents the same clinical picture as maternal depression. It manifests itself in a poor mood, despair, lower self-esteem, irritability, attention and concentration problems, and a low frustration threshold. Children of fathers with postnatal depression were found to have affective and behavioral disorders by 3½ years old, which persisted throughout their childhood years and up to their teen years.

Other Psychiatric Disorders

Apart from depression related to pregnancy or childbirth, other, preexisting psychiatric disorders in a parent—be it the mother or father—might become exacerbated as a result of pregnancy. We address this subject in chapter 15.

Conclusion

The transition into parenthood is a developmental stage that most human beings, both women and men, go through. It is a multidimensional stage involving biological, psychological, and social aspects. The transition into parenthood demands the reorganization not only of one's internal world but also one's relationship with one's parents and partner. Becoming a parent can reinforce and mature a parent's psychological apparatus, but it can also shake it up or destabilize it. In their work, professionals need to identify possible crises during pregnancy, childbirth, or the first year of life to ensure the infant's healthy development.

References

Brazelton, T. B., & Nugent, J. K. (2011). *The Neonatal Behavioral Assessment Scale* (4th ed.). London, England: Mac Keith Press.

Chuvin, P. (2006). Quand l'abandon n'était pas un crime: In *L'Enfant et la Famille*. Les collections de l'Histoire, Number 32, 8–13. Sainte-Geneviève Cédex.

Cox, J. L., Holden, J. M., & Sagovsky, R. (1987). Detection of postnatal depression: Development of the 10-item Edinburgh Postnatal Depression Scale. *British Journal of Psychiatry, 150*, 782–786.

Dolto, F. (1999). *La langue des images.* Paris, France: Editions Bayard.

Feldman, R., Granat, A., Pariente, C., Kanety, H., Kuint, J., & Gilboa-Schechtman, E. (2009). Maternal depression and anxiety across the postpartum year and infant social engagement, fear regulation, and stress reactivity. *Journal of the American Academy of Child and Adolescent Psychiatry, 48*, 919–927.

Fivaz-Depeursinge, E., & Corboz-Warnery, A. (1999). *The primary triangle.* New York, NY: Basic Behavioral Science.

Golse, B., & Bydlowski, M. (2001). La transparence psychique [Psychic transparency]. *Le Carnet PSY, 63*, 30–33.

Gordon, I., Zagoory-Sharon, O., Leckman, J. L., & Feldman, R. (2010a). Oxytocin and the development of parenting in humans. *Biological Psychiatry, 68*, 377–382.

Gordon, I., Zagoory-Sharon, O., Leckman, J. L., & Feldman, R. (2010b). Oxytocin, cortisol, and triadic family interactions. *Physiology & Behavior, 101*, 679–684. doi:10.1016/j.physbeh.2010.08.008

McHale, J. (1997). Overt and covert co-parenting processes in the family. *Family Process, 36*, 183–201.

Olds, D., Henderson, C. H., Cole, R., Eckenrode, J., Kitzman, H., Luckey, D., . . . Powers, J. (1998). Long-term effects of nurse home visitation on children's criminal and antisocial behavior: 15-year follow-up of a randomized controlled trial. *JAMA, 280*, 1238–1244.

Papoušek, H., & Papoušek, M. (1987). Intuitive parenting: A dialectic counterpart to the infant's integrative competence. In J. Osofsky (Ed.), *Handbook of infant development* (2nd ed., pp. 669–713). New York, NY: Wiley.

Raphael-Leff, J. (2005). *Psychological processes of childbearing* (4th ed.). London, England: Anna Freud Centre.

Stern, D. (1985). *The interpersonal world of the infant.* New York, NY: Basic Books.

Stern, D. N. (1995). *The motherhood constellation: A unified view of parent–infant psychotherapy.* New York, NY: Basic Books.

Stoleru, S., Morales Huet, M., & Grinschpoun, M. F. (1985). De l'enfant fantasmatique de la grossesse a l'interaction mère-nourrisson [From the fantasmatic child of pregnancy to the mother–infant interaction]. *Psychiatrie de l'Enfant, 28*, 441–484.

Tyano, S., & Keren, M. (2010). Single parenthood: Its impact on parenting the infant. In S. Tyano, M. Keren, H. Herrman, & J. Cox (Eds.), *Parenthood and mental health: A bridge between infant and adult psychiatry* (pp. 31–38). Hoboken, NJ: Wiley-Blackwell.

Weinberg, M. K., & Tronick, E. Z. (1998). Emotional characteristics of infants associated with maternal depression and anxiety. *Pediatrics, 102,* 1298–1304.

Winnicott, D. W. (1956). Primary maternal preoccupation. In D. W. Winnicott, *Through paediatrics to psycho-analysis: Collected papers* (pp. 300–305). New York, NY: Brunner-Routledge.

Winnicott, D. W. (1960). The theory of the parent-infant relationship. *International Journal of Psychoanalysis, 41,* 585–595.

Recommended Reading

Bailham, D., & Joseph, S. (2003). Posttraumatic stress following child birth. *Psychology, Health & Medicine, 8,* 159–158.

Condon, J. T., Boyce, P., & Corkindale, C. J. (2004). The First-Time Fathers Study: A prospective study of the mental health and wellbeing of men during the transition to parenthood. *Australian & New Zealand Journal of Psychiatry, 38,* 56–64.

Sagi, A., Lamb, M. E., & Lewkowicz, K. S. (1985). Security of infant–mother, –father, and –metapelet attachments among Kibbutz-reared Israeli children. *Monographs of the Society for Research in Child Development, 50,* 257–275.

Skari, H., Skreden, M., Malt, U. F., Dalholt, M., Ostensen, A. B., Egeland, T., & Emblem, R. (2002). Comparative levels of psychological distress, stress symptoms, depression and anxiety after childbirth—A prospective population-based study of mothers and fathers. *BJOG: An International Journal of Obstetrics and Gynecology, 109,* 1154–1163.

CHAPTER 3
Basic Concepts in Infant Psychiatry

The Multifactorial Developmental Model

For decades, theorists were on a quest to find a single model that would account for the development of personality. Freud and his disciples put forward the medico–psychological model. Some 50 years later, neuroscience and genetics came along, creating the illusion that human development could be wholly explained in neurophysiological terms. More recently, a school of thought tried to explain its development on the sole basis of sociological factors. None of these approaches could singlehandedly explain the various pathways of development from birth to adulthood. Consequently, the model that has guided us in writing this book was the multifactorial and transactional model.

As the transactional model has posited, the development of the person is shaped by biological, psychological, social, and cultural variables, as well as by positive and negative life events. We suggest conceptualizing the interplay among these parallel axes as a three-dimensional cube, as illustrated in Figure 3.1. The rate of development on each of the three axes is not always identical, and life events may affect each of them in a different manner.

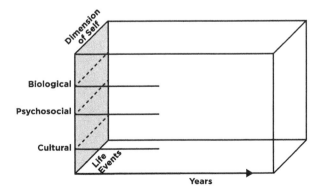

Figure 3.1. Three-dimensional cube illustrating the interplay among biological, psychological, social, and cultural variables.

The first (top) axis groups the individual's biological characteristics: physiological rhythms, temperament, motor skills, sensory activity, genetic make-up, and brain structure.

The second axis groups the individual's psychosocial traits: cognitive development (e.g., language development, thought development, theory of mind [ToM]), intrapersonal emotional development (e.g., the ability to regulate impulses, moral development), and interpersonal emotional development (e.g., attachment, sociability).

The third axis groups the individual's cultural characteristics. This covers the set of cultural norms and values assimilated by the child over the course of his development from his parents and educators.

The life-events factor groups all those events and experiences that the child goes through in her development. This thus adds the third dimension to the model, alongside the dimensions of time and development of the self. Any life event may change the expected development on each of the three axes listed.

Risk Factors and Protective Factors

In 1975, Sameroff and Chandler introduced the multifactorial (transactional) model, with its emphasis on risk factors and protective factors. To understand how each of these factors influenced child development, they followed babies born into families of different psychological, genetic, and environmental profiles. Having followed them from birth to young adulthood, Sameroff and Chandler defined the protective factors and risk factors involved in a child's normative development. At any point in time, it is the interplay between these factors that determines the child's course of development and emotional state. Beside these factors, the child's development is constantly influenced by positive and negative life events. Here are some of the principles underlying the model:

- The sum of risk factors weighed against the sum of protective factors determines the level of risk that the child is at. Before this model was developed, each risk or protective factor would be weighed in light of a value-based hierarchy. Sameroff and colleagues demonstrated that what matters for the child's development outcome is the amount of factors rather than their nature.

- Impairment in an infant's functioning may be due to risk factors on different development axes. For example, a cognitive delay may be due to a risk factor along the psychosocial axis, such as poverty or a deprived environment, or it may be a reaction to an acutely stressful situation. Therefore, the identification of a symptom tells clinicians nothing about its etiology.

- The same risk factor can affect different babies differently, depending on their respective characteristics—namely, on their other risk and protective factors. Postpartum depression, for example, will induce an insecure style of attachment only in some infants, whereas others are protected by their genetic and constitutional setup.

We now list the risk factors and protective factors that play a role in the child's development.

Risk Factors

Risk factors can be divided into three categories: risk factors originating in the child, risk factors originating in the parents, and risk factors originating in both the child's and parents' environment.

Risk factors originating in the child

On the biological axis, these include factors of constitutional vulnerability that are either innate (such as a difficult temperament) or acquired (such as prematurity, chronic physical disease, developmental delays, or disability).

On the psychological–social axis, the significant risk factors are mainly negative interpersonal experiences (such as rejection, abuse, neglect, or insecure attachment).

Risk factors originating in the parents

On the biological axis, these include age (too young or too old), both parents' IQ, low maternal level of education, and physical or mental illness (including postpartum depression).

On the psychological axis, personality disorders, posttraumatic history, substance abuse (alcohol and drugs), as well as chronic conflicts between parents and family dysfunction are also highly significant risk factors in a baby's development. Similarly, single parenting is often a risk factor, as described in the previous chapter.

Risk factors originating in both the child's and parents' environment

These factors mainly include the absence of familial or social support, exposure to a violent neighborhood, and poverty—which often means food scarcity, inaccessibility of appropriate health care, emotional burden on the parents, as well as a lack of physical and psychological availability for the child.

Protective Factors

Resilience is the broad term for the child's as well as the adult's ability to find within himself and outside the resources to grow out of adversity. Indeed, it is now known that some children go through difficult experiences without developing any psychopathology in response, whereas others will react to lesser situations with high levels of anxiety or dysfunction. Resilience is the complex interaction between protective and risk factors in the child as well as in his close environment (Rutter, 2012).

Protective factors originating in the child

Protective factors on the biological axis include, among others, IQ, temperament, and gender. A child with a high level of IQ is often able to discern environmental risk factors and eschew them. As for temperament, her adaptation to the environment (goodness of fit) helps the child survive. Gender is a more complex issue: For instance, on the one hand, girls are more resilient to maternal depression than boys, and they have less communicative disorders (autism), behavioral disorders, and attentive disorders. On the other hand, when girls do develop these disorders, they usually have it harder than boys.

Protective factors on the psychological axis include a good parent–child relationship, secure child attachment to each parent, and exposure to peer relationships.

Protective factors originating in the parents

On the biological axis, these include physical and mental health and IQ.

On the psychological axis, these include secure style of communication, positive childhood experiences, adaptive defense mechanisms, the ability to manage negative emotions, and interpersonal communication characterized by empathy and the ability to be in an intimate relationship. Another protective factor is a normally functioning parental relationship based on open interpersonal communication and openness to discuss issues relating to the children's education in mutual respect of the other parent's values. Other than IQ, the mother's level of education was also found to be a protective factor. The more educated she is, the more likely she is to identify signs of distress in the baby as they appear and seek appropriate professional help.

On the cultural axis, familial and social support and religion are significant protective factors. By helping parents cope with negative life events, they also protect the child indirectly. The term "angels in the nursery" (Lieberman, Padron, Van Horn, & Harris, 2005) has been suggested as a flip side to the expression "ghosts in the nursery" previously used as a metaphor for the risk factors (Fraiberg, Adekson, & Shapiro, 1975).

In the clinical assessment of the infant and her parents, clinicians must therefore try to detect the intrapersonal, interpersonal, environmental, and cultural risk factors and protective factors influencing the child's development. Let us illustrate this multifactorial approach with a clinical case:

CASE STUDY

A., a 1-year-old baby to parents in their 40s, was referred to us with eating difficulties. As it turned out during the session, this was an in vitro baby born prematurely and significantly underweight. A. was kept at the hospital's neonatal intensive care nursery for about 3 months because of life-threatening, prematurity-related complications (including brain hemorrhage and eating difficulties).

As part of the assessment, we listed the risk factors specific to this case. On the biological axis, we identified three major risk factors: the developmental risk secondary to the brain hemorrhage and the prematurity, the problematic eating, and the parents' relatively advanced age. On the psychological axis, we factored in the effects of the long hospitalization on both the baby (including the experience of physical pain, limited mobility, and inadequate environmental stimulation) and the parents (including feelings of anxiety, helplessness, and uncertainty). During our session, we discussed all of these factors with the parents. Protective factors were also identified in this case, including the parents' willingness to get psychological help and understand the impact of the traumatic experience on their parenting behaviors in general and, more specifically, on those related to the child's eating.

This case illustrates how the integrative, multiaxial approach unquestionably helps clinicians gain a better sense of the symptoms with which an infant comes in for consultation and treatment. We now proceed to review each of the significant variables on the various development axes.

The Biological Axis of Development

On the biological axis of development, we chose to address the following factors: genetic make-up, brain structures involved in the child's normative and abnormal development and mental health, memory, physiological rhythmicity, language, temperament, and cognition.

Genetic Make-Up

The field of medical genetics has made great strides in the past two decades thanks to advanced laboratory technologies. Nevertheless, it is still hard to pinpoint the genetic components underlying various psychiatric disorders because these involve tremendous complexity and likely more than one gene. The relatively new field of epigenetic research has shown how psychiatric disorders stem from interactions between genetic and environmental variables. Comparing the development of identical twins separated and raised in different environments helps researchers determine the respective contributions of genetics and environment to the appearance of a given disease. If a given trait is manifest in both twins, even though separated at birth, it can reasonably be assumed to be genetic. However, things are not that simple, given the presence of dormant genes that are only "awakened" by environmental factors. This is where the interplay between genetic and environmental factors comes into play. These interactions can also explain why we often come across children or adults in our practice who are genetically predisposed to a certain disease without manifesting it. Conversely, we encounter patients suffering from a supposedly genetic disease that no other family member suffers from.

What is seen here is environmental risk factors being integrated into the individual's genetic constitution. How does this combination of genetics and environment come about? Thapar and Rutter (2008) have offered a few leads. As is now known, children inherit many of their parents' traits and characteristics, and each child carries genetic traits received from both the mother and father. From birth on, a child is also exposed to environmental risk factors, many of them related to her parents—their character, functioning, behavior, and interrelationship. A psychiatric disorder in a parent affects the baby's development on two levels: It impairs the parent's functioning and has a genetic component that might have also passed on to the child. For example, depression in one of the parents increases the genetic risk of its appearance in the child, while affecting the parent–baby relationship, because the parent is unable to offer the child the needed security of attachment. On the other side of the genetics–environment equation, there is the effect of the genetic make-up on the choice of environment made by the individual. For example, a child genetically prone to Attention Deficit Hyperactivity Disorder might, because of her impulsive behavior, associate with "bad" kids. In their midst, the prone child may develop behavioral problems that would not have appeared were it not for the bad environment. Let us also recall that a given abnormal behavior, which may express a specific genetic inheritance, influences how the environment (adults and peers) will respond to the child. Negative responses are a risk factor in themselves because they often amplify the child's problematic behavior and may produce a vicious circle that can send the child into a tailspin.

Research by O'Connor and Parfitt (2009), conducted on twins, corroborates this conceptualization of the vicious circle because they found that adoptive parents of children with high genetic risk of developing antisocial behavior exhibited more negative types of parental patterns than adoptive parents of kids with low genetic risk of behavioral disorders. The data regarding the child's genetic risk were unknown to the parents in both groups. The negative parenting behaviors turned out to be a risk factor in themselves, responsible to a large degree for the depression that these children later developed. A second study looked at the development of children with a communication disorder—a disorder whose appearance and gravity are largely rooted in genetics. In the cases in which parents responded to a child's strange behaviors by distancing themselves away, the child became more introverted.

To conclude, the dichotomous conception that distinguishes between genetic-based and environment-based disorders is no longer accepted today. Even when the environmental component is paramount, as in a posttraumatic disorder, significant variability would be expected in the babies' or toddlers' responses on the basis of their genetic make-up. This understanding of the interaction between genetics and environment carries tremendous clinical implications. For instance, genetic risks may be prevented from expressing themselves by reinforcing protective factors.

The Brain

Brain development starts a few days after the ovum has been fertilized, and it continues after birth through childhood and adolescence. The first 3 years of life, however, are characterized by accelerated brain growth. In fact, this accelerated growth already begins during the third trimester of pregnancy, as demonstrated by innovative imaging technologies.

Contrary to what was once believed, that brain growth and development over the years depended only on the child's genetics and constitution, it is now known that environmental experiences directly influence brain development — in particular the specialization of certain regions — as early as during pregnancy. These biological processes take place in parallel with the psychological and cognitive processes that take place as the young child discovers his body and environment.

During the first years, the nervous infrastructure for all mental processes related to emotions, memory, behavior, and interpersonal relationships comes into being. The brain-tissue infrastructure structures itself around the baby's interactions with others — a process that has been named brain-to-brain relationships, on which the domain of interpersonal neurobiology centers. These processes have been demonstrated by empirical studies conducted on apes to see which variables affect the size of the neocortex (the part of the cerebral cortex that developed in high-ranked mammals). It was found that the number and the complexity of social relations between the apes were correlated with a bigger, better developed neocortex. The baby's internal emotional states, her impulses, are almost totally regulated by interactions with others; hence, the baby's need for human companionship is an existential one. Her ability to communicate with human beings is the result of the changes taking place in the brain and at the same time their cause. The vital need for human communication also explains why small children who grew up in institutions during the 1940s without the benefit of social interaction developed extreme depression (defined as anaclitic by Spitz, 1965), which not uncommonly even led to their death.

Several complex processes are involved in the development of the nervous system in the fetal period and the first years of life. Brain cells develop and migrate to the areas where they belong (as per the genetic code), the neurons become more sophisticated and grow "arms" named dendrites and axons, and connections (synapses) are formed between the neurons and the glial cells. Early childhood experiences shape brain structure in the following ways:

- Positive or negative experiences reinforce, weaken, or extinguish synapses. For instance, synapses in the limbic system, responsible for an individual's emotional life, are endangered not only when a baby has negative or traumatic experiences but also when he is not exposed to essential experiences, such as attachment relationships, as often happens in institutional care and neglectful environments.

- Experiences thicken the myelin layer. Myelin is the white substance that envelops the axons and determines the speed of information transfer between neurons.

- Recurring experiences gradually thicken the synapses in various areas in the body. This is how experiences are registered in memory.

The central locus where these processes take place is the limbic system deep inside the brain, which has one arm extended to the right cerebral hemisphere and another to the left one. This system is responsible for regulating attention, memory, emotion, and behavior. A key structure within this system is the amygdala. Almost ripe at birth, the amygdala reaches full maturity by the end of the first year. The right-hemisphere extension is responsible for many aspects of emotional communication and interpersonal communication, whereas the one in the left hemisphere mediates verbal communication. As the limbic system also sends extensions to the frontal cortex, it is often seen as governing people's emotional life. It is no wonder, therefore, that early traumatic experiences that are not "balanced" by protective experiences can have such a devastating effect on a child's emotional, cognitive, and social development.

From the totality of neurons in the brain, a unique group was detected that plays a key role in development: the mirror neurons. Italian scientists (Rizzolati, Fogassi, & Gallese, 2001) worked with macaque monkeys, conducting electrophysiological recordings of their brain activity in two situations: when the monkeys were peeling a banana and when they were watching another monkey peel a banana. To their surprise, the researchers found that the exact same group of nerve cells was activated in the brain in both cases, in the premotor cortex. They named this group of neurons "mirror neurons." In 2005, the same type of neuron was also discovered in the human brain. Furthermore, these neurons are activated not only during motor activities but also in emotional states. Since then, a more extensive mapping of the brain was carried out, and identical cells were also found in the insula area—a structure that has been linked with the detection of benevolent versus deceitful faces. These neurons fire up automatically and unconsciously, and they seem to play a special role in the development of the ToM and empathy. We return to them later in the chapter.

Memory

Development is impossible without memory because memory is responsible for recording and assimilating experiences in the brain. Memory already exists in the fetal period—babies remember sounds and smells that they had been exposed to in their mother's womb. This early memory, called implicit memory, differs from explicit memory, which develops beginning at 18 months old as language develops. Implicit memory is unconscious and therefore carries no sense of déjà vu events. Still, it directly influences present behaviors and emotions. What makes this kind of memory unique is its multichannel nature: An experience acquired through one particular sense may register via another sense. Thus, for example, an audio stimulus may be registered as a picture, and touch might be experienced as sound. How can this phenomenon be explained? One possibility is overlapping areas in the somatosensory cortex. Another possibility is that certain areas of the brain receive information from several senses and are capable of translating sensory stimuli of one kind into another. Implicit memory accompanies individuals through life and may come up in intense emotional situations.

Explicit memory is an essentially conscious process attended by an inner feeling of "I am now recalling something that was." Where does this memory reside in the brain? Imaging studies of brain development showed that hippocampus cells within the limbic system must attain a certain degree of maturation for this kind of memory to kick into action.

This being the case, do babies remember? The answer to this question carries clinical implications, especially when trauma is involved. If babies do remember experiences and feelings, then clearly those who go through difficult events are at risk of developing a posttraumatic disorder essentially similar to Posttraumatic Stress Disorder in older children.

Physiological Rhythmicity

From birth, human beings are regulated by two time dimensions: their internal, own time and that of the external world. A fetus's heartbeat is synchronic with her mother's, and this can be said to be the way in which time is first experienced. After birth, things change, and the baby's internal rhythms—cycles of hunger and satiety, wakefulness and sleep, comfort and discomfort, and so forth—encounter reality. From this moment on, two dimensions of time collide: subjective time, which Colarusso (1979) called "maternal time," or internal time, and objective, external time, which he dubbed "paternal time." Maternal time is the one with which the baby comes into the world. Paternal time is that of reality, the environment. This is similar to the distinction drawn by Freud between the "pleasure principle" and the "reality principle." The frustrating reality interrupts the ongoing, endless pleasure continuum and requires that the individual delay immediate gratifications and adapt to it. Everyone has a maternal and a paternal time dimension, regardless of gender. Hence, the balance between maternal and paternal time depends on the parents' responses and the coordination between them. Parents who think that babies must not be frustrated do not allow their baby to internalize the existence of paternal time. This pattern of parenting is the opposite of what Winnicott (1960) defined as optimal: "Good enough" parents are the best because they allow for both frustration and gratification of the child's desires.

Language

A distinction should be made between speech and language. Language is a necessary condition for speech; there is no speech without language. Language, on the other hand, can exist without speech. Language is the cognitive and emotional ability that allows speech. Thus, the absence of speech does not necessarily indicate a problem in language development because it is sometimes related to some motor difficulty. Piaget (1962) and Chomsky (1965) saw language as a way to represent the outside world; Vygotsky and Lurie emphasized the interpersonal communicative aspect of language, whereas psychoanalysts see it as a way to express the inner world.

In the first stages of development, cognitive structures precede the structures involved in the development of language. The child knows what he wants to say before he has acquired the tools to do so. During subsequent development stages, at around 5 years old, the situation is reversed, and language is more developed than cognition. Words such as "because" and "if" will be incorporated into the child's speech before he understands their meaning. Language likewise undergoes two stages at the emotional level. Initially, the parent labels the baby's emotional state as the parent understands it (e.g., "you are sad," or "you are happy"). These words are part of the parent–child emotional relationship, which has rules of its own. In the second stage, language expands and moves from this set of rules to become an independent structure. The cognitive and affective dimensions of language gradually balance out.

At 6 months old, the babbling stage appears, and parents respond to the baby using a special language: motherese. This response is important for further development. When a parent fails to respond to the baby's babbling—for example, because of postpartum depression—language acquisition might be delayed. Babbling is an important stage in discovering the sound arrangement of language, and it is not meant to express specific content. During the baby's preverbal period, each parent's melody and speech intonation—whether soft or aggressive—contribute to shape the emotional component of language. One way of conveying a message containing emotional content to children is through stories and songs read out loud to them from infancy on.

At 11–16 months old, the first words appear. Each child of this age has her own vocabulary. Some toddlers do not utter a single word at 16 months, whereas others already have 100 words under their belt! The average is approximately 30 words.

From 16 up to 26 months old, language becomes increasingly structured, and vocabulary grows richer by increments of 4–10 new words daily. The toddler begins to assimilate the rules of phonology (the language's system of sounds) and morphology (the language's system of word forms).

On the neurophysiological–cerebral level, language development was formerly attributed to the left hemisphere only. It is now known that both hemispheres take part in the formation of language, each in its own way, and each at different stages of language development. The information flows between both hemispheres through the bridge connecting them: the corpus callosum. The myelination of the bridge starts at 1 year old and ends at around 10 years old. To demonstrate the reciprocal interaction between the two cerebral hemispheres, the development of play in children can be followed as well as the relationship between play and language. It is now known that the right hemisphere, the one most active in affective development, is the one responsible for the development of play. However, it does not operate independently. It has the ability to transmit an emotional message through the corpus callosum to the left hemisphere, which will convert the emotional message into verbal action. The transmission of the emotional information to the left hemisphere allows better control of the emotions and fantasies registered or created in the right hemisphere. This process could explain the ability of 3- and 4-year-olds to understand a game and its emotional significance for them. Children at this stage of development enjoy talking to themselves while playing. This illustrates how the development of play and the development of language come together in the interplay between the two hemispheres.

Skinner (1989), one of the founders of behavioral theory, held that language, like any other form of behavior, is acquired through learning, conditioning, and reinforcements given to the articulation of certain sounds and word combinations. In the babbling period, for example, babies utter many sounds spontaneously, but the parents and other significant figures around them respond to certain sounds they deem significant and thus reinforce the emergence of these very sounds. When the child vocalizes clearer sounds, interpreted by the parents as actual words, he is reinforced even further. When a baby says "ink," he is given a drink; and when he says "ad," his dad immediately shows up smiling to him. The baby understands: The syllable he had emitted successfully brought him his father, and it is worth trying again. When his mother tells him — "Say cake!" — and he repeats, he receives a cake. The baby slowly realizes and assimilates the power of words.

Social learning theory

Alongside behavioral theory, other researchers, foremost among them Bandura (1977), developed a slightly different conception of language development. According to them, language is learned through observation and imitation and not necessarily through conditioning and reinforcement. Children hear well-formed speech in their mother tongue and imitate this model of speech. In her mind, the child builds connections linking a certain word and a given situation that exists in the world at that moment. When she hears the words "no more," and the porridge plate is empty, then "no more dice," and the dice box is empty, she begins to understand how the words relate to reality. The phrase "no more" begins to take on a meaning. From the porridge and box, the child will, of course, infer about other "no more" situations. The emphasis in this theoretical construct is on the baby's ability to draw conclusions and infer from one thing to another.

Behavioral-emotional theory

Golse (2001), French psychoanalyst and child psychiatrist, has tried to integrate the analytical and behavioral approaches. He has maintained that the emotional component is also important in the development of language: Language needs others; the message requires an address. This angle can explain why children who grow up in institutions are often linguistically behind even when their intellectual level is normative.

The professional literature underlines the role and importance of the "mother tongue" in the development of the child's language. In our opinion, the "mother tongue" should not be the only reference, and the "father tongue" should also be given its due place. This certainly holds true in bilingual families, in which the father and mother address the child in different languages. Both the mother tongue and the father tongue are also significant in families in which both parents speak the same language; although they use the same vocabulary, their tone of speech and choice of words are also different. In fact, the child is exposed to two emotional world views that manifest themselves verbally. Just as people internalize father time and mother time, they have in their repertoire both their mother tongue and father tongue.

Temperament

Temperament is an innate attribute that largely determines how an individual will respond to external stimuli. Thomas and Chess (1977) defined four principal patterns of response to an external stimulus that can be characterized on the basis of measuring the following nine inborn variables:

- *Physiological regularity*: regularity of the sleep–wake cycle, hunger and satiety, and other cyclical actions.

- *Level of physical activity*.

- *Adaptation time*: the time it takes the baby to get used to a new situation.

- *Reaction threshold*: the level of intensity required for a stimulation to elicit a response from the baby.

- *Response intensity*.

- *The type of initial response to a stimulus or a new situation*: Does the baby approach the new stimulus without hesitation or recoil from it?

- *Mood*: a child's tendency to respond to an external stimulus by being happy, being sad, smiling, or crying.

- *Distractibility*: the extent to which any stimulus coming from the outside distracts the baby and makes it hard for him to keep up the activity he was engaged in.

- *Attention span and persistence*: the baby's ability to persevere in a task despite frustrations caused by the environment.

On the basis of these nine variables and their permanence over the years in thousands of babies, Thomas and Chess (1977) defined four types of temperament: easy, difficult, slow-to-warm-up, and mixed. Sixty-five percent of the children examined were classified into categories, as follows: 40% were of easy temperament, 10% were difficult, 15% were slow-to-warm-up, and 35% were mixed.

Kagan, Reznick, and Snidman (1988) defined temperament based on the baby's initial approach to or withdrawal from new stimuli and divided infants into only two groups: introverts and extroverts. They found that each group had distinct psychological and physiological characteristics. They also found that highly introverted babies were at greater risk of developing social phobia when reaching school age.

The concept of temperament is not equivalent to the notion of personality. Temperament is but one aspect of personality. Furthermore, even though temperament is a mostly innate trait, and is relatively stable over time, the individual's adaptability to her environment—what researchers call goodness of fit—is another factor influencing the individual's sense of self. Adults can be aware of their temperament and try to change their behavior to fit their surroundings.

Parents respond to the baby's temperament in line with their own temperament and personality. Thus, for example, a parent with a difficult temperament would likely perceive his like-tempered child as "doing things for spite" and would feel considerable anger or helplessness toward it. The slow-to-warm-up baby is also not always understood by her parents. They often see her as passive, too shy, a baby with no interest in her environment, and they even tend to be overprotective, critical, or intrusive toward her.

Cognitive Development

In the second half of the 20th century, Piaget's (1962) theory of development reigned supreme. Widely implemented in the health and educational systems, it allowed physicians and teachers to understand and measure the stages involved in the maturation of the child's intellectual capacities. Many a curriculum was based on it.

Underlying Piaget's theory is the understanding that cognitive development depends on the maturation of areas in the brain, and it proceeds in a fixed pattern of leaps and bounds, with major changes taking place at 18 months, 7 years old, and 12 years old. This is an epigenetic theory, which views the completion of each stage as a prerequisite for moving on to the next.

During the first 18 months, a child learns through sensory and motor exploration, which is why Piaget called this stage the sensorimotor stage. The child slowly differentiates himself from his surroundings and even learns that intentional actions on his part can influence his environment (e.g., extending a hand and pulling on an object will bring on music). The baby also understands that an object continues to exist even when out of sight (object permanence). This is an important stage in a child's development, preparing him for that stage where he will understand that the parent continues to exist even when out of sight (object constancy). It is therefore highly important to allow babies to explore their physical surroundings with all their senses, to touch food and get dirty, to put things into their mouths, and to move freely. Freedom of movement encourages exploration—the main learning tool that serves people throughout life. In the first 2 years of life, the environment is mainly explored through movement and the senses.

The second stage of cognitive development, according to Piaget, is the pre-operational stage (from 2 to 7 years old). The transition into this stage depends on language development. At this stage, the child's thinking is still egocentric; she has a hard time acknowledging the existence of a viewpoint other than her own, and she can sort objects on the basis of one criterion only, such as color, shape, or size.

The next stages in cognitive development take place at later ages, and they are not dealt with in this book. Toward the end of the 20th century, many researchers and theorists started to critique Piaget's theory. They opposed the rigid schematic conception of cognitive development. Cognition, they claimed, develops differently in every child and is also influenced by the interplay between the child and his environment. This is evidenced by the delayed cognitive development of most babies growing in institutions or neglectful families.

The Psychological Development Axis

In the next pages, we review the theories and major basic terms related to the baby's inter- and intrapersonal psychological development.

Development at the Interpersonal Level

Theory of Mind (ToM)

As shown earlier, Piaget's premise was that all children share the same stages of cognitive development. In their works, Winnicott (English pediatrician and psychoanalyst), followed by Daniel Stern (American psychiatrist and psychoanalyst), drew conclusions regarding the development of babies on the basis of direct observation of healthy babies, without feeling in any way obligated to follow in the footsteps of theoreticians before them. They boldly conceptualized new approaches to understanding development. Both were highly impressed by babies' observable ability, already at birth, to understand their immediate environment and respond accordingly. In their writings, Winnicott and Stern paved the way for the works of Baron-Cohen, who conceptualized the ToM in 1995.

ToM is a cognitive theory that develops in the human brain and allows the individual to understand that people's actions, as well as her own, are driven by an inner world, intentions, beliefs, and knowledge. When this theory develops, a child can draw conclusions regarding her own mental and affective state and differentiate it from that of others. She then also realizes that other people's desires, intentions, and beliefs differ from her own. This is, thus, a complex cognitive skill that is basically innate while requiring interpersonal interactions to develop. The ToM is currently perceived as the foundation for the development of social intelligence, or the "social brain" as many call it. Baron-Cohen studied its development and even tried to find how it differed in children with deviant development. Baron-Cohen, Tager-Flusberg, and Cohen (1993) discovered, for example, a serious deficit in its development among children who suffered from autism, as opposed to healthy children and children affected with intellectual disability.

The normative development of the ToM is thought to go through the following stages:

- At 6 months old, a baby distinguishes between still objects and human figures.

- At 12 months old, joint attention will have developed—that is, the baby's cognitive ability to lend his attention to something together with someone else, such as looking at a tractor on the street together with his mother. Social referencing also develops—namely, the baby's ability to alleviate the anxiety that arises in unfamiliar situations by looking at the parent's calm facial expression.

- At 14–18 months old, a toddler will start to understand that a relationship exists between the behaviors of those around her and their intentions (intentionality). By way of example, a baby might understand that if her mother leaves her handbag in the room and leaves the house, it is a sign that she intends to come back!

- By 24 months old, a toddler is able to identify himself in the mirror and realize that the child facing him is none other than himself. This is a further stage in the distinction between the me and the not-me. At this stage, the child already uses the word "I." This is an essential stage in the development of the ToM—namely, the ability to understand that other people are unlike him in their beliefs and thoughts.

- At 3 or 4 years old, the child distinguishes between reality and imagination, and between her own beliefs and those of others. During the next years, up until 7 years old, she will also develop the ability to understand superstitions, metaphors, and humor as well as to tell apart jokes and lies. Toward preadolescence (at 9 or 10 years old) comes the ability to evaluate what is proper and fitting to say in various social scenarios, that special sense called tact.

Parents play an important role in the development of the ToM. They speak to the child, expressing beliefs, thoughts, intentions, and feelings, and they point out links to behaviors and actions. Sroufe (Sroufe, Egeland, Carlson, &

Collins, 2005) looked at children's emotional understanding when they were 3½ years old, and then 18 months later, when they turned 5 years old. The researchers found that children of mothers who gave spontaneous expression to their feelings within this 18-month interval were endowed with a higher level of emotional understanding when they reached 5 years old.

Fonagy (2001) called the aptitude to articulate the emotional motives behind behavior "reflective functioning." Oppenheim and Koren-Karie (2002) called this ability "empathic understanding," and they developed a measuring tool for it, named the Insightfulness Assessment. Interestingly, the presence of older brothers or sisters contributes to the development of ToM in the younger sibling, among others, and to his ability to understand emotional states.

Development of empathy

The ability to feel empathy, to understand another's feelings, is yet another stage in the development of social intelligence. It is based on the cognitive understanding of emotional states in others, but there is more to it than that: It involves the ability to feel close to another, to be in another's shoes. Studies using brain imaging to demonstrate emotional processes showed that empathy required the activation of areas in the brain responsible for expressing feelings (amygdala, cingulate). These areas would indeed seem to malfunction in people who suffer from autism and possibly even certain individuals with personality disorders.

The development of empathy in a child greatly depends on her parents' ability to be empathetic. Parents lacking empathy thus raise likewise deficient children, and it is therefore not surprising to find a relationship between abuse and neglect on the one hand and on the other hand the development of personality disorders, which are characterized by considerable difficulty in understanding others.

Beside one's innate infrastructure and the relationships with the parents, other variables play a role in the development of empathy, such as peer relationships. Social relations present an opportunity for a child to picture what others might be seeing, feeling, or thinking—a chance to put herself in the other's shoes. Hence, we strongly advocate encouraging little children to spend time with their peers, at home, in the playground, in nursery schools, or in day care centers.

Styles of attachment

The concept of attachment, so common in professional literature on baby development, is borrowed from ethology, the scientific branch studying animal behavioral patterns. Bowlby (1969), the first to have used it to describe human behavior, was greatly influenced by the works of two prominent ethologists: Lorenz and Harlow. Lorenz (1937) described the inborn phenomenon called imprinting in ducks—the tendency that ducklings have to follow the first female duck they see after birth. Harlow (see Suomi, van der Horst, & van der Veer, 2008) showed that young monkeys preferred the presence of a tender and close parent who did not feed them to that of a distant parent who did. Bowlby claimed that babies were born with the biological drive to seek the proximity of a protective human figure at a time of emotional or physical distress. He called this "the drive for attachment." A distinction should be made between the baby's attachment to his parent and the notion of bonding, which denotes the parent's affective bond to the baby that starts already during pregnancy.

After the term "attachment" was conceptualized, researchers had to establish a typology of attachment and find tools to test for each baby's individual style of attachment. Ainsworth, Blehar, Waters, and Wall (1978), who worked a lot on attachment theory, elaborated the Strange Situation paradigm, which has been widely used to date. This is a test conducted in a room that the baby is unfamiliar with, in the presence of the baby's caregiver and an unfamiliar examiner. The caregiver and baby enter the room, and clinicians observe the extent of the baby's exploratory behavior (the extent to which she investigates and plays with the toys in the room). At some point, on the examiner's cue, the caregiver exits the room, leaving the infant alone with the examiner to respond as she will in her own particular way, by either crying, calling out loud or displaying distress, remaining indifferent and continuing to play, or freezing solid or becoming agitated. Three minutes later, the caregiver returns to the room, and clinicians watch the reunion between the caregiver and the baby, mainly looking to see how the baby greets her caregiver: whether she approaches her caregiver and calms down or continues to cry and be angry, whether she clings to the caregiver or remains indifferent and continues to play. A particularly worrying reaction is when the baby is reticent about going up to her caregiver, looking scared and petrified.

It would seem that, starting from the second month, a baby internalizes the way in which his caregivers, most often his parents, treat him during moments of distress. These internalizations—what Stern (1985) called "schemas of being with"—add up, and by the end of the first year, different styles of attachment can be observed within a normative baby population.

Ainsworth et al. (1978) defined three types of attachment:

- *Secure attachment*: A baby presenting this type of attachment clearly manifests attachment behaviors toward the parent in situations of distress. She cries, approaches, and seeks the parent's physical closeness, and after the storm subsides, she quickly settles down and back to the investigative activity.

- *Insecure avoidant attachment*: A baby characterized by this type of attachment does not display his distress, does not acknowledge the parent's return to the room, does not seek the parent's proximity, and goes on playing as if nothing had happened. This style is often observed in babies of parents who suffer from mental illnesses such as depression, psychosis, or Obsessive Compulsive Disorder and who respond to their child's distress with insensitivity. This form of attachment reflects the baby's way of dealing with an emotional situation he finds difficult: Instead of manifesting neediness and receiving a hurtful response, the baby "muffles" his need for proximity and his attachment system.

- *Insecure resistant/ambivalent attachment*: A baby with this style of attachment vents her distress with great intensity. Not reassured by the parent's proximity, she persists in her crying and anger toward the parent, unable to return to her previously inquisitive activity. This pattern is mostly observed in babies whose parents suffer from mood swings (e.g., Borderline Personality Disorder) or high levels of basic anxiety.

- *Disorganized attachment*: An additional type of attachment, termed disorganized, was defined by Main and Solomon (1990) after observing the separation and reunion behaviors in the Strange Situation paradigm of babies growing up in verbally or physically violent dysfunctional families. A baby whose attachment is disorganized is unable to cope with the distressful situation. At separation, he displays considerable distress, but with the parent back in the room, his behavior becomes confused: He draws close to and moves away from the parent, and he sometimes freezes solid as if fearing the parent.

The attachment system we have just defined is closely related to the exploratory system, the one that urges people to venture out, with wholesome curiosity, to explore the immediate environment, then more distant surroundings as they grow older. Both systems are hard-wired in people and are active throughout life. The exploratory system is vital to learning and to emotional and intellectual development, whereas the attachment system is vital for the development of a basic sense of security and protection in times of distress. Secure attachment, which is present in the majority of the population, provides a sense of psychological "anchoring," a secure base from which to go forth and explore the world, as illustrated in Figure 3.2.

Figure 3.2. The security cycle: Secure attachment allows exploration and learning. Image copyright © 2016 Cooper, Hoffman, and Powell. Circle of Security International. Reproduced with permission.

Secure attachment also plays a key role in the development of autoregulation. The caregiver's facial expression and body language lend room and legitimacy to the negative emotions that arise in the baby in distressing and stressful situations while mitigating them. The infant internalizes the response of the beneficial figure and will, later on in life, be able to regulate herself without her parents' help. This is why secure attachment is listed among the protective factors. It is now known, for example, that a baby with a difficult temperament who is at risk for developing an attention deficit disorder will be less prone to developing one if she has a secure type of attachment.

A distinction is to be made between the concepts of attachment and relationship. Attachment forms part of the child's relationship with his parents, whereas relationship spans additional areas, such as play and learning, setting boundaries, education, and sociability. Insecure attachment is a risk factor for the emergence of a disorder in the parent–child relationship but by no means a predictor of things to come. The same goes for secure attachment, which does not preclude the possible existence of a problem in the relationship. A child can be certain of his parents' support when serious trouble hits, even if his daily relationship with them remains fraught with tensions and conflict around all matters of a nonurgent nature.

Sroufe et al. (2005)—researchers of child development—followed children with different styles of attachment into their young adulthood. They demonstrated a relationship between styles of attachment in infancy and the nature of interpersonal and social relationships formed by those children when they reached school age. Children who had a secure style of attachment at 1 year old were observed to be more sociable at 5 years old than children with an insecure style of attachment at 1 year old. They displayed better adaptability to the system, flexibility in their interpersonal relationships, a high degree of sensitivity to others, and strong problem-solving skills.

Hesse and Main (2006) pointed to a direct relationship between one's attachment style in infancy and the organization level of one's personality at adolescence and adulthood. They demonstrated that the style of attachment remains active and fairly stable throughout life, as follows:

- Secure attachment exhibited during childhood tends to carry over into adolescence and adulthood as well; in other words, those who have it as children grow up to become adults who are capable of empathy and appreciate the importance of close relationships.

- Those with insecure avoidant attachment tend to become adolescents and adults with a dismissing style of attachment who minimize the importance of the emotional component in their relationships.

- Children with an insecure resistant/ambivalent attachment develop a preoccupied style as adults—that is, they become susceptible individuals who constantly analyze their interpersonal relationships.

- Those characterized by a disorganized style of attachment as children tend to stay so as they become adults: Situations of emotional distress, whether their own or those of people close to them, threaten them very much and make them seem frightened and frightening.

Fonagy (2001) showed that highly negative—or highly positive—life events can change a person's attachment pattern. Lieberman and Pawl (1988) showed that psychotherapy—even at adulthood—can also change a person's attachment style for the better.

As we have noted above, secure attachment is a protective factor for the development of a healthy personality, whereas insecure attachment is a risk factor that engenders vulnerability. That being said, it is important to note that neither one can predict the appearance of a psychiatric disorder. The exception here is the disorganized style of attachment, which predicts the emergence of behavioral disorders at school age and the emergence of Borderline Personality Disorder at adulthood. Furthermore, a child presenting this type of attachment who experiences a stressful situation at adulthood is at a high risk of developing Posttraumatic Stress Disorder.

Are attachment representations transmitted from one generation to another, from parents to their children? It seems so. Replicated studies found a very high correlation (75%) between parents and children in terms of attachment style. Thus, here too, as in every intergenerational transmission, a complex multifactorial bio–psycho–social mechanism underlies the process. Several studies using imaging have shown, for example, that the same neurobiological process occurs in the child's and the parent's brain during an attachment-based interaction.

To better understand insecure attachment behaviors, consider the metaphor of testing the strength of a string, in which the string represents the attachment relationship. When one has doubts about the strength of the string, one will stretch it, even at the price of causing it to snap. The same applies in the case of an insecure attachment: The infant "stretches" it with provocations just to test its strength. A parent who fails to understand where these provocations are coming from will respond angrily, weakening even more the security in the relationship.

Finally, let us emphasize that an insecurity of attachment and Reactive Attachment Disorder are two different things. The latter refers to a clinical situation in which a baby completely lacks a permanent attachment figure. In these situations, common among children who grow up in institutions or hop between foster families, the child is unable to develop normative social skills, fails to establish deep personal relationships, and is sad; in addition, her development is most often delayed. Such were the institutionalized children described by René Spitz (1965) in the works he published after World War II: babies who suffered from anaclitic depression that led them to their death. Zeanah et al. (2009) extended the term Reactive Attachment Disorder to those children with a permanent but neglectful parental figure. Often, these children resort to self-endangering behavior in the presence of the parent (e.g., a child who climbs up on the windowsill expecting the parent to pay attention to him and "save" him). Another clinical expression of an attachment disorder is a pattern of role reversal between toddler and parent, in which it is the former who watches over and commands the parent, having internalized an image of a weak parent who cannot be counted on.

"Developmental Organizers": Developmental Milestones

In the 1950s, René Spitz defined three "developmental organizers" — namely, three turning points in the development of a baby's object relations:

- The first organizer is the "social smile." This appears at 2–2½ months old and signifies the start of the baby's dialogue with her human environment.

- The second organizer is "stranger anxiety." Manifested by the baby at around 8 months old, it reflects the baby's ability to tell familiar people apart from strangers. As mentioned, this anxiety develops owing to a positive attachment experience to constant caregivers in the first 6 months of life. Spitz wrote in his observations (e.g., Spitz, 1965) that babies in institutions did not experience stranger anxiety precisely because they did not experience attachment. Following his work, other clinicians noticed other situations in which stranger anxiety did not appear, such as lengthy hospitalizations and autism.

- The third organizer is uttering the word "no." A toddler starts saying "no" at about 18 months old. What this signifies is that the child perceives himself as a separate entity with desires of his own. This is also a new way for the child to express aggression and resistance. Spitz saw this development as a critical phase in the socialization process that the child undergoes, the process by which he becomes part of human society and submits to its rules. From this moment on, discussions and debates will be able to replace physical aggression. When parents perceive the "naysaying" negatively and view it as "rebellious" or "spiteful" behavior rather than the toddler's need for self-expression, they might become filled with anger and a great deal of aggression. These feelings make them threaten and punish the child, which often drives him to dig his heels in even deeper. Being misunderstood irritates the toddler, and his behavior grows even more rebellious. Parents should see the toddler's "no" as a mark of normative development, requiring a focused and matter-of-factly response, without taking offense.

The Skin as Symbol of the Transition Between the Interpersonal and Intrapersonal Axes of Development

On the way from the interpersonal psychological factors to the intrapersonal factors influencing behavior, there is the skin. On the physical level, the skin mediates the sensory experiences between the body and its surroundings, but metaphysically speaking, it carries symbolic meaning as a medium between the self and others through touch—hence, the important role played by touch in the development of the baby's relationship with her environment from her time of birth. The current recommendation is to lay the newborn baby on the mother's skin to create a sensation of continuity with the intrauterine environment. The skin connects the baby with the outside world and protects her from external harm. Anzieu (1989), a French psychoanalyst, coined the concept of Skin-Ego. The ego envelops the soul like the skin envelops the body, and, just like the skin, the ego also evolves from childhood on as an enclosing, containing entity protecting the soul from unconscious impulses, from the demands of the superego, and from various external factors. Because the skin mediates between what lies inside the body and what lies outside, it also acts as a demarcation line between people's external and internal body images.

External body image

From a young age, individuals develop their external body image. This image has three dimensions: the way people think they look; the way people think others see them; and their actual, objective bodily dimensions. Some emotional disorders, such as eating disorders, involve problematic gaps between these three dimensions.

Internal body image

Everyone also has an internal body image. Individuals can imagine their various organs. This image has both a conscious element and an unconscious one. People harbor their own unique perceptions as to the structure of their heart, lungs, stomach, brain, skeleton, eyes, and so forth. This image has to do with how different individuals view aches and diseases in different areas of their body.

Development of the Baby's Intrapersonal Emotional World

In this section, we discuss the basic concepts of different theories relevant to the development of the baby's intrapersonal emotional world. Let us start, in due historic order, with a description of Freudian theory, and go on to present newer constructs by post-Freudian scholars, for the most part psychoanalysts, who actually treated children.

Freud (1953–1974) built his theory on the early stages of development through the retrospective reconstruction of childhood memories as reported by adult patients of his as they lay on the couch. In contrast, modern researchers based their understanding of human development on direct and longitudinal observations of the infant and his interaction with his close environment, from infancy to young adulthood.

Freud described two fundamental characteristic human impulses: the life impulse (Eros) and death impulse (Thanatos). The energy that feeds the life impulse, the libido, is the life-preserving energy. The one that feeds the death impulse is destructive energy, aggression. Freud determined that in each stage of development, the libido concentrates itself in a specific part of the body and that psychological disorders appear when individuals get permanently fixated in a given stage of development, usually because of difficulties in their relationship with their parents. In his view, these fixations lead to the emergence of personality disorders in the future.

Let us recall the initial stages of development described by Freud, noting where the libido is focused in each. In the oral stage, from birth to 2 years old, the libido centers around the mouth; in the anal stage, from 2 to 3 years old, the libido centers around the anus; in the phallic stage, from 3 to 5 years old, the libido centers around the genital area; and in the oedipal stage, the libido centers in the opposite-sex parent. The oedipal stage is also attended by fears of castration. In addition to these stages, Freud also described how the child internalizes the mother and father figures as having a separate identity to her own. This internalization, later called object constancy by Margaret Mahler (Mahler, Pierre, & Bergman, 1975), gives the child the unconscious sense of the parent's constant presence, even when not physically there. This feeling is a source of great security for the child. Flaws in one's positive internalization of the parent lead to low self-image and a feeling of insecurity—a lack of trust in both oneself and others.

With her original thinking, psychoanalyst Françoise Dolto (1994) contributed her share to an understanding of normative and pathological baby behavior. Unlike Freud, for whom castration was an all-negative thing, a cause of mainly anxiety and loss, Dolto saw its positive aspects. Castration, she believed, allowed a child to wean himself from the pleasure involved in each of the developmental stages—a necessary process to move on to the next stage. It therefore symbolized a child's passage from one development stage to the next. She described several developmental castrations: umbilical castration, which disconnects the fetus from his mother's uterus; oral castration, which prevents the baby from continuing to enjoy breastfeeding, freeing the mouth to move on to its next function, speech; followed by anal castration; genital castration; and oedipal castration. Each castration is in fact a parental prohibition imposed on a given pleasure to allow the child to move on to a more mature stage of development. Beside this original developmental approach, Dolto offered two more important concepts: speaking the baby and telling it the truth.

Darwin noted that 5-month-old babies smiled at their own reflection in the mirror, a phenomenon termed the "mirror stage." Delving deeper, Zazzo (1981) discovered stages of development common to all babies: At 3 months old, a baby looks at the mirror and smiles to herself as she would at this age to any human figure. From 8 months old, a baby takes an interest in her reflection in the mirror while observing the reflection of the adult by her side. During her second year, the child is embarrassed, sometimes even to the point of avoiding a glance at the mirror. It seems that this is when the toddler starts to realize that she is watching herself. This is also the age when the child already says "I." Between 18 months and 2 years old, the child recognizes herself in the mirror. This is verifiable using the "stain" test, in which a toddler is made to stand in front of a mirror with a red spot drawn on her nose. If she tries to remove the stain from the figure reflected in the mirror, this means that she still fails to recognize herself in the mirror.

Psychoanalysts also took an interest in the relationship between the way in which the child understands his reflection in the mirror and intrapersonal processes. According to Wallon (1949) and Lacan (1949), it is through the baby's observation of his reflection in the mirror that his initial narcissism is born and the baby starts to identify with the parent as he sees himself in the parent's arms and internalizes this image.

Dolto (1994) likewise emphasized the importance of this stage in the child's development, not only in the visual dimension but also in terms of the participation of all the senses in the experience. The parent in whose arms the infant is held and who stands by his side actually gives his identity a name. When the parent points at the mirror saying "Here's Danny," the physical body and its symbolic meaning fuse together.

Donald Winnicott (1960) emphasized the key role of the human environment in a baby's development. His most famously quoted phrase is "There is no such thing as an infant alone, and no such a thing as a mother alone." Winnicott gave future generations two more seminal concepts: the "good enough parent" and the "transitional object."

According to Winnicott (1960, 1990), some amount of frustration is necessary for the baby's development (as Dolto, 1994, has noted under the term of developmental castrations, as we saw above), and so the "good enough" parent is the one who not only knows how to gratify the child but also how to frustrate her to the extent befitting her age. Winnicott also coined the concept of "facilitating environment," or "good enough environment." This is an environment that does not dictate in which direction the child should develop. It adapts itself to the baby's changing needs and evolves to fit her stages of maturity. It is an environment that accompanies the baby, the toddler, and then the child but also knows to let go and gradually release its grip.

Winnicott (1960) also coined the term "transitional object." The infant, he claimed, dealt with frustrating situations by means of a soft object—a rag, a teddy bear, a blanket, a pillow. For the baby, this transitional object symbolizes his parents' presence, and he invests his libido in it. This is an object located between reality and fantasy, in that it represents the parent, and the infant uses it to soothe and pacify himself, especially in situations of frustration or separation.

In contrast to what has been taught in the past, published studies have shown there to be no connection between the existence of a transitional object and the quality of the parent–baby relationship. American psychoanalyst Daniel Stern based his theory on direct observation of babies with their parents (e.g., Stern, 1985, 1995). He was the first to study intra- and interpersonal processes from a research perspective. Stern analyzed each stage in the baby's development of self. When a baby is engaged in mental or motor activities, she has some sense of herself, even though her sensations are neither conscious nor verbal. Each time she shuts her eyes, for example, she sees black; each time she moves her head, the picture changes; and each time she moves her hands, she gets some sort of sensory feedback. It is the baby's actions that create those experiences, which keep recurring and form the baby's core self. The baby therefore feels creative—she is the one creating her own internal organization with her own senses—and thus gains a sense of physical and emotional continuity.

Stern described the baby's sense of self as he develops: At each age, he experiences himself differently, and these sensations stack up, accumulate. These are not stages, and they are not transitional periods that come and go, but a whole inventory of sensations maintained throughout life. One of the main clinical implications of Stern's conception lies in the emphasis on the preverbal component of the self that resides in everyone. This component often expresses itself during psychotherapy.

Stern (1995) also studied the parent–baby relationship. Among others, he proposed the concept of affect attunement. The mother becomes emotionally attuned to the baby, thus signaling to her that she can read her facial expressions and understand her. According to Stern, this is not conveyed through words or through a simple imitation of the baby's facial expression. In fact, affect attunement takes form in the parental affective reaction, which has to be similar, but not identical, in intensity, form, and duration to the baby's. It is in this way that parental empathy is communicated. This process might look like this: The baby expresses happiness by making rising and descending sounds, to which the mother responds with a gesture similar in intensity, duration, and form, such as rising and falling hand movements. Affect attunement is thus a process of emotional conversion into equivalent but different elements. This intuitive parental behavior allows parents to signal their understanding, yet separateness, to the baby. In this way, the baby develops a separate identity. The process begins with the attention paid by the parent to the baby, which signals the parent's understanding of her emotional state. This is, incidentally, a cornerstone in the development of the ToM and empathy.

The Psychosocial Axis of Development

How the Social Network Influences Development

Through its parents, the baby learns to assimilate the norms and values of the society in which he is brought up. In addition, studies have shown the benefit derived by babies from interacting with the other. These studies, based on group observations of babies in day care, found that babies were able to interact by the age of 12 months and to cooperate at 15 months: They "chat" by uttering sounds and comfort a crying baby in different ways. They smile at each other, even drawing closer and touching each other. These are the very behaviors they exhibit toward their parents. This is, then, a social competence that develops at a very tender age. When babies already know each other, they can develop interpersonal relationships unmediated by toys. With no toys around, babies are able to keep longer at a common activity together with other babies. Moreover, babies whose parents were befriended formed the best bonds of friendship. These studies show just how important it is to encourage babies in their first year of life to spend time with infants their age. This time spent together contributes greatly to the development of social competence. It is unfortunate that the idea whereby a baby is better off growing up in the sole company of his parents and extended family during his first 3 years in life continues to prevail in some circles.

Cultural Influences on Development

We use the term culture to refer to a system of meanings and values shared by a group of individuals. These meanings and values, passed on from one generation to the next, are also reflected in the way children are treated and in the caregiving role assigned to each member of the child's close family, including grandparents. A baby growing up in a family of Ethiopian origin, for example, is attended by all members of the family; it is thus to be expected that attachment behaviors within this particular population will differ from those seen among babies growing up in Western nuclear families.

Modern society, along with its rules and values, is in constant flux, which also influences the development of children. Many families emigrate, bringing their cultures and values into the new country. Is the understanding that has been gained regarding the development of children in Western society also relevant to the development of children raised in other cultures? Indeed, most child development theories have originated in Western societies. They mostly address the intrafamilial components related to child development without regard to cultural factors or those values on which the family members were brought up for generations. It is known today that cultural factors are also at play among the risk factors and protective factors, and studies have started to approach the topic, especially in these troubled times of forced immigration.

As concerns emigrant families, their degree of integration into the new society obviously also influences the child's development, and integration often depends on the parents' decisions: Do they let the child acculturate to the new country's state educational system? What language should they speak with the child, and up to what age? Should they preserve the family's original habits, or assimilate the norms of the new culture? Should they turn to public services for advice, support, or treatment?

Differences of opinion often appear between families and health professionals in regard to the definition of abnormality. Emigrant families may often oppose the establishment, unwilling to give up their legacy and the patriarchal discipline or adopt rules and values that are supposedly more effective and advanced.

This issue is highly important in Israel, a country of immigrants, yet it is sometimes forgotten during evaluations and therapies. Incidentally, a very common question among parents who have only recently immigrated to Israel is the question of bilingualism—whether the parent should speak to their child in her mother tongue or the local idiom, or whether the child benefits from speaking two or more languages at home. We would like to emphasize that bilingualism does not affect a child's development, as long as there is no primary language delay, and could even contribute to it greatly in the long run. This being said, one has to take into account that speech in these children might be a few months late to appear.

Life-Events Axis

Since the start of the present century, the importance of social and environmental factors in children's development has been well-recognized. In the past, the theories and studies were mainly concerned with the biological and psychological facets of development. It has now become clear that life events largely account for developmental diversity. The life-events axis is the only unpredictable axis. The previous approach was overly deterministic, leaving no room for the unexpected and its place in development. It is now known that life events can influence the baby, sometimes directly and sometimes through his parents. In fact, the parents mediate the experience even when the baby had experienced it firsthand.

Life events are commonly divided into events taking place within the family cell—disease, loss, birth of a sibling, relocation, and unemployment—and those occurring outside the family—natural disaster, war, accidents, and so forth. Studies have shown that not all babies respond to a difficult life event traumatically. A baby's response is influenced by her personality, her (short) past, resilience, the circumstances of the event, and mainly by the intensity of the parent's response.

Although these studies are still in their infancy, there is no way to generalize and predict the emotional impact of a negative event of some sort or other. Clinicians must wait for the mechanisms mediating the emotional response to a traumatic event to be better known.

Intuitive Parenting

German researchers Papoušek and Papoušek (1987) conceptualized the term "intuitive parenting" from watching hundreds of mothers and babies throughout their work. This denotes a parent's unconscious biological ability to encourage her child's development in a way that matches his current stage of development. Rather than being governed by rational decisions, these parental actions happen on their own. In the relatively rare cases in which this ability is lacking, a parent can be taught how to support her child and encourage his development.

Parental Projections

Parental projections play an important role in the baby's development, for better or worse. Cramer and Palacio-Espasa (1993) identified three types of parental projections on their children:

- *Libidinal projections*: positive wishes and desires for the child's future that also leave ample room for the child's independent development.

- *Conflictual projections*: wishes and desires that are not well suited to the child but which the parent has a hard time letting go of even when realizing that they are only meant to serve the parent's own needs.

- *Narcissistic projections*: wishes and desires that are only meant to serve the parent's needs, with no regard for the child's true "self." These projections are obviously pathological, leading to disorders in the parent–child relationship.

Psychiatric Evaluation of the Infant

The psychiatric evaluation of an infant is meant to (a) determine whether the very young child has symptoms that correspond to one or more disorders based on the *DC:0–5™: Diagnostic Classification of Mental Health and Developmental Disorders of Infancy and Early Childhood* (DC:0–5; ZERO TO THREE, 2016), (b) consider the possibility of differential diagnosis, and (c) propose a treatment plan after the final diagnosis has been determined. The evaluation is informed, of course, by the theoretic approach advocated by the examining physician. We would, however, like to provide a few guidelines based on the multifactorial approach described above. The baby is always examined in the presence of both parents.

Who Refers the Parents to Professional Counseling and Why?

Parents may either come to clinicians directly or be sent by health professionals (community Well-Baby centers, pediatricians, psychiatrists, and social workers). Counseling is sought for a variety of reasons: either abnormal behaviors in a baby, or delayed development that seems to be emotionally based, or parental dysfunction rooted in various causes (e.g., postpartum depression, parental psychopathology). The main question behind the consultation is whether a disorder really exists or whether it is just a case of parental inexperience that only requires developmental guidance, with a few practical tips thrown in.

The most common reasons underlying referrals of babies and toddlers to evaluation include the following: eating problems, sleeping problems, severe tantrums and unrest, excessive stranger anxiety, separation anxiety, aggression toward self and others, difficulties in communication and social interactions, psychogenic constipation, hair pulling, problems in the parent–baby relationship, parental dysfunction, and parental psychopathology that affects the young child (e.g., postpartum depression, severe personality disorders).

Evaluation Process

A baby's clinical assessment involves several components:

- The parents describe why they have sought counselling and recount the child's development from the time that the mother got pregnant to the time of the consultation.

- The clinician examines the child, observing his behavior, checking his physical and affective condition, and identifying his level of development.

- The parents describe their lives, including losses, crises, illnesses, and traumatic events.

- The quality of interactions between the parents and the baby is evaluated.

- The clinician sums up all the information collected and the observations made, gives a diagnosis, and suggests a treatment plan.

Evaluation Setting

The examination room is strewn with games and toys suited for infants, and the child is free to pick her toy of choice. We believe the choice of a particular toy to be significant.

When the parents enter the room with the baby, they choose a place to sit. This is another choice we attribute significance to, as is the decision of where to put the baby or which of the parents he will stay close to. Our clinical experience has taught us that the choice of seating—on the chair or on the carpet, close to the baby or to the other parent, close to or away from the examiner—often reflects the family dynamics. Naturally, account must be taken of cultural factors, which often dictate the seating arrangement. The parents' choice of seats, posture, and behavior as they come into the room are not necessarily conscious, affording a glimpse into their emotional world.

It is essential for the baby to be present in the room during the interview with the parents, because the baby's very presence elicits certain behaviors in the parents that teach us a great deal about relationships in the family and because it is important to follow the baby's behavior during the session. We know that babies understand what is going on in the room, the words, and the body language of those present. For example, when we inquire about the course of the pregnancy, significant life events, or about the choice of the baby's first name, the infant may abruptly stop playing, turn her head toward the parent or in our direction, with curious eyes, pricked-up ears, either smiling or crying.

By the same token, it is highly important to have both parents attend the consultation. Therapists often tend to be content with the mother's presence. They assume that she is the child's principal caregiver and that she can provide all the pertinent information needed to reach a diagnosis. This assumption is obviously erroneous. The father's presence in the room during the consultation is more than necessary, for several reasons: because he plays a major role in his child's development; because he is a source of additional, outside information on the mother–child relationship; and because, in his absence, it is impossible to assess the marital relationship.

In cases in which another family member plays an important role in raising the child, one should consider adding them to the consultation as well.

House calls, where a baby can be observed in his natural environment, are not a routine part of the evaluation but should sometimes be favorably considered. This might be the case, for example, when a discrepancy exists between the child's behaviors as reported by the parents and his actual behavior in the office, or when a parent cannot easily visit the clinic because of some mental or physical problem.

The Infant's Developmental History

During the meeting, we ask the parents to tell us how the pregnancy went emotionally and physically, whether the mother had a hard time conceiving, what expectations each of them had with regard to parenting, and whether the baby born resembles the one they had imagined during pregnancy. We also ask to hear about the delivery and how the mother had experienced it, about the process of selecting the baby's name (which often reflects parental projections and the quality of their coparenting), about the milestones in the child's physical development, and about the way in which the symptoms that led them to seek counseling evolved. We ask the parents to describe their baby's temperament, breastfeeding and eating habits, her daily routine, her transitional object (if she has one), her sleeping habits, and who watches over her. We also inquire about the support provided to the couple by the family (grandparents, other relatives, friends).

The Parents' History

It is greatly important to receive information about the parents' life to assess the emotional baggage they bring with them into their parental role. Furthermore, the intergenerational transfer processes, as mentioned, play an important role in the baby's development. The information provided to us by the parents allows us to identify the protective and risk factors characterizing each family. Among other things, we ask the parents to describe the atmosphere that prevailed in their own parents' home during their childhood, how they view their parents, the kind of relationship they had and have with them, how they experienced adolescence, and whether they were exposed to traumatic events in life. Talking with the parents likewise allows us to get a feel for their emotional state and child-raising practices.

Observing the Parent-Infant Interaction

This is when the semistructured phase of the evaluation starts. First, the parents are invited to play freely with the baby. Then, we ask the parents to play a game with the child that requires problem solving and seeking help. Finally, we ask them to pick up the toys together with the child and put them back in place. We may also do a "mini-separation," asking the parent to leave the room for 3 minutes. All these things allow us to examine how the parents set the child limits, and to what extent the child perceives them as secure attachment figures.

During the assessment, we observe the child's mood and physical condition. Among others, we take note of the following variables: nutritional state, abnormal appearance, involuntary or repetitive movements, gross and fine motor skills, language, understanding, attention, concentration, level and content of play, the level of aggression toward objects and parents, acceptance of parental authority or the examiner's authority, level of exploratory behavior, degree of proximity to the parent, attitude toward the examiner, and interpersonal communication.

Structured Tools for Examining the Baby and Her Relationship With Her Parents

The structured tools have the advantage of being objective and standardized. Following are the principal tools used:

- *Assessment of the child–parent interaction using the Coding Interactive Behavior Scale* (Feldman, 1998): This scale includes 42 indicators, grouped into parental relational characteristics (sensibility, reactivity,

intrusiveness, and the ability to set boundaries), the child's characteristics (engagement, withdrawal, alertness, and temperament), and
descriptors of the dyadic relationship (reciprocity, tension, and conflict).
The scale has proved its worth as a parent–infant relationship assessment and treatment-outcome tool in studies conducted on both healthy
and high-risk children. This method has another advantage: When
the parent–child interaction is videotaped, viewing it together with the
parents allows clinicians to draw the parents' attention not only to the
child's behavior but their own. Thus, for example, situations may be
pointed out in which the parent "failed to notice" or misunderstood
words or signals coming from the child.

- *The Strange Situation paradigm*: This test is designed to characterize
  the child's style of attachment to his caregiver (Ainsworth et al., 1978).
  It examines how the child responds when the familiar adult leaves him
  for 3 minutes with the examiner (a stranger) and especially how he
  greets the returning caregiver. These reactions guide clinicians in defining his style of attachment (secure, insecure, or disorganized).

- *Bayley test* (Bayley, 2006): This is the most widely accepted structured
  test used to assess child development stages from 3 months old to 2½
  years old. It examines the child's cognitive potential, motor skills, as well
  as behavior and affective states. It is important to note that this test does
  not measure intelligence, only cognitive potential.

- *Lausanne Triadic Play paradigm*: This is a paradigm developed
  in Switzerland by Elizabeth Fivaz-Depeursinge and colleagues
  (Fivaz-Depeursinge & Corboz-Warnery, 1999; Fivaz-Depeursinge,
  Corboz-Warnery, & Keren, 2004) to assess the communication patterns
  between both parents and their infant using structured play. Among the
  aspects assessed are the involvement of each participant, the distribution
  of roles, the joint attention, and the shared pleasure. This procedure
  makes it possible to diagnose problems in the family's communication
  patterns, both between parent and child and within the couple.

- *McHale Coparenting Interview*: This tool (McHale, 1997) helps examine the extent to which parents work "as a team" with regard to the
  child: Do they support each other? Do they acknowledge each other?
  Do they believe in each other? In other words, this tool examines the
  extent to which the parents display a "united front" and are able to form
  a common stance on controversial issues.

- *Parental Insightfulness Assessment*: This tool was developed by
  Oppenheim and Koren-Karie (2002) of Haifa University with a view
  to examine how parents understand the emotional motives behind

their child's behavior. During the test, both the parent(s) and therapist watch a video recording of the parents' interaction with their child. The parents are asked to describe what they think the child thought and felt during the interaction and what they themselves think and feel now as they watch the videotaped interaction with their child. The tool can thus be used to gauge three components of empathic insight: the extent to which the parent understands the emotional motive of the behavior exhibited by the child, the complexity of the parent's understanding of the child, and finally the extent to which the parent is open to see in the child new aspects that she was previously unaware of. This procedure can often give one an idea of how the parent would respond to therapy.

- *Home Observation and Measurement of the Environment tool* (Bradley & Caldwell, 1977). This tool is used to assess the quality of the child's physical environment—in terms of safety and developmental stimulation—as well as the nature of the interaction between the child and his parents in their natural surroundings.

- *Video recordings of interactions*: Recording baby–parent interactions is a very common practice in infant psychiatry. This form of documentation allows clinicians to monitor the child's situation over time and evaluate whether it has changed. Furthermore, videotaped excerpts can be watched together with the parent. Viewing them together in this way helps parents to better understand their child's behavior and to become aware of many things that had escaped them in real time in regard both to themselves and the child.

- *Questionnaires*: Parents may be asked to fill in various questionnaires designed to evaluate the various aspects of their parenting (self-esteem as a parent, anxiety level, depression level, and level of support received by the family). The parent also fills in questionnaires related to the infant's behavior (e.g., Brief Infant and Toddler Socio-Emotional Assessment, Briggs-Gowan & Carter, 2004; Vineland, Sparrow & Cicchetti, 2011).

DC:0–5™: Diagnostic Classification of Mental Health and Developmental Disorders of Infancy and Early Childhood (DC:0–5)

As mentioned at the start of this chapter, emotional and behavioral disorders in babies can take on many forms. Moreover, different babies will express the same disorder in different ways. A disorder in the parent–child relationship, for example, can translate into incessant crying, an eating or sleeping disorder, hair-pulling, tantrums, or physical aggression. Clinicians must not rely on a single symptom, as dominant as it may seem, in determining their diagnosis. Thus, for example, a baby isolating himself from the outside world, enclosed in his own bubble and shunning any contact with his environment is not necessarily presenting signs of autism because these symptoms may be the manifestation of Posttraumatic Stress Disorder. Hence, it is a clinician's job to detect a set of symptoms, offer different plausible diagnoses, and choose the most pertinent one.

We recommend formulating the young child's clinical condition with reference to the DC:0–5. The classification is based on five independent axes, each of which reflects one aspect of the clinical picture.

Axis I refers to the child's Clinical Disorders—that is, clusters of symptoms that are severe enough to impair the child's or the family's functioning, and that are pervasive across different contexts. It includes eight categories, each divided into subcategories. For each of those, clear and specific criteria are detailed in the DC:0–5 and are beyond the scope of this book. Hence, we mention here only the categories and subcategories:

- **Neurodevelopmental Disorders**
    - » Autism Spectrum Disorder
    - » Early Atypical Autism Spectrum Disorder
    - » Attention Deficit Hyperactivity Disorder
    - » Overactivity Disorder of Toddlerhood
    - » Global Developmental Delay
    - » Developmental Language Disorder
    - » Developmental Coordination Disorder
    - » Other Neurodevelopmental Disorder of Infancy/Early Childhood

- **Sensory Processing Disorders**
    - » Sensory Over-Responsivity Disorder
    - » Sensory Under-Responsivity Disorder
    - » Other Sensory Processing Disorder

- **Anxiety Disorders**
    - » Separation Anxiety Disorder
    - » Social Anxiety Disorder (Social Phobia)
    - » Generalized Anxiety Disorder
    - » Selective Mutism
    - » Inhibition to Novelty Disorder
    - » Other Anxiety Disorder of Infancy/Early Childhood

- **Mood Disorders**
    - » Depressive Disorder of Early Childhood
    - » Disorder of Dysregulated Anger and Aggression of Early Childhood

» Other Mood Disorder of Early Childhood

- **Obsessive Compulsive and Related Disorders**
  - » Obsessive Compulsive Disorder
  - » Tourette's Disorder
  - » Motor or Vocal Tic Disorder
  - » Trichotillomania
  - » Skin Picking Disorder of Infancy/Early Childhood
  - » Other Obsessive Compulsive and Related Disorder

- **Sleep, Eating, and Crying Disorders**
  - » Sleep Disorders
    - ◆ Sleep Onset Disorder
    - ◆ Night Waking Disorder
    - ◆ Partial Arousal Sleep Disorder
    - ◆ Nightmare Disorder of Early Childhood
  - » Eating Disorders of Infancy/Early Childhood
    - ◆ Overeating Disorder
    - ◆ Undereating Disorder
    - ◆ Atypical Eating Disorder
  - » Crying Disorder of Infancy/Early Childhood
    - ◆ Excessive Crying Disorder
    - ◆ Other Sleep, Eating, and Excessive Crying Disorder of Infancy/Early Childhood

- **Trauma, Stress, and Deprivation Disorders**
  - » Posttraumatic Stress Disorder
  - » Adjustment Disorder
  - » Complicated Grief Disorder of Infancy/Early Childhood
  - » Reactive Attachment Disorder
  - » Disinhibited Social Engagement Disorder
  - » Other Trauma, Stress, and Deprivation Disorder of Infancy/Early Childhood

- **Relationship Disorders**
  - » Relationship Specific Disorder of Infancy/Early Childhood

Axis II, named the caregiving relational context axis, characterizes the level of adaptation of the dyadic and triadic/family relationships. This axis is not about categorical disorders but about the dimensional rating of the quality of the caregiving the young child is exposed to.

Axis III records physical health conditions and considerations that have a significant impact on the young child's socioemotional functioning.

Axis IV records environmental stress factors that might affect the baby. The criteria that define a life event as stressful are its intensity, the child's stage of development at the time of the event, and the degree of protection received by the child from a significant adult at that time. Following are the main categories of the extensive checklist of Psychosocial and Environmental Stressors:

- Challenges within the infant's/young child's family or primary support group
- Challenges in the social environment
- Educational or child care challenges
- Housing challenges
- Economic and employment challenges
- Infant's/young child's health
- Legal or criminal justice challenges
- Other

Axis V records the baby's competencies in the domains of emotional, social–relational, language–social communication, cognitive, motor, and physical development. In each of these domains, the child's competencies are rated as "exceeds developmental expectations," "functions at age-appropriate level," "inconsistently present or emerging," or "not meeting developmental expectations."

Along the chapters of this book, we show how to use the DC:0–5 classification when we refer to clinical vignettes.

Conclusion

This chapter was devoted to defining core concepts and terms in the field of infant mental health. These definitions will help the reader understand numerous matters addressed in this book. Clearly, we could not discuss all professional terms. We picked those most pertinent to understanding the text, and those we deemed most useful to the clinical work. Let us note that the terms we use when describing the different treatments appear in chapter 17, which covers the therapeutic approaches used in infant mental health. Readers wishing to go deeper on certain subjects can use the References and Recommended Reading lists provided at the end of each chapter.

References

Ainsworth, M. H., Blehar, M., Waters, E., & Wall, S. (1978). *Patterns of attachment: A psychological study of the Strange Situation*. Hillside, NJ: Erlbaum.

Anzieu, D. (1989). *The skin ego*. New Haven, CT: Yale University Press.

Bandura, A. (1977). *Social learning theory*. Englewood Cliffs, NJ: Prentice Hall.

Baron-Cohen, S., Tager-Flusberg, H., & Cohen, D. J. (Eds.). (1993). *Understanding other minds: Perspectives from autism*. Oxford, England: Oxford University Press.

Bayley, N. (2006). *Bayley Scales of Infant & Toddler Development: Administrative manual*. San Antonio, TX: Harcourt Assessment

Bowlby, J. (1969) Attachment. In *Attachment and loss: I* (pp. 177–198). London, England: Hogarth.

Bradley, R., & Caldwell, B. (1977). Home Observation for Measurement of the Environment: A validation study of screening efficiency. *American Journal of Mental Deficiency, 81*, 417–420.

Briggs-Gowan, M. J., & Carter, A. S. (2006). *The Brief Infant–Toddler Social and Emotional Assessment (BITSEA)*. San Antonio, TX: Psychological Corporation.

Chomsky, N. (1965). *Aspects of the theory of syntax*. Cambridge, MA: MIT Press.

Colarusso, C. A. (1979). The development of time sense—From birth to object constancy. *International Journal of Psycho-Analysis, 60*, 243–251.

Cramer, C., & Palacio-Espasa, F. (1993). *La pratique des psychotherapies mères-bébés* [The practice of mother–baby psychotherapies]. Paris, France: Presses Universitaires de France.

Dolto, F. (1994). *Tout est language* [Everything is language]. Paris, France: Gallimard.

Feldman, R. (1998). *Coding Interactive Behavior (CIB) scale*. Unpublished manual. Bar Ilan University, Israel

Fivaz-Depeursinge, E., & Corboz-Warnery, A. (1999). *The primary triangle*. New York, NY: Basic Books.

Fivaz-Depeursinge, E., Corboz-Warnery, A., & Keren, M. (2004). The Primary Triangle: Treating infants and their families. In A. J. Sameroff, S. C. McDonough, & K. L. Rosenblum (Eds.), *Treating parent–infant relationship problems: Strategies for intervention* (pp. 123–151). New York, NY: Guilford Press.

Fonagy, P. (2001). *Attachment theory and psychoanalysis*. New York, NY: Other Press.

Fraiberg, S. H., Adelson, E., & Shapiro, V. (1975). Ghosts in the nursery: A psychoanalytical approach to the problems of impaired infant–mother relationships. *Journal of the American Academy of Child & Adolescent Psychiatry, 14*, 387–421.

Freud, S. (1953–1974). *The standard edition of Freud's complete work* (Vol. 22). London, England: Hogarth Press.

Golse, B. (2001). *Du corps à la pensée* [From body to thought]. Paris, France: Presses Universitaires de France.

Hesse, E., & Main, M. (2006). Frightened, threatening, and dissociative parental behavior in low-risk samples: Description, discussion, and interpretations. *Development and Psychopathology, 18,* 309–343.

Kagan, J., Reznick, S., & Snidman, N. (1988, April 8). Biological bases of childhood shyness. *Science, 240,* 167–171.

Lacan, J. (1949, July). *Le stade du miroir comme formateur de la fonction* [The mirror stage as a formator of function]. Paper presented at the 15th International Congress of Psychoanalysis, Zurich, Switzerland.

Lieberman, A. F., Padron, E., Van Horn, P., & Harris, W. (2005). Angels in the nursery: Intergenerational transmission of beneficial parental influences. *Infant Mental Health Journal, 26,* 520–540.

Lieberman, A. F., & Pawl, J. (1988). Clinical applications of attachment theory. In J. Belsky & T. Nezworski (Eds.), *Clinical implications of attachment* (pp. 327–347). Hillsdale, NJ: Erlbaum.

Lorenz, K. (1937). On the formation of the concept of instinct. *Natural Science, 25,* 289–300.

Mahler, M. S., Pierre, F., & Bergman, A. (1975). *The psychological birth of the human infant.* New York, NY: Basic Books.

Main, M., & Solomon, J. (1990). Procedures for identifying infants as disorganized/disoriented during the Ainsworth Strange Situation. In M. T. Greenberg, D. Cicchetti, & E. M. Cummings (Eds.), *Attachment in the preschool years: Theory, research, and intervention* (pp. 121–160). Chicago, IL: University of Chicago Press.

Marvin, R., Cooper, G., Hoffman, K., & Powell, B. (2002). The Circle of Security Project. Attachment-based intervention with caregiver–pre-school child dyads. *Attachment and Human Development, 4,* 107–124.

McHale, J. (2007). *Charting the bumpy road of coparenthood: Understanding the challenges of family life.* Washington, DC: ZERO TO THREE.

O'Connor, T. G., & Parfitt, D. B. (2009). Applying research findings on early experience to infant mental health. In C. H. Zeanah, Jr. (Ed.), *Handbook of infant mental health* (3rd ed., pp. 120–131). New York, NY: Guilford Press.

Oppenheim, D., & Koren-Karie, N. (2002). Mothers' insightfulness regarding their children's internal world: The capacity underlying secure child–mother relationships. *Infant Mental Health Journal, 23,* 593–605.

Papoušek, H., & Papoušek, M. (1987). Intuitive parenting: A dialectic counterpart to the infant's integrative competence. In J. Osofsky (Ed.), *Handbook of infant development* (2nd ed., pp. 669–713). New York, NY: Wiley.

Piaget, J. (1962). The stages of the intellectual development of the child. *Bulletin of the Menninger Clinic, 26,* 120–128.

Rizzolati, G., Fogassi, L., & Gallese, V. (2001). Neurophysiological mechanisms underlying the understanding and the imitation of action. *Nature Reviews Neuroscience, 2*, 661–670.

Rutter, M. (2012). Resilience as a dynamic concept. *Development and Psychopathology, 24*, 335–344.

Sameroff, A. J., & Chandler, M. J. (1975). Reproductive risk and the continuum of caretaking casualty. In E. D. Horowitz, H. Hetherington, S. Scarr-Salapatek, & G. Siegel (Eds.), Review of child development research (Vol. 4, pp. 187–244). Chicago, IL: University of Chicago Press.

Skinner, B. F. (1989). The origins of cognitive thought. In *Recent issues in the analysis of behavior* (pp. 13–25). Columbus, OH: Merrill.

Sparrow, S. S., Cicchetti, D. V., & Balla, D. A. (2005). *Vineland Adaptive Behavior Scales, Second Edition (Vineland–II)—Survey Forms Manual.* Circle Pines, MN: AGS Publishing.

Spitz, R. A. (1965). *The first year of life.* New York, NY: International University Press.

Sroufe, L. A., Egeland, B., Carlson, E. A., & Collins, W. A. (2005). *The development of a person: The Minnesota Study of Risk and Adaptation From Birth to Adulthood.* New York, NY: Guilford Press.

Stern, D. (1985). *The interpersonal world of the infant.* New York, NY: Basic Books.

Stern, D. N. (1995). *The motherhood constellation: A unified view of parent–infant psychotherapy.* New York, NY: Basic Books.

Suomi, S. J., van der Horst, F. C. P., & van der Veer, R. (2008). Rigorous experiments on monkey love: An account of Harry F. Harlow's role in the history of attachment theory. *Integrative Psychological & Behavioral Science, 42*, 354–369.

Thapar, A., & Rutter, M. (2008). Genetics. In M. Rutter, D. Bishop, D. Pine, S. Scott, J. Stevenson, E. Taylor, & A. Thapar (Eds.), *Rutter's child and adolescent psychiatry* (5th ed., pp. 339–358). New York, NY: Wiley-Blackwell.

Thomas, A., & Chess, S. (1977). *Temperament and development.* New York, NY: Brunner/Mazel.

Wallon, H. (1949). *Les origines du caractère chez l'enfant* [The origins of character in children]. Paris, France: Presses Universitaires de France.

Winnicott, D. W. (1957). *Mother and child: A primer of first relationship.* New York, NY: Basic Books.

Winnicott, D. W. (1960). *The theory of the parent–infant relationship.* Lecture given at the International Psychoanalytical Conference, London, England.

Winnicott, D. W. (1990). *The maturational processes and the facilitating environment.* London, England: Karnac Books.

Zazzo, R. (1981). Miroir, images, espaces [Mirror, images, spaces]. In
P. Mounoud & A. Vinter (Eds.), *La reconnaissance de son image chez
l'enfant et l'animal* [The recognition of his image in children and animals]
(pp. 77–110). Neuchâtel, Switzerland: Delachaux & Niestlé.

Zeanah, C. H., Jr., Egger, H. L., Smyke, A. T., Nelson, C. A., Fox, N. A.,
Marshall, P. J., & Guthrie, D. (2009). Institutional rearing and psychiatric
disorders in Romanian preschool children. *American Journal of Psychiatry,
166,* 777–785.

ZERO TO THREE. (2016). *DC:0–5™: Diagnostic classification of mental
health and developmental disorders of infancy and early childhood* (DC:0–5).
Washington, DC: Author.

Recommended Reading

Bales, K. L., & Carter, C. S. (2009). Neuro-endocrine mechanisms of social
bonds and child–parent attachment, from the child's perspective. In
M. de Haan & M. R. Gunnar (Eds.), *Handbook of developmental social
neuroscience* (3rd ed., pp. 246–264). New York, NY: Guilford Press.

Bower, T. G. R. (1974). *Development in infancy.* San Francisco, CA: Freeman.

Caldwell, B. M., & Bradley, R. H. (1984). *Home Observation for Measurement
of the Environment.* Little Rock: University of Arkansas at Little Rock.

Carver, L. J., & Cornew, L. (2009). The development of social information
gathering in infancy. In M. de Haan & M. R. Gunnar (Eds.), *Handbook of
developmental social neuroscience* (pp. 122–131). New York, NY: Guilford
Press.

Caspi, A., & Shiner, R. (2008). Temperament and personality. In M. Rutter,
D. Bishop, D. Pine, S. Scott, J. Stevenson, E. Taylor, & A. Thapar (Eds.),
Rutter's child and adolescent psychiatry (5th ed., pp. 182–198). New York,
NY: Wiley-Blackwell.

Decety, J., & Meyer, M. (2009). Imitation as a stepping stone to empathy. In
M. de Haan & M. R. Gunnar (Eds.), *Handbook of developmental social
neuroscience* (pp. 142–158). New York, NY: Guilford Press.

Dew, I. T., & Cabeza, R. (2011). The porous boundaries between explicit and
implicit memory: Behavioral and neural evidence. *Annals of New York
Academy of Science, 1224,* 174–190.

Dunbar, R. (2003). The origin and subsequent evolution of language. In
M. H. Christiansen & S. Kirby (Eds.), *Language evolution: The states of the
art* (pp. 219–234). Oxford, England: Oxford University Press.

Fraiberg, S. H. (1980). *Clinical studies in infant mental health: The first year of
life.* New York, NY: Basic Books.

Luthar, S. S. (2010). *Resilience and vulnerability: Adaptation in the context of
childhood adversities.* New York, NY: Cambridge University Press.

Mayes, L. C., Magidson, J., Lejuez, C. W., & Nicholls, S. S. (2009). Social relationships as primary rewards: The neurobiology of attachment. In M. de Haan & M. R. Gunnar (Eds.), *Handbook of developmental social neuroscience* (pp. 342–377). New York, NY: Guilford Press.

Michiko, C., & Ghosh Ippen, C. (2009). The socio-cultural context of infant mental health: Toward contextually congruent interventions. In C. H. Zeanah, Jr. (Ed.), *Handbook of infant mental health* (pp. 104–119). New York, NY: Guilford Press.

Mills, D., & Conboy, B. T. (2009). Early communicative development and the social brain. In M. de Haan & M. R. Gunnar (Eds.), *Handbook of developmental social neuroscience* (pp. 175–206). New York, NY: Guilford Press.

Myowa-Yamkoski, M., & Tomonaga, M. E. (2009). Evolutionary origins of social communication. In M. de Haan & M. R. Gunnar (Eds.), *Handbook of developmental social neuroscience* (pp. 207–224). New York, NY: Guilford Press.

Powell, B., Cooper, G., Hoffman, K., & Marwin, R. (2007). The Circle of Security Project: A case study: "It hurts to give that which you did not receive." In D. Oppenheim & D. F. Goldsmith (Eds.), *Attachment theory in clinical work with children* (pp. 172–202). New York, NY: Guilford Press.

Sameroff, A. J. (2008). Risk and protective factors. In C. H. Zeanah, Jr. (Ed.), *Handbook of infant mental health* (3rd ed., pp. 133–230). New York, NY: Guilford Press.

Sameroff, A. J., & Fiese, B. H. (2000). Models of development and developmental risk. In C. H. Zeanah, Jr. (Ed.), *Handbook of infant mental health* (2nd ed., pp. 3–19). New York, NY: Guilford Press.

Sheridan, M., & Nelson, C. A. (2009). Neurobiology of fetal and infant development: Implications for infant mental health. In C. H. Zeanah, Jr. (Ed.), *Handbook of infant mental health* (3rd ed., pp. 40–58). New York, NY: Guilford Press.

Vygotzky, L. S., & Lurie, A. (1997). The history of the development of the higher mental functions. In R. Reiber (Ed.) *The collected works of L. S. Vygotzky*, Vol 4. New York, NY: Plenum Press.

CHAPTER 4
I, My Crying, and My Surroundings

Danny Is a Hero

Mommy said to me: Danny,
My child is courageous and wise.
He's not like them little silly boys,
He'll never have tears in his eyes.

I'm not a crybaby like others.
I never, ever cry.
So tell me, mom, why do these
Tears come rolling down from my eye?[1]

Introduction

Crying is an inborn, universal behavior that carries psycho–biological mean-ing. It remains, throughout life, the most common mode of expressing pain, sorrow, and loss. Babies cry, and their parents respond in different ways, each according to their personality and influenced by their culture of origin. Crying is a natural behavior that signals distress; it is a complex physical and behavioral phenomenon which involves, among others, the production of sound, facial contortion, and changes in body posture. When babies cry, they shut their eyes, open their mouths wide, stretch their hands, and clench their fists. Babies "practice" these crying motions while still in the womb. Uterine video footage allows researchers to view the sequence of actions that precedes loud crying already during pregnancy. Hence, the fetus already has the structural system in place that can later serve to broadcast distress to the world.

Notwithstanding the idiosyncratic crying patterns of individual babies, crying has universal characteristics that are independent of any given society or culture. For example, babies start crying increasingly more during their first

---

[1] Miriam Yalan-Shteklis, "Danny Is a Hero," appears in *I Gave Nurit a Flower*, p. 14, published by Kinneret Zmora-Bitan. Reprinted with permission.

weeks of life, peaking at around 1 year old; crying then starts to decline in quantity, stabilizing at 3 or 4 years old. The only intercultural difference we have found in the research literature is in the overall amount of crying a baby does as measured during the day. Babies in cultures in which mothers carry them in a sling most of the time tended to clock less daytime crying.

By Myself

Mommy said: bye bye my child.
Goodbye my darling, then she left.
And now she's gone,
And I'm alone.
I kept alone for long, I tried—
And then I cried.

Then I said to Mister Bear:
That's enough—
You be a good bear, don't despair.
Sit by my side.
Sit down my dear,
And mom, you'll see, will soon be here.

A bear like you is not allowed
To sob, or bang the door real loud.
A big big bear will never weep
He'll sit still and in silence keep.
A big big bear is nothing like
A silly tyke . . .
Right?
Right, my darling?
But why, oh why, does my mom leave
And I'm alone?
I kept alone for long, I tried—
And then I cried . . .[2]

What better way to express the sorrow of parting than crying? "And then I cried," says the child at the end of the first stanza, in a separate line, and the echo of his crying fills the entire space. In the next two stanzas, the child tries to overcome his grief, calm himself, and stop crying just as "big children are supposed to do." To achieve this, he uses his teddy bear, the transitional object that becomes his child. As a parent, he relies on what he had often heard his parents say. He knows what a little boy needs to do

---

[2] Miriam Yalan-Shteklis, "By Myself," appears in *I Gave Nurit a Flower*, p. 42, published by Kinneret Zmora-Bitan. Reprinted with permission.

*when his mom goes out and leaves him alone, and he declaims the whole
lesson to the teddy bear: "A big big bear will never weep/He'll sit still and
in silence keep." Furthermore, even though his is a loving mother who
makes a point of taking proper and gentle leave of her child, and even if
the child knows full well that a son to a good mother is not supposed to cry,
because to cry is to be "a silly tyke," he is unable to fill the void left by the
mother's absence—and the tears come streaming down of their own accord.*

Before words appear, crying is the language of babies and toddlers, allowing them to signal both physical and emotional unease. Through crying, the
baby expresses hunger, fatigue, pain, sickness, difficulty due to overstimulation,
frustration, boredom, fear, and loneliness. The purpose of crying is to draw the
attention of caregivers, with the physical closeness, security, and holding that
come with it—whichever helps to alleviate the distress, if only momentarily.
Crying is thus a very basic and primary prosocial behavior, which appears right
after birth and precedes the social smile, most probably because of the role it
plays in survival. In comparing human babies and baby monkeys, the latter
were found to stop their crying when its underlying cause disappeared, whereas
human babies kept at it even after the cause went away.

It is commonly held that crying is only triggered by internal stimuli until 2½
months old. Interestingly, this is also the age in which the social smile appears.
This is important because it indicates the development of social understanding.
At 2½ months old, a baby also responds to external stimuli, by either smiling
or crying.

Neuroimaging technology allows researchers to track changes in crying
characteristics and understand their meaning by "peeping" into the baby's
brain. Involuntary crying, which appears right after birth, is linked to the operation of the limbic system (the region likely responsible for processing emotions).
The cerebral cortex is hardly involved in this type of crying. As the cerebral
cortex matures in the first year, babies display the ability to control their crying;
this ability is enhanced with time and gradually turns into prosocial behavior, as
Bowlby (1979) designated the type of crying that appears at 7–8 months old. At
this age, indeed, a baby is cognitively able to anticipate the effect of her crying
on her surroundings. In other words, her tears increasingly target others. The
type of crying, its quantity, and its intensity are also modulated to fit the adult
figure present in the baby's immediate environment. It follows that the absence
of crying too should raise a red flag: If a baby has stopped resorting to crying to
communicate distress, it means that she has despaired of the possibility that a
responsible grown-up would address her distress. In many cases, babies exposed
to emotional neglect no longer cry.

Crying is not only influenced by the responses of the baby's adult caregivers but also influences these adults, activating certain areas in their brain.

Neuroimaging technology allows researchers to monitor this process. Among others, crying activates the listener's amygdala, which is connected to the cerebral cortex and the autonomic nervous system and is associated with the regulation of emotions. Indeed, when parents hear a baby cry, their heart beats faster and their amygdala activity accelerates. A baby's laughter triggers a different physiological response in them (Seifritz et al., 2003). Gender differences are also evident: Women respond to another baby's crying exactly as they do to their own baby's. The male response is actually aggressive. Moreover, in a breastfeeding mother, her infant's cry also raises breast temperature, triggering—within 7 minutes—a heavy sensation in the chest and milk secretion.

A baby's crying mainly affects his parents because they are so emotionally invested. It triggers their intuitive parenting—namely, the need to guard the baby, to protect his life. In this way, the baby's secure attachment to his parents gradually builds. It is not easy for parents to deal with their baby's crying. Each parent has a different coping mechanism, and even this can change with circumstances. This mechanism has been described by various researchers as an unconscious choice between "fight" and "flight." This terminology comes from the physiological field, in which it refers to the individual's physical response to situations of stress. Freud also made this distinction when discussing unconscious mechanisms available to the individual facing stressful situations.

Many studies have looked at baby crying (e.g., LaGasse, Neal, & Lester, 2005). The older the baby, the louder her crying, and the more others perceive it as a sign of distress. Crying in a baby with a difficult temperament elicits a more negative response from the parents, who see it as something irritating and a sign of a spoiled child. As for parents, the younger they are, the more irritated they may get by crying, experiencing it as a form of rejection. Men feel that way more than women. Furthermore, parents who are more empathic and less self-centered are more sensitive to the baby's distress. Regarding cultural differences, studies have found that Western mothers tend to view crying as a signal of distress and hasten to take the baby into their arms. African mothers wait longer and give their baby a pacifier. In comparing parents with adults who are not parents, differences were found in how they interpreted crying: Mothers better identified pain-related crying in babies than women who were not mothers. Fathers were able to better identify hunger-related crying than men who were not fathers. It was also found that mothers to a single child interpreted crying as a sign of distress more often than mothers who had multiple children (Barr, Hopkins, & Green, 2000).

A parent who suffers from a psychiatric disorder is prone to interpret crying negatively, feeling more rejected and tending to view the baby as a rather demanding creature. Mothers with a psychiatric disorder often prefer using a pacifier or waiting passively, instead of picking up and holding the baby. Mothers diagnosed with depression tend to be less sensitive to different nuances of crying and generally less attentive to it. Finally, it was found that parents who ignored their baby's crying—that is, parents who "do not hear it"—tended to think it was prompted by fatigue. "He needs sleep," they tell themselves mostly, as if guided by a set coping mechanism, regardless of circumstances.

From around 6 months old, crying no longer indicates only fatigue, hunger, or unease. At 8 months old, for example, it often reflects the "stranger anxiety" characteristic of this age, which René Spitz (1965) termed the "second organizer" (see chapter 3). Crying as a form of protest appears in the toddler's second year as her ability to say "no" (the third organizer) evolves. As language improves, the amount of crying diminishes with age.

Crying, like sleeping and eating, thus forms part of a baby's normative development, and parents most often understand its underlying message, especially when used to communicate hunger or fatigue. Mostly, but not always, and when they fail to understand, they respond in a variety of different ways, some of them sound and others pathological. Such reaction usually depends on the parent's personality and past experiences. Hence, although a baby's crying can conduce to the creation of a secure relationship and facilitate healthy growth, it might sometimes lead to a tense parent–infant relationship.

Persistent and Excessive Crying

Persistent crying is among the leading concerns that prompt parents to seek medical advice during a baby's first year. It is often a very thin line between crying that calls for diagnostic and therapeutic intervention and crying that does not. We come back to this point later on in this chapter but not before we go over different types of persistent crying, which all appear in our clinical work.

Persistent crying is commonly divided into two groups: persistent crying in the first 3 months of life, and persistent crying that endures thereafter.

Persistent Crying in the First 3 Months

Roughly 20% of babies cry significantly more than most for no apparent reason (Ziegler, Wollwerth de Chuquisengo, & Papoušek, 2008). Their excessive crying sends their parents to the pediatrician in search of possible causes. These babies exhibit four major distinctive characteristics: Their crying is longer, louder, and inconsolable, and it tends to appear in the afternoon and evening hours. When presented with such babies, a pediatrician must first rule out physical illness or milk allergy. He checks for weight loss, fever, hematemesis (vomiting of blood), and blood in stool. He also makes sure that there is no diarrhea. Next, the doctor must consider whether it is a case of infant colic due to an immature bowel. Wessel (1954) defined infant colic as crying that obeys the "rule of threes" in that it appears at least 3 hours per day, at least 3 days in a week, for at least 3 weeks. This type of crying is no longer attributed today, as it was before, to some problem in the gastrointestinal system; instead, it is attributed to self-regulation. Self-regulation is indeed the foremost developmental task in a baby's first 3 months. It turns out that around 30% of breastfeeding babies display persistent crying at 6 weeks old, compared with only 12% of babies who are fed various formulas. This is why most pediatricians recommend stopping breastfeeding for babies who cry a lot in their first weeks of life and feeding them formula milk (contrary to the position of many breastfeeding counselors).

Another common cause of persistent crying in the first months of life is a difficult temperament, as defined in chapter 3.

How does a baby stop crying on her own? It is now known that some babies can soothe themselves, or in other words regulate themselves, independently, whereas others, who cannot, depend on outside help. A few simple actions can make self-regulation easier for a baby and help her help herself: reducing the level of external stimulation, identifying those situations that bring on crying (e.g., keeping a journal can help), cradling the baby with her fists close to her mouth (a position that encourages thumb sucking), and initiating physical contact (holding the baby in one's arms, gently rocking her, and massaging her). It is worth noting here that at times nothing will do, and the baby will go on to cry the "fit" out. Parents need to identify the point where they start to feel too much anger and frustration and interpret the baby's crying as mere "stubbornness." When this happens, they need to lay the baby down in the cradle and take some time off. As long as this is done gently, accompanied by soothing words, they need not fear harming the baby.

It is commonly assumed that holding babies who suffer from persistent crying in one's arms helps calm them. This assumption was reinforced by the educative approach called the Continuum Concept, which advocates the baby's need for constant presence near his mother's body, day and night, and for keeping to a minimum the level of frustration. According to this principle, this kind of parental behavior leads to little crying, but this has not been proven in controlled studies (Papoušek, Schieche, & Wurmser, 2008). Many parents adopt this approach for fear of frustrating their baby.

When Should Professional Help Be Sought?

The ability to get through the first 3 months unscathed largely depends on the parents' emotional state. Young parents who are insecure in their parenting might view persistent crying as proof of their inability to be good enough parents. This interpretation might produce a vicious circle, making it harder for the baby to regulate herself with each passing day and amplifying the parent's frustration and sense of helplessness. This vicious circle jeopardizes the parent–infant relationship and, in some cases, causes parents to distance themselves from the child and to neglect her. It is worth noting here that parents who suffer from a psychiatric disorder, such as postpartum depression or psychosis, might perceive the baby's crying as persecutory behavior, aimed at tormenting them. This distorted understanding might result in mistreatment of the baby and even extreme acts such as murder. These relatively rare situations require immediate therapeutic intervention. Family-health-center nurses or family pediatricians are sometimes the first to identify them.

CASE STUDY

A mother to a first-born baby, 2½ months old, showed up at the pediatrician's office in a state of exhaustion and despair due to her son's incessant crying. The baby was found to be physically healthy, and the pediatrician referred both mother and baby to our infant mental health unit for fear that the mother's emotional state might endanger the baby. During consultation at our clinic, we learned that the mother was a 38-year-old woman who had married a man 14 years her senior a year earlier and was prone to depression and anxiety. She went through a childhood overshadowed by an unprocessed family bereavement following the stillbirth of her twin brother. Her pregnancy, although highly desirable, coincided with the loss of her mother, who passed away after a hard, protracted disease. During the 7 days of mourning observed in Judaism, she held her stomach, saying: "He must be hearing all of us cry, and maybe he too is crying in there."

The baby was born healthy after a pregnancy carried to term, even though the mother was confined to bed rest following premature contractions. The first week following birth went well, but the mother was finding it increasingly harder to cope with the baby's crying. She became restless and nervous, terrified of being left alone with him, and she found herself spending most hours of the day in tears, calling on her late mother for help. It was decided to start dyadic psychological treatment, involving both the mother and child, while referring the mother to an adult psychiatrist for antidepressant medications. The father did not attend the consultation, and therefore no evaluation of the family's functioning could be done.

About 4 months into therapy, the mother's emotional state improved. During therapy, she repeatedly brought up the death of her twin brother, and although she never knew him, this appeared to fuel her fear of losing her newborn son. This preoccupation manifested itself in her inability to leave her son for even a brief moment, even at night. The therapeutic process helped her make the link between her difficulty to tolerate her baby's crying and her childhood experiences around the unspoken depression her own mother had suffered from since the death of the twin baby. She told us how she used to imagine her twin brother growing to become better than her, and how her mother's veiled messages made her feel that she had grown at his expense in the womb. These ambivalent feelings—both toward her mother, with whom she had had a tempestuous and dependent relationship, and toward her imaginary twin brother—were projected onto her baby boy, distorting her initial relationship with him. The early detection and referral by the pediatrician, the parent-infant psychotherapy, and the antidepressant medication given to the mother helped both mother and son to step out of the vicious circle in which they were caught.

The *DC:0-5™: Diagnostic Classification of Mental Health and Developmental Disorders of Infancy and Early Childhood* (DC:0-5; ZERO TO THREE, 2016) formulation of this case would be as follows:

- Axis I: Clinical Disorders
  - » Excessive Crying Disorder
  - » Relationship Specific Disorder of Infancy/Early Childhood (with mother)

- Axis II: Relational Context
  - » Level 3—Compromised to Disturbed mother-child relationship

- Axis III: Medical Condition
  - » None

- Axis IV: Psychosocial Stressor
  - » Maternal mental health problems

- Axis V: Developmental Competence
  - » Functions at age-appropriate level

Persistent Crying at 3 Months Old and Beyond

Nogah was a crybaby. Asking her to do anything, be it even come to eat or brush her teeth, brought out a renewed outburst of tears.

The preceding paragraph summarizes the opening to Yaacov Shavit's book about Nogah,[3] a girl who speaks in tears. The book takes crying as a phenomenon to its absurd extreme: Nogah's sea of tears, like Alice's sea of tears in Lewis Carroll's Alice in Wonderland, *floods her home, flows down the stairs, and turns the whole neighborhood into a mighty river in which all its inhabitants—women, men, and children—delightedly bathe. It is only when all her street dwellers implore her not to stop crying that Nogah stops her tears and "shuts down" the sea.*

The story expresses both the girl's drowning in her sea of pain and the parents' "drowning" as they helplessly face their children's unfathomable, endless crying. In this story, crying is stopped as a kind of rebellion, a childish "spite," as if to say, "If you don't want me to stop crying, then I'll stop on purpose, and there's nothing you can do about it."

Around 40% of babies who cry profusely in their first 3 months continue to do so after their fourth month. Common causes include a difficult

---

[3] Yaakcov Shavit, 2006, *Teary Nogah*, published by Sifriat Hapoalim.

temperament, a primary innate regulatory disorder, or a disorder in the parent–baby relationship stemming from parental tension or anxiety, a serious conflict between the parents, or maternal depression (as illustrated in the previous case). Other than that, almost any state of emotional distress in the baby entails persistent crying. Let us now elaborate on some of the common causes mentioned.

Babies with a "difficult" temperament (see chapter 3) do cry a lot and appear unhappy most of the time. A difficult temperament is not a disorder in itself but might become one if the parent responds to its manifestations in anger or even rejection. Such behavior might lead to a disorder in the relationship between the toddler and his parents.

A baby's persistent crying could also indicate a Sensory Processing Disorder, as detailed in chapter 5.

Excessive crying may be indicative of a disordered parent–baby relationship. Babies may express emotional distress in several ways, in particular through crying, eating problems, sleeping problems, aggressive behaviors, anxious behaviors, and a depressed mood. Crying is the most direct and immediate form of expressing distress, with other symptoms usually appearing only when the baby is several months old. Crying signals distress but also protest. It is Bowlby (1979) who described crying as a form of protest, as an initial expression of a baby's dissatisfaction with the quality of care she receives. For example, persistent crying is one of several ways documented by the scientific literature in which babies try to "awaken" their depressive mother. A baby or toddler who senses too much tension between her parents will also resort to crying at times to draw their attention and thus end their bickering.

Researchers who have looked at the familial constellation of persistent criers have often found the parent–baby relationship or the relationship between the parents themselves to be disturbed. The more a baby cried, the more this threatened to affect the parents' responsiveness and emotional involvement. Particularly evident was a drop in their ability to spot the positive signals. An interesting relationship was also observed between the way in which the mother had experienced the birth and the intensity of the baby's crying. Babies of mothers who had experienced a traumatic delivery cried harder.

The relationship found between the quality of the relationship and the baby's crying naturally raises the "question of the chicken or the egg." Is the disorder in the baby–parent relationship the cause or the effect of the increased crying? A prospective study (Schmid, Schreier, Meyer, & Wolke, 2010) that followed a large sample of parents and children in the general population, from pregnancy to 6 months old, pointed to a direct relationship between signs of depression in mothers or fathers in the 20th week of pregnancy and persistent crying in the baby's first year. The acceptable practice in the past was to focus solely on the mother's emotional state during or immediately after pregnancy. Clinicians now realize that the father's emotional state equally deserves attention. Fathers who were depressed during pregnancy or the first year of the baby's life had no less an impact on their baby's development than mothers who experienced a similar condition. These findings can be interpreted in several ways: Depression may make fathers respond more negatively to their baby's normative crying, thus creating a closed vicious circle of hardship. In addition, a depressed father's difficulty communicating with his baby may be an indirect result of other influencing factors, such as dissatisfaction with the conjugal relationship, employment problems, or other tensions adversely affecting the relationship between the parents. Last but not least, in extreme cases, persistent crying might be one symptom of neglect or abuse.

Treating Persistent Crying

We have shown in this chapter how varied the reasons for the appearance of persistent crying are. Consequently, the process of evaluating the baby and his parents must be completed in full and the underlying cause of crying understood before clinicians can opt for the right treatment. If clinicians find, for example, that a baby's persistent crying stems from a serious disorder in his relationship with his environment, it is this relationship that will be the focal point of the therapy. Moreover, if it turns out that the baby suffers from a consti-tutional regulation problem, the parents will have to learn to help him regulate himself while remaining flexible and accepting the baby's characteristics. Hard as this therapy is, most parents go along with it. Furthermore, upon realizing that they are not the source of the disorder, they often feel relieved, gradually shedding the feelings of frustration and guilt with which they came when seek-ing help. Parents will be similarly relieved to find out that their baby "simply" has a difficult temperament.

Parents frequently seek help after a long journey of trial and error in han-dling the baby's crying, having received many suggestions and having explored different courses of action. They often come to clinicians bursting with anger, frustration, and disappointment, and they are often rife with disputes and mu-tual accusations, exhausted from arguments about how to cope with the crying. This is why the required therapy is dyadic or triadic, focusing on the baby's relationship with her parents and the relationship between the parents, even if the disorder is constitutional at base. Such treatment will also involve an occu-pational therapist to help the parents find the right amount of stimulation for their baby. The parents will also be given training with a focus on structuring a daily routine that would include both moments of common play and moments in which the child plays on her own.

CASE STUDY

G., a 4-month-old baby, was referred to our clinic because of persistent crying that was very hard to soothe as well as nervousness, fussiness, and avoidance of eye contact with his mother. The parents reported that he also suffered from difficulties falling asleep and frequent arousals both night and day and that he required many prolonged breastfeeding sessions. On arrival at the clinic, the mother was exhausted, constantly on the verge of crying, and seemed stretched to the limit of her forces, sad, and nervous. She felt that she was a bad mother and was overcome with negative feelings of anger, frustration, and failure. She attended the session alone because her husband, who was a student at the time, was about to take his final exams. The baby and his parents were referred by their pediatrician after the mother had a nervous breakdown, during which she had developed very negative thoughts toward the baby.

During our first meeting, it turned out that the mother was the provider in the family. During 7 years of living together, the couple had maintained a good relationship. Still, some time before coming to us, differences broke out between them regarding sources of income and the division of labor at home. The parents had no support from their respective families. The mother felt that her mother-in-law did not accept her, and her relationship with her own parents was also tense.

This was a first birth after two miscarriages. The mother's pregnancy was accompanied by repeated hemorrhaging and nightmares—she was concerned that she would give birth to a sick child. Despite these difficulties, she kept imagining that "she would be a perfect mother." She ended up giving birth 3 weeks ahead of the due date and by cesarean section, following 17 hours of ineffectual labor. Her initial bonding with the baby was good, and the first 3 weeks went by without any particular difficulty. In the fourth week, the mother suffered from a nipple inflammation and had a hard time breastfeeding; the baby started going into inconsolable spells of prolonged crying. The mother started exhibiting signs of depression. The father was not on hand to help her, busy as he was with his studies and completely oblivious to the severity of the problem.

In our second meeting with the parents and the baby, we observed their interactions. When the mother tried to grab G.'s attention, by talking and touching, he turned his head defiantly sideways. The mother left him no room to initiate the interaction. The more he recoiled, the more intrusive she became, bending over the baby, who sat in an infant seat, to get his attention. G. cooperated more with his father, but his low frustration threshold was constantly evident. He cried persistently for no reason, and his parents were hard-pressed to soothe him. Each one of them responded differently to his crying: The mother looked desperate and very angry, uttering sentences such as "You only smile when I'm not looking at you, don't you?" or "You don't like my milk, right?" The father did not seem the least worried. If anything, he seemed to be composed and in a good mood, and he kept on trying to calm his son. Still, he was quite helpless at supporting his wife.

A medical examination of the baby carried out alongside the evaluation process in our unit found that he suffered from a moderately severe gastro-esophageal reflux (gastric juice coming back up because of weakness of the sphincter between the esophagus and the stomach). G. was also diagnosed with low muscular tonus and oversensitivity to noise. Other than that, his neurodevelopmental evaluation came out normal.

In establishing our understanding of this case, we were back to the "chicken or egg" conundrum. Was G. crying and averting his gaze to regulate his mother's intrusiveness and anxiety, which were the result of her basic lack of confidence in her motherhood and her wish to be a perfect mom? Or was the burning pain of the reflux and the muscular weakness what made sitting hard for G. and caused his persistent crying, which, in turn, made the mother feel rejected?

The DC:0-5 diagnoses in this case would be as follows:

- Axis I: Clinical Disorders
  » Excessive Crying Disorder
  » Sensory Over-Responsivity Disorder
  » Relationship Specific Disorder of Infancy/Early Childhood (with mother)
- Axis II: Relational Context
  » Level 3—Compromised to Disturbed mother–child relationship
  » Level 2—Strained to Concerning caregiving environment
- Axis III: Medical Condition
  » Gastrointestinal reflux—moderately severe
- Axis IV: Psychosocial Stressor
  » Mother mental health problems
- Axis V: Developmental Competence
  » Inconsistently present or emerging

In the light of these, we put in place a combined treatment, including physiotherapy sessions for the baby, occupational therapy to guide the parents on the adequate amount of stimulation for G., and parent–child psychotherapy. The dyadic therapy centered on the source of the mother's highly negative, almost persecutory, interpretations of G.'s behavior, on the assumption that his withdrawn behavior and persistent crying ignited an unprocessed and threatening anger in the mother. Projected onto the baby, this anger produced a highly ambivalent relation between him and his mother. Indeed, we discovered during therapy that here was a functioning woman, but one who craved attention and having her abilities recognized, a woman who found it hard to articulate her feelings and needed considerable support. The triadic treatment—attended by the mother, the father, and the baby—helped the father understand his wife's distress. For his part, G.'s self-regulatory skills gradually improved as well as his relationship with his mother. The weekly treatment sessions lasted approximately 5 months, and they ended after considerable improvement had been observed in the baby's condition and the interactions at home. The improvement proved stable at the follow-up session held when G. was 18 months old.

Course of the Clinical Syndrome of Persistent Excessive Crying Beyond the First Months of Life

When clinicians deal with the prognosis of persistent excessive crying, a very useful criterion is the severity of the crying. Indeed, babies whose crying never called for professional intervention in the first place developed without any particular problems (Schmid et al., 2010). In contrast, those who required professional counseling in their first year were later observed to have a higher prevalence of sleeping disorders, eating disorders, insecure attachment to their parents, and anxious behaviors at 3 years old. Among these children, 72% presented a poor playing capability, social withdrawal, and tantrums, as opposed to only 45% of children who did not suffer from regulation and crying problems in the past. More oppositional behaviors were also observed in the early persistent criers (28% compared with 13% in the general population). When reaching school age, 19% of these children suffered from various disorders, such as Attention Deficit Hyperactivity Disorder, oppositional behaviors, conduct disorders, separation anxiety, social withdrawal, aggression, and sibling rivalry.

A longitudinal study (Ziegler et al., 2008) examined the development of premature babies at four points in time during their first 5 years: at birth, at 5 months, at 20 months, and then at 56 months. The group of premature babies diagnosed with regulation disorders was divided into two: those who had a simple regulation problem—that is, those presenting only one symptom (persistent crying, sleeping problems, eating difficulties)—and those with a complex regulation problem—that is, those showing more than one symptom. The findings at the end of the first 5 years into the study were that a regulation disorder attended by persistent crying at 5 months old tended to lead into a sleeping disorder at 5 years old. This development might be related to the parents' response to the crying, such as letting the baby spend the rest of the night in their bed to calm him. However, 7%–8% of the babies who suffered from a complex regulation disorder, especially those who also exhibited an eating problem, were found to have difficulties in adaptive social skills at 5 years old. Thus, a persistent crying disorder in infancy requires professional attention and, in many cases, therapeutic intervention.

Breath-Holding Spells

This dramatic phenomenon is not such a rare occurrence. The baby starts crying and stops breathing, to the point of turning blue (cyanosis). Its first occurrence usually draws such a dramatic response from her surroundings that the baby quickly learns to use it as a means of preventing her entourage from frustrating her and making her cry. These spells disappear on their own if ignored, something that most parents and even medical teams are unable to do! It is important to send the baby a clearly articulated message that the parent is not afraid of her crying. This being said, the psychological circumstances involved are sometimes more complex, as the following case illustrates:

CASE STUDY

B., a 1-year-old baby suffering from cerebral palsy, was referred to our clinic by the Well-Baby nurse, who was under the impression that the mother had a hard time coming to terms with her daughter's relatively minor cerebral palsy, and by the pediatrician, who was concerned by the high frequency of the spells. The child functioned normally at the day care, with no breath-holding spells.

B., the first and only child of her young parents, had a very traumatic and preterm birth, with acute respiratory distress secondary to diaphragmatic hernia. She underwent surgery right away and spent 4 months in intensive care. Given slim chances of survival at the start of the hospitalization, the parents were later afraid to take her back home even when told that her condition had significantly improved. Back home from the hospital, the parents had to deal with the baby's eating difficulties, a very common problem in premature babies. This task weighed very heavily on the mother, who herself suffered from eating problems. In her mind, the baby's eating problems were directed at her. Faced with her refusal to eat, she developed anger, frustration, and anxiety, and at some point started feeding her by force, to which B. responded with breath-holding spells. This was her way to express her frustration at the mother's anger toward her.

In our first meeting with the baby and both parents, the sadness shared between the baby and her mother was conspicuous. The mother looked at her child and said, "Fate has screwed us both over . . . I don't know how much to expect of her, even though I know she is smart." Together, we tried to unravel this perplexing statement, and the mother said that when she was a child, she had been diagnosed with a chronic medical illness. She grew up not only with the feeling of being different from the other kids but also, more crucially, with a serious lack of affective support from her parents ("They didn't take good care of me . . . and so now I insist on going through with B.'s treatments, even when she cries in physiotherapy"). When she reached puberty, her older brother died. "When B. was born and they told me she wouldn't make it, I felt a lump in my throat . . . the exact same sensation I had when I heard of my brother's death." She responded to her brother's death with an eating disorder, which lasted many years and still persists, albeit attenuated.

During her pregnancy with B., the mother, given her eating disorder and negative body image, had a hard time dealing with getting big and became ambivalent about her pregnancy. This emotional stance manifested itself unconsciously in her failure to regulate her medical condition properly. Consequently, she and her fetus suffered several hypoglycemic attacks (a dangerous drop in blood sugar level, which leads to fainting). B.'s father was a very soft and supportive young man, but he was afraid of taking care of his baby and left all the caregiving to his wife. Still, the level of tension was reduced when they were all together.

The DC:0–5 diagnoses in this case would be as follows:

- Axis I: Clinical Disorders
  » Relationship Specific Disorder of Infancy/Early Childhood (with mother)
  » Neurodevelopmental disorder: mild cerebral palsy

- Axis II: Relational Context
  » Level 3—Compromised to Disturbed mother–child relationship

- Axis III: Medical Condition
  » Breath-holding spells

- Axis IV: Psychosocial Stressor
  » Maternal Eating Behavior Disorder

- Axis V: Developmental Competence
  » Delay in motor development

In the light of this formulation, the chosen treatment was dyadic psychotherapy with a few triadic meetings, as much as the father could take time off work. We also recommended individual psychotherapy for the mother, to which she agreed.

As the treatment process progressed, the mother began to slowly realize just how much all those life events influenced the birth and her parenting behaviors toward B. She gradually started showing greater sensitivity to B.'s own characteristics, strengths, and weaknesses. Metaphorically speaking, we might say that the mother made room for her toddler to "breathe." The child started cooperating with the physical therapy, the frequency of her breath-holding spells diminished very significantly at home (never appeared at the day care), and therapy ended after a year.

Is the Absence of Crying a Sign of Health or Disorder?

Hana Goldberg's Pink Tears[4] *tells the story of Motek, a little female kitten that no one wants to play with, even when everyone is playing together. However, Motek looks on without letting her tears "go up" to her eyes. When evening falls and everyone goes home, so does she. Her parents, worried at the sight of their sad daughter, ask her how she is. Motek slips by and shuts herself up in her room. Yet again, she holds back the tears, pushing them back as hard as she can, and goes to sleep.*

---

[4] Hana Goldberg, 2001, *Pink Tears*, published by Hakibbutz Hameuchad.

Although the crying remains bottled up inside, Motek's body seems to "do the talking" in its stead: At first, a black stain appears on her chest (where the heart is); it then increasingly spreads, and her entire body turns black with unending sorrow. One morning, Motek looks in the mirror and sees a totally black Motek with angry eyes. At the sight of her alarming bodily transformation, the pent-up tears break free from their prison, leaving behind them rose-colored trails. Turning increasingly pink, Motek can now go down to her friends downstairs and lick pecan, cherry, and strawberry ice cream with them and even do a triple somersault in the air. Because sometimes the only way to release tears is to see the impact left on the body by tears locked inside it.

Some babies never cry, and this too should be a great cause for concern. Babies cry when they emerge into the world, showing that they are alive. Crying is also one component of temperament, and it is vital for survival. It allows babies to call out to others for help in times of distress.

The known physical causes underlying the absence of crying are severe prematurity (lungs that are insufficiently developed to produce crying), serious distress at birth, and serious congenital disease (such as hypothyroidism, cardiac insufficiency). Sometimes, babies stop crying for psychological reasons. This happens in extreme existential situations, which have taught the baby to extinguish his crying. Such situations can develop when the caregiver is indifferent to the baby's crying or responds to it violently.

CASE STUDY

A., a 2-year-old toddler, was brought in for a one-time consultation by her foster parents. They felt that she was a difficult child who did not fit in with their family. She had been born to two parents with schizophrenia, removed from their custody before she was 1 year old, and moved to a foster family. She did not bond well with the foster mother, who struggled to meet the needs of both the girl and her biological son, who was also a toddler. During the evaluation, the little girl was very quiet and looked sad. When she bumped into a table during the session and hit herself, her response to the pain was highly peculiar: Her mouth twitched in pain, but no sound came out of her throat, as if she was restraining her crying. As the session went on, it became clear to us that the girl felt the unspoken rejection conveyed by the foster mother, trying to please her and hold back her tears for fear of provoking her anger.

Conclusion

A baby's crying holds tremendous power. A baby uses it to cry out for help as well as to seek support and protection. Crying, however, can also stir up rejection, anger, and even violence in adults. Some parents find it hard to bear their infant's crying, perhaps because it reminds them—whether consciously or not—of some pain or crying that they had experienced in their youth that their parents had failed to understand. Every baby has her own kind of crying, the one with which she came to the world, the one dictated by her genetic and biological make-up. Every parent expects to hear the baby's first cries. Every parent also needs to deal with the baby's crying. Most parents do this successfully, but some do not, and they need professional help. These are usually parents whose mental or conjugal situation is difficult; parents who once had complicated experiences that had left them scarred; or parents who view their baby's crying as "manipulative," "spoiled" behavior, or as a sign of "pathological dependence." These are the parents that clinicians are called on to help, and the sooner the better.

References

Barr, R. G., Hopkins, B., & Green, J. A. (2000). *Crying as a sign, a symptom and a signal.* London, England: High Holborn House.

Bowlby, J. (1979).*The making and breaking of affectional bonds.* New York, NY: Tavistock.

LaGasse, L. L., Neal, A. R., & Lester, B. M. (2005). Assessment of infant cry: Acoustic cry analysis and parental perception. *Mental Retardation and Developmental Disabilities Research Reviews, 11,* 83–93.

Papoušek, M., Schieche, M., & Wurmser, H. (Eds.). (2008). *Disorders of behavioral and emotional regulation in the first year of life: Early risks and intervention in the developing parent–infant relationship* (K. Kronenberg, Trans.). Washington, DC: ZERO TO THREE.

Schmid, G., Schreier, A., Meyer, R., & Wolke, D. (2010). A prospective study on the persistence of infant crying, sleeping, and feeding problems and preschool behavior. *Acta Paediatrica, 99,* 286–290.

Seifritz, E., Esposito, F., Neuhoff, J. G., Lüthi, A., Mustovic, H., Dammann, G., . . . Di Salle, F. (2003). Differential sex-independent amygdala response to infant crying and laughing in parents versus nonparents. *Biological Psychiatry, 54,* 1367–1375.

Spitz, R. A. (1965). *The first year of life.* New York, NY: International University Press.

Wessel, M. A. (1954). Paroxysmal fussing in infancy, sometimes called colic. *Pediatrics, 14,* 421–435.

ZERO TO THREE. (2016). *DC:0–5™: Diagnostic classification of mental health and developmental disorders of infancy and early childhood* (DC:0–5). Washington, DC: Author.

Ziegler, M., Wollwerth de Chuquisengo, R., & Papoušek, M. (2008). Excessive crying in infancy. In M. Papoušek, M. Schieche, & H. Wurmser (Eds.), *Disorders of behavioral and emotional regulation in the first year of life: Early risks and intervention in the developing parent–infant relationship* (pp. 85–116). Washington, DC: ZERO TO THREE.

Recommended Reading

Cramer, B., & Palacio-Espasa, F. (1993). *La pratique des psychotherapies mères-bébés* [The practice of mother–baby psychotherapies]. Paris, France: Presses Universitaires de France.

Lester, B. M., Boukydis, C. F. Z., Garcia-Coll, C. T., Hole, W. T., & Peucker, M. (1992). Infantile colic: Acoustic cry characteristics, maternal perception of cry, and temperament. *Infant Behavior and Development, 15,* 15–26.

Lucas, A., & St. James-Roberts, I. (1998). Crying, fussing and colic behavior in breast- and bottle-fed infants. *Early Human Development, 53,* 9–18.

Papoušek, H., & Papoušek, M. (1987). Intuitive parenting: A dialectic counterpart to the infant's integrative competence. In J. Osofsky (Ed.), *Handbook of infant development* (2nd ed., pp. 669–713). New York, NY: Wiley.

Richman, N. (1981). Sleep problems in young children. *Archives of Diseases in Childhood, 56,* 491–493.

Wolke, A., Rizzo, D., & Woods, C. (2002). Persistent infant crying and hyperactivity problems in middle childhood. *Pediatrics, 109,* 1054–1060.

CHAPTER 5
I Am Giving You a Hard Time Because I'm Having Trouble Regulating Myself

Carlo Collodi's The Adventures of Pinocchio *tells the story of the wooden puppet known as Pinocchio. Carved by his father Geppetto from a block of wood, Pinocchio obviously has trouble self-regulating from the get-go. When Geppetto finishes carving out his figure, the newborn gives him an impudent and demanding look as his nose continues to grow fast of its own free will and his hand shoots up to yank the wig off the head of the horrified father. Next, his newly sculpted legs send Pinocchio flying out of the workshop. The description of the wonder puppet's birth ends with the heart-piercing wails of the infant, who has banged his head on the cobblestones. The father is left feeling rejected, doubting his ability to be a parent.*

Pinocchio's character, especially as initially portrayed, definitely bears many of the marks of a regulatory disorder typically observed in children. It is evident, right from the start, that the block of wood found by the carpenter is highly sensitive, packing an intense response to every little push of its "buttons": aggressive shouting, glaring provocations, and nervous giggles. Moreover, when Pinocchio sallies forth into the world, this over-reactivity only intensifies. He wanders about restlessly and cannot bear the slightest feeling of hunger; his actions are impulsive, at least at first, and he is devoid of any ability to weigh their consequences; he is quick to despair when his desires are not instantly fulfilled; he has a hard time communicating with his father-creator; and he cannot stand frustration.

Later on, a tortuous process occurs whereby Pinocchio is increasingly able, with the help of those around him, to get a grip on his impulses and better organize the reality in which he lives. It should be noted in this context that Collodi has a firm grasp of the tremendous difficulty involved in overcoming the disorder: Time and again, Pinocchio is sidetracked by the countless stimulations around him; time and again, his regulatory and

organizational abilities are dashed against the surrounding temptations,
which he cannot but respond to straight away.

Introduction: Regulation, Attention, and Development

Physiological and psychological regulation, or the organization of inner sensations and states, is one of the young child's major developmental tasks during his first 2 years (Schore, 1994; Tronick, 2007). His ability to regulate himself depends on biological and environmental factors. Some define "regulation" broadly, seeing it at play in all areas of development—that is, motor, cognitive, communicative, behavioral, and social. Others take a more reductive approach, only linking regulation to the processing of sensory stimuli.

The physiological regulation system operates through three channels: the tactile system, the vestibular system (responsible for maintaining the body's balance), and the proprioceptive system (which receives information on body posture and body movements from the muscles and joints). Incidentally, these systems also contribute to the development of the body schema, as described by Dolto (1994; see chapter 3).

The understanding of the central role of emotional regulation in baby development deepened in the 1990s. Numerous studies (Greenspan, 1992; Greenspan & Wieder, 2006; Schore, 1994; Stern, 1985) have shown that during normative development, a baby first learns to regulate her physiological state, and only then her emotional state. The combination of these two is what is needed for organized responses to new experiences. Regulation is thus formed through the baby's daily encounter with her environment, with the adult caregiver playing a key role in the process: The adult provides the baby with regulation strategies, which the baby gradually assimilates (Williamson & Anzalone, 2001). For example, the adult might offer a pacifier or a transitional object to help the baby fall asleep or settle down, and the child slowly internalizes this behavior. The strategies learned from the adult are progressively generalized by the baby and then also applied in regulating emotional states, tuning alertness and attention, and organizing all those complex behaviors that characterize interpersonal relations.

Although the parent and the environment have an important role to play in the gradual organization of the regulatory system, they are not alone. Another key factor shaping it is the baby's genetic make-up. Temperament, for example, is a prominent component in the innate regulatory system. Chess and Thomas (1986) defined it on the basis of nine characteristics: activity level, physiological rhythmicity, response threshold, response intensity, approach or withdrawal given a new and unfamiliar stimulus, adaptability, mood, attention span and duration, and ease of distractibility (see chapter 3). On the basis of these characteristics, Chess and Thomas defined four different types of temperament: easy, difficult, slow-to-warm-up, and mixed.

A baby's ability to regulate himself is thus shaped by a combination of innate biological and environmental variables. These interrelations are more complex than one might imagine. Take, for example, the place of heredity in emotional, sensory, and cognitive regulation. Parents who have an infant with regulatory difficulties on their hands, with or without an attention deficit disorder, often share very similar or outright identical personality traits with that child—impulsiveness, hyperactivity, and a hard time keeping focus over time. The similarity between child and parent often leads to confrontations and clashes between them. The frustrated parent often feels incompetent as a parent and even "guilty" of the child's "bad character," expressing such distress as anger toward the child. The distress and anger, in turn, might amplify the parent's sense of helplessness—the feeling of being unable to function as a parent—and, in serious cases, lead to rejection of the child and even physical or verbal violence. Some parents actually tend to identify with their child, who reminds them of themselves as children—the suffering they felt at the time and the environment's failure to understand them. Parents will sometimes choose to deny the child's problem for the very same reasons. Whether they reject the child or identify with him, parents frequently find it hard to set the child consistent and clear barriers.

CASE STUDY

An 11-month-old baby girl was hospitalized in a general hospital's pediatric ward because of prolonged fever. During hospitalization, she was seen by a child psychiatrist for what looked like oversociability toward strangers and emotional detachment from her mother. Especially conspicuous was the absence of physical contact between her and her mother. On arrival at the ward, we were greeted by the team, who said, "There's something wrong with the mother, she's rejecting her daughter." This was our impression too when we began our examination. However, when the mother was asked to take her daughter into her arms, the child pulled back. "You see," said the mother, "she doesn't want me." When the mother was asked since when she felt that way, she recounted their sad story, which had already started in the first month following birth.

The mother told us about an inexplicable silence that had fallen over the baby each time she fed her. Repeated physical examinations were normal, leaving the pediatrician clueless. In the second month, the mother found out that her daughter was more comfortable eating while lying down in bed with the bottle propped up by a towel. "It tore me up that she would prefer to be alone; I felt she didn't like me, didn't want me as her mother, but what could I do? . . . At least this way she ate well . . . She doesn't like being touched to this very day." Asking the mother to describe her baby's reactions to noises, lights, and changes from very early on helped us make the *DC:0–5™: Diagnostic Classification of Mental Health and Developmental Disorders of Infancy and Early Childhood* (DC:0–5; ZERO TO THREE, 2016) Axis I diagnosis of Sensory Over-Responsivity Disorder. The clinical presentation of the mother–infant interaction warranted yet another diagnosis, also on Axis I, of Relationship Specific Disorder of Infancy/Early Childhood. We may argue that very early intervention at 2 months could have prevented the mother from feeling rejected and deeply hurt, as it would have helped her understand the physiological reason for her baby's behavior.

Here are a few more examples of behaviors that one should consider when diagnosing a sensory processing disorder:

- A 3½-year-old boy who was suspended from the neighborhood nursery school because of aggressive behavior toward other children.

- A 2½-year-old girl who is constantly moving, getting up at 6:00 in the morning, never sleeping at noon, and only falling asleep at 11:00 at night.

- A 3-year-old girl who has to be constantly watched over, having already visited the emergency room on three previous occasions after swallowing detergents.

- A 2-year-old boy whose interest in his many toys lasts only several minutes, and who breaks even his favorite games.

The New Concept of Sensory Processing Disorders

In 1992, Greenspan first introduced the concept of regulatory disorders as a mixed developmental and emotional disorder, defining regulatory disorders as atypical behaviors accompanied by evident difficulties in several areas: in processing sensory information (over- or undersensitivity of the senses), in processing sensory-motor information (especially in the mouth region), in spatial organization, and in regulating one's emotional state. This view has been accepted to this very day by many clinicians working with infants.

Because of the very small number of empirical studies that supported this very broad definition of regulatory disorders and the tendency to overdiagnose children with this disorder, the DC:0–5 team was led to restrict the diagnostic criteria and to rename it as Sensory Processing Disorders. This diagnosis currently refers to infants/young children who experience clinically significant and impairing responses to sensory stimuli. These responses are independent of other pathological and neurodevelopmental conditions. Three categories are defined in the DC:0–5 manual:

1. Sensory Over-Responsivity Disorder
2. Sensory Under-Responsivity Disorder

3. Other Sensory Processing Disorder (this last category is for those children with a persistent and pervasive pattern of atypical sensory response who do not, however, meet all the criteria for either the Over-Responsivity or the Under-Responsivity types).

Children less than 3 years old with motor and impulse-regulation difficulties will, according to the DC:0–5 manual, be diagnosed with the new diagnostic category of Overactivity Disorder of Toddlerhood.

Sensory Over-Responsivity Disorder

This clinical disorder is characterized by a persistent pattern of exaggerated, intense, or prolonged responses to sensory stimuli (tactile, auditory, olfactory, vestibular, taste, visual, proprioreceptive, or interoreceptive). This over-responsivity occurs in more than one context, and it causes significant impairment in either the infant's daily functioning or her family's. Neuroimaging studies have shown that infants with Sensory Over-Responsivity Disorder, compared with typically developing infants, have difficulty processing multimodal stimuli, such as a combination of auditory and visual stimuli. There is some preliminary evidence suggesting dysfunction of white matter in the posterior area of the brain. Also, sensory over-responsivity shows moderate stability throughout childhood. Identical twins have more similar manifestations of sensory over-responsivity than nonidentical twins, suggesting an inherited origin.

The developmental feature of sensory over-responsivity symptoms is that excessive crying and difficulty to be soothed in the first years often turn into avoidance or opposition when the older child is expected to engage in activities involving exposure to the stimuli.

Infants with Sensory Over-Responsivity Disorder often have comorbid disorders, including eating and sleep problems. At preschool age, these children are at risk for emotional and behavioral problems, and at school age, they are at risk for academic difficulties and anxiety disorders.

Prematurity, intrauterine growth retardation, and global developmental delays are risk factors for Sensory Over-Responsivity Disorder. Although the disorder is constitutional in nature, environmental factors play a very important role, including lack of movement and tactile stimulation (as in situations of neglect), exposure to drugs during pregnancy, and community violence.

Sensory Over-Responsivity Disorder, although biological in nature, makes it very hard for a baby to form positive interactions with his environment, including his attachment figures (usually his mother and father). These are irritable babies who tend to exhibit a lot of crying and irritability and to over- or under-react to everyday stimuli (e.g., smells, noises, heat, lights); they are experienced as highly difficult and frustrating babies. It is no surprise, then, that they pose a challenge to those aspiring to be "good enough parents." Moreover, they are particularly challenging for parents who themselves suffer from regulatory difficulties or parents with a vulnerable personality.

It is important to emphasize the distinction between this disorder and a difficult temperament. The latter characterizes the normal development of approximately 10% of babies, whereas a Sensory Over-Responsivity Disorder indicates a pathological condition. Whether the Sensory Disorder is an extreme form of a difficult temperament is still being debated.

Differential diagnosis of Sensory Over-Responsivity Disorder

Between 24 and 36 months old, the differential diagnosis includes the DC:0–5 diagnosis of Overactivity Disorder of Toddlerhood. In addition, it is sometimes a challenge to distinguish anxiety responses from sensory responses in very young children. A typical example is an infant's fearful reaction to a vacuum cleaner: If the child reacts fearfully only to one stimulus, oversensitivity is unlikely to be diagnosed. After 36 months old, it is possible to pick out those children who have a harder time than their peers maintaining a sustained level of attention under different conditions.

Last but not least regarding differential diagnosis is the diagnosis of Autism. According to the DC:0–5 manual, atypical sensory responsivity is a criterion for Autism Spectrum Disorder; Autism Spectrum Disorder and Sensory Over-Responsivity Disorder are mutually exclusive diagnoses.

Posttraumatic Stress Disorder of Infancy (also see chapter 11) must always be ruled out, especially when the infant's exaggerated response occurs to very specific stimuli, which may actually be reminders of a traumatic event.

Sensory Under-Responsivity Disorder

Contrary to Sensory Over-Responsivity Disorder, the core feature of Sensory Under-Responsivity Disorder is a persistent pattern of minimal, neutral, or very brief responses to sensory stimuli that is inconsistent with normative developmental expectations, that occurs in more than one context, and that involves one or more sensory domains. The criterion of impairment in the child's or family's functioning is mandatory, as it is for all clinical conditions described in this book.

Depression of Infancy, Posttraumatic Stress Disorder of Infancy, and Deprivation Disorder must be ruled out because under-responsivity is often part of the clinical presentation of these disorders.

Comorbid Relationship Specific Disorder of Infancy/Early Childhood may be diagnosed if the DC:0–5 criteria are fulfilled.

Overactivity Disorder of Toddlerhood

This new diagnosis, defined by the DC:0–5, designates difficult-to-handle children 24–36 months old who exhibit impairing hyperactivity and impulsivity. The impairment entails exclusion from activities, problems in relationships with others (such as physical aggression, difficulty in waiting for a turn, and difficulty in reciprocal exchanges), and self-endangering behaviors. This diagnosis should not be given in cases in which the high activity level is episodic, reactive, or context-specific.

The core problem of these children is not sensory processing but the regulation of their impulses and motor visuospatial organization. As such, they tend to be very challenging to their parents, especially when these parents have behavioral and emotional regulation difficulties of their own. Indeed, these very young children very often fall and get injured because of their impulsivity and overactivity. Some of these children also have very short sleep duration.

Clinicians' knowledge on the extent of overlap between Sensory Over-Responsivity Disorder and symptoms of Attention Deficit Hyperactivity Disorders in toddlerhood is insufficiently grounded, because until the publication of the DC:0–5, the diagnostic category of Regulatory Disorders included both children with sensory processing difficulties and children with early signs of attention problems and motor impulsivity. As mentioned above, a distinct diagnostic category of Overactivity Disorder of Toddlerhood has been created for those older than 24 months and younger than 36 months. Obviously, there are still no published data using this new category. Still, from our clinical experience, quite a few parents to older children diagnosed with Attention Deficit Hyperactivity Disorder at childhood tell us that their children also had sensory processing problems as babies. Among others, they describe a severe sleep disorder. Indeed, the scientific literature suggests some correlation between severe sleep disorders in infancy and Attention Deficit Hyperactivity Disorders in childhood. On the basis of the reported findings, one of every four babies who suffer from serious sleep disorder is at risk of developing attention problems at preschool age, even more so when the former is compounded by additional risk factors, such as a difficult temperament. It follows that a sensory processing disorder accompanied by a serious lasting sleep disorder and familial dysfunction may be a high-risk factor for developing an Attention Deficit Hyperactivity Disorder from childhood on.

For those young children with Overactivity Disorder of Toddlerhood who develop Attention Deficit Hyperactivity Disorder after 3 years old, genetic factors, heritable patterns, and caregiving adversity are risk factors.

Let us now return to Pinocchio, who struggles to regulate his sensations, emotions, and behavior. As he develops, he encounters two types of "mentors": his parents—his father Geppetto and the Fairy with Turquoise

Hair—on the one hand, and tempter figures he crosses paths with—the mischievous boys, the fox and the cat—on the other hand. Geppetto, "his father," and the Fairy with Turquoise Hair, "his mother," each try, in their own way, to set him boundaries and teach him a daily routine consisting of studies and work. The fairy usually stands her ground and sets him clear boundaries, whereas Geppetto finds this hard to do, especially when overwhelmed by his worries and anxieties. The tempting characters, which represent external stimuli, derail him from the straight and narrow—that is, the path offered by his parents. The parental figures try to help him regulate himself and organize the chaotic reality around him, whereas the tempters stoke his impulses and make him "forget" his promises to his parents. Pinocchio's tutoring process draws to a close as he begins to internalize the meaning of the boundaries given to him by his fairy mother and believe in his ability to bring some preliminary order into his inner world: He is thus able to rescue his father from the stormy sea in which he nearly drowns and to go back to his mother and experience a sense of mastery and happiness. On his first homecoming night, he dreams that his mother turns him into an ordinary child and buys him new clothes. To him, these dream clothes represent his transformation. He then wakes up to discover that all he has dreamt of has come true: The piece of wood frequently manipulated by the tempters has disappeared, and in its place now stands the child of "his parents"; the family now starts to function as a regular family and gets to enjoy "a child like all others."

The Diagnostic Process for the Difficult-to-Handle Infant/Toddler

There's a man who lives in town, he's a man of great renown:
It's the topsy-turvy man, quite confused, and not from wine.
In the morning wakes the man and wonders, sitting up in bed:
Is my sleep behind me now, or do I have all night ahead?
In the sky shines a balloon, is it sun or is it moon?
Time to rise or time for bed? Clocks won't tell you, I'm afraid!
Oh yes, right, I now recall, surely as the sun does shine,
Now is obviously tomorrow, since last night the clock chimed nine.
That's our topsy-turvy man, quite confused, and not from wine.[1]

Sensory processing disorders, as well as Overactivity Disorder of Toddlerhood, are very important to diagnose early in view of the huge relief

---

[1] *The Distracted Man From Kfar Azar* by Leah Goldberg. Text copyright © 1968 Leah Goldberg. Used with the permission of Am Oved Publishers Ltd. Tel Aviv, Israel. All rights reserved. www.am-oved.co.il.

brought to parents when these difficult situations, which bear upon the parent–child relationship, are labeled and accounted for. For the first time, parents understand why their baby is so hard to handle. Following what we have mentioned above about the important role of the environment, the assessment must include a comprehensive report of the infant's development and the parents' own history as well as close observation of the interaction between the infant and his caregivers.

Occupational therapists play a key role in the diagnostic process. Their assessment is based on close observation of the infant's sensory processing and visuospatial organization as well as her self-regulation skills. They also use the Dunn Sensory Profile Questionnaire (Dunn & Bennett, 2002), which addresses eight areas of sensory processing: hearing, eyesight, taste, smell, movement, touch, activity level, and body position.

In addition, it should be emphasized that whenever the clinical picture meets the criteria for a Relationship Specific Disorder of Infancy/Early Childhood, it needs to be noted on Axis I, as comorbid diagnosis to the Sensory Over-Responsivity Disorder.

Treatment of Difficult-to-Handle Infants

The treatment plan for infants and toddlers with a sensory processing disorder or an overactivity disorder includes, by definition, the determination of the optimal type and amount of stimulation for them. For example, when an infant suffers from a low stimulation threshold and hypersensitivity, his caregivers will try to reduce the amount and force of stimuli around him (by, say, dimming the light in his room, turning down the music, protecting him from extreme temperatures, and avoiding exposure to crowds). Conversely, an infant who suffers from a high stimulation threshold and hyposensitivity will benefit from a stimulus-rich environment—for example, by being rocked in a hammock. A "sensory diet" could be implemented (Kimball, 1999), with diverse activities to help children focus their attention, adapt to the environment, and better regulate themselves. Stanley Greenspan and Serena Wieder, researchers who specialized in these treatments, underlined the importance of identifying a baby's sensory-regulation difficulties early on (e.g., Greenspan & Wieder, 2006). They elaborated an integrative developmental therapy for these types of sensory-regulation problems. A very young child who is particularly sensitive to noise, for example, will be offered games with changeable volume, allowing the parents to gradually turn up the amount and level of noise that the child is exposed to. As the child grows older and his language evolves, he can be taught to anticipate the situations in which he might encounter the offensive sensory stimuli and be encouraged to describe his feeling in words. Talking about his difficulties will make his parents more empathic and less critical toward him and will reduce the amount of punishments. Studies that have followed toddlers suffering from Attention Deficit Hyperactivity Disorder over time have shown that the more tolerant and stable the families in which they grew up, the better they functioned as adolescents.

The issue of medications in infant mental health is especially challenging because of the reluctance of both physicians and parents to give children at this age psychiatric drugs. In regard to the treatment of Attention Deficit Hyperactivity Disorder, the currently acceptable recommendation is to give Ritalin or a similar drug only to children 5 years old and up. When a toddler's regulatory difficulties are so severe as to impair everyday function and endanger the child or her surroundings, low doses of antipsychotic drugs should be considered.

CASE STUDY

K., 20 months old at time of referral, was born following an unplanned pregnancy to a mother who probably used drugs. He was a difficult baby from Day 1. He would cry for hours on end with back arching, and he was hard to console. He also had eating difficulties and vomited often. Any external stimulation made him extremely restless. His motor development was slow, and his muscle tonus was low. Every bodily contact exacerbated his restlessness. Furthermore, he would make sudden transitions, without external stimulation, from a state of unrest to one of indifference and under-reactivity. Physiotherapy given to K. during his first year helped him achieve the motor milestones and was therefore discontinued by the mother. The parents saw a pediatrician again when K. was 18 months old. They complained of persistent crying, rebelliousness, and severe tantrums both at home and at day care. The pediatrician referred the parents to our clinic for diagnosis. What we found striking during our first evaluation was K.'s lability of affect and functioning. The parents reported that there were days when he seemed cheerful and happy, and others when he would wake up in anger and launch into tantrums, flinging himself on the floor and banging his head against anything near.

K's sensory profile showed indeed that he had a hard time dealing with the slightest sensory changes, especially when tired. Even touch did not help him calm down. His parents—his mother in particular—felt helpless, angry, and frustrated, and we assumed that he banged his head on the floor partly to get what he wanted from them. K.'s DC:0–5 Axis I diagnosis would be Sensory Over-Responsivity Disorder, coupled with Disorder of Dysregulated Anger and Aggression of Early Childhood (see chapter 8). Neurological examination was normal. In light of these, we recommended mother–child dyadic combined occupational and psychotherapeutic treatment. The goal of therapy was twofold: to treat K.'s sensory disorder and show the mother just how much the sensory processing problem was tied to the child's aggressive temper tantrums.

During treatment, we emphasized how important it was to reduce the amount of stimulation at home and set appropriate limits for short, definite periods of time. The mother learned to identify the telltale signs of a brewing tantrum and was thus able to help K. stop the frustrating activity before the onset of the crisis. For example, K. refused to eat during family meals. Instead of eating, he would play with his food, smear it, and finally spill it. He seemed to take more pleasure in feeling the food with his hands than eating it. After his mother understood his need to touch the food, she softened up and allowed him to play with it while eating, but not to spill it over, to abide by the preestablished boundaries. Gradually, K.'s general situation improved, as did his relationship with his parents. At 3 years old, he was well-integrated into prekindergarten, even though his constitutional vulnerability was still there and the adults had to help him regulate himself. At 5 years old, on entering kindergarten, he had a hard time coping with all the stimuli around him, was diagnosed with Attention Deficit Hyperactivity Disorder—in addition to his sensory processing disorder—and was put on medication (Ritalin) in parallel to a supplementary round of occupational therapy.

Evolution of the Difficult-to-Handle Young Child

A longitudinal study conducted by Tirosh, Bendrian, Golan, Tamir, and Dar-Cohen (2003) followed 319 babies from infancy to 11 years old. Fifty-five of them had trouble regulating themselves at 3 months old (on the basis of the previous *Diagnostic Classification of Mental Health and Developmental Disorders of Infancy and Early Childhood, Revised Edition* [DC:0–3R; ZERO TO THREE, 2005] diagnostic criteria). The study showed that, compared with the control group, these 55 babies indeed suffered from Attention Deficit Hyperactivity Disorder at 4½, 8, and 11 years old. However, when the data were subjected to more accurate statistical analysis, also taking into account family risk factors, the difference between the study group and the control group was no longer statistically significant. This brought the researchers to conclude that regulatory problems (as diagnosed in the broad sense) in and of themselves did not necessarily lead to Attention Deficit Hyperactivity Disorder. Other risk factors in the child's immediate environment are at play. A pattern of negative mother–baby interactions, for example, may be a stronger predictor of psychopathology at a more advanced age than constitutional vulnerability.

Another longitudinal study (Becker et al., 2010) involving a random sample of children from birth to 7 years old found that 40% of them showed varying degrees of attention deficit problems to 5 years old; however, only 5% of all children continued to suffer from these disorders at an older age. Those whose disorder did persist also exhibited a high incidence of interpersonal and behavioral difficulties, anxiety, and motor clumsiness. This study tried to establish the risk factors and protective factors for the development of Attention Deficit Hyperactivity Disorder. It found that the protective factors were a high maternal intelligence quotient, a stable family, the absence of other physical problems, as well as good cognitive and verbal skills in the child. The risk factors included family dysfunction in general and maternal emotional problems in particular. Rejection, alienation, or excessive strictness on the parents' part exacerbated aggressive, impulsive, and rebellious behaviors, especially in those children who were biologically and genetically prone to develop attention and behavioral disorders.

CASE STUDY

P., a single child to her parents, was referred by her pediatrician to our infant mental health clinic at 2 years and 8 months old because of restlessness, irritability, and very frequent tantrums at home and at day care. Her mother described herself as suffering from Attention Deficit Hyperactivity Disorder. The marital relationship was described as good. P. was delivered normally following a desired, planned, and normal pregnancy. The mother developed pre-eclampsia after giving birth, but she was released from hospital with the baby. P. was described as having been a difficult-temperament baby, with excessive crying and difficulty to self-soothe. On her first examination in our clinic, P. entered the room without hesitation and started talking fast and abundantly in a grown-up style of speech. She passed from one game to another without pausing by any of them. Her spirits were high. She fell a lot, as if oblivious to the obstacles on her path. Her parents looked helpless in dealing with her. They were unable to set her boundaries, and their reaction alternated between anger and pity. The mother found it particularly hard to "see herself reflected in her daughter." For the most part, the father left his wife to handle the situation alone.

The differential diagnosis, based on DC:0–5, would include the following Axis I diagnoses: Sensory Over-Responsivity Disorder, Overactivity Disorder of Toddlerhood, and Relationship Specific Disorder of Infancy/Early Childhood. Given no history of clear sensory processing problems, we opted for the last two diagnoses. The treatment plan was based on a combination of triadic psychotherapy with occupational therapy. Even though P.'s functioning at day care was significantly impaired, medication was not given at this stage. Gradually, as psychotherapy progressed, the mother's ability to set her daughter boundaries improved, as did the girl's general condition.

About a year following treatment, P.'s condition deteriorated, and she relapsed into her restlessness, irritability, and frequent tantrums in day care, with added reports of aggressive behavior toward its other children. During our examination, she looked sad, had trouble controlling herself, often apologized for her behavior, and exhibited instability. Her argumentativeness toward her mother seriously escalated. Pediatric, neurological, and blood tests were within normal range. Given the level of impairment in the child's functioning at home and at day care, medication was administered, along with parental guidance and individual play psychotherapy aimed at helping P. deal with her anxieties and aggressive impulses. At follow-up, when P. was

6 years old, it was decided to continue both medication and psychotherapy to allow her to fit into a regular first-grade class.

Conclusion

All the disorders discussed in this book involve a combination of biological, psychological, and social dimensions. When it comes to sensory processing disorders and overactive infants/toddlers, the biological component is dominant, but environment also strongly influences the child's subsequent functioning. Few studies have been conducted in this area, but because this is a rather widespread phenomenon, we thought it important to review them and see what can be learned from them. In fact, behavior disorders and atypical forms of interpersonal communication might stem from a sensory processing disorder.

To conclude, sensory, behavioral, and emotional regulation can be said to be a core component in each individual's mental health. The regulatory system probably starts to form already in the womb, as shown by work done using ultrasound. Later, after birth, the regulatory capacities will also be influenced by environmental and cultural factors, among them the parents' regulatory skills (their aptitude to regulate themselves and help the baby regulate himself). Sensory processing disorders and overactivity disorders exist and manifest themselves from infancy, and their early detection is crucial. Treating only the child is not enough, and one also has to treat the relationship between the parents and their infant. Sometimes, parents also need a therapeutic process of their own.

References

Becker, K., Biomeyer, D., El-Faddagh, M., Esser, G., Schmidt, M. H., Banaschewski, T., & Laucht, M. (2010). From regulatory problems in infancy to attention-deficit/hyperactivity disorder in childhood: A moderating role for the dopamine D4 receptor gene? *Journal of Pediatrics, 156*, 798–803.

Chess, S., & Thomas, A. (1986). *Temperament in clinical practice.* New York, NY: Guilford Press.

Dolto, F. (1994). *Tout est language* [Everything is language]. Paris, France: Gallimard.

Dunn, W., & Bennett, E. (2002). Patterns of sensory processing in children with ADHD. *OTJR: Occupation, Participation, and Health, 22*, 4–15.

Greenspan, S. (1992). *Regulatory disorders: Infancy and early childhood.* Madison, CT: International Universities Press.

Greenspan, S. I., & Wieder, S. (2006). *Engaging autism: Using the floor time approach to help children relate, communicate, and think.* Cambridge, MA: Da Capo Press.

Kimball, J. (1999). Sensory integration frame of reference: Theoretical base, function/dysfunction continua, and guide to evaluation. In P. Kramer & J. Hinojosa (Eds.), *Frames of reference for pediatric occupational therapy* (2nd ed., pp. 119–159). Baltimore, MD: Lippincott Williams & Wilkins.

Schore, A. M. (1994). *Affect regulation and the origins of the self.* Hillsdale, NJ: Erlbaum.

Stern, D. (1985). *The interpersonal world of the infant.* New York, NY: Basic Books

Tirosh, E., Bendrian, S. B., Golan, B., Tamir, A., & Dar-Cohen, M. (2003). Regulatory disorders in Israeli infants. *Journal of Child Neurology, 18,* 748–754.

Tronick, E. (2007). *The neurobehavioral and social–emotional development of infants and children.* New York, NY: Norton.

Williamson, G. G., & Anzalone, M. E. (2001). *Sensory integration and self-regulation in infants and toddlers: Helping very young children interact with their environment.* Washington, DC: ZERO TO THREE.

ZERO TO THREE. (2005). *Diagnostic classification of mental health and developmental disorders of infancy and early childhood* (Rev. ed.). Washington, DC: Author.

ZERO TO THREE. (2016). *DC:0–5™: Diagnostic classification of mental health and developmental disorders of infancy and early childhood* (DC:0–5). Washington, DC: Author.

Recommended Reading

Alon, L., Cohen Ophir, M., Cohen, A., & Tirosh, E. (2010). Regulation disorders among children with visual impairment: A controlled study. *Journal of Developmental Physical Disabilities, 22,* 57–64.

Barton, M. L., & Robins, D. (2000). Regulatory disorders. In C. H. Zeanah, Jr. (Ed.), *Handbook of infant mental health* (2nd ed., pp. 311–325). New York, NY: Guilford Press.

Dale, L. P., O'Hara, E. A., Keen, J., & Porges, S. W. (2011). Infant regulatory disorders: Temperamental, physiological, and behavioral features. *Journal of Developmental and Behavioral Pediatrics, 32,* 216–224.

DeGangi, G. (2000). *Pediatric disorders of regulation in affect and behavior.* New York, NY: Academic Press.

Greenspan, S. (1995). *The challenging child.* Reading, MA: Addison Wesley.

Liebenluft, E. (2011). Severe mood dysregulation, irritability, and the diagnostic boundaries of bipolar disorder in youth. *American Journal of Psychiatry, 168,* 129–142.

Monk, T. H., Burk, L. R., Klein, M. H., Kupfer, D. J., Soehner, A. M., & Essex, M. J. (2009). Behavioral circadian regularity at age 1 month predicts anxiety levels during school-age years. *Psychiatry Research, 178,* 370–373.

CHAPTER 6
White Nights for Me . . . and My Parents

In many lullabies, there is a tie between nightfall—the stars that come out, the sun that goes down, and the shadows collecting in the room—and bedtime. Lullabies can apparently allay the separation anxiety attending the process of falling asleep.

In "Lullaby for Elisheva" by Miriam Yalan-Shteklis,[1] the girl tucks in her doll exactly when the clock announces the hour in a childish voice as "a quarter past," the time when the doll's heavy eyelids should close in preparation for her night's sleep: "Mine's a big and grown-up doll/By a nice name I her call/This I called her—Elisheva/Now my doll must go to sleep/Tick tock, tick tock, goes the clock/It's a quarter past already, said he/Hush now, sleep now, my dear doll/Elisheva, you're my all."

Introduction

Kreissler, a French pediatrician and psychoanalyst, viewed a baby's sleep as a highly sensitive gauge of his physical and emotional well-being (see Kreissler, Fain, & Soule, 1974). Our clinical experience has taught us that sleep is related to how people function physically and emotionally, not just in infancy but throughout life. Sleep disorders are often a first red flag—in childhood, adolescence, and adulthood—that some psychopathology such as depression, anxiety, or psychosis is in the making. The popular expression "to sleep like a baby" is common in many cultures, originating in the notion that a baby's sleep reflects the peace and quiet characteristic of people's first months in life. In fact, this romantic view, rather than reflecting what babies actually experience, is what adults project on them.

Each child has her own sleep architecture, which changes over her first 3 years. Sleeping difficulties, temporary or permanent, are relatively common throughout childhood. In fact, difficulties falling asleep and frequent arousals until 1 year old are a widespread, transient phenomenon related to

---

[1] Miriam Yalan-Shteklis, "Lullaby for Elisheva," appears in *I Gave Nurit a Flower*, p. 16, published by Kinneret Zmora-Bitan. Reprinted with permission.

physiological processes that take place as the brain matures. This is why we only use the term sleep "disorders" from 1 year old on.

In his book, *The Interpersonal World of the Infant*, Daniel N. Stern (1985) addressed the ways in which a baby assimilates his experiences. According to Stern, the way in which the baby internalizes his human environment is influenced by the way in which the activities involved in his daily care are carried out—the feeding, the diaper change, the bathing, and, for our purposes here, the laying down in bed. Stern maintained that a baby who falls asleep with a lullaby, soft words, or a story in the background finds himself in a different emotional state compared with a baby who is just "laid in bed" and left to his own devices. Some people even carry with them into adulthood the memory of moments experienced before being overtaken by sleep and the voice of the adult lulling them into sleep.

Up to some 20 years ago, studying baby and toddler sleep was technically difficult. One had to remove the baby from her natural home environment and bring her into the lab. The move itself was bound to distort the test results. Nowadays, as the late Avi Sadeh, a well-known sleep researcher, described in his 2001 book *Sleeping Like a Baby*, a simple device resembling a wristwatch, called an actigraph, is used. Attached to the baby's foot, the device can track her sleep pattern in her own bed, in her natural surroundings.

When parents come to our clinic with complaints about their baby's sleep disorders, we look into the relationship between the mother and father and their relationship with the baby. We ask the parents about the conditions found in the environment in which the baby is growing up as well as about the baby's health condition and temperament. We find out whether there are overt or hidden conflicts in the couple. Let us take, for example, parents who complain that their baby is unable to fall asleep alone in his bed, thus pushing one of them out of the conjugal bed. What we often discover is that abandoning the conjugal bed stems from a declared or repressed desire not to sleep together. Tensions in the family, which bring out anxiety or aggressiveness in the parents, could also cause sleep disorders in the very young child.

Sleep deprivation, in turn, affects parents and their response to their baby. We know of cases, from the literature and clinical practice, in which baby sleep disorders give rise to considerable tension between parents and might push them to temper tantrums and sometimes even physical abuse of the baby. A longitudinal study (Owens & Burnham, 2009) showed that recurring nighttime arousals in infants that persisted beyond 2 years old (a phenomenon known to occur in 6% of infants) were often linked to maternal depression and marital strife. It is important to note that lack of sleep lowers the baby's frustration threshold, makes the baby irritable, and puts the baby in a bad mood.

Sleep: Aspects of Normative Development

The Link Between Brain Development and Sleep Architecture

Ultrasound scans performed during pregnancy showed that, as early as the 32nd week of pregnancy, a clear pattern of deep, restful sleep (non-REM sleep) and a clear pattern of active sleep (REM sleep, also called dream sleep) can be observed in fetuses. A gradual increase in active-sleep hours is also evident from Week 32 to Week 40. Interestingly, the same sleeping pattern has been observed in premature babies at the same gestational age. The relatively high percentage of dream sleep in the last trimester of pregnancy coincides with the fast maturation of the brain during this period, underscoring the unique role of REM sleep in brain development.

During the first year of life, the change in sleep architecture also reflects the maturation of the circadian system, the system responsible for sleep cycles (day–night cycles). The synchronization of the baby's sleep cycle with nature's cycles — that is, light and dark, day and night — is a gradual process. From birth to 3 months old, the sleep–wake cycle depends on the hunger–satiation cycle and feeding times, regardless of the day–night cycle. From 5 months old on, most babies already manage longer sleep intervals at night, thanks to secretions of the "sleep hormone" melatonin. As for daytime, during her first months the baby spends more time in sleep, most of it of the active type, related as mentioned to the brain's maturation process. The gradual drop in active sleep during the first year is accompanied, of course, by an increase in hours of "restful sleep." By 2 weeks old, for example, half of the baby's sleeping hours are spent in active sleep, as opposed to only 30% at 9 months old. At the end of the first year, the toddler's sleep architecture, as it appears when measuring the brain's electric activity, is identical to that of an adult. Sleep cycle duration also changes gradually during the first 2 years of life: From a 1-hour cycle, it then increases to 1½ hours, as in adults. Infants begin their night sleep with active (REM) sleep, whereas adults start the night with deep (non-REM) sleep.

Beyond the first year, each sleep cycle starts off with deep non-REM sleep involving four substages. The end of the fourth substage is followed by dream sleep (REM), which is characterized by rapid eyelid movement, increased heart and breath rate, and low muscle tone. Around five such cycles take place every night. Nighttime dream time totals around 90 minutes.

What children dream of is revealed to others only when they start talking. There are universal contents, which recur in the dreams of same-aged children worldwide: Toddlers dream of monsters and sometimes events taken from their everyday life — the birth of a brother or sister or other happy or stressful events. It is important to talk to a child about his dreams because they afford a glimpse into his inner world and often allow parents and clinicians to understand what prevents him from sleeping well. Sometimes a child awakes from a nightmare (a dream with terrifying content). Nightmares usually occur during the last part of the night—they can last even half an hour—and their content remains inscribed in the child's memory even after waking up. Night terrors, however, appear during deep sleep and are hazy in terms of content; moreover, the child has no memory of them after waking up.

To learn what environmental factors play a role in inducing continuous sleep in babies, we suggest looking at the research work of Anders, Goodlin, and Sadeh (2000). They studied babies 9 months old, some of whom slept well, whereas others suffered from frequent arousals. In this study, the mothers were asked about each baby's sleep quality, and 12 hours in the life of each baby were documented on video. Analysis of the research data showed that none of those babies defined as "silent" by their parents woke up more than twice per night. However, those defined as "signalers" woke up 3–6 times at least per night. Examining the family's sleep habits turned up that the "silent" babies did not need rocking to fall asleep and that most of them had a transitional object (see chapter 3) that helped them resume peaceful sleep after awakening. Moreover, they were able to fall back asleep despite being at a distance from their parents, whereas the "signalers" demanded their mother's close physical presence each time for falling back asleep. About 70% of babies stop waking up at night around 3 months old, and about 13% stop waking up at night around 6 months old. Approximately 90% of babies sleep through the night at 1 year old.

As mentioned at the start of this chapter, a close relationship exists between sleep and the brain development. It is now known, for example, that "deep sleep" (non-REM) is the time when the child's physical growth takes place through the agency of the growth hormone. Researchers have suggested that sleep also influences brain plasticity—that is, the brain's ability to change its structure and functioning. This ability is particularly heightened up to 3 years old but continues to exist, albeit to a much lesser degree, throughout life (this is, by the way, the main rationale for early diagnosis and treatment in infancy and early childhood).

The developmental changes that take place in sleep architecture allow a child, usually by 3 years old, to build up gradually to a short period of sleep during the day and continuous sleep at night.

The Process of Falling Asleep

Falling asleep is an intermediate stage between wakefulness and sleep at both the physiological and psychological levels. It is already in place when people come out into the world and allows the circadian system (with controlled sleep cycles) to adapt to the differences between day and night. At the psychological level, falling asleep means disconnecting from wakefulness, from people's surrounding—agreeing to let go of the environing reality with all that this implies and, in the case of children, mainly the sense of security afforded by adults through their very presence. It is thus clear how the ability to fall asleep and the child's inner peace and security are connected. If a child sees sleep as a secure state of being, she will easily fall asleep; otherwise, she might not give in to sleep so readily. Several factors play a role in this subjective perception, among them the degree of security conveyed by the parent to the baby during her waking hours. Hence, a link is found between the existence of a secure style of attachment and falling asleep rapidly in infancy and even in subsequent years.

Mira Meir's book, Once Upon a Time There Was a Boy Who Did Not Want to Sleep Alone,[2] *describes a child who is unable to fall asleep alone. By remaining unnamed, the child becomes an archetype for any child who has this difficulty. The conventional wisdom in Israeli culture, out of which the story was born, is that a child must sleep alone. Many parents, however, find this principle hard to accept and allow the child into their bed. The storyteller in this story suggests an alternative solution for coping with the threatening "aloneness" without having to resort to sleep in the parents' bed: The child decides to take his teddy bear into his bed. However, on the following night, it turns out that the teddy bear is sad because it too needs a friend to fall asleep. In the same way, every night brings with it another friend to the bed, and another, until the bed becomes fully occupied with no more room left for the child. So now, every night, another friend goes back to its place, until one night the child decides that now he wants to sleep quietly alone. From that day on, the child sleeps quietly in his own bed all through the night.*

In Mira Meir's story, the child himself assumes responsibility for his fear of sleeping alone. It is he who comes up with the solution to the problem—at first for himself, and then for the teddy bear, the bunny, the little monkey, the snake, and the cat. He ends up realizing that this togetherness with multiple characters also comes at a price: He himself has no more room left in his own bed. He therefore starts emptying the bed of his "friends" and ends up deciding to sleep in it alone. Passing the responsibility to the child allows him to feel that the power to save himself lies in his own hands— that even if the process takes a while, it is bound to come to an end, and for the better. The author avoids interpreting the child's fear of sleeping alone. She does not explore the reasons for this avoidance and thus leaves the interpretation to the reader—the parent and the child, each according to their individual needs, to their personality.

---

[2] Mira Meir, 2010, *Once Upon a Time There Was a Boy Who Did Not Want To Sleep Alone,* published by Sifriat Hapoalim.

In Laura Numeroff's When Sheep Sleep,[3] *the story's hero remains unnamed. The anonymous hero tells the story in the second person: Her idea is to count sheep if you are having trouble falling asleep. The child, who has a hard time falling asleep, represents all similarly challenged children. She too does not turn to her parents to find a cure. She adopts a solution that her parents had probably offered before: counting sheep. This child too does not sit around idly. She does not even try to understand why she has a hard time falling asleep. She asks herself what does one do and immediately takes action.*

In this case too, there is no immediate solution to her distress. The child realizes that the solution she was offered by her parents is insufficient: She counts sheep, but they fall asleep, whereas she remains awake. The resourceful child does not give up. She counts deer, but they are quick to shut their eyes — as are the cows in the meadow, the pigs wallowing in mud, the mischievous puppies, the birds, the cats, the little bears, and the rabbits. All the animals are quick to fall asleep, dreaming sweet dreams. Finally, the child concludes that the very effort to count sheep has done the trick, and made her tired enough to fall asleep. In this story, just as in the previous one, the child finds the answer to her predicament — her own solution, which combines the strategies suggested by her parents with an independent version that finally brings about the hoped-for calm.

The transition from arousal to sleep is a gradual one usually accompanied by rituals designed to make the process of falling asleep pleasant and relaxed. Typical rituals include the bath, putting on the pajamas, reading a story, and listening to a lullaby (usually by a baby's significant caregiver). This is the place to point out the importance of the transitional object — the teddy bear, cloth diaper, or blanket that helps the baby to feel secure and to part from her parents. It is Winnicott who understood the importance of the transitional object, an object symbolizing the figure to whom the child is attached and making separation easier for the child (see, e.g., Winnicott, 1960, 1990). Winnicott showed how the young child projects onto her transitional object — whose smell, taste, color, and viscosity never change — all those feelings of love and anger she feels toward her parents, both when falling asleep and when being separated from them during the day. Further on in this chapter, we address those situations in which the difficulties around falling asleep become persistent and require professional intervention.

---

[3] *When Sheep Sleep* by Laura Numeroff. Text copyright © 2006 Laura Numeroff. Used with the permission of Express Permissions on behalf of Abrams Books for Young Readers, an imprint of Harry N. Abrams, Inc., New York. All rights reserved. www.abramsbooks.com.

The Question of Co-Sleeping
(Sleeping in the Parents' Bed)

Parents often say, "Our infant sleeps great in bed with us . . . so why insist on him sleeping in his bed alone? Isn't it possible that babies have a genuine need for closeness?" The cultural aspects of sleep are brought to the fore when it comes to co-sleeping. Let us take, for example, the results of the research work conducted by Richman (1981), who looked at the sleeping habits of White and Black babies in the United States. In this study, 70% of parents in Black families declared that they slept with their child until 4 years old, compared with only 35% within the White population. Co-sleeping within the White population was often linked to stressful situations experienced by either the child or the parents. Co-sleeping can thus be considered normative in one culture and abnormal in another context. One may wonder what is served by co-sleeping: the child's emotional needs, those of his parents, or perhaps those of all members of the family.

Some parents sleep with their children in keeping with the so-called Continuum Concept, which advocates that parents should refrain from setting boundaries and frustrating the child during her first 2 years. This concept is inconsistent with the definition of the "good enough" parent, according to which setting boundaries and "meting out" appropriate doses of frustration are a catalyst toward the development of a healthy, well-adapted individual.

The incidence of sleep disorders in families that live by the Continuum Concept is no lower than it is in the general population. Our clinical experience shows that these parents often have unresolved issues with their own parents regarding separateness, separation, and frustration, and they find the rationalization they need in the Continuum Concept. It is not unfounded to say that parents' behavior during the putting-to-bed ceremony reflects their psychological position regarding the baby's ability to detach from them and achieve emotional independence.

To conclude, sleeping habits clearly have a cultural aspect. Tribal tradition dictates where a baby will sleep, with whom, and starting at what age. In Western society, sleeping habits imparted by parents are also influenced by new medical knowledge. The current tendency is to have the baby sleep in the parents' room until he is about 3 months old and then to move him to his own bed and of course allow him to use a transitional object.

Sleep Disorders in Infancy

Definition of Sleep Disorders in Infancy

As shown in the beginning of the chapter, difficulties falling asleep and sleeping through the night are quite common in a child's first years. Consequently, the line between phenomena that lie within the norm and ones that require professional intervention is sometimes very thin. According to the *DC:0–5™:Diagnostic Classification of Mental Health and Developmental Disorders of Infancy and Early Childhood* (DC:0–5; ZERO TO THREE, 2016), sleep difficulties can be diagnosed as a disorder from 6 months old onward because the majority of typically developing babies are able to sleep through the night by that age.

The DC:0–5 manual classifies sleep disorders in infancy into four categories: Sleep Onset Disorder, Night Waking Disorder, Partial Arousal Sleep Disorder, and Nightmare Disorder of Early Childhood. The disorders are defined empirically, not etiologically, and require impairment in the child's or the family's functioning as an obligatory criterion to prevent overpathologizing of sleep patterns that may be only slightly deviant.

Sleep Onset Disorder is defined as whenever a very young child takes more than 30 minutes to fall asleep most nights of the week for at least 1 month. Night Waking Disorder is defined as whenever a child who is at least 8 months old wakes up several times per night, cries out, and does not return to sleep spontaneously. Partial Arousal Sleep Disorder is defined as whenever a child who is at least 1 year old has frequent, recurrent episodes of sudden arousals from sleep, without being awake (night terrors), or frequent episodes of arising from bed and walking in the house. In both cases, the child has no recollection of the event in the morning. The symptoms must be present for at least 4 weeks.

Night terrors account for only 1%–3% of sleep problems and, for the most part, first appear after 9 months old. Children who suffer from them are observed lying in bed with open eyes expressing fear or panic while often screaming. Their breathing and heart rates are accelerated, and hyperkinesia of the limbs is also often observed. To the onlooker, these children give the impression of trying to escape and protect themselves from some external threat. This state can often be misinterpreted by parents as a state of wakefulness, but attempting to wake them up indicates that they are in a state of confusion and are incapable of any communication. Terrors usually appear in the first third of the night during deep (non-REM) sleep, characterized by slow brainwaves. The attack lasts from several minutes to 30 minutes, after which the child falls asleep, remembering nothing of the incident the next day; she does not even resist going back to her bed, as she would if this was a nightmare. Unlike a nightmare, in which the contents of the dream carry symbolic meaning, night terrors have none. The only way to diagnose this disorder is to monitor sleep using an actigraph and see at what stage of sleep the fit takes place. If it appears during deep (non-REM) sleep, it is night terrors. If it appears during active (REM) sleep, these are nightmares.

Nightmare Disorder of Early Childhood is defined as repeated occurrences of bad dreams that awaken the child and cause clear distress, even though the young child may not recall or report their content. The child must be at least 1 year old, and the symptoms must last at least 1 month.

Prevalence of Sleep Disorders in Infancy

Epidemiologic studies—mostly in the United States and Europe—that have looked at the prevalence of Sleep Onset Disorder are highly variable in terms of the diagnostic criteria used in their research design. It seems that approximately 10%–15% of infants and toddlers have a sleep onset duration of greater than 30 minutes, but when the criterion of impairment is used, these figures drop to 5%–10%. Nightmares and partial arousals are common in the preschool-age group, but only 1%–3% experience nightmares "often."

Etiology of Sleep Disorders in Infancy

Sleep disorders in early childhood have been linked with an infant's/young child's biological factors as well as family factors.

Biological factors

It turns out that heritability of all types of sleep problems is high. Difficult temperament and difficulty to be soothed put young children at risk for sleep problems, especially Sleep Onset Disorder and Night Waking Disorder. Medical problems, such as gastrointestinal reflux and neurodevelopmental disorders, are also risk factors. Atypical diurnal cortisol patterns have been reported among young children with Sleep Onset Disorder and Night Waking Disorder, but it is unclear whether they are a cause or effect of sleep deprivation.

Family factors

Family factors that have been linked with sleep disorders in early childhood can be divided into three main categories: parents' sleep-related behaviors, parents' cognitions about sleep, and parents' psychopathology.

Parents' sleep-related behaviors and cognitions

A baby's ability to self-soothe and fall back asleep spontaneously after awaking largely depends on the parents' sleep-related behaviors. For instance, infants whose parents hold them, feed them, and rock them while being put to bed are at higher risk for sleep disorders than infants who are put to bed while still awake with minimal parental assistance. Babies awake from sleep on multiple occasions, moving, mumbling. There is no call to rock them straight away, pick them up, or feed them. Mostly, they should simply be allowed to fall back asleep quietly in their bed. When parents intervene with an immediate response to the arousal, the baby will expect them to do so every time he wakes up in the dead of night. Nighttime arousals in healthy babies after 5 months old are unlikely to indicate hunger. Infants whose parents react to their arousals by feeding them (either breastfeeding or bottle feeding) are also more likely to have difficulties falling asleep, and their arousals are reinforced. Underlying these parental behaviors are cognitions and beliefs, such as resistance to setting limits, or the belief that babies need an immediate response to reduce their crying.

The typical scenario for the Sleep Onset Disorder in 2- and 3-year-old children generally goes as follows: The child stalls for time to delay her bed-time under different pretenses—wanting water, having to pee, wanting another hug, one more story, 5 more minutes, and so forth. The parents play along with the toddler, getting sucked into her schedule, and the ceremony drags on and on. Why do parents find it hard to set the toddler boundaries? Sometimes, especially in the case of a first child, the difficulty can be chalked up to inexpe-rience, but sometimes it comes from a deeper place, which is usually related to their past. Oftentimes, in toddlers 3 years old and up, in particular, the difficulty falling asleep is accompanied by rebellious behavior during the day, which testifies to a tense parent–child relationship fraught with anger.

Parental psychopathology

Maternal separation anxiety is very often linked to difficulty in setting limits and letting the infant fall asleep by himself. Also, postnatal maternal depression, especially if preceded by depression during pregnancy, has been linked to sleep onset problems and night arousals in infancy. Parents' own sleep problems have also been linked to infant sleep difficulties. Marital tension, as we have men-tioned in the introduction, is sometimes the underlying cause of the infant's sleep difficulty.

Insecure attachment

A correlation between insecure attachment in both mother and infant and sleep disorders in infancy has been reported. How should one understand this connection? The baby may experience being put in bed as a separation from the parent and feel distressed. Parents with an insecure style of attachment (toward their own parental figures) might transmit their own insecurity to their baby. Such parents tend to view the baby's arousals as a cry for help and actually stand in her way to falling back asleep on her own. In rarer cases, a baby's sleep problem reflects her parents' ambivalence toward her—for example, when she has a serious disease and an uncertain future. This ambivalence—their love for the baby alongside the great difficulty involved in raising her—produces contradictory behaviors: overprotectiveness toward the baby on the one hand and keeping a distance from her on the other hand.

CASE STUDY

A., a toddler 1 year and 8 months old, was referred to our clinic by a pediatrician because of difficulties falling asleep. The mother stayed at home, and the father was an employee who got back home from work late in the evening. During our initial session, the parents said that A. would only fall asleep every night around 1 a.m., adding "In fact, he never sleeps really well." The parents reported that in A.'s first year, his father was unemployed and hence was the main caregiver. A.'s mother had a very hard time bonding with him. It turned out that the mother had been suffering from an Obsessive Compulsive Disorder for years, finding it very hard to form interpersonal relationships. While still pregnant with A., she was preoccupied with the question of whether she would be capable of loving her son. This question, which kept spinning in her mind, produced considerable anxiety and stress. Indeed, after A.'s birth, she had a hard time connecting with him emotionally. He was too demanding, she felt, and a hindrance to performing her rituals from morning to evening.

When A. turned 1 year old, his father found a job that kept him away from home for long hours, even at night. From the baby's perspective, his father vanished from his life, leaving him alone with his mother, with all that this implied. These new circumstances left the mother in a state of distress and significant emotional burden, and she found it hard to contain the baby. "Sometimes, I don't feel like taking care of him," she said during our meeting. "I cannot bring myself to love him, just as I had feared would happen." It is important to note that A. was the only one on the receiving end of this attitude on the mother's part. Her relationship with his baby brother was normal. Thus, A. and his mother would loiter every day waiting for the father to come back home. When he did, the mother would hand him A. and go about her rituals into the wee hours. As the sleeping problem persisted, the parents grew more tired and the child more nervous. Fearing that the mother might get violent with the toddler, the couple decided to enlist the help of a babysitter three afternoons a week. This help was supposed to prevent the possibility of the mother and A. being left together alone.

In examining A., we found him to be slightly big for his age (i.e., chubby; very much like his father). He bonded easily, perhaps too easily, with the examiner and asked to play with her. He was in a good mood for the better part of the session, but when this changed, we were often at a loss to understand the reasons for it. A. would suddenly burst out crying and would respond very angrily to even the slightest frustration. He seemed to understand everything spoken around him, used words befitting his age, but his imaginary play was poorer than expected. The father's interaction with A. was quite normal, except for a tendency he had to placate A. too fast on every little thing. The mother seemed distant, but A. did not "give up" on her. A small smile from her in his direction was enough to make him approach her right away, as if he had only waited for that smile to draw closer to her.

The DC:0–5 diagnoses would be as follows:

- Axis I: Clinical Disorders
  - » Sleep Onset Disorder
  - » Relationship Specific Disorder of Infancy/Early Childhood

- Axis II: Relational Context
  - » Level 4—Disordered to Dangerous mother–infant relationship
  - » Level 2—Strained to Concerning caregiving environment

- Axis III: Medical Condition
  - » None

- Axis IV: Psychosocial Stressor
  - » Maternal Obsessive Compulsive Disorder

- Axis V: Developmental Competence
  - » Functions at age-appropriate level

The mother did not attend our third meeting. She told her husband, "I don't like A., so I don't want to go to therapy." During that meeting, we apprised the father of the severity of the situation and explained to him that if this went on, we would have to report it to the Welfare authorities. We made it clear that regular, continuous treatment should start immediately, with the mother's participation of course. We referred the mother to an adult mental health clinic to receive medication and behavioral treatment to help her deal with the Obsessive Compulsive Disorder afflicting her. We also recommended psychotherapy in our clinic with a focus on her relationship with A. We suggested that the father should also take part in these sessions alternately.

Because A. was a planned and wished-for baby, the threat of losing him appealed to the mother's healthy side, and she agreed to cooperate with us. Gradually, as she underwent treatment at our clinic and the adult mental health clinic, her emotional condition improved, as did her relationship with her child. A few months later, both parents also reported an improvement in A.'s sleep disorder. As far as we know, he now sleeps well.

A highly anxious parental attitude toward the baby accompanied by an unconscious fear of loss and death sometimes underlies the baby's sleep disorder. Even in infancy, the notion of death is present in the bedroom. Some parents are gripped by anxiety every time they put their baby to sleep. They sometimes wake up several times at night to verify that he is still breathing, without always being aware of the anxiety that drives them and its repercussions. Fearing Sudden Infant Death Syndrome is understandable, and many parents use an infant monitor called "Babysense" to allay their anxiety. However, if these anxieties persist even after the child is 6 months old, it might be useful to consult a professional.

CASE STUDY

B., a 10-month-old baby, was brought to our clinic by her exhausted parents because of multiple arousals (about 10 per night). Our initial examination showed that B., an only child, was a healthy looking, well-developed baby. Her mood was good. Her relationship with her parents seemed smooth at first sight. The parents described their conjugal relationship as normal, reporting only few differences between them, and certainly none when it came to B.'s education. They said that they had already consulted a pediatrician and received advice on how to deal with sleep disorders at this age, but to no avail. When we asked the parents to describe their sleeping patterns, we were surprised to hear that each one of them woke up during the night, at different times, to check up on the baby and make sure she was still alive. The parents saw no connection between this behavior of theirs and B.'s arousals. As we enquired further, each parent related a traumatic event they had experienced in the past. Both events were somehow related to nighttime: The father had lost his best friend during a war when they lay in ambush together at night, and the mother had received a phone call at night with news of her brother's death in a terrorist attack when she was abroad. Of course, they were unaware of the linkage between these two traumatic events and B.'s sleeping problem. The child's only DC:0–5 diagnosis would be Night Waking Disorder on Axis I. The therapy was triadic. Talking about the painful experiences of loss each of them were still going through, and how it related to their unconscious fear of losing their baby, is what eventually helped solve the problem of B.'s multiple arousals. The parents stopped visiting her bed at night (the father still woke up but learned to control the urge and stay in bed). B. went back to "sleeping like a baby"—that is, she woke up 2-3 times at night but was able to fall back asleep on her own.

Interestingly, sleep and death are also linked in Greek mythology: Hypnos (hypnosis), otherwise known by his Roman name Somnus (insomnia), was the god of sleep, whereas Thanatos, his twin brother, was the god of death. The two, identical twins, were born to the goddess of the night, Nyx, daughter of none other than Chaos. The twins, the god of sleep and god of death, resided in the underworld in a foggy cave in whose center slowly flowed the river of forgetfulness.

In Greek mythology, then, sleep and death are identical twins. They are bound by a Gordian knot. Their twinning reflects the notion of death anxiety being an integral part of sleep, but Hypnos himself is described as a winged young man with beneficial power who brings men and gods the gift of vitalizing sleep. The stories in the mythology can therefore be seen to represent the duality characterizing humans' perception of sleep: death anxiety alongside hope for a life of revival and vitality.

In sleep, the day that has died and gone by fuses with the new day about to be born: Death touches life. During a person's sleep at night, she entrusts the goddess of the night, daughter of Chaos, with her soul and takes refuge in the shadow of the cave of the god of sleep and the god of death. Does doing so amount to reckless neglect? Will the god of sleep prevail over the god of death? Will the beneficial gift offered by the god of the night quench the sleeper's body and soul?

This duality is likewise evident in the Jewish sources. The morning prayer opens with thanks given to God, "living and eternal King, that you have compassionately restored my soul within me," and ends on "Blessed are you my Lord, who restores souls to corpses dead"; whereas in the "He who grants strength to the tired" blessing, the individual blesses God for having reinvigorated and rejuvenated his tired soul after the previous day's toil and returned it to him on the morning of the next day, restful and recharged with vitality.

Overlapping eating and sleeping times

Another quite common cause for the appearance of multiple and persistent arousals in babies is sleep times turned into feeding times either because of an eating problem during the day or night breastfeeding past the age when the baby can sleep through the night without eating—that is, around 5 months in healthy babies. After that time, whenever an arousal is understood by parents as a sign of hunger, falling asleep thus becomes associated in the baby's mind with sensations of fullness, and with time she might view eating as a necessary condition for falling asleep. The conditioning thus created between eating and sleep is by no means desirable for babies.

Beyond 5 months old, nocturnal eating also affects the rate of maturation of the circadian cycle—that is, the 24-hour periodicity of each of the physiological activities that take place in one's body. Instead of the rhythmic cycle of hunger–satiation–digestion–sleep–wake becoming a day–night cycle in which sleeping happens at night and eating during the day, the baby will have no experience of uninterrupted sleep.

Babies who suckle after 9 months old might also awaken frequently at night. That breastfeeding is continued at night has more to do sometimes with the mother's need than the baby's hunger. Indeed, breastfeeding may give the mother a sense of self-confidence in her motherhood, to such a degree that there is no place left for the rest of the family, including the father. The latter might even quit the conjugal bed and leave it to the baby and the breastfeeding mother. This situation often produces significant marital tension. The process of weaning off nighttime breastfeeding is important for both baby and mother. It gives the mother her body and independence back and accentuates the difference between day and night for the baby. When this process fails and the baby insists on continuing to eat at night as well, becoming a kind of small "tyrant" controlling her mother's body, professional intervention is sometimes required. These are the cases in which we will not only diagnose a sleep disorder but also one in the mother–baby relationship.

Neurodevelopmental disorders

Sleep disorder can sometimes be one symptom of a neurodevelopmental disorder. In other words, the neurodevelopmental disorder is what impairs the physiological action mechanism of sleep. In other cases, sleep disorder is a side effect of medication administered to treat a neurodevelopmental disorder. Sleep disorders are frequent in 30%–80% of children suffering from intellectual disability, and 70%–75% of children suffering from a disorder on the autism spectrum suffer from sleep disorders already in infancy. These high figures have compelled the DC:0–5 Task Force to determine that sleep problems secondary to a neurodevelopmental disorder will not be diagnosed as a separate subcategory of a sleep disorder but will be included under the diagnosis of the neurodevelopmental disorder.

Children with Attention Deficit Hyperactivity Disorder sometimes also suffer from sleep disorders, but this seems more related to their general oppositional behaviors than to the attention problem itself.

Differential Diagnosis of Sleep Disorders in Infancy

In diagnosing a sleep disorder, clinicians must first rule out physical illnesses, including obstructive sleep apnea, restless leg syndrome, milk allergy, gastroesophageal reflux, atopic dermatitis, asthma, pain (such as undiagnosed infection of the ear), neurological disorders involving convulsions, and sensory processing disorders. Clinicians must also rule out sleep disorders brought on as a side effect of medications given to the baby. Infant depression, although rare, can also express itself in too much sleep.

The Diagnostic Process

During the evaluation process in our clinic, we need to obtain a full, orderly history of the sleep disorder from the parents and document it. We need the parents to tell us how frequently the child wakes up from sleep, what characterizes his difficulties when trying to fall asleep, how they see these difficulties, and how they respond when the child awakes. As we have explained in detail in chapter 3, the baby's presence is very important for the diagnostic process.

We inquire about the pregnancy and delivery, about significant events, and about stressful moments they had experienced, such as the loss of a significant figure in their lives, accidents, or diseases. We also ask them about the child's development from birth on, paying attention to how each of them perceives their infant's development. We try to understand how the parents understand the appearance of the symptom and the factors to which they attribute the disorder. The frequent question that parents put to us about the proper length of time to let the baby cry sometimes hides a painful memory of their own crying that their parents failed to hear. Detecting this psychological identification with the child helps the parents and us understand what sleep means to them.

As in any evaluation process of infants and parents, it is important to let the parents express themselves freely and describe their feelings, both positive and negative, without passing judgment. If we feel that one of the parents has many things to say, but has a hard time saying them in the presence of the other parent, we will consider summoning only that parent to the next meeting.

Parents who seek counseling with regard to their baby are usually dedicated and caring parents, parents attuned to her crying and concerned for her physical and emotional well-being. Nevertheless, parents often protest the personal questions they are asked, failing to understand how they relate to the matter that brought them to us. What does their own childhood have to do with their child's sleeping problem? How does a long-past loss, which had cost them many sleepless nights, tie into their baby's arousals in the present? Sometimes it takes parents a while to realize that a connection exists between their past and their current parenting.

As mentioned above, marital functioning is also very important to investigate in relation to the infant's sleep pattern.

Treating Sleep Disorders in Infancy

In many stories, parents—and sometimes even grandmothers—step in to resolve the sleeping crisis. In Anu Stohner and Henrike Wilson's Good Night, Stars!,[4] a little bear asks its parents to play the "good-night" game with it. The weary parents, greatly deterred by the prospect of a drawn-out game, make other suggestions. But here too, there are no magic solutions: The process is long and hard, just as it is in the extra-literary reality. The good-night game suggested by the little bear is a rhyming game in which the mother and father take part. The little bear invites its parents to come up with a fitting rhyme for each of its opening phrases as it addresses various things it sees around it (e.g., stuffed animals) and bids them good night. Fifteen charming rhymes are thus formed. At the end, the little bear starts yawning and addresses the stars, inviting them to join it in its sleep. The little bear, all yawns, lies in bed and musters its last-remaining forces to bid the light goodnight. One rhyme later, the little bear is lying down on

---

[4] Anu Stohner and Henrike Wilson, 2009, Good Night, Stars!, published by Kinneret Zmora-Bitan.

its back, its eyes almost closing. This is yet another story in which it is the child who offers a solution to the difficulty he has falling asleep, one that will very much delay the end, but the parents who play along with it do not give up and persist in their shared game.

In the past, most pediatricians considered sleep disorders in infancy to be a transient phenomenon that does not call for treatment. "It will pass with time," they used to say. Today, in the wake of studies showing that sleep disorders in infancy can be persistent and detrimental in the long term to the functioning of both the baby and the family, the approach has changed, and early intervention is often resorted to. There are several types of intervention.

Behavioral Therapy

Behavioral therapy is the most common and effective treatment, in both the short and long run, for multiple arousals in babies and toddlers and for difficulties they have going to sleep or falling asleep. Behavioral therapy is based on three principles:

- *Extinction*: This is the process of neutralizing the attention that parents devote to the baby's crying and cries. In fact, when parents do not respond to these behaviors, the baby learns to self-soothe. Success with this treatment largely depends on the parents' ability to stand aloof without feeling guilty. This is no easy task, which means that taking a gradual approach to the process is preferable in most cases. The 5-minute method, developed in Israel by Avi Sadeh (2001), is one of the recognized behavioral methods. Using this method, one lays the child in her bed, calms her with soothing words, steps out of the room, and steps back in at increasing intervals if the baby needs soothing; this is done until the baby stops crying. This method, proven effective in dealing with difficulties falling asleep and repeated arousals, can be used for treatment only when the parents are game and are prepared to cope with the baby's crying.

- *Creating a routine around sleeping*: This principle is about reinforcing parental behaviors that create a relaxed atmosphere for the baby and help him lessen his level of alertness and regulate his emotional state.

- *Psycho-educational guidance for parents*: In line with this principle, parents are given explanations regarding desirable and undesirable behaviors. As part of this guidance, parents are taught to lay the baby down in bed (as early as 3–4 months old) when she is drowsy yet still awake, explaining to the parents how important it is for the child to have a transitional object and become accustomed to an unchanging, well-organized bedtime routine (bath, pajamas, story). Consistent behavior on the parents' part is key if the treatment is to succeed.

Psychodynamic Therapy

As shown in the clinical case below, some parents are unable to go through with the behavioral treatment because of deep-seated psychological—and for the most part unconscious—causes. When the sleep disorder is a manifestation of some disorder in the baby–parent relationship, we will usually recommend triadic psychodynamic therapy, involving both parents and the baby, in accordance with the principles presented in chapter 17, which discusses types of therapy in infancy.

Medications

Pediatricians often recommend antihistamines or benzodiazepines to treat children's sleep disorders, even when they are very young children. This approach is ineffective in the long run. Resorting to medications is recommended only in complex clinical situations (e.g., autism, intellectual disability, physical disease).

Massage

Massage probably influences melatonin secretion and the development of normal circadian rhythms in very young children. One study (Field & Hernandez-Reif, 2001) reported that preventive massage was found to be effective in treating babies who suffered from sleeping problems: After being given a massage, babies fell asleep faster, awoke less during the night, and were even more alert during the day. This method is still new and requires additional studies to test and validate it.

We end the chapter with a case that shows the different aspects of sleep problems as a symptom in infancy.

CASE STUDY

L., a single child to educated parents in the fourth decade of their lives, was referred to our clinic at 1 year and 10 months because of an eating problem. L. still suckled and refused solid food other than candy and biscuits. She was born following a desirable, normal pregnancy, and delivery was uneventful. Still, she was a "crybaby" ever since birth, and breastfeeding in the parents' bed very soon became a way to both soothe and feed her. L.'s motor development was normative, but she was clearly behind in language development. She uttered only sounds, not even syllables, let alone a few words. The mother testified that she had been raised by parents who pampered her and asked almost nothing of her, and that she had not felt prepared enough for motherhood. She could not recall any stressful event in her past. The father grew up in a home where the parents argued a lot, and he was more attached in childhood to his father. He was not the least bit aware of his emotional world or that of those around him, including his daughter. Thus, for example, he refused to entertain the possibility that a nasty road accident in which he was involved at 3 years old and that crippled his mother could in any way be related to the way he felt today about his daughter. This being said, he was very much involved in raising L. As for the mother, breastfeeding was practically the only way for her to express her motherhood. In everyday life, she had a very hard time setting L. boundaries and was mainly guided by considerations of convenience ("having peace and quiet"). This is also why she never made any effort to take L. out of the parents' bed and move her to one of her own. When they turned to us for advice, the relationship between the parents was very tense. The father tended to be picky about every little detail of everyday life (as was the custom at his parents' house), and this obviously had an adverse effect on their marital relations.

During our initial session, L. and her father sat on the carpet next to the therapist, whereas the mother sat on a chair. This form of sitting unconsciously reflected the mother's difficulty to play with her daughter "at eye level." L. turned out to be a high-strung child with a low frustration threshold who had a hard time soothing herself. All through the meeting, she did not play one bit but stayed close to her father, hardly interacting with her mother. Her late language development made it hard to assess her general level of understanding. Her parents reported no diseases from which she suffered.

After two meetings, we established the following diagnoses on the basis of the DC:0–5 classification:

- Axis I: Clinical Disorders
  - » Night Waking Disorder
  - » Undereating Disorder
  - » Relationship Specific Disorder of Infancy/Early Childhood
  - » Language developmental delay

- Axis II: Relational Context
  - » Disturbed dyadic and triadic relationship

- Axis III: Medical Condition
  - » None

- Axis IV: Psychosocial Stressor
  - » Marital discord

- Axis V: Developmental Competence
  - » Below expected level of competence

On completing the diagnostic process, we suggested triadic interactional guidance, aimed at improving their interpersonal relationships and the parents' insightfulness. L. also underwent an auditory test to rule out a hearing problem as the source for her late language development. Weaning off the breast was defined as the first step in therapy. The mother was guided to talk about it with the child so that the child would not experience weaning as a rejection: "Mommy has no more milk left in her boobies, but don't worry, mommy also knows how to love you without boobies."

After the third session, and with no advance warning, L. and her parents vanished and did not show up at the clinic for about 2 months. They resurfaced when L. was 2 years and 1 month old, laying their absence on technical reasons. As it turned out, breastfeeding was indeed stopped as agreed during our last session, but, contrary to our recommendation, the girl was given no explanation as to why it stopped. The reason the parents gave for this was their mistrust in L.'s ability to "understand emotional language." They came back to us because L.'s sleep problem had taken a turn for the worse and they could no longer deal with her crying. The helplessness they felt made them behave unreasonably. One day they brought L. to day care while still sleepy and in her pajamas; they found it hard to handle the chore of waking her up in the morning and getting her ready and the arguments that broke out between them as a result. In the same session in which they reported this incident, we also learned that since breastfeeding was stopped, L. would fall asleep only when touching her father's nipple! The parents saw nothing wrong with this behavior.

Following their meeting with us, the parents understood the need to ensure consistent and orderly treatment, and they actually started coming every week as necessary. At this stage, the goal of therapy was to help the parents stand united in front of their daughter. After 7 months of therapy, the mother's relationship with the toddler greatly improved. It is as if the mother had found her path to motherhood without having to rely on breastfeeding. The parents were able to build a family routine, including meals together, and their ability to understand L.'s behavior significantly improved. Slowly, the sleeping and eating problems also went away. As to the late development of language, L. was treated by a speech therapist and started talking. During therapy, the parents noticed that they themselves did not talk much between them, and they made it their mission to improve in this domain as well.

As this case shows, treatment of early childhood psychopathology is a complex process. It initially sets out to extinguish a given clinical symptom or to treat a given disorder, but it often ends up achieving additional objectives.

Conclusion

Sleep disorders in infancy reflect a wide range of difficulties, from ordinary parenting problems that only require giving parents simple guidance to deeper psychopathology that calls for diagnosis and professional psychotherapy. In considering whether the disorder in question requires professional attention, clinicians must keep in mind that arousals and difficulties falling asleep are part of the normative development of sleep architecture during the first year of life. With that said, when parents of a baby who is less than 1 year old fail to respond as they should, creating habits that encourage arousals or feeling intense anger and frustration that compromise the quality of their relationship with their baby, professional counseling should be sought, and the sooner the better.

References

Anders, T. F., Goodlin, J., & Sadeh, A. (2000). Sleep disorders. In C. H. Zeanah, Jr. (Ed.), *Handbook of infant mental health* (2nd ed., pp. 326–338). New York, NY: Guilford Press.

Field, T., & Hernandez-Reif, M. (2001). Sleep problems in infants decrease following massage therapy. *Early Child Development and Care, 168,* 95–104.

Kreissler, L., Fain, M., & Soule, M. (1974). *L'enfant et son corps. Etudes sur la Clinique psychosomatique du premier âge* [The child and his body: Studies on the Psychosomatic Clinic of the First Age]. Paris, France: Presses Universitaires de France.

Owens, J., & Burnham, M. M. (2009). Sleep disorders. In C. H. Zeanah, Jr. (Ed.), *Handbook of infant mental health* (3rd ed., pp. 362–376). New York, NY: Guilford Press.

Richman, N. (1981). A community survey of characteristics of one- to two-year-olds with sleep disruptions. *Journey of the American Academy of Child Psychiatry, 20,* 281–291.

Sadeh, A. (2001). *Sleeping like a baby.* New Haven, CT: Yale University Press.

Stern, D. N. (1985). *The interpersonal world of the infant: A view from psychoanalysis and developmental psychology.* New York, NY: Basic Books.

Winnicott, D. W. (1960). *The theory of the parent–infant relationship.* Lecture given at the International Psychoanalytical Conference, London, England.

Winnicott, D. W. (1990). *The maturational processes and the facilitating environment.* London, England: Karnac Books.

ZERO TO THREE. (2016). *DC:0–5*™: *Diagnostic classification of mental health and developmental disorders of infancy and early childhood* (DC:0–5). Washington, DC: Author.

Recommended Reading

Daws, D. (1989). *Through the night: Helping parents and sleepless infants.* London, England: Free Association Books.

Guedeney, A., & Kreissler, L. (1987). Sleep disorders in the first 18 months of life: Hypothesis on the role of mother–child emotional exchanges. *Infant Mental Health Journal, 8,* 307–318.

Mindell, J. A., Kuhn, B., Lewin, D. S., Meltzer, L. J., Sadeh, A., & American Academy of Sleep Medicine. (2006). Behavioral treatment of bedtime problems and night wakings in infants and young children. *Sleep, 29,* 1263–1276.

CHAPTER 7
I Have a Hard Time Eating

All children, except one, grow up, writes James Mathew Barrie in the opening line of Peter Pan. *Peter runs away from home as soon as he can after overhearing his father and mother discuss what the future holds for him as a grown-up. Peter's immediate response to the parental prognosis is a firm resolve: He has no wish to grow up at all; on the contrary, he wants to remain a little boy and play all his life.*

Nurit Zarchi's book Solitude Games[1] *recounts the childhood and adolescence of Kalia, the author's double, from a grown-up woman's perspective. Toward the end of the book, Kalia, herself now a mother, describes a recurring dream in which she leaves her baby in one of the drawers, only to discover later that she had forgotten where she had placed her hungry child. To her ever-growing dismay, she is unable to find the child, regardless of how thoroughly she searches, drawer by drawer, box by box. Her hands shake, her pulse revs up, horror sweeps over her, and the baby is gone and cannot be fed, and she wonders what will happen.*

The absence underlying Kalia's self-definition is not just a cursed fate that has befallen her. This absence becomes "DNA" passed on from generation to generation: motherless girls experiencing themselves as giving birth to motherless children; because being a woman–mother means repeating the familiar maternal pattern and, in this case, a mother incapable of feeding her hungry baby.

Introduction

Eating is an existential act. People eat because they want to live. It is therefore no surprise to find out that changes in appetite accompany most illnesses—physical as well as emotional—in babies, children, adolescents, and adults.

---

[1] Nurit Zarchi, 1999, *Solitude Games*, published by Yediot Aharonot.

In a baby's first year of life, he completely depends on the figure feeding him, usually the parent. The way in which the baby eats conjures up powerful positive or negative images for the adults. They view babies who eat well as "healthy" and "easy," and those who refuse food as "difficult" and "stubborn." Moreover, there are also babies who ask for more and more, as if never satiated. Parents see those babies as "demanding." As we show later in this chapter, paying attention to negative attributions of this kind is important because they are liable to impair the parent–infant relationship.

> The maternal figure as represented in world literature, and more so in Jewish literature, is closely linked to food, and food is perceived as the quintessence of motherhood. In other words, the physical act of feeding is seen in culture as a metaphor for the mother's ability to give her children the gift of life. A mother is considered good if she nourishes her offspring well or a "stepmother" if she struggles to do so. The story of Hansel and Gretel (the Brothers Grimm) illustrates this as follows:

> In this fairy tale, the plot is driven by hunger, which is always related to a woman: to the stepmother in the beginning and to the old woman—the hag from the forest—in the second part. Both feminine figures—the life-denying "stepmother" and the one who seemingly gives life—are shaped in the story from the child's perspective, who has but one yardstick by which to measure a mother: her ability or inability to provide nourishment.

> The stepmother is, after all, not the mother in that she views banishing the children into the woods as a way out of the famine that has hit the family. In other words, in her refusal to feed her children she sentences them to death and thus becomes a "stepmother" to them, a mother who has failed to fulfill the foremost task of any mother. From a mother like this, the kids have no protection: Even the breadcrumbs that Hansel has crumbled and scattered from the last piece of bread given to them before setting off for the woods do not last, and the children are abandoned to their fate.

> The life-denying mother is contrasted in the tale with the seemingly "other woman"—"the very old woman." The house from which the children were banished was the epitome of scarcity, whereas the house revealed deep inside the forest abounds with goodies and treats (cake, bread, and sugar). In contrast to their brutal expulsion from their own home, the old woman invites them to take refuge in her house and to feast on its delicacies. However, the truth soon comes out: The invitation to indulge in gluttony is nothing but a ploy to fatten them up for cannibalistic purposes. The very old woman turns out to be a hag—a devouring mother incapable of seeing

her children as separate from herself, to the point of being even capable of transforming them into food.

On the Process of Eating and Feeding: The Twofold Value—Caloric and Psychological—of a Spoonful of Food

Feeding a child in infancy is not only meant to fill a physiological need. It also takes a child on a journey to becoming familiar with her body, to building her self-image as someone capable of acting, taking initiative, and eating independently.

A distinction should be drawn between eating and feeding: Eating denotes those actions taken by a baby—that is, chewing and swallowing. Proper eating requires physical health, hunger, and desire (libido).

Feeding, however, is one facet of the baby–caregiver relationship. It is important for the process to be felt by both baby and parent as an enjoyable, stress-free experience to allow initiative and experimentation on the baby's part, without paying too much attention to tidiness. According to Chatoor's (2010) definition, optimal feeding takes place in a pleasant ambience, at the right pace for the baby, while avoiding power struggles and distractions through stimuli unrelated to the meal as well as any negotiation about food. A child should only eat when he wants to.

A child is no longer supposed to be fed by an adult by around 18 months old, when toddlers become developmentally capable of self-feeding. In infancy, successful feeding happens when eating and feeding are optimal. When both feeding and eating are impaired, or when either one of these processes is, a significant impairment can be seen in the infant's eating behaviors. It is this principle that accompanies this chapter and serves as a basis for understanding situations in which babies refuse to eat and do not grow. Mealtime thus plays a major role in a baby's emotional development. It is experienced in both the baby's body and mind. Mental images form around the process of eating and feeding, such as in the following examples:

- "This hand, with which I eat, is mine, I control it"—the act of eating allows the baby to construct her body image;

- "This person knows how to give me nice-tasting food at the right timing, she can be counted on"—a pleasant experience that corresponds to the child's needs and allows him to acquire basic trust in others;

- "Mom relies on me to let her know when I'm hungry"—a sense of independence builds up the baby's self-esteem; or

- "This I want . . . this I don't"—a sense of being able to choose, allowing the baby to feel in control of what enters her body.

Eating in infancy involves all the senses: taste, smell, touch, sight, and hearing. The sense of **smell** is the first to be activated after birth. It has been demonstrated that babies can remember the smell of their mother's breast already when they are 3 days old. When presented with a few pairs of breasts, they choose to eat from their mother's.

As the baby's hand and the mother's arm **touch** during nursing, the baby is made aware, for the first time, of his body's boundaries. With the sense of touch, the baby gradually starts to build what is termed his external body image or his physical self. Touch defines the "heat" of proximity and the "coldness" of distance for the baby.

The sense of **sight** also plays an important role in the parent–baby interaction during feeding. Eye contact between mother and baby during feeding is of paramount importance, as this is a moment of mirroring, meaning that the baby sees herself in the mother's eyes (Winnicott, 1960).

The baby's sense of **hearing** is quite well-developed at birth—she listens to her adult caregivers, especially the ones who feed her. The parent's speech, which accompanies feeding, acts as a kind of background music that enhances the baby's enjoyment of the food. The mother's tone of speech, the rhythm of her voice, the tenderness of her talk, and its content will accompany the child for many years and influence her eating for better or worse.

The sense of **taste** naturally plays a special role in nursing. The baby enjoys the taste of milk and gets used to consuming food at body temperature.

Finally, on the level of the inner sensations linked with eating, we assume that the sensation of the milk flowing through the esophagus into the stomach sows the first seeds in forming the baby's internal body image of the digestive system. In their work, Kaminer, Munitz, and Tyano (1978) showed that the human unconscious holds an image of the body's internal organs. We call this image the *internal body image*. It starts to form in infancy, when eating.

In Yaakov Shabtai's novel Past Perfect,[2] *Meir Lifshitz, a 42-year-old engineer from Tel Aviv, describes his memories of his many encounters with his mother in their home kitchen, which recreated the primordial sensory-motor connection between the mother and the baby. Time and again, Meir revisits the kitchen in his parents' home, his mother's exclusive realm, where he and she are engulfed in the lamp's yellow circle of light, cut off from the whole world. The feeding by the mother, with the warmth emanating from her person and her cooking, and the eating by the son, who relishes each and every bite of her delicacies, especially the taste and texture of the butter cookies that melt in his mouth, tell the reader how strong their relationship is.*

---

[2] Yaakov Shabtai, 1987, *Past Perfect*, published by Viking Press.

Breastfeeding and Weaning

It is now known that breastfeeding greatly contributes to strengthening the baby's immune system as well as his bond with his mother. Their reciprocal touches trigger the secretion of oxytocin—the attachment hormone. This hormone is also vitally important because it negates the action of cortisol, the distress and stress hormone.

One of the differences between breastfeeding and bottle feeding is the direct contact between the mother's skin and the baby's. The uniqueness of this touch can be appreciated from studies conducted in a neonatal intensive care nursery, which described how a premature baby responds to being laid on her mother's or father's chest a few times each day (the "kangaroo" method). This contact was found to have a beneficial impact on the baby's physiological indicators, including body temperature, oxygenation levels, pulse, and breathing.

With that said, breastfeeding is not always the better choice. One example would be a highly anxious mother who can hardly bear the uncertainty of not knowing her baby's actual milk intake. For a mother like this, each time her baby cries, this will be interpreted as a sign of hunger and a reason to give the baby her breast. Consequently, the baby will eat a small amount each time; the mother will end up exhausted; and the feeding interaction will be shrouded in a stressful, unpleasant atmosphere. The mother might be offended by the baby's refusal and might give up with a sense of failure. Difficulties might also arise when a baby injures her mother's nipple when sucking while the mother—although suffering in pain—insists on continuing to nurse because she has no doubt in her mind that being a good mother means breastfeeding at all costs. Such a mother is liable to secrete high levels of cortisol—the stress hormone—at the expense of oxytocin, in which case what was supposed to be a mutually enjoyable process will turn into a mutually stressful one. Finally, let us recall that some babies suffer from physical conditions (e.g., a heart defect) that make them tire more at the breast than at the bottle. In such cases, a mother's insistence on breastfeeding is harmful to the baby.

Social factors also weigh heavily in deciding whether to breastfeed. Nowadays, mothers are strongly encouraged to nurse in view of the advantages mentioned above, but one must keep in mind that breastfeeding is not necessarily right for every woman. When a mother is ambivalent about the whole thing, her relationship with the baby might suffer as a result. In such cases, enjoyable bottle feeding is preferable to forced breastfeeding for both baby and mother.

Breastfeeding Duration and Frequency, and Weaning Off It

As a backlash perhaps against the time when Dr. Spock and the regimented Kibbutz education reigned supreme, Israeli society now tends to avoid frustrating the child and lets him do "what he wants." This position has also seeped into nursing: The common view is that a baby should be allowed to suckle every time—and for as long as—he wants to; his needs are to be satisfied all the time, without limits, staying, in Colarusso's (1979) terms (see chapter 3), within the "maternal time" dimension to the exclusion of "paternal time." The proponents of this stance have eyes only for the advantages of nursing while ignoring its symbolic meaning. They do not think about the day after, the day when the baby will have to be weaned and the weaning process might turn from a normative one to a struggle between baby and mother.

Indeed, psychologically speaking, weaning is no less important than nursing because it symbolizes the child's separation from her mother and the father's admission into the mother–child dyad. Weaning off the breast helps the baby realize that her mother is not just a breast—that even when the breast "is lost," her mother remains by her side. Dolto (1994) called the weaning process "the oral developmental castration" in that frustration pushes the baby to the next stage in her development. Winnicott (1960) also saw frustration as a necessary component of "good enough" parenting—in which "good enough" parents are those who also know how to frustrate their child, in a way adapted of course to her current stage of development. Weaning is also meaningful in terms of the relationship between the parents. The mother's breast goes back to being a sexual object, and the father can also partake in feeding the baby.

As we show later in this chapter, eating problems in infancy sometimes arise because the mother has a hard time giving up breastfeeding, for psychological reasons on top of social pressure. For example, nursing sessions are often the mother's only time off the work load that she is subjected to, her only chance for alone time with the baby. If she suffers from basic insecurity in her maternal competencies, close physical contact with her baby can reassure her. Finally, when the couple's relationship is tense, continuing to breastfeed can serve as an excuse to avoid sexual intercourse.

Eating Disorders in Infancy

Eating disorders in the first 3 years of life are a relatively widespread problem. Causes for concern that parents may have about their baby include unrest or falling asleep while eating, refusal to switch from the breast to the bottle, refusal to move on to solids, or selective eating. Between 1% and 5% of all hospitalizations in pediatric wards, and a quarter of referrals to pediatric clinics in the community, are due to problems of this kind. In serious cases, eating disorders could result in failure to thrive—that is, varying degrees of lateness in psychomotor and bodily development (weight, height, and head circumference). In the past, a distinction used to be made between organic failure to thrive and psychological failure to thrive, but this dichotomous approach has been abandoned with the understanding that the symptoms were due to the reciprocal influence of biological and psychological factors. Chatoor and colleagues (Chatoor, 2010; Chatoor et al., 1997) suggested classifying eating disorders on the basis of the time and stage of development where they appear. They proposed six subgroups of Feeding Behavior Disorders: (1) Feeding Disorder of State Regulation, (2) Feeding Disorder of Caregiver–Infant Reciprocity, (3) Infantile Anorexia, (4) Sensory Food Aversion, (5) Feeding Disorder Associated With Concurrent Feeding Disorder, and (6) Posttraumatic Feeding Disorder.

This classification has been left out of the *DC:0–5™: Diagnostic Classification of Mental Health and Developmental Disorders of Infancy and Early Childhood* (DC:0–5; ZERO TO THREE, 2016) because it mixed etiology and phenomenology. The changes came from reviewing major studies published in the past 10 years and reports from clinicians collected through surveys. The main changes consist in terminology, such as "Eating Disorders" instead of "Feeding Behavior Disorders," as well as a focus on the child's observed eating symptoms rather than the classification of eating problems by inferred etiology. A new category—Overeating Disorder—has been added because it is increasingly recognized as a significant clinical condition. Another major change relates to the differentiation between eating disorders that are observed beyond any specific caregiver–child relationship context and those confined to one specific relationship.

The approach that has been adopted in the DC:0–5 manual is descriptive rather than etiological. Three categories of eating disorders are defined in the DC:0–5 on the basis of the infant's eating behavior: Overeating Disorder, Undereating Disorder, and Atypical Eating Disorder. The diagnosis of Relationship Specific Disorder of Infancy/Early Childhood is used in those cases in which the eating or feeding disturbance is only one manifestation of the relationship disorder. The various reasons behind the development of the eating disorder will be formulated on completion of the evaluation and will form the basis for planning the treatment, as we show later in this chapter.

Finally, the level of impairment in either the child or the family's functioning because of the eating disturbance is the main criterion by which the clinician will ultimately decide whether a diagnosis is warranted. The presence of poor weight gain or nutritional deficiencies is a parameter of severity and should therefore be noted as well, but failure to gain weight is not a criterion anymore for the diagnosis of Undereating Disorder.

Overeating Disorder

Overeating is a behavior rarely seen in children less than 2 years old because some degree of autonomy, as well as verbal and motor skills, is required to search for the food. By contrast, cases of overfeeding are quite common in children less than 2 years old, in particular during the first year of life. Whenever overfeeding is a manifestation of an early parent–infant relational disorder under the DC:0–5 criteria, an Axis I diagnosis of Relationship Specific Disorder of Infancy/Early Childhood is warranted. Similarly, whenever the overeating pattern is limited to a specific relational context (dyadic, triadic, family), the diagnosis of a Relationship Specific Disorder of Infancy/Early Childhood, with overeating as one of its manifestations, is relevant.

The core features of Overeating Disorder are the young child's excessive preoccupation with food and eating, as manifested by a pattern of seeking food between mealtimes or scheduled feedings, persistently asking for excessive amounts of food during meals, taking food from others or foraging in trash cans, stuffing food in the cheeks while eating, as well as talking and playing repeatedly around food themes. To warrant the diagnosis, the young child must exhibit distress if prevented from engaging in these behaviors, and the abnormal eating behaviors must be pervasive, beyond any specific relational context.

The differential diagnosis includes food unavailability and hunger, side effects of medication, or medical conditions (e.g., Prader-Willi syndrome, hypothyroidism). The child may also be displaying nonspecific symptoms of anxiety, irritability, or anger.

Comorbid diagnoses of a Sensory Processing Disorder, Depression, and Reactive Attachment Disorder are also to be considered.

There are no published data on the course of Overeating Disorder among infants. On the basis of our clinical experience, overeating does not always resolve spontaneously, and parents tend to seek professional help only when the child is putting on weight and their attempts to limit his food craving are unsuccessful. There are no published longitudinal data to suggest any link between overeating in infancy and binge eating or bulimia nervosa at a later age, and therefore different terms are used.

The main potential consequences of Overeating Disorder include the child's obesity, lack of participation in age-appropriate social activities, and ultimately peer rejection. This is why it is important to diagnose and treat the problem as early as possible. The introduction of Overeating Disorder in the first years of life as a new diagnostic category may encourage researchers and clinicians to study the phenomenon in depth.

CASE STUDY

A., a 2½-year-old girl, was referred to our infant mental health program because she persistently asked for food, both at home and at day care, and ate significantly more than her peers. In the initial session, we saw a chubby little girl with a sad expression who clung to her father, avoided her mother, and displayed limited exploratory behavior. By contrast, her language skills were advanced, as was her ability to pick up on the vibe around her. She appeared to be hypervigilant. As a baby, A. had been perceived as "fussy," and the mother would soothe her with bottles of milk (the mother did not breastfeed her because the idea repelled her). The mother's description of A.'s eating behavior was that "She would drink from the bottle as if I was starving her." A. entered day care at 2 years old; she manifested separation difficulties and started requesting food all day long. She became oppositional at home while very compliant and shy at day care.

The observed mother–child interaction revealed overt hostility with negative attributions toward the child mixed with strong guilt feelings on the mother's side. The mother reported suffering from severe Obsessive Compulsive Disorder with many rituals that impinged on her emotional availability. The observed triadic mother–child–father interaction revealed that A. had a closer relationship with her father than she did with her mother. The father assumed a mediating role between his wife and daughter, and the overall family atmosphere during their interaction was sad and tense. An individual session with the parents revealed the mother's childhood history of physical and emotional abuse and her own difficulties with sexuality, intimacy, and empathy, in addition to her Obsessive Compulsive Disorder. The father grew up in a warm, extroverted family setting. They had significant difficulties coparenting their child.

Although the overeating seemed to have developed in the context of a conflicted mother–child relationship, the fact that the overeating behavior occurred at day care in addition to home indicated that it had been generalized and had become a characteristic of the child that manifested itself cross-contextually. The oppositional behavior, on the other hand, was limited to her relationship with her mother—not with her father and not at day care—and therefore met criteria for Relationship Specific Disorder of Infancy/Early Childhood with oppositional behavior as its main symptom.

The DC:0-5 diagnoses would be as follows:

- Axis I: Clinical Disorders
    - » Overeating Disorder (persistently asked for food, at home and at day care, and ate significantly more than her peers)
    - » Relationship Specific Disorder of Infancy/Early Childhood (with mother)

- Axis II: Relational Context
    - » Level 4—Disordered to Dangerous mother–child relationship
    - » Level 3—Compromised to Disturbed caregiving environment

- Axis III: Medical Condition
    - » Mild overweight

- Axis IV: Psychosocial Stressor
    - » Maternal psychopathology

- Axis V: Developmental Competence
    - » Functions at age-appropriate level

The recommended treatment for this child included triadic and dyadic sessions as well as referral of the mother to cognitive-behavioral treatment. The treatment lasted a year, the overeating disorder resolved, and the mother–child relationship improved but remained tense, with sleep and oppositional behavior still evident. We observed a significant improvement in A.'s ability to verbalize her feelings of sadness and anger whenever her mother was emotionally unavailable to her and preoccupied with her compulsions and obsessions. Both parents showed improvement in their communication and coparenting skills.

Undereating Disorder

In 2015, Kerzner and colleagues categorized children with undereating behaviors into three main problematic eating behaviors: limited appetite, selective intake, and fear of feeding. The feeding styles of caregivers were also categorized as responsive, controlling, indulgent, and neglectful. The advantage of this approach is that it is based on the infant's observed behaviors and not on etiological factors, which are often inferred. As for overfeeding, the caregiver's style of feeding the infant was encompassed within their specific relationship.

The DC:0–5 criteria for Undereating Disorder relate to situations in which young children consistently eat less than expected for their age or exhibit maladaptive eating behaviors—such as a consistent lack of interest in eating, a fearful avoidance of eating, a difficulty to self-regulate during feedings (e.g., repeatedly falling asleep or becoming agitated), eating only while asleep, refusing to make the transition to solid foods, eating only when specific conditions imposed by them are met by the caregivers (e.g., in front of the television set, with toys and stories), or being extremely picky eaters. Significant impairment of the child or the family must be present to warrant the diagnosis, as we have described above. Common associated features include prolonged mealtimes, stressful mealtimes, lack of appropriate autonomous feeding, nocturnal eating (after 1 year old), prolonged breast- or bottle-feeding, and failure to taste new textures.

It is important to note that the criterion of weight loss or lack of expected weight gain is not a mandatory one. Indeed, some young children may refuse to eat solids yet drink several bottles of formula during the day and thus stay on their weight curve in spite of their maladaptive eating pattern.

Undereating often starts at around 9 months old when transitioning into more independent and diverse eating. These infants tend to be extremely selective about their food (eating only very specific foods), to eat slowly (they might sometimes hold food in their mouths for a long time without swallowing), and to consume very little food. In extreme cases, a baby will actually refuse to open her mouth, or vomit. Typically, the parent–infant interaction at mealtimes is very tense. The parent feels helpless, and this helplessness can take on various forms, including force feeding, using all manner of toys and distractions, and cooking up a host of different dishes in the hope of finding the "miracle food" that the child will finally consent to eat. This preoccupation usually comes at the expense of any other activity with the baby. Food becomes the main order of business on the baby's and the parents' agenda, and everything revolves around it in an ever-stronger negative atmosphere that sometimes escalates to the point of actual physical violence. A battle of spoons—a battle of wills: This is what Chatoor (2010) called what happens between the parent and the child at mealtime. Indeed, the parent's strong desire to be in control clashes with the infant's need for separateness and independence. Clinical work with these mothers has taught us just how much the difficulty involved in allowing the baby's separateness is often tied to difficulties they once had with their own parents. Mothers who suffer from eating disorders themselves struggle particularly hard with the task of feeding their infant.

Treatment needs to focus on the fight for power and control waged between parent and child. During therapy, parents learn how important it is to give the toddler independence as far as his body is concerned. When parents carry the weight of unresolved issues of their own related to eating, body image, control, and independence, psychotherapy needs to be longer and go deeper. The guiding principle for treatment is to let the parent control **when**, **where**, and **what** the child eats while leaving the child in control of **how much** he eats.

CASE STUDY

A., 1 year and 10 months old, refused to taste solid food and only ate formula milk from a bottle. No physical reason for her refusal was found. Her growth curve indicated insufficient weight gain, and her parents were extremely worried. Her psychomotor development was normative, but her language lagged behind. When she could not have her way, she would bang her head on the floor. This behavior terrified her parents, who did everything they could to avoid frustrating her. This is also why they did not dare insist on her eating solid food. A. still suckled at night.

A., an only child, was born following a normal, highly desirable pregnancy that came after several years of fertility problems. A.'s mother had also been "difficult with food" as a child, and she remembered how her mother used to chase her around with a spoon. The parents' concerns were further compounded by a family history involving the death of the father's niece at 3 years old following a severe illness. The diagnostic process focused on the question of A.'s refusal to move on to solid food and eat independently. The parents believed the reason was physical, but the medical tests, as mentioned, yielded nothing out of the ordinary. We tried explaining to the parents that their daughter refused to eat for psychological reasons. They had a hard time seeing their baby as an independent entity with capabilities and wishes of her own, and the child unconsciously identified with this perception (a process called "projective identification"). Her parents were afraid to frustrate her because they perceived her as a fragile baby. They mainly feared her tantrums and gave in to almost every one of her whims.

During the therapeutic process, we encouraged the parents to set limits assertively, yet without anger or aggressiveness. The therapist showed them how to do this each time the baby flew into a rage. Only after the parents were able to frustrate their daughter to a reasonable degree in other areas of everyday life did we start tackling the eating problems. The principle underlying the treatment was to let the toddler control the amount of food she puts into her mouth and to guide the parents to decide the time, place, and content of meals. In A.'s case, her parents were afraid to give her leeway and independence for fear that she would "eat nothing and lose weight." To alleviate their anxiety, we had to summon them to see our team's pediatrician every other day. The pediatrician would examine the girl and show the parents that she was in decent physical shape. The therapeutic process lasted about 7 months. Initially, A.'s general behavior improved, she became more mature, and her language came along beautifully. Her eating behavior improved subsequently.

Undereating Disorder Combined With an Active Physical Illness

In complex cases involving a concomitant medical diagnosis, one has to make sure that the undereating pattern is not fully explained by it or by some side effect of medication. The most common medical diagnoses include milk allergy; structural abnormalities that affect the naso-oropharynx, larynx, trachea, and esophagus; neurodevelopmental disabilities; oral hypersensitivity and oral-motor dysfunction; systemic illnesses; and organic causes of pain, such as esophagitis due to gastroesophageal reflux.

Treatment of the eating disorder in these situations is most often complex. The therapist has to examine how the baby's physical illness affects the parenting patterns in general and the eating interaction in particular. The therapist must understand the nature of the baby's physical illness to identify the relative respective weights of the emotional and physical components in the appearance of the eating disorder. The therapist also needs to have the medical team treating the physical illness take into account the baby's emotional aspects and the way it affects her general and eating behavior.

CASE STUDY

A., a toddler 2 years and 10 months old who suffered from a renal disease, awaited a kidney transplant. However, because he did not eat enough, his nutritional condition did not allow him to undergo the operation. His parents were justifiably very worried by the postponement of the operation and tried to feed the child in every way possible, at all times, day and night, even against his will. As time passed, and the date for surgery kept being postponed, the more stressed out, frustrated, and anxious they became. At some point, they even started getting mad at A. for "not understanding why it is so important for him to eat." The angrier they grew, the more the toddler resisted eating. The medical team called on a child psychiatrist for consultation.

During the session, the child psychiatrist addressed the toddler directly, using words he could understand; she talked about his disease, his fear, and his parents' fear. We were surprised to learn that although he had received medical treatment for his disease since birth, no one saw fit to talk to him about it. When the parents realized that the child understood despite his young age, their pattern of behavior toward him changed. This brought down the anxiety and anger levels on both sides, but insufficiently so. Therefore, an anti-anxiety medication was added to lessen the child's anxiety, and indeed, this improved his eating. The boy attained the necessary weight to undergo the transplant, and following surgery, as his physical condition improved, the eating disorder also disappeared completely.

Undereating Disorder as Secondary to Trauma to the Digestive System

Traumatic medical treatments around the mouth (e.g., oro-gastric intubation, repeated aspiration of mucus) may be the cause of undereating because these are painful medical procedures that the baby has learned to fear. Such babies then manifest considerable tension or anxiety when served food. The preferred treatment is behavioral, focusing on the child's gradual exposure to food. It is a slow process requiring patience, perseverance, and creating a relaxed atmosphere.

It is also important to note that damage to the digestive system does not necessarily exclude the existence of other pathogens, such as family conflicts or problems in the parent–child relationship. In these more intricate cases, treatment must also address these aspects.

Differential Diagnosis of Undereating Disorder

Undereating may be a symptom of a sensory processing disorder, depression, Posttraumatic Stress Disorder, and Reactive Attachment Disorder, which means that these diagnoses must be ruled out. Whenever the eating problem is observed only within a specific parent–child interactive context, a primary diagnosis of Relationship Specific Disorder of Infancy/Early Childhood should be preferred to Undereating Disorder.

Undereating as a Symptom of Sensory Processing Disorder

Undereating with consequent failure to thrive in the first 3 months of life usually appears because of a difficulty that the baby has to attain physiological equilibrium, assuming, of course, that some physical serious illness has been ruled out. These infants display a conspicuous, persistent difficulty — already from birth — in regulating physiological processes inside their bodies. Typical symptoms for such babies include irregular breathing accompanied by hiccups; low or high muscle tone or jerky movements; oversensitivity to environmental stimuli involving great difficulty focusing their attention; labile moods in terms of quality and intensity; and disorganization, evident in physiological functions such as eating, sleeping, and excretion.

Treatment of undereating as one of the symptoms of a sensory processing disorder includes parental guidance and adjusting the intensity and quantity of the stimulation given to the baby (not only around food). It is sometimes hard to treat babies who present this kind of disorder because their sensory processing difficulties arouse feelings of helplessness, anxiety, and anger in their parents, to the point of having feelings of rejection toward the baby, especially during mealtimes. Occupational therapists play a key role in therapy, skilled as they are in constructing a stimulation plan that is specially tailored to the baby. At the same time, the emotional component is treated, with a view to prevent the emergence of a disorder in the parent–child relationship or to treat it if it already exists.

CASE STUDY

B., a 1-month-old baby, was taken to a pediatrician because he was not putting on weight. He cried a lot and would fall asleep every time he was offered food. As a result, he did not eat enough. B.'s mother was worn out. She had to hold the baby in her arms and breastfeed all day long. Strong feelings of frustration and anxiety overwhelmed her. Her husband stood by her side but was helpless at the same time. Medical examinations ruled out any serious medical condition. During our evaluation, the mother told us that B. had been born prematurely, at a lower weight than expected for his gestational age (a sign of intrauterine growth retardation). B. did not suffer from any complication related to prematurity but was already hard to feed. He was his parents' firstborn, and his unexpected premature birth came as a great disappointment to them, or, as the mother put it, "This was not what we had expected; we did everything to ensure that things went smoothly, we so didn't want for this to end this way." The eating difficulties only added to the mother's feelings of incompetence.

The DC:0–5 diagnosis for this case would be Sensory Under-Responsivity Disorder rather than Undereating Disorder because the baby's primary difficulty was to stay awake during mealtimes. No criterion for a relationship disorder was met, but there was a need to help the mother feel less guilty and more self-confident. The treatment team included an occupational therapist—to help the parents adjust the amount of stimulation to the baby's needs—and a psychologist. B. became better regulated and started gaining weight, and in parallel, the mother–infant relationship became fully adaptive.

Undereating as a Symptom of a Relationship Specific Disorder

Babies who manifest undereating behaviors secondary to severe lack of caregiving usually arrive at the pediatric emergency room because of very poor physical condition. A pediatrician who diagnoses parental failure must involve the welfare services, and the parents must commit to intensive therapy or else lose custody of their child.

CASE STUDY

G., a 4-month-old only child of a couple that separated during pregnancy after the father abruptly left the house, suckled but failed to gain any meaningful weight. She barely emitted sounds, seldom smiled, and frequently turned her head sideways. The pediatrician, unable to find a physical explanation for G.'s worrying condition, referred her to have her hearing and vision tested. The test results were within the norm. With early signs of autism suspected, G. and their mother went to a child psychiatrist.

The child psychiatrist diagnosed a severe disorder in the primary relationship between the mother and the baby as well as maternal depression. The first order of treatment was to find out whether the mother was motivated to improve how she functioned as a parent. When she was clearly told that the social worker was duty bound to report the case and that the baby might be taken away from her, the mother understood the severity of the situation and "snapped out" of grieving the loss of her relationship with her mate.

The mother's life story revealed a series of separations from significant others. Not only did the baby represent the abandoning father in the mother's eyes but her identity as a mother was not yet well-established, and she exhibited such low parental skills in her everyday care of the girl that help had to be brought into the house. The mother agreed to intensive treatment requiring emotional and technical work. She visited the clinic twice a week. She also consented to taking antidepressants. The baby's condition gradually improved thanks to the 1-year-long mother–infant psychotherapy. At the same time, the mother started psychotherapy for herself.

Atypical Eating Disorders

Rumination Disorder

Rumination disorder is a rare disorder that appears from 3 months to 1 year old. A baby who suffers from it regurgitates the food he had swallowed, chews it, reswallows, and so on. He does this mostly when alone, remaining motionless during the act, detached from his surroundings, with a countenance of pleasure written on his face. Rumination can involve medical complications, including dehydration, delayed growth due to malnutrition, hypokalemia (low level of potassium in the blood), and peptic ulcer. A quarter of cases end up in death. The etiology of this disorder is varied and includes profound intellectual disability, depression, and attachment disorders due to abuse or neglect.

Pica

Pica is another rare disorder, defined as regular absorption of nonnutritive substances manifesting itself in a child for at least 1 month. It mainly occurs in 10%–30% of babies who suffer from profound intellectual disability or severe neglect. Some have even linked pica to autism. Medically speaking, pica is sometimes caused by anemia.

Several types of pica are to be distinguished: geophagia (ingestion of sand and dirt), the type most common in children; ferrophagia (ingestion of substances with iron content), which often appears in toddlers who suffer from anemia accompanied by an iron deficiency; lithophagia (ingestion of stones); coprophagia (ingestion of feces); amylophagia (ingestion of objects containing starch); and trichophagia (ingestion of hair). Ingestion of other substances — such as paper, insects, matches, and metals — also falls under this diagnosis. Common medical complications secondary to this disorder include the following: lead poisoning, bowel obstruction, gastrointestinal perforation, infections, and death.

Recommended treatments for rumination and pica are behavioral therapy (involving positive and negative reinforcements) and dynamic treatment focusing on the parent–child relationship. In severe cases, in which the child's life is in danger, sedatives or medications against stomach spasms (antispasmodics) are sometimes administered.

Hoarding

Hoarding relates to a child's storing food in unusual places (e.g., under a pillow, in a closet, in a desk drawer). Finding food in unusual places supports the diagnosis. These children can be either overweight or underweight, depending on what they do with the hidden food. To the best of our knowledge, hoarding has not been described in children less than 2 years old. Before food hoarding can be diagnosed, hunger, neglect, maltreatment, and Obsessive Compulsive Disorder must be ruled out.

Pouching

Pouching relates to a child holding food in her mouth for long periods of time without swallowing it. Dental caries are often an associated sign in cases in which pouching happens on a daily basis for several hours. To the best of our knowledge, there are practically no publications about food pouching in children less than 2 years old, and yet clinicians occasionally witness this behavior.

No data have been published on the risk and prognostic features of pouching during infancy. Still, on the basis of clinical experience, infants who have been put on a nasogastric or gastrostomy tube may develop pouching behaviors in the process of tube weaning. Traumatic events that involve painful medical procedures may play a role as risk factors. Ruling out any medical condition that prevents the child from swallowing is warranted before pouching is diagnosed.

Evaluation of Eating Problems in Infancy

The purpose of evaluating an infant with an eating problem is to determine whether a primary diagnosis of Eating Disorder of Infancy/Early Childhood is warranted or whether the eating problem is one symptom, among others, of another diagnosis. The optimal treatment plan will be tailored accordingly to each specific infant and family. Diagnosis is best carried out by a multidisciplinary team comprising a pediatrician, a child psychiatrist, a psychologist, an occupational therapist, a dietician, and a social worker. The diagnostic process should include the following stages:

- *Examination by a pediatrician*: A physical examination is performed, and there is a referral for laboratory tests if some physical illness is suspected.

- A *meeting with the parents*: The purpose of the meeting is to obtain from the parents the history of the illness and hear how they perceive the baby and understand the disorder. During the meeting, it is important to encourage the parents to express their feelings toward the baby who refuses to grow or eat (most often there are feelings of anger and frustration as well as a sense of failure and poor self-esteem). It is also important to dwell on the baby's daily routine and to evaluate the parents' skills and their ability to support the baby.

- *Observing the parent–baby interaction*: The focus of attention is the quality of the play and feeding interaction. This observation makes it possible to evaluate the extent to which the parents are available, sensitive, and in synchrony with the baby at the nonverbal level and capable of expressing emotions. It also provides an impression of the general atmosphere characterizing the interaction between the baby and his parents. It is important to ascertain whether the interaction during play is the same as during mealtime. This is particularly significant when it comes to mothers who find situations in which control must be shared conflictual. In their case, the interaction with the baby will be positive during play as opposed to tense and unsatisfying during mealtime.

- *Evaluation of the baby's eating skills*: This is done in terms of chewing and swallowing. This evaluation, usually carried out by an occupational therapist or a speech therapist, aims to rule out a physiological etiology underlying the eating disorder.

- *Evaluation of the baby's nutritional condition*: This is conducted by a pediatric dietitian to make sure that the baby's nutrition is calorically balanced and adapted to her age and weight.

- *Evaluation of the baby's development*: This evaluation, performed by the developmental psychologist, is important to assess the extent to which the eating disorder affects the child's development.

Prognosis

The outcome of Eating Disorders of Infancy/Early Childhood greatly depends on the factors that have led to their development. Validated long-term studies that compare different therapeutic approaches are still not available. A significant percentage of infants with a serious eating disorder will continue to have growth problems, coupled with cognitive and behavioral difficulties of varying degrees. Our clinical experience has taught us that when a disorder in the parent–child relationship underlies the eating problem, this sometimes leads to the subsequent appearance of disorders in other areas—for example, around toilet training and compliance with rules.

Conclusion

Eating disorders are a very common phenomenon in infancy, and a distinction must be drawn between those that require both psychological and medical treatment and those that require nothing more than parental guidance. To determine the most efficient treatment, clinicians must take into account both the severity of the physical condition (i.e., the severity of retardation in growth and development) and the severity of the disorder in emotional terms (i.e., the scope of damage caused to the parent–baby relationship). Evaluation and treatment are best provided by a multidisciplinary team. There are still not enough studies that have followed babies who suffered from eating disorders in infancy long enough to allow researchers to establish the relative efficacy of various treatment approaches.

References

Chatoor, I. (2010). *Diagnosis and treatment of feeding disorders in infants, toddlers, and young children*. Washington, DC: ZERO TO THREE.

Chatoor, I., Getson, P., Menvielle, E., Brasseaux, C., O'Donnell, R., Rivera, Y., & Mrazek, D. A. (1997). A feeding scale for research and clinical practice to assess mother–infant interactions in the first three years of life. *Infant Mental Health Journal, 18*, 75–91.

Colarusso, C. A. (1979). The development of time sense — From birth to object constancy. *International Journal of Psycho-Analysis, 60*, 243–251.

Dolto, F. (1994). *Tout est language* [Everything is language]. Paris, France: Gallimard.

Kaminer, I., Munitz, H., & Tyano, S. (1978). The heart image as a model of internal organ body image. *Psychotherapy and Psychosomatics, 30*, 187–189.

Kerzner, B., Milano, K., MacLean, W. C. Jr, Berall, G., Stuart, S., & Chatoor, I. (2015). A practical approach to classifying and managing feeding difficulties. *Pediatrics, 135*, 344–353.

Winnicott, D. W. (1960). *The theory of the parent–infant relationship.* Lecture given at the International Psychoanalytical Conference, London, England.

ZERO TO THREE. (2016). *DC:0–5™: Diagnostic classification of mental health and developmental disorders of infancy and early childhood* (DC:0–5). Washington, DC: Author.

Recommended Reading

Ammaniti, M., Lucarelli, L., Cimino, S., D'Olimpio, F., & Chatoor, I. (2010). Maternal psychopathology and child risk factors in infantile anorexia. *International Journal of Eating Disorders, 43*, 233–240.

Feldman, R., Keren, M., Rosval, O., & Tyano, S. (2004). Specifying the role of touch in infant feeding disorders: Maternal, child, and environmental correlates. *Journal of the American Academy of Child and Adolescent Psychiatry, 43*, 1089–1097.

Saarilehto, S., Keskinen, S., Lapinleimu, H., Helenius, H., & Simell, O. (2001). Connections between parental eating attitudes and children's meager eating: Questionnaire findings. *Acta Paediatrica, 90*, 333–338.

Sherkow, S. P., Kamens, S. R., Megyes, M., & Loewenthal, L. (2009). A clinical study of the intergenerational transmission of eating disorders from mothers to daughters. *Psychoanalytical Study of the Child, 64*, 153–189.

Stein, A., Woolley, H., Murray, L., Cooper, P., Cooper, S., Noble, F., . . . Fairburn, C. G. (2001). Influence of psychiatric disorder on the controlling behavior of mothers with 1-year-old infants. *British Journal of Psychiatry, 179*, 157–162.

CHAPTER 8
I Am Angry, I Bite and Hit

In the story of creation as told by Greek mythology, the three deities of fury (the Erinyes or Furies) were born after Cronus (the god of time) castrated his father Uranus (deity of the sky). The three were named Alecto ("the endless"), Tisiphone ("the voice of vengeance"), and Megaera ("jealous rage"). Their role was to exact vengeance on anyone breaching the ancient laws relating to family and to subject them to the harshest punishment possible for violating the social order. To demonstrate the speed at which rage ignites as well as the facial expression of a person in the throes of a tantrum, the furies were depicted as winged and extremely ugly figures. Victims of the tantrums were tortured until they lost their mind. This description of the victims as "mad" expresses the notion that rage drives people crazy and that, when it erupts, there is no telling where it might lead. The Furies resided in Erebus, the darkest pit in the underworld, which represents the depths of the unconscious. Rage thus erupts from the depths of the unconscious.

The Greeks evidently understood that family was the cradle of rage, being the most primordial, most vulnerable place. Hurt within the family, the place considered the safest, summons the madness of rage as a means of defense. The family is the crossroads where pure instinct meets culture, the place where rage breaks out of the unconscious to take revenge on the object that had injured the individual's wholeness and self-esteem. In its way out of the underworld to pursue its vendetta outside, it has to learn from scratch the restrictions placed by culture on world-shattering rage.

According to the mythology, aggression teams up with rage: Both are sparked within the family circle. In current parlance, one might say that rage always comes bundled with a desire to hurt, destroy, and damage the offender and to repay him in kind. Rage raises the level of aggression, and the latter seeks the right object and appropriate forms of punishment.

Introduction

This chapter on aggressive behaviors in very early childhood is concerned with a complex, multifaceted issue. Indeed, in discussing the evaluation of infants and toddlers with aggressive behaviors, we must take our bearings and ask ourselves these questions: (1) What are the social norms within which we operate? (2) What is the value system by which we measure behaviors? and (3) Where do we draw the line between normative behavior and abnormal — possibly even pathological — behavior? Behavioral disorders also have social, moral, and educational aspects to them. Infants and toddlers are perceived by many as "cute little things who do not have the slightest notion of why hitting others is so wrong," and many adults are unaware of the importance of monitoring their aggressive behaviors and setting them clear limits.

Aggressive and oppositional behaviors resemble those disorders discussed in previous chapters in that here, too, the line separating the normative from the abnormal is thin and variable, seeing as some level of innate aggressiveness is needed for survival.

Aggression should be distinguished from violence. Aggression is instinctive and innate; it can take on different orders of magnitude and forms as well as be extroverted or introverted. Freud (1920), the father of psychoanalysis and a biologist by training, believed that human beings were born with two drives — the libido (life drive) and aggression (the death and destructiveness drive) — which they try to keep in balance throughout life. Golse (2002) identified three major motives behind the very young child's aggression: to preserve existence and protect one's living space, to test the security of the attachment figure, and to control others. Human aggression can be either "reactive," brought on by frustration or anger, or it can be "instrumental," serving as a tool for individuals to satisfy their immediate needs. Violence is the most extreme manifestation of aggression. In infancy, girls and boys are quite alike in expressing aggression. Further down the road, when language has developed sufficiently, boys usually stick with physical aggression, whereas girls tend to use words to express their aggression, especially words that threaten the relationship with the other ("I won't be friends with you"). This type of aggression, called relational aggression, is no less painful than physical aggression because it often leads to bullying and ostracizing a child from the group of peers.

Children's literature, like literature for adults, reflects the typical gender differences of its time. Contemporary children's literature features mostly the rather restrained girls, who unload their anger with words or tears, more commonly than it does aggressive and violent girls; on the male side, boys who express their anger by physical means occur more often than those who hold it in and cry. Still, literature also portrays some fascinating characters that cross gender boundaries, despite censure from their surroundings. An aggressive girl is dubbed a "Tom Boy," and a lachrymose boy is called a crybaby, even though he is usually a real man, a hero:

I'm not a crybaby like others.
I never, ever cry.
So tell me, mom, why do these
Tears come rolling down from my eye?[1]

In the poem "Mikha'el" by Miriam Yalan-Shteklis,[2] a nameless girl waits for Mikha'el, a boy with a well-defined identity: "But he never shows up, he never shows up, Mikha'el." Her wish to see Mikha'el arrive, because he "had promised twice/that he'd come in the afternoon," is not realized. She "waited" and "waited" and "cried" and "cried" and wore a "very pretty" dress; she sat thinking silently and stood on the balcony, went down to the garden, and even laid her dolls to sleep "so that they won't disturb" her and Mikha'el. In other words, she contains her frustration and anger and only cries.

The Russian folk tale Sister Alyonushka and Brother Ivanushka *is another instance of gender difference being maintained. Brother Ivanushka and Sister Alyonushka, orphaned after the death of their parents, the king and queen, set out on a journey to roam the world. The boy grows very thirsty, craving to drink out of different water sources they come across, but his sister warns him time and again to quell his desire for water lest something bad should befall him. Ultimately, the lad fails, drinks from one of the water sources, and turns into a young goat. The gender difference is evident: The girl is accustomed to moderation and restraint, whereas the boy, who likewise obeys his gender stereotype, fails to overcome his impulse and frequently gives in to his desire.*

Although this tale is not about aggression, it reflects the gender stereotype whereby the boy is unable to assimilate cultural values and curb his impulse, just as he is unable to avoid aggressive behavior. Failure to internalize cultural values entails punishment. Culture defends its principles.

Breaking ranks with these girls who represent perfection stands one who has partially crossed the boy–girl divide: Pippi Longstocking, the heroine of Astrid Lindgren's eponymous series of books. Pippi takes on five boys, beating them effortlessly, and flouts every social convention to boot: She

---

[1] Miriam Yalan-Shteklis, "Danny Is a Hero," appears in I Gave Nurit a Flower, p. 14, published by Kinneret Zmora-Bitan. Reprinted with permission.
[2] Miriam Yalan-Shteklis, "Mikha'el," appears in I Gave Nurit a Flower, p. 44, published by Kinneret Zmora-Bitan. Reprinted with permission.

refuses to attend school, dresses sloppily, washes her hair in a murky swamp to avoid having to pay the hairdresser, and wholeheartedly aspires to become a buccaneer when she grows up. Why this "boy-like" behavior? The rationale provided in the story itself is that Pippi had lost her mother soon after being born, spent many years in the company of men when she joined her father the captain on his seafaring journeys, and now, at the time that the story takes place, is growing up with neither father nor mother. In other words, her gender otherness is accounted for on clear psychological grounds, thus excluding any comparison with children who grow up under normal circumstances (a mother, a father, and a home).

Aggression and Violence in Infancy: Developmental Aspects

According to Winnicott (1985), every healthy young child who trusts his father and mother defies conventions and tries to test his destructive force, deterring power and ability to control others. He does so from infancy, but if the home is resilient to his destructive attempts, the child will learn to self-regulate through play and speech. For this to happen, the child must be aware from birth that boundaries exist, as does a flexible yet consistent structure. This is an important condition for the development of the child's ability to regulate both emotions and behaviors—an ability he still lacks during infancy and with which he needs outside help. When starting out in life, children have not yet learned to withstand frustrations and deal with their impulses. They need an environment that is loving, strong, and protective, yet at the same time flexible, or else they might come to fear their own thoughts and fantasies. The toddler's aspiration for independence and selfhood is often a cause of frustration, leading to disobedience, aggression, and tantrums, hence the term "developmental oppositional behavior." In fact, about 70% of toddlers display aggression and tantrums at around 2 years old, hence the term "terrible twos." These kinds of behaviors appear, indeed, at the age when toddlers can already walk and their sense of confidence increases, as does their cognitive ability to understand causality.

Still, there are early signs of potentially problematic aggressive or rebellious behaviors that require professional counseling, such as the following:

- *Excessive demands on the toddler's part.* This is sometimes mistakenly perceived by parents as "unavoidable" or "age-related." Parents have to stand strong without giving in to the child's demands. It is Winnicott (1985) who defined the "good enough" mother as one who knows, right from the baby's first months in life, not only to satisfy his needs but also to frustrate him.

- *Disobedience that manifests itself in resistance to rules, instructions, and social norms.* The ability to say "no" is, as is now known, a major developmental phase that appears at around 18 months old. Consequently, some consider the disobedience that comes at 2 years old perfectly normative. However, when it crosses a certain line, it might indicate a problem that calls for treatment.

- *Tantrums, with stamping of the feet, screams, crying, and—at times— breaking of objects.* Such behavior usually reflects frustration, anger, and emotional distress. Because particularly aggressive and frequent tantrums in infancy are sometimes predictors for the development of anxiety and depression at school ages, they are important to detect and intervene in, as we show below.

CASE STUDY

D., a 2½-year-old toddler and her parents' second child, was referred for diagnosis by her nursery school teacher because of violent behavior and a very low frustration threshold. Her verbal and cognitive development were high for her age. Straight into the session, the parents reported D.'s tendency to throw severe tantrums over minor frustrations and that all their attempts to calm her came to naught. On first examination, we saw a little girl who ordered her parents where to sit. Furthermore, she stood between them and the therapist, as if she did not allow them to speak or the therapist to intervene in her relationship with her parents. The therapist pointed this out to the parents, but they failed to see why she was so fussy about the seating arrangements. The mother was even slightly annoyed, saying "That's okay, she's allowed, she doesn't know you, it's natural."

"That's right, she doesn't know me, and I would expect her to be anxious and cling to you, but she doesn't strike me as being afraid," retorted the therapist.

"You're right," the father sighed, "She's not anxious, she's simply controlling us."

The mother turned to him, wrapping both arms around her daughter. "She's too little for all your rules," she said, upon which the child launched into baby talk that in no way resembled her tone of voice when she had ordered her parents around. Once again, she asked the mother to stand up and take the seat she had pointed to initially, and the mother was about to oblige. The therapist asked her to remain seated, adding, "There are things that children can decide, such as what to play, and things that only the parents decide, such as where to sit." D. looked at the therapist, then into her parents' face, and flew into a rage. The tantrum lasted up until the end of the meeting and was accompanied by physical aggression toward the mother. The mother put up no protest.

The parents' differences of opinion already came up in this first session: The mother believed that the child should not be frustrated, whereas the father intuitively felt that this parental attitude was detrimental to the child; however, fearing a conflict with his wife, he stood by helplessly. For the next session, only the parents were invited, with a view to try and gain a better understanding of the background underlying the current state of affairs between them.

During the meeting, it turned out that D. had contracted acute leukemia when she was 1 year old, had successfully undergone all treatments, and had made a full physical recovery—requiring only a follow-up every 6 months. In answer to the therapist's question, "How did you get through those tough times?" the mother replied, "We never did, we're still there," and the father explained, "The girl is the one who had made it through them; we are still traumatized, because . . . ." However, he could not finish his sentence because the mother abruptly cut him short and asked, "What does this have to do with the problem that brought us here, the girl's violence?" The therapist explained to them that this was exactly what they had to try to figure out together, adding, "Let us try to see what emotions arise in each of us here in the room. For example, let's try to understand why D. started affecting a baby's voice at that specific moment, who said what then, and how the tantrum came about. Maybe there is a connection between the ordeal you went through and the hard time you have setting boundaries for your child, as if she were still a miserable, vulnerable baby who has to be compensated for the suffering she had been through." Upon hearing this, both parents started to weep silently (this was also a hard moment for the therapist), and the mother said, "To my mind, she really is still a baby, and I don't see the need to frustrate her on top of everything. As far as I'm concerned, she can do whatever she likes; what really matters is that she's alive."

"Whatever she likes? Even hit you?" asked the therapist. Silence filled the room. "Maybe I feel like I deserve to suffer because she suffered so much; I gave birth to her with the leukemia," answered the mother.

The mother's angry and aggressive attitude gave way to her deeply felt pain and feelings of guilt, and we were able to link this to the difficulty she had setting boundaries for her daughter. The parents slowly came to realize how confused their daughter was and how hard she found it to distinguish between what was allowed and what was forbidden as well as between being a big girl (i.e., healthy and able to cope with frustrations) and being a baby (i.e., ill, unable or not required to be independent and her own self). D. had become a child-tyrant deserving of compensation for her suffering. This confusion underlay the tantrums, making life hard for her both at home and at nursery school. After the girl felt her parents standing up to her, unafraid to frustrate her, yet still around in moments of true distress, she calmed down. She still needed close monitoring.

The *DC:0–5™: Diagnostic Classification of Mental Health and Developmental Disorders of Infancy and Early Childhood* (DC:0–5; ZERO TO THREE, 2016) diagnoses in this case would be as follows:

- Axis I: Clinical Disorders
  - » Disorder of Dysregulated Anger and Aggression of Early Childhood

» Relationship Specific Disorder of Infancy/Early Childhood
- Axis II: Relational Context
  » Level 2—Strained to Concerning relationship with father
  » Level 3—Compromised to Disturbed relationship with mother
  » Level 2—Strained to Concerning caregiving environment
- Axis III: Medical Condition
  » History of cancer and of painful procedures
- Axis IV: Psychosocial Stressor
  » None
- Axis V: Developmental Competence
  » Exceeds developmental expectations in cognitive and language domains
  » Inconsistent competencies in emotional and social–relational domains

To conclude, behavioral and emotional regulation is one of the child's key developmental tasks from birth on. The ability to regulate depends on cognitive development, language development, and the child's biological constitution, but not only on them. Parents, too, play an important role in their child's acquisition of regulatory capabilities. When a child acquires speech, his parents must help him and teach him to express anger in words rather than actions. Moreover, parents should be role models because imitating parental behavior is one of the most important environmental factors shaping the child's behavior.

When Does Normative Developmental Aggression Become Pathological?

In the nursery rhyme "My Friend Tintan" by Miriam Yalan-Shteklis, Danny, the hero of and speaker in the poem, adopts an imaginary friend, a kind of imaginary double, who eats from his plate, sleeps in his bed, and is always by his side. As long as the double is well-behaved, he is like a twin, a close friend, a partner who offsets the loneliness of the poem's speaker. However, when Tintan is gripped in an outburst of aggression and irritates others, Danny then provides a reminder that Tintan is really just a friend and not he himself, despite their striking resemblance:

But at times he's bad, bad to no end!
The poor cat's tail he'll pull and bend,
His egg he will refuse to eat,
And only shout and stomp his feet!

And then they all are mad at me,
And then they all blame it on me,

Oh, Danny-Danny-Danny-Dan!
Not knowing that the deed was done
By none else than my friend Tintan.[3]

Tugging on the cat's tail, refusing to eat, the yelling and thrashing about
are associated in the poem with boyish behavior and its overtly physical
expression of aggression. This behavior earns Danny the title "bad boy,"
and not just "bad" but "bad to no end," whom "all" get angry with and
"blame," and justifiably so. Although Danny understands full well that
such aggressive behavior is judged intolerable by the representatives of the
entire civilization — namely, his parents — his ability to contain and curb
it at this stage is limited. Giving his aggression free reign thus requires a
scapegoat in the form of Tintan to take the rap for failures and to allow
Danny to remain mommy's darling boy.

A 2-year-old can truly be very aggressive toward her parents and siblings
and other children her age, even toward herself. The question asked is whether
this happens deliberately in infancy. Some claim that underlying any form
of violence is the intention to hurt someone or to damage something. Others
reject the notion that intention can lie behind a very young child's aggressive
behavior, believing that her cognitive ability is not sufficiently far advanced to
perceive other people's intention. This point of view is inconsistent with studies
indicating that toddlers are capable of identifying intentions in others.

Those who hold that intention could indeed fuel violence as early as
infancy rely on longitudinal studies (Shaw, Gilliom, Ingoldsby, & Nagin, 2003;
Tremblay et al., 2004) that showed that 2-year-old children who displayed very
high levels of aggression were at high risk of developing into violent children
later in life. Certain familial factors also contribute to increasing this risk,
among them having many siblings, mothers with antisocial personality disorder,
a mother's young age, and a mother's coercive or punitive style of disciplining.
Dysfunctional families and low socioeconomic status are additional risk factors,
which often go hand in hand with those above.

A child's level of violence in infancy also predicts future social competence.
A study that followed the development of 1,195 children from 2 to 9 years old
(Odgers et al., 2008) focused on the relationship between the form of violence
at a young age, in terms of intensity and duration, and social competence at an
older age. The study suggested that prolonged episodes of low-intensity aggression in infancy that persisted after 3 years old (25% of the sample) predicted
interpersonal problems further down the line. Prolonged, moderately intense
aggression that substantially subsided on entering school (12% of the sample)
predicted good social adaptation at 12 years old. However, in cases of prolonged

---

[3] Miriam Yalan-Shteklis, "My Friend Tintan," appears in *I Gave Nurit a Flower*, pp. 30–31,
published by Kinneret Zmora-Bitan. Reprinted with permission.

high-intensity aggression (3% of the sample), serious adaptation difficulties were to be expected in adolescence. Protracted, moderately intense aggression (15% of the sample) predicted emotional-regulation disorders together with attention deficit disorders at school age. Finally, 45% of children who had already manifested abnormal aggression at 2 years old—without, however, any linear continuity—were observed to have the hardest adaptation difficulties at 12 years old. Hence, the very appearance of violence at 2 years old influences future development, depending on its initial intensity, continuity, and consistency. As time goes by, a vicious cycle of violence in the child and social rejection from his peer group sets in and often leads to depression and sometimes to suicidality in adolescent years.

CASE STUDY

B., an 18-month-old toddler, was referred to us urgently by the manager of the day care he attended. She threatened to send him away from there because of his severely violent behavior toward his peers and himself. She described B. as a sad, intelligent, and—very often—angry child. During our first meeting, he was extremely anxious; however, contrary to what would be expected of a young child in an unfamiliar situation, he did not go near his parents. Instead, he stood behind a chair, moaning like an injured animal. This behavior persisted throughout the evaluation. B. took no interest in games, and he did not smile even once. His parents, for their part, did not try to call him or take him into their arms. From what they said, we gathered that they perceived him as a child who did things to spite them, despite all their efforts.

During our next sessions, it turned out that B.'s father had lost his mother at 9 years old and that his father, who treated him violently, abandoned him. B.'s father even went criminal and served a prison sentence for a particularly violent act. When he got out of jail, he decided to clean up his act, met B.'s mother, and wed her. B. is their common child. The mother was born into a destitute family to parents who only knew how to provide instrumental care to their children, without any emotional communication. After B. was born, the relationship between his parents started to deteriorate. They had a very hard time making the shift into parenthood. B. was born with a difficult temperament and cried a lot. One evening, the father told us, when B. was 2 months old, he had lost his patience and banged B. against the wall. Greatly alarmed by what he had done, the father went to a psychiatric clinic and started medication. The mother said that she had failed to protect B. from his father's aggression because she was submissive and dependent. About 2 months after B. was born, the mother got pregnant for the second time, and B. had a baby brother when he was 11 months old. B. took his brother's birth very hard out of jealousy, and the parents, who found it hard to deal with his aggressive behavior, left him enclosed for hours on end in his playpen. By and by, the parents developed a preference toward their second son, who was born with an easy temperament and did not frustrate them. B.'s rage only increased, manifesting itself in real violence directed at other children at day care, his baby brother, his mother, and also himself (he would bite himself when crying).

When the therapist and parents sat down together to watch video footage of one of the therapy sessions and focused on the nonverbal interaction between the mother and the baby, the mother realized how scared she was of her child, already seeing an "abusive man" in him. This association came to light at one point when the baby approached her with quick steps and she raised up her hand up as if to shield herself. The same session saw the father present confusing behavior toward his son. He conveyed both verbal violence and a desire to fix his past experiences: "I'll kill you if you become a criminal like me," he said.

The parents expected the treatment to make them better parents. They realized that they were not good enough parents. This very realization was taken by the therapist as a promising sign of change.

His DC:0–5 diagnoses would be as follows:

- Axis I: Clinical Disorders
  - » Disorder of Dysregulated Anger and Aggression of Early Childhood
  - » Relationship Specific Disorder of Infancy/Early Childhood (with mother and father)

- Axis II: Relational Context
  - » Level 4—Disordered to Dangerous relationships with each parent
  - » Level 4—Disordered to Dangerous caregiving environment

- Axis III: Medical Condition
  - » None

- Axis IV: Psychosocial Stressor
  - » Parental personality disorders (antisocial and borderline types)

- Axis V: Developmental Competence
  - » Functions at age-appropriate level

Treatment lasted for about 1 year, under the Social Welfare's supervision, because abuse had been reported. Some of the sessions were attended by the toddler with his mother, some by the toddler and both parents, and others by his younger brother and both parents. Most sessions were held at the clinic, but some took place at their home. It is worth noting here that B.'s parents did not perceive these home sessions as an invasion of their intimacy. In fact, they felt that the therapists expressed respect toward them—respect they had not gotten from professionals who had treated them in the past.

The therapeutic work centered on finding an alternative understanding of B.'s aggressive behaviors other than his just being a nasty little boy, as his parents perceived him. Let us take, for example, his sleeping problems. B. would cry a lot when it came time to go to bed, and he woke up a lot during the night. This frustrated both parents and made them highly aggressive.

Their anger only served to amplify B.'s. The parents had never made the connection between this behavior and the child's fear of losing their love following days packed full of frustrations and anger. At the start of the treatment, the mother's response to B.'s behaviors was to say, "What a spoiled child. My parents would put me in bed willy-nilly; who gave a flying fig about my feelings!"

The mother reiterated this line several times during treatment. On one such occasion, the therapist pointed out the connection between the emotional deprivation that had marked her childhood and her husband's on the one hand and their parental behavior on the other hand. Despite this new insight, the change in parental behavior was very slow, partly because of B.'s difficult temperament. The day care personnel were also having a hard time containing the child's behavior, which led us to add medication to the psychological treatment. This combination brought about an improvement both at home and at day care. After 1 year of treatment at our unit, the family pursued 2 more years of treatment at a clinic for preschool children, but at some point, the parents gave up and decided to send the child to boarding school. In retrospect, the prospects for this child may have been better if he had been removed from his abusive parents and placed in a long-term foster care family. The problem, though, was that the parents asked for treatment, which made us think and hope that there was a good-enough chance of keeping the child within his family together with his younger brother.

Expressions of aggression and violence in infancy and toddlerhood are thus not to be taken lightly, and seeking professional counseling in these cases is very much recommended. Because, as longitudinal studies have repeatedly shown, without therapeutic intervention, these children are at very high risk of becoming depressed, anxious, addicted to drugs or alcohol, and suicidal as adolescents and young adults. When they become parents, they are highly at risk of becoming negligent or violent toward their child, as the previous vignette illustrates.

Prevalence of Pathological Aggression and Violence in Infancy

Violence in toddlers is a significant clinical problem. For example, among all children referred to our infant mental health unit, 18% seek our help between 1 and 2 years old—and 24% between 2 and 3 years old—because of oppositional, aggressive, and (in some cases) violent behavior. Several researchers have looked at the prevalence of aggression and violence among infants and toddlers. A scale (Wakschlag & Danis, 2009) was developed on the basis of checking the number of times per day that very young children manifested aggression. By doing so, they turned a once-subjective evaluation of aggression and violence into an objective, reliably measured variable, and they showed that 5% of 2-year-olds were significantly violent physically.

Etiology of Pathological Aggression and Violence in Infancy

Winnicott was the first to describe the relationship between emotional deprivation and neglect during infancy and violence and delinquency later in life. He learned about this relationship through his clinical work, and it was indeed validated years later by longitudinal studies of aggressive and violent infants and toddlers (e.g., see Winnicott, 1985). These studies have reinforced the assumption that to understand the development of early aggression, account should be taken of biological, psychological, and socioenvironmental factors.

Biological Factors

For obvious ethical reasons, most biological studies on aggression are conducted on animals, making it difficult to extrapolate from their results to human beings. Still, several studies were undertaken to try to detect the constitutional factors of excessive aggression in infants and toddlers. Next, we mention the most significant among them.

Neurophysiological factors

A study of the autonomic nervous system (Shaw, Gilliom, & Giovannelli, 2000), the system that also regulates heart rate and skin conductivity, has indicated a lower base level of activity in the most aggressive children compared with typically developing children under normal conditions, and a higher-than-normal level when they were under stress. These data indicate a physiological difficulty in abnormally aggressive children to regulate anger and negative emotions, which leads them to inappropriate aggressive behavior.

Neurological factors

Comparisons between aggressive and calm toddlers in terms of electrical brain activity as plotted by electroencephalograms showed a lower than normal delta-wave frequency in the former, especially in the frontal cerebral region (Shaw et al., 2000). This finding usually indicates cerebral immaturity and can also explain the difficulty to regulate impulses. Cerebral imaging testing of highly aggressive children has made it possible to identify a dysfunction in the frontal cortex region and in deeper cerebral regions, such as the limbic system. Indeed, their limbic system presented asymmetric functioning: a drop in the left hemisphere functioning as opposed to increased activity in the right one. Moreover, dysfunction of the right hemisphere of the brain in adults with delinquent behaviors was shown to characterize those who had themselves fallen prey to violence in childhood. These new biological data surely reinforce the connection established by Winnicott (1985) between emotional deprivation and adult delinquency.

To sum up the findings indicating the role of the brain in the early emergence of aggression, it would seem that abnormal aggression stems from dysfunction in several regions of the brain responsible for emotional regulation. This dysfunction takes place at two levels: the deep, subcortical level, which plays a primary role in operating the emotional system, and the higher frontal-cortical level, which is in charge of identifying situations that call for regulation. Deficits at these levels help to better understand why abnormally aggressive toddlers have a hard time identifying situations that require emotional control.

Constitutional factors

A child's difficult temperament, which is an innate factor, can also contribute to the emergence of behavioral disorders. In her pioneering 1966 study, Robins already showed the existence of a correlation between a baby's difficult temperament and the subsequent development of behavioral disorders. Odgers et al. (2008) threw some complexity into the mix, saying that it was the combination of two variables—the baby's temperament and inadequate parental behaviors—that led to dysregulation of aggression in toddlers and then, eventually, to behavioral disorders.

In addition, different studies have found that language development was often deficient in overly aggressive toddlers. This might suggest imbalance between motor skills and language: "When I don't know how to say it in words, I express it in actions."

Fania Bergstein's nursery rhyme, "The Pencil Is Angry,"[4] and that of Miriam Yalan-Shteklis, "Anger," aptly describe the shortcomings of language in confronting the inner storm whipped up by feelings of rage and aggression.

In Fania Bergstein's wonderful poem, the angry toddler projects his feeling onto the pencil, an implement mainly designed for writing, which might therefore serve as a verbal mediator between him and the world. The child could have recounted his adventures in all tranquility had the pencil not persisted in its "wooden" rage. And what characterizes the pencil's anger? The wooden pencil cannot, by nature, bend or change, and it continues to stand upright; furthermore, the pencil cannot allow the child to express what he really feels. It puts up a wall between the child's inner world and the outer world, and it refuses to obey the known spelling rules, or, in other words, it rebels against the cultural conventions within which it is supposed to operate.

In the second stanza, the poetic "I" continues to project his "bad" and lazy side onto the pencil: He is not the one who is reprehensibly angry—he is

---

[4] Fania Bergstein, 1967, "The Pencil Is Angry," appears in *Azure and Red*, p. 10, published by Hakibbutz Hameuchad.

not the lazy one who fails to find appropriate, cultural words with which to express his rage. It is rather that wooden "stranger," the pencil, who betrays its role and refuses to play by the rules.

In Miriam Yalan-Shteklis's poem, the house cat assumes the role of the pencil: The irritated cat, a fickle pet, represents the animalistic, "uncultured" side of the poetic "I" (which comes out when he is mad) but also the pet who might snuggle up to its owners and enjoy a loving pat. Here is how the cat is portrayed:

Anger

*Anger, anger, anger,
The cat is wrapped in anger,
Ang-ang-angry at a friend —
One grey kitten — to no end.
At bim, at bam, at bim bulan,
Angry-ang at everyone.*

*And he is furious, all frown
And doesn't want to settle down
And didn't eat and didn't drink
And not ta-ta, and not ta-tink . . .
And only wrapped he is in anger,
Anger, anger, anger.*[5]

A cat who is wrapped in anger might garble the spoken language ("Ang-ang-angry at a friend"), refuse any prospect of calming down ("And doesn't want to settle down"), ignore even his own hunger and thirst ("And didn't eat and didn't drink"), and immerse himself whole in the anger that leaves him empty ("And only wrapped he is in anger").

The cat in the first stanza of the poem can still name his enemy, the source of his anger, "one grey kitten." However, as time goes by, he becomes speechless. "At bim, at bam, at bim bulan," the cat gets his tongue into a twist and can no longer even tell apart friends and foes: "Angry-ang at everyone."

The cat in the second stanza magnifies the bankruptcy of language when it comes to verbalizing the nature of the anger: Language not only fails to get to the bottom of the anger ("At bim, at bam, at bim bulan," in the first stanza) but it even comes up short of talking about it in negative terms:

---

[5] Miriam Yalan-Shteklis, "Anger," appears in *I Gave Nurit a Flower*, p. 24, published by Kinneret Zmora-Bitan. Reprinted with permission.

"And not ta-ta, and not ta-tink." By the end of the poem, for want of other words, the cat gets stuck, literally, at "anger, anger, anger, anger," unable to find even one synonym for his anger (e.g., resentment, rage, wrath, fury, irritability), perhaps because no verbal creativity can sprout from where anger springs.

Psychological Factors

Abnormal aggression and violence in infancy and toddlerhood can stem from numerous psychological factors. We mention the most significant ones.

Let us start with parental disciplinary behavior: Authoritative, coercive, and incoherent discipline does not allow the young child to regulate her aggression, and it reinforces her "normative" disobedience. As Rutter and Stevenson (2008) showed, inconsistent parenting that mixes up absence of boundaries with hostile criticism toward the child increases the likelihood of rebellious and aggressive behavior appearing during and after infancy.

Violent parental conflicts are a common cause of aggressive behavior in children. It has been demonstrated that from 6 months old, a baby's response to violent disputes between his parents includes behavioral withdrawal and exaggerated anxiety vis-à-vis any new stimulus. Then, at the age in which they acquire imitative capabilities, these children will become violent and aggressive, like their parents, both at home and outside it (Nelson, Hart, Yang, Olsen, & Jin, 2006).

A young child's early exposure to violent, unacceptable interpersonal communication in her parents implicitly gives her permission to act on the pleasure principle alone and to disrespect the ground rules of society. As a toddler, for example, the parents will allow her to touch everything or climb things without fear; then, at school age, they will take her side against the teachers, even if she had seriously breached school discipline. These parents' failure to regulate their own aggression transforms normative developmental aggression into problematic, ongoing violence. The child then internalizes scary, threatening parental figures with no self-control, and she develops a disorganized style of attachment. She is then incapable of either regulating herself or feeling protected by her own parents. Normative developmental aggression then becomes pathological aggression and violence because there was no one around to moderate it in time. This often happens in families in which transgenerational family ties are fraught with anger and aggression (as illustrated in the previous vignette), which can culminate in interpersonal violence. At times, the parent projects his own negative parental images onto the baby, "labeling" her in some specific terms, and from this point on addressing her as per these negative attributions. The baby, in turn, will identify with these negative projections, growing up to match them (a process called projective identification).

According to the sociologist Dodge (1993), aggression that develops abnormally in infancy and is then transformed into a behavioral disorder at an older age is caused by a distortion in the development of social cognition. According to him, this distortion occurs when a parent responds to the baby's negative behaviors while ignoring his positive ones. This cognitive pattern makes the toddler misinterpret behaviors in his environment and react violently to neutral stimuli that he perceives as hostile.

CASE STUDY

A. was 2½ years old when he came in for a consultation. His parents were helpless and terrified in view of his growing violence at home and at day care. A., a single child, was adopted at 1 year old. Prior to adoption, he had been raised in an orphanage abroad, where he suffered from emotional and developmental deprivation that often characterizes such institutions. After arriving at his adoptive parents' home, he appeared to adapt very quickly to his new environment, as if he had put all of his bad experiences behind him. His parents believed that he had simply forgotten those thanks to their love and dedication. They now failed to understand the origin of his aggression and even took offense, saying, "What more could we have given him? Our entire life revolves around him." A. was a charming toddler, physically advanced for this age but behind on his language development. In our first meeting at the clinic, he initially came across as a nice and shy little boy, but only minutes later, feeling confident in our presence, he started testing the limits provocatively. The father gave up immediately, whereas the mother got angry and cried.

"What is A. trying to tell us with this behavior?" asked the therapist.

"What! Are you telling us that he knows why he is being a bad boy?!" replied the father with a question.

"Is it possible that he doesn't feel good with us, that we don't understand him at all, and that he is mad at us for that?" asked the mother, shocked and sad.

"Or perhaps, quite to the contrary," answered the therapist, "he likes you so much that he is terribly afraid to lose you, and one of the more common ways available to young children to test the strength of their relationship with their surroundings is to try and stretch it as much as possible."

"Why should he fear losing the relationship? We never leave him. We don't even have a babysitter!" wondered the father.

"True, but still, he already went through a separation before," commented the therapist softly.

"What do you mean?"

"Well . . . , he left the orphanage. From where he stands, he is at risk of being transferred again . . . The more he becomes attached to you, the greater the fear of losing you."

"Could it be, then, that for him the transition was hard, even if the orphanage was not a good environment?" asked the father, surprised.

"Possibly," answered the therapist softly, aware of the "bomb" she had dropped in the room.

While they were talking, A. was playing quietly with the dollhouse.

"Look, Dad, the crocodile is trying to get into the house!" he said all of a sudden, a big plush crocodile in his hands.

"No way, he's too big, he can't enter," said the mother, while the father kept silent, not knowing how to respond.

"Look, here, he did manage to get inside," A. pursued the game.

"Oh no, we must protect the children in the house . . . Who is going to protect them?" the therapist joined in.

To which A. immediately replied, "Dad and Mom!"

A.'s parents were flabbergasted by their child's symbolic play skills and by the idea that his aggressive behavior toward them actually expressed a fear of being abandoned.

As the triadic treatment went on, the parents still had a hard time reading their son's behavior correctly. They were apprehensive about approaching emotional subjects, most of all the adoption issue. The turning point came when they brought in A.'s photo album for one of the sessions, "because A. loves browsing through it, and we also wanted you to see it." Everyone looked together at the photos taken during A.'s first days in Israel. One of the photos showed the baby wearing a serious facial expression, questionably scared or sad.

"Look at the face you made when you came to Israel," said the therapist to the child with a smile . . . "As if you were asking yourself: Wow! What is this new place they suddenly brought me to? Who are these people who are with me all the time and keep giving me so much stuff? I'm not used to this . . . It feels good, but it also scares me a little."

The room filled with silence. A. looked at the therapist, turned his head toward his parents, met their teary eyes, and brought his gaze back to her.

"That's right, your dad and mom are very emotional because they remember how hard it was for you to move from the children's home to your home in Tel Aviv," the therapist continued.

"We never talked about the adoption in this way . . . The adoption was a given fact, we never discussed what we each felt," the father commented.

A. quit looking at the album and started playing with the dollhouse, as if to tell us adults: "You go on discussing this between you; I've had enough for one day!" Indeed, the next sessions were primarily devoted to understanding the source of the parents' emotional difficulty to talk about their past. At the same time, as if by chance, A.'s level of violence gradually came down to the norm for his age, and his language became more articulate. Treatment ended after 6 months.

In this case, the DC:0–5 diagnoses are as follows:

- Axis I: Clinical Disorders
  » Neurodevelopmental disorder: Developmental Language Disorder
  » Disorder of Dysregulated Anger and Aggression of Early Childhood

- Axis II: Relational Context
  - » Level 2—Strained to Concerning relationship with mother and father
- Axis III: Medical Condition
  - » None
- Axis IV: Psychosocial Stressor
  - » Post institutional rearing; adoption
- Axis V: Developmental Competence
  - » Under developmental expectation in language domain

Socioenvironmental Factors

Certain socioenvironmental factors contribute to the more frequent appearance of violence already in early childhood. One such factor is the media but also poor living conditions and exposure to violence in neighborhoods, at day care, and in situations of social stress.

Regrettably, young children's exposure to social violence is constantly on the rise. In the United States, one in 10 children less than 6 years old who visits a pediatric clinic has witnessed at least one stabbing or shooting in her life, half of these at home and half on the street. Moreover, many studies have found that kids who grew up in conditions of extreme poverty and chronic hunger were likely to suffer from fits of violence and rage later in life.

Among others, society influences child development by controlling the content of media broadcasts. Woods, Wong, and Chachere (1991) demonstrated a strong relationship between exposure to violence on screen and the degree of violence in children. Meltzoff and Moore (2000) examined how television affected babies 14 months old: They assimilate and imitate violent behaviors they see there (such as the dismantling and smashing of objects). One has to bear in mind that until 3 or 4 years old, a toddler does not clearly distinguish between reality and imagination. Children who experience the world through the screen—and, unfortunately, kids in Israel watch too many hours of television compared with other countries, including the United States—absorb a large dose of aggression, especially in families in which television watching is not controlled or mediated by an adult who follows the events being watched with age-appropriate commentary to match the toddler's understanding.

Babies who grow up in war-stricken societies, where violence is woven into the fabric of everyday life, are even more prone to develop abnormal aggression because violence in these societies is mostly institutionalized and seen as justified behavior required for self-defense. Yolanda Gampel (2017) described her concept of "social radioactivity" regarding the connection between war and the individual's aggression. She described how social violence seeped into people's consciousness through their senses and sensations, becoming fixed at both the conscious and unconscious levels. This "radiation" injures, damages, and leaves its mark at the seams between body and emotion. Its residues add up: They are not the outcome of a single event but of exposure to numerous events. These "residues" affect mental structure and functioning at all ages—in babies, children, adolescents, and adults. This social violence can no longer be denied, and there is no escaping the exposure to it. It penetrates people's soul and influences them at any age, even if they are not aware of it.

Diagnosing Aggressive or Violent Infants

When diagnosing a very young child with aggressive behavior, a mental health professional must determine whether it is a case of normative developmental aggression or rather pathological aggression expressing a Disorder of Dysregulated Anger and Aggression of Early Childhood (DDAA) and requiring treatment. Among other things, the practitioner needs to establish whether the child is overly aggressive in response to frustrating situations or whether he displays aggression without any external trigger.

How, then, does one differentiate pathological aggression from developmentally normal aggression? On the basis of what criteria? Wakschlag and colleagues (Wakschlag & Danis, 2009; Wakschlag et al., 2012) suggested a model comprising four parameters: aggression, temper tantrums, noncompliance, and empathy.

- *Aggression*: The normal developmental task is to regulate anger and aggression using adaptive and problem-solving competencies. The toddler's aggression will be defined as pathological given frequent bouts of reactive or instrumental aggression accompanied by hostility.

- *Temper tantrums*: The normal developmental task is to achieve emotional regulation. A departure from this goal will lead to medium-intensity tantrums in response to daily situations involving frustration. The toddler's condition will be defined as pathological given frequent severe tantrums accompanied by aggression toward self or others and by breaking things.

- *Noncompliance*: The normal developmental task is to internalize the boundaries set by the parents. Developmentally normative disobedience is limited to specific situations and negotiable. The pathological level is defined as situations of overall, persistent disobedience.

- *Empathy*: The normal developmental task is to show concern for others and morality. Lack of empathy is pathological in itself, and it can be observed already by 3 years old in social situations in which the toddler seems to take pleasure in other children's predicaments.

The DC:0–5 manual provides a diagnostic algorithm for the diagnosis of DDAA, under the category of Mood Disorders, based on four clusters of symptoms: anger, noncompliance, reactive aggression, and proactive aggression. It should be emphasized that this diagnosis is not about transient displays of challenging behaviors but must rather be present for at least 3 months in more than one setting and in more than one relationship. If these four clusters of symptoms are observed only in the context of a specific relationship, then the right diagnosis will be Relationship Specific Disorder of Infancy/Early Childhood. In addition, it is very important to note that the disorder cannot be diagnosed in children less than 24 months old because of the developmental capacities required to fully display it, although difficulties in temper and behavioral regulation may be seen before 24 months old.

Differential Diagnosis and Comorbidity of DDAA

Major Depressive Disorder should be considered and pronounced rather than DDAA if vegetative signs are present—namely, sleep and eating disturbances together with a persistent lack of pleasure and interest in activities. Generalized Anxiety Disorder, Posttraumatic Stress Disorder, Acute Stress Reaction, Sleep Onset Disorder, Sensory Over-Responsivity Disorder, and Relationship Specific Disorder of Infancy/Early Childhood are all diagnoses to rule out because they often manifest themselves in irritability. Also, neurodevelopmental disorders—such as Developmental Language Disorder and Autism Spectrum Disorder—need to be ruled out. Finally, several medications prescribed by pediatricians can cause dysregulation.

In regard to comorbidity, most of the diagnoses mentioned above can also occur with DDAA as long as the symptoms do not overlap and distinct features of each diagnosis are present. For example, a young child may be given comorbid diagnoses of DDAA and Overactivity Disorder of Toddlerhood/Attention Deficit Hyperactivity Disorder.

Course of Pathological Aggression Over the Years

Failure to eradicate developmental aggression during the early years may lead to emotional and behavioral dysregulation in childhood and adolescence. Research data have built up, showing the complex interplay among genes, caregiving environment, and the timing of adverse life events in the development of chronic anger and behavioral dysregulation. Poor parental mental health, deficient prenatal care, and exposure to toxins and stressors have been identified as risk factors—so have coercive parenting, lack of warmth, and poor family functioning. The greater the number of risk factors, the greater the chances of aggressive temper tantrums and violence in infancy turning into an oppositional disorder, a behavior disorder, depression, or anxiety in adolescence. Clinicians must therefore be aware of these risk factors to be able to detect them early and intervene in time to try to prevent the development of DDAA.

Preventive and Early Therapeutic Interventions

A distinction should be made between preventive intervention and early therapeutic intervention. The former aims at the early detection of 2-year-olds and older children who are at risk of becoming violent. Parents, the nursery teacher, the pediatrician, the social worker, or any family member who observes a child's behavior and finds it abnormal should recommend sending this child to professional diagnosis. The parents' vigilance cannot always be counted on because their child's behavior sometimes re-creates familiar patterns from their own childhood, which they are thus very likely to view as normative behavior.

In regard to early therapeutic intervention, this kind of intervention is called for when the toddler already presents signs of severe violence or when her parents do not respond as they should. The therapist will first identify the risk factors and protective factors and then draw up a unique treatment plan tailored to the family. Indeed, because of the important role the parents have in regulating the young child's aggression, both parents and child should undergo psychotherapy, aimed at enhancing the parents' and the child's capacity to regulate their emotions and behaviors and at understanding the emotional meaning of the child's aggressive behaviors. Among other things, parents learn how to use positive reinforcers to consolidate desired social behaviors and to extinguish undesirable ones.

Whenever domestic violence is suspected or identified, the clinician is bound by law to involve the social welfare services and to consider placing the child in a safer environment.

In regard to the practice of medicating highly aggressive children who are younger than 3 years old, our recommendation is to try to avoid it. In rare cases, however, when words are not efficient enough in diminishing the toddler's level of violence and when the child causes others physical hurt (as described in one of the case studies presented in this chapter), there is no choice but to administer drugs for a limited duration.

Conclusion

Abnormal aggression and violence in infancy are a cause for worry and for referring a toddler to see a professional. By "abnormal," we mean cases in which emotional and behavioral dysregulation are a daily occurrence, last long, remain unchanged following adult intervention, and obstruct the child's functioning.

There are various types of risk factors: Some have to do with the toddler, others with his parents and environment. At-risk toddlers are born with a vulnerability combined with parents whose self-reflective capability as well as frustration and impulsiveness thresholds are at their lowest. Factors such as a low income level, delinquent surroundings, and the absence of social support are environmental risk factors. The importance of early detection and intervention lies in the fact that some of these toddlers might otherwise suffer from significant psychopathologies later in life.

References

Dodge, K. A. (1993). Social-cognitive mechanisms in the development of conduct disorder and depression. *Annual Review of Psychology, 44*, 559–584.

Freud, S. (1920). Beyond the pleasure principle. In *The standard edition of the complete psychological works of Sigmund Freud*, Vol. XVIII (pp.1–64). London, England: Hogarth Press.

Gampell, Y. (2017). Evil. In R. Lazar (Ed.) *Talking about evil. Psychoanalytical, social and cultural perspectives* (pp. 1–16). London, England, and New York, NY: Routledge.

Golse, B. (2002). Agressivité, haine, et destructivité: Les racines de la violence (Aggression, hate, destructiveness: The roots of violence). In O. Halfon, F. Ansermet, J. Laget, & B. Pierrehumbert (Eds.), *Sens et non sens de la violence: Nouvelles expressions, nouvelles approches* (pp. 31–46). Paris, France: Presses Universitaires de France.

Meltzoff, A. N., & Moore, M. K. (2000). Imitation of facial and manual gestures by human neonates: Resolving the debate about early imitation. In D. Muir & A. Slater (Eds.), *Infant development: The essential readings* (pp. 167–181). Malden, MA: Blackwell.

Nelson, D. A., Hart, C. H., Yang, C., Olsen, J. A., & Jin, S. (2006). Aversive parenting in China: Associations with child physical and relational aggression. *Child Development, 77*, 554–572.

Odgers, C. L., Moffitt, T. E., Broadbent, J. M., Dickson, N., Hancox, R. J., Harrington, H., . . . Caspi, A. (2008). Female and male antisocial trajectories: From childhood origins to adult outcomes. *Developmental Psychopathology, 20*, 673–716.

Robins, L. N. (1966). *Deviant children grown up: A sociological and psychiatric study of sociopathic personality.* Philadelphia, PA: Lippincott Williams & Wilkins.

Rutter, M., & Stevenson, J. (2008). Development in child and adolescent psychiatry over the last fifty years. In M. J. Rutter, D. Bishop, D. Pine, S. Scott, J. S. Stevenson, E. A. Taylor, & A. Thapar (Eds.), *Rutter's child and adolescent psychiatry* (5th ed., pp. 3–18). New York, NY: Blackwell.

Shaw, D. S., Gilliom, M., & Giovannelli, J. (2000). Aggressive behavior disorders. In C. H. Zeanah, Jr, (Ed.), *Handbook of infant mental health* (2nd ed., pp. 397–398). New York, NY: Guilford Press.

Shaw, D. S., Gilliom, M., Ingoldsby, E. M., & Nagin, D. S. (2003). Trajectories leading to school-age conduct problems. *Developmental Psychology, 39,* 189–200.

Tremblay, R. E., Nagin, D. S., Séguin, J. R., Zoccolillo, M., Zelazo, P. D., Boivin, M., . . . Japel, C. (2004). Physical aggression during early childhood: Trajectories and predictors. *Pediatrics, 114,* e43–e50.

Wakschlag, L. S., & Danis, B. (2009). Characterizing early childhood disruptive behavior. In C. H. Zeanah, Jr. (Ed.), *Handbook of infant mental health* (3rd ed., pp. 392–408). New York, NY: Guilford Press.

Wakschlag, L. S., Henry, D. B., Tolan, P. H., Carter, A. S., Burns, J. L., & Briggs-Gowan, M. J. (2012). Putting theory to the test: Modeling a multidimensional, developmentally-based approach to preschool disruptive behavior. *Journal of the American Academy of Child and Adolescent Psychiatry, 51,* 593–604.

Winnicott, D. W. (1985). *Deprivation and delinquency.* London, England: Routledge.

Woods, W., Wong, F. Y., & Chachere, J. G. (1991). Effects of media violence on viewers' aggression in unconstrained social interaction. *Psychological Bulletin, 109,* 371–383.

ZERO TO THREE. (2016). DC:0–5™: *Diagnostic classification of mental health and developmental disorders of infancy and early childhood* (DC:0–5). Washington, DC: Author.

Recommended Reading

Baillargeon, R., Zoccolillo, M., Keenan, K., Pérusse, D., Wu, H. X., Boivin, M., & Tremblay, R. E. (2007). Gender differences in physical aggression: A prospective population-based survey of children before and after 2 years of age. *Developmental Psychology, 43,* 13–26.

Carter, A., Briggs-Cowan, M., McCarthy, K., & Wakschlag, I. (2009). *Developmental patterns of normative misbehavior in early childhood: Implications for identification of early disruptive behavior.* Paper presented at the Evolution of Disruptive Behavior Problems in Young Children symposium, annual meeting of the Social Research and Demonstration Corporation, Denver, CO.

Côté, S., Vaillancourt, T., LeBlanc, J., Nagin, D. S., & Tremblay, R. E. (2006). The development of physical aggression from toddlerhood to preadolescence: A nation wide longitudinal study of Canadian children. *Journal of Abnormal Child Psychology, 34,* 71–85.

Crick, N. (1996). The role of overt aggression, relational aggression, and prosocial behavior in the prediction of children's future social adjustment. *Child Development, 67*, 2317–2327.

Kochanska, G., Coy, K., & Murray, K. (2001). The development of self-regulation in the first four years of life. *Child Development, 72*, 1091–1111.

Minuchin, S., & Fishman, H. C. (1979). The psychosomatic family. *Journal of the American Academy of Child and Adolescent Psychiatry, 18*, 76–90.

Stieben, J., Lewis, M., Granic, I., Zelazo, P., Segalowitz, S., & Pepler, D. (2007). Neurophysiological mechanisms of emotion regulation for subtypes of externalizing children. *Development and Psychopathology, 19*, 455–480.

Zito, J., Safer, D., Dosreis, S., Gardner, J., Boles, M., & Lynch, F. (2000). Trends in the prescribing of psychotropic medications to preschoolers. *Journal of the American Medical Association, 283*, 1025–1030.

CHAPTER 9
I'm Scared

Goldilocks the Doll Is Tired

Goldilocks the doll is tired
And the bear is plain worn out
Shadows in the room have gathered
Whispering in my ear Good Night

Lying in her bed is Nurit
Next to her a teddy sits
And a cat and little rabbit
And they all just want to sleep

Then at once Nurit arises
Daddy, Dad, she calls out loud
Come here quick, the darkness bugs me
He's a bad boy, drive him out

Goldilocks the doll is laughing
Bear is laughing even more
Why would you expel the darkness?
He's a good boy after all.[1]

Early childhood anxieties and fears figure prominently in children's literature. These anxieties and fears awaken from their daytime slumber immediately after bedtime and wait to pounce at the exact moment when the parents exit the room — leaving the children to face the demons, monsters, and nightmares alone. In Miriam Yalan-Shteklis's poem, the toys hear the lonely girl's cry and try to banish the anxiety; they portray the monster — in this case darkness — as a "good boy." Was their ruse successful in allaying Nurit's fears? Hopefully, yes. Such are, at least, the norms of children's literature. Many children's books are concerned with fears and anxieties because these are most common in children. They offer different models for

---

[1] Miriam Yalan-Shteklis, "Goldilocks the Doll Is Tired," appears in *I Gave Nurit a Flower*, p. 8, published by Kinneret Zmora-Bitan. Reprinted with permission.

tackling the problem and especially promise a happy ending. This promise allows both child and parent to feel in control of things.

Introduction

Fear and anxiety are universal emotions essential to human existence. The line between normative and pathologic fears and anxieties is, thus, very thin. Moreover, there are normative developmental fears and anxieties — that is, ones that constitute milestones in the cognitive development of the young child, who gradually comes to realize that the world around him is complex and sometimes dangerous. The earliest to develop is stranger anxiety, appearing around the 8th month of life (see chapter 3). Then, at 1 year old, when the child already understands the potential danger inherent in separating from his beloved figures, separation anxiety also comes about. These anxieties — necessary stages in the infant's emotional, cognitive, and social development — pass with time. In fact, when stranger anxiety and separation anxiety do not appear in the first 2 years of life, some pathology is to be suspected. Up until their first year of school, many children thus express different fears related to development, such as fear of animals, monsters, or the dark. The difference between these developmental fears and anxiety disorders in infancy and early childhood is discussed later in this chapter.

Anxiety disorders are among the most common problems in childhood, affecting 9%–20% of children. Their prevalence during infancy is unknown because many clinicians and researchers have regarded distressing anxiety in infants as either a normative phase of development or a temperament trait that only predisposes for later mental health problems. It is clear today that anxiety at a young age can impair the infant's and her family's functioning and that it increases risk for later anxiety and depression.

In the scientific literature, two main approaches to diagnosing anxiety disorders in infancy are proposed: the dimensional approach and the categorical approach. In the dimensional approach, the appearance of anxiety symptoms is viewed as an amplification of a basic anxiety level present in every young child. The magnitude of the anxiety is sometimes so high as to affect the family's functioning. A child's anxieties often force parents to reorganize their work around him or to even stop working altogether. In the categorical approach, a clear distinction is made between normal and abnormal. Those who use it diagnose anxiety disorders based on criteria in the DC:0–5™: *Diagnostic Classification of Mental Health and Developmental Disorders of Infancy and Early Childhood* (DC:0–5; ZERO TO THREE, 2016). These types of anxiety disorders include Separation Anxiety Disorder, Social Anxiety Disorder, Generalized Anxiety Disorder, Selective Mutism, and Inhibition to Novelty Disorder.

Etiology of Anxiety Disorders in Infancy

Maternal Stress and Intrauterine Environment

Many researchers have tried to trace the origins of anxiety in infancy. Field, Diego, and Hernandez-Reif (2006)—for example—showed a direct relationship between high levels of maternal depression and anxiety during pregnancy and a low reactivity threshold in babies at 8 weeks, a higher prevalence of a difficult temperament at 4 months, and difficulty regulating attention at 8 months. These findings raised the question of whether situations of maternal stress and anxiety during pregnancy may cause structural changes in the fetus. It turns out that the fetus's degree of vulnerability to maternal anxiety depends on the fetus's genetic make-up and, more precisely, the short arm of the serotonin-transporter gene (HTTLPR-5).

Temperament

Approximately 15% of preschool children display excessive anxiety, shyness, and social withdrawal when meeting unfamiliar people or confronted with new situations. These children, designated as "behaviorally inhibited" by Kagan (1997) or "slow-to-warm-up" by Chess and Thomas (1996) can already be detected at 14 months old. This type of temperament, which is innate, has unique physiological and cerebral characteristics discernable when using imaging techniques. The physiological response of such children to new situations resembles the typical anxiety response (e.g., an accelerated heart rate, a high level of cortisol in the morning, or a particularly low stress threshold). Brain functional imaging of these "inhibited" babies showed distinctive characteristics in the amygdala region that set them apart from other children (Goldsmith & Lemery, 2000). Furthermore, electroencephalogram tests showed overactivity of the prefrontal cortex region as well as greater asymmetry than would be expected between the right and left hemispheres. Babies who show signs of excessive anxiety only a few months after birth, in the form of an inhibited temperament, have been found to be at high risk for developing Social Anxiety Disorder at 3 years old and up. Some of them are in fact already impaired in their functioning. These findings support the notion that early inhibition is not a precursor to anxiety, but anxiety itself. In other words, an inhibited-type temperament may, at least in some infants, be an early manifestation of an innate anxiety disorder.

Young children are usually equipped with a healthy mechanism allowing them to cope with anxiety-producing situations. The role of this mechanism is to shift the child's focus from the anxiety-producing object to a neutral one. Babies and toddlers with inhibited temperament have a difficult time at this task.

Insecure Style of Attachment

What is the link between an insecure style of attachment and the appearance of anxiety disorders in young children? Several studies have been published on the subject, with sometimes contradictory conclusions. Some researchers have suggested a link between an insecure resistant-ambivalent style of attachment and the subsequent appearance of Social Anxiety Disorder, whereas others have refuted this link. It appears that insecure attachment contributes to the development of an anxiety disorder only when other risk factors are present, whereas secure attachment can mitigate the effect of existing risk factors and thus prevent the development of an anxiety disorder (Brumariu & Kerns, 2008).

Parental Depression or Anxiety

A family history of anxiety disorders or depression raises the risk of young children developing anxiety disorders (Murray et al., 2008). The intergenerational transmission mechanism is complex, combining biological and psychological risk factors. In fact, studies have shown that babies of parents with anxiety have high cortisol levels. Regarding psychological transmission, mothers with anxiety were found to be less sensitive to their babies than typical mothers, and their countenance tended to be negative for the most part (Nicol-Harper, Harvey, & Stein, 2007). It was further found that babies imitated and adopted their parents' anxious behaviors, such that these traits and behaviors became an integral part of themselves.

Parental Behavior

Researchers have also examined how parents influenced their toddler's level of anxiety with their behaviors and attitude toward her. It was found that excessive and intrusive control by the parent of the child's activities—which has been termed as negative control in the professional literature—and failure to allow the child the adequate degree of autonomy for her age contribute to the development of anxiety in the toddler. As these parents see it, they are helping their toddler deal with tasks and challenges. What they fail to acknowledge is that this excessive control can be detrimental to the child's development because it does not allow her to develop independent mechanisms for coping with stressful situations. In other words, they do not allow the child to regulate her own anxiety, and she learns to rely on external factors when confronted with stressful situations.

The question is of course where one draws the line between, on the one hand, help and guidance and, on the other hand, intrusiveness and coercion. Put differently, when is help truly offered as an aid for dealing with problems, stress, and trauma, and when is it nothing but a form of intrusion meant to control the child and impose specific forms of behavior on him? This depends, of course, on the parents' personality: the balance between the need to intervene, supervise, guide, and control and the ability to see the baby or the toddler as an independent being with wants and capabilities of his own. These parental attributes will largely determine the amount of leeway made available to the baby or otherwise prepare the ground for the development of an anxiety disorder.

Most children's stories about anxieties and fears portray the families involved as supportive and understanding as well as knowing how to handle the anxious child. David Grossman's story Itamar the Dream Hunter[2] *is no different. This is a story about a father and his son who defeated the blue demon with the sad red eyes and the sharp horns that appeared in Itamar's dreams and overshadowed him. In the dream, the demon appears on the seashore, chasing Itamar. Itamar starts crying out, but no one hears his shouts. In real life, however, his father quickly arrives at his bedside. The two immediately establish the "ItaDad" (Itamar and Dad) alliance and devise a cunning plan to entrap demons—one that would free Itamar of his feeling of helplessness when confronted with the demon that casts a huge shadow over him.*

The story ends in victory for the alliance. The demon is caught in the trap that the two had set up for it, and all that remains of it are a few blue stains. Both partners in the ItaDad alliance pat each other on the back in admiration: The father is impressed with Itamar's stance against the demon, and the son is impressed with the father's brilliant design of the trap.

Monsterella, *a story by Racheli Baharal,[3] likewise describes a child who is preoccupied with the question of what would happen if a giant purple monster showed up suddenly and wanted to sneak into their home. Here, too, the parent comes to the rescue: She tries to soothe the child and suggests putting up a sign at the entrance to the house that prohibits entry to monsters, digging a deep moat filled with water around the house, and installing a heavy iron door. However, all her suggestions—as logical and realistic as they might be—fail to reassure the child, who is terrified of the monster's powers to overcome any obstacle. In the end, a way out is found that the child can accept: They will imprison the monster in a cage. The monster would become sad, and then, to console it, they would take it out of its cage, pat it on the head, and give it a name. The child gives the scary monster the pet name "Monsterella," thus freeing the monster of its scary identity.*

---

[2] David Grossman, 1990, *Itamar the Dream Hunter*, published by Am Oved.
[3] Racheli Baharal, 2004, *Monsterella*, published by Yessod.

In Mercer Mayer's There's a Nightmare in My Closet,[4] *the child is not assisted by his parents, coming up with a remedy for his fears on his own. The book describes an ingenious boy who has a nightmare in his closet—a demon that appears at night, one that must be "taken out of the closet" and be befriended. In this well-known story, the boy—accompanied by the moon in the window—discovers that the monster itself has significant anxieties, and that the way to help it, and be helped by it, is to put it in his bed. The savior in this story is thus the child himself, who is willing to confront his demon head-on. In this way, he finds a way of his own to calm his anxieties.*

Adverse Life Events

Life events occurring during infancy could give rise to the subsequent development of anxiety disorders. These are mostly life events that threaten the physical existence of the toddler or her parents or that seriously disrupt the young child's everyday life, such as divorce (especially when the child uses her parents as a trump card or a battering ram against each other), a parent's hospitalization, or loss of a parent's source of income. Several studies have looked at the link between the type of event and the nature of the disorder that would develop later in life. For instance, it has been suggested that a high-conflict divorce tends to engender mostly anxiety, whereas the loss of a parent is rather accompanied by depression and specific fears (phobias).

Diagnosis of Anxiety Disorders in Infancy

To diagnose an anxiety disorder of any type in an infant, several criteria must be met according to the DC:0–5: The anxiety must (a) cause or lead to avoidance of activities associated with the anxiety or fear, (b) occur during two or more everyday activities, (c) be uncontrollable for the most part, (d) persist for at least 2 weeks, (e) impair the child's or family's functioning, and (f) hinder the child's expected development. Each type of anxiety disorder has its specific diagnostic criteria.

Separation Anxiety Disorder

As we already noted, separation anxiety is a normal phenomenon, which appears around 10–11 months old, peaks at 10–18 months old, and progressively declines by 3 years old. Separation and anxiety in the first 3 years often expresses itself in inconsolable crying, clinging, hiding, and tantrums. The anxiety is defined as Separation Anxiety Disorder if at least three of the following

---

[4] Mercer Mayer, 2008, *There's a Nightmare in My Closet*, published by Paw Prints.

symptoms appear for at least 1 month and the infant's or his family's functioning is impaired:

- The child is highly distressed when separating from home or from a major attachment figure.

- The child is excessively worried about any event that might lead to separation from an attachment figure (such as being kidnapped).

- The child persistently refuses to go to day care or any setting outside of home and lives in constant fear of being alone.

- The child refuses to be left alone in a room, accompanying the adult wherever she goes, be it even the bathroom, because of his inability to contain his anxiety or calm down in some other way.

- The child refuses to fall asleep without the presence of a caregiver.

- The child has frequent nightmares relating to separation.

- The child frequently complains about physical pain such as stomach aches, vomiting, or headaches.

CASE STUDY

G., 18 months old, came to our clinic with his parents after 2 months of failed attempts to put him in a day care. He was unable to take leave of his parents in the morning. During our first session, the parents emphasized how anxious G. was when they were away from him. At home, they said he would only stay in the same room that they were in. He would not let them distance themselves from him, be it even to go to the toilet or take a shower. "He needs to maintain constant eye contact with us," said the mother, at exactly which point G. crouched under the therapist's nose, as if seeking to maintain eye contact with her as well. The parents painfully described the traumatic delivery and the cardiac arrest episode that he underwent at home when the mother was with him alone. They mentioned G.'s difficult temperament and his excessive stranger anxiety, which were the hallmark of his entire first year. When they finished their story, the mother added, "I have had my eye on him ever since." To this, the therapist replied with a question: "So you also need to maintain eye contact with him; he's not the only one?" A long silence fell in the room, followed by a new understanding of the separation and loss anxiety shared by the toddler and his parents. We decided to start triadic therapy aimed at increasing the child's independence and his ability to explore his surroundings—in the treatment room initially, then at home—while gradually reducing the parents' anxiety level. Three months into treatment, G. was able to become integrated into day care. This case illustrates the interaction between the parents' separation anxiety and that of the toddler and, hence, the need to treat both.

Phobias

The term phobia, or fears, refers to situations in which a toddler's exposure to an object or to specific circumstances arouses in him an acute and overwhelming anxiety manifested in crying, clinging, panic, or tantrums. The child often freezes or clings to an adult. He will steer clear of any stimuli that are threatening in his eyes. Sometimes, out of love for the toddler or compassion, the parents go along with this avoidant behavior, failing to realize that this only serves to reinforce the disorder and encourage its continued existence. For this condition to be diagnosed as a disorder, one must ascertain that it has existed for at least 4 months.

CASE STUDY

A 2½-year-old girl came in for a psychiatric evaluation because of extreme fear around ants. Her parents reported that she otherwise functioned normatively. During the first meeting, the mother described herself as "fearful," but other than that there was no indication found of psychopathology in the family. Consequently, we suggested targeted behavioral therapy—namely, therapy directed at a single symptom (fear of ants)—based on the principle of desensitizing the toddler to ants through gradual exposure to the terrifying stimulus. First, we drew an ant together with the girl, then looked at pictures of different-sized ants, and read children's books on ants. Finally, we went outside and slowly, gradually, approached an ant nest. This progressive exposure to the threatening stimulus helped the child overcome her anxiety, which went away after eight sessions. It is important to note that after this singular anxiety vanished, none other appeared.

As opposed to a child with Generalized Anxiety Disorder, a child with a phobia goes back to function normatively after the specific symptom is extinguished.

Inhibition to Novelty Disorder

This is a new diagnostic category, which has been added in the DC:0–5 to cover cases of extreme behavioral inhibition that impair the infant's functioning. These infants show an overall, pervasive difficulty to approach new situations, toys, activities, and people: They freeze or withdraw, and they display marked, persistent, and pervasive negative affect. This stands in contrast to the slow-to-warm-up infants, whose reluctance to approach new situations is short in duration. The symptoms of Inhibition to Novelty Disorder cause distress to the infant and her caregivers, and they interfere with relationships with peers and adults and with developmentally expected activities. The infant must be less than 24 months old. A toddler who remains symptomatic past that age will usually display symptoms of the other types of anxiety disorders, especially Social Anxiety Disorder or Generalized Anxiety Disorder, as seen in older children.

CASE STUDY

S., an 11-month-old baby girl, was referred by a Well-Baby community center to our unit because of "extreme passivity and delay in developmental milestones." Unusually, the father was the one who brought the baby to the first consultation session. S. was the only child of a young couple in their late 20s. The mother was described as "shy since forever." The marital relationship was good until the mother got pregnant. Since then, the father was extremely anxious about their baby (he had a history of losses in his family). The mother felt hurt and excluded: "He does not see me anymore; all his attention has turned to S." She reacted by withdrawing from the baby.

The DC:0–5 diagnoses would be as follows:

- Axis I: Clinical Disorders
  - » Inhibition to Novelty Disorder
  - » Relationship Specific Disorder of Infancy/Early Childhood (with mother and father)

- Axis II: Relational Context
  - » Level 3—Compromised to Disturbed relationship with mother and father
  - » Level 3—Compromised to Disturbed caregiving environment

- Axis III: Medical Condition
  - » None

- Axis IV: Psychosocial Stressor
  - » Paternal anxiety disorder

- Axis V: Developmental Competence
  - » Inconsistently present competencies

Both dyadic and triadic psychotherapy took place for almost a year. The paternal anxieties, as well as the mother's poor self-esteem, and their links to the parents' personal history in their respective families of origin were worked through. In parallel, the parents' cognitive perceptions of S. as a weak, almost handicapped, infant were sorted out, and behavioral reinforcements were given to S. to help her become less withdrawn and helpless. A follow-up session at 3 years old revealed a well-developed and functional child, albeit still very shy. She had two good friends in kindergarten, who were also her only playmates. It took her a long time to open up to the kindergarten teacher, and she spoke in a very low voice in the presence of strangers. She did not like going to birthday parties, even her own. She would be diagnosed with Social Anxiety Disorder with mild impairment in functioning. However, the parental and parent–child relationships were stable and healthy.

This case illustrates the biological roots of the Inhibition to Novelty Disorder, as reinforced by anxious parental behaviors and pathological triadic dynamics. The significant improvement at the relational level contributed to lowering the impact of the child's biological vulnerability.

Social Anxiety Disorder (Social Phobia)

Toddlers with Social Anxiety Disorder manifest persistent fear or panic in social situations that expose them to unfamiliar people, including other children. This fear surfaces, for example, during family gatherings, birthday parties, and even during assembly time in day care. On such occasions, the anxiety manifests itself in panic attacks, crying, tantrums, freezing, latching on to an adult, and sometimes even in withdrawal or temporary mutism. These symptoms should be present for at least 2 consecutive months to be diagnosed as a disorder.

As noted earlier, a toddler's social behavior is influenced by his own temperament but also by his parents' social behavior. Murray et al. (2008) observed many toddlers who had this disorder along with their parents. They found that the children's stranger anxiety intensified following a recurring anxious response on the parent's part. In fact, the degree of openness displayed by the parent toward strangers or in new situations is communicated to the baby from birth, reinforcing or weakening his innate biological predisposition to feel safe or apprehensive around strangers—adults and children alike. In their research, Murray et al. (2008) studied a sample of 158 mother–child pairs in which half the mothers had social anxiety. They found that the mothers with social anxiety responded to their child in a unique way, especially if he had an "inhibited" temperament. They did not encourage the child to approach strangers or new social situations, as the other mothers did. Parents with anxiety thus tend to "convey" their anxieties through their own behavior in social situations, and this particularly amplifies the innate vulnerability of their infant with inhibitions.

Selective Mutism

Selective Mutism is a syndrome characterized by total silence in one setting as opposed to free and fluent conversation in others. This syndrome can appear at 2½–3 years old (before the age when Social Anxiety Disorder appears), and some researchers see it as an extreme case of social anxiety. Toddlers who have Selective Mutism are usually shy by nature, and their parents often report that its appearance was preceded by an introverted attitude. Furthermore, 20%–50% of children with Selective Mutism also have late language development. In one study, Cohan and Chavira (2008) looked at 130 children 5–8 years old who had Selective Mutism at a younger age and found that this group could be divided into three clinical subgroups: Selective Mutism accompanied by anxious behavior, Selective Mutism accompanied by oppositional behavior, and Selective Mutism accompanied by language retardation. The third group of children was the most dysfunctional compared with the other two.

As in the case of social anxiety, parents often contribute unintentionally to reinforcing Selective Mutism. They often go along with the child's symptoms — for example, by talking or answering in her stead on all those social occasions in which she decides to remain silent.

CASE STUDY

Y., a 2-year and 7-month-old only daughter of a single mother, was referred to our unit by a Well-Baby nurse. The nurse noticed that the girl kept stubbornly silent every time she came in for a consultation at the Well-Baby center. However, the mother reported that Y. spoke freely at home, even if her vocabulary was poor. The evaluation revealed a highly anxious toddler with language retardation and a socially isolated mother who had social anxiety from a young age. Particularly striking was the mother's refusal to leave the girl at home with a babysitter or any other stranger. We attributed this refusal to a concern the mother had that Y. would go into states of acute anxiety without the babysitter knowing how to calm her.

We started out with dyadic mother–daughter psychotherapy, but Y.'s situation showed no signs of improvement in the first 3 months. We attributed this lack of progress to the difficulty the mother had letting go of her overprotective behavior, and we invited the mother to attend the next session alone. During this session, it turned out that Y.'s Selective Mutism not only reflected a social anxiety set against a hereditary and familial background but also a deeply complicated situation involving a family secret. Y., it transpired, was born of a relationship between the mother and a married man. The man visited their home on a regular basis and knew that Y. was his. Never explicitly told that he was her father, Y. still called him "Dad" a few times, possibly suspecting something, but the mother would quickly divert her attention.

This secret partly accounted for the Selective Mutism and lack of headway in therapy. Y. was not allowed to talk about her family outside of home without the mother's permission. After the therapist was entrusted with the secret, it became possible to start dealing with it—and dealing with family secrets is no easy task. In the end, the fact that the mother revealed her secret to the therapist and contemplated a possible solution, keenly invested as she was in her child's emotional well-being, brought about an improvement in Y.'s condition, and her Selective Mutism resolved. She remained a shy child (as her mother was too).

Generalized Anxiety Disorder

Generalized Anxiety Disorder is defined as the presence of anxiety and worry during most days of the week for at least 6 consecutive months and in at least two settings or different activities in which the toddler takes part. A toddler with this disorder has a hard time containing the anxiety and constantly tries to draw security from the adults around him, becoming very much dependent on them. Generalized Anxiety Disorder is usually accompanied by agitation, fatigue, difficulties concentrating, a low stimulation threshold, tantrums, and difficulties falling asleep.

> *Billy, the hero of Anthony Browne's story* Silly Billy,[5] *was worried about hats, shoes, clouds, rain, giant birds, and much more. However, darkness, strangers, and monsters—which terrify most children—did not worry him. A cloud of worry hung over Billy about common everyday stuff. What did his parents do? His father tried to reason with him and explain the difference between real things and mere figments of the imagination. Billy, however, was not reassured. His mother took a more emotional, protective approach: She declared that they, his parents, would always keep him safe. However, even this solemn promise failed to reassure Billy. One night, when he slept over at his grandmother's house, he confessed his worries to her. His grandma told him that in her childhood she too worried just like him, except that after a while she came up with a way to deal with her worries. Then she rushed into her room and brought out tiny worry dolls, which she entrusted to Billy. What he had to do, she told him, was to share all his concerns with the dolls, then put them under his pillow and fall safely asleep. Worry dolls are special dolls: They worry every night instead of the child so that he may sleep undisturbed. And, indeed, it worked. Yet, after a while, Billy started worrying again: He feared that the worry dolls would not sleep enough and tire. He decided to craft worry dolls for grandma's worry dolls with his own hands; his dolls would worry instead of her worry dolls. Now that he had made the dolls and given them names, he was able to sleep through the night again. Did Billy's worries end there? Would he have to craft dolls for the dolls' dolls? The story does not say.*

Differential Diagnosis of Anxiety Disorders in Infancy

Before determining that an infant or toddler has an anxiety disorder, a clinician must rule out other diagnoses with similar symptoms, such as Acute Adjustment Disorder, Posttraumatic Stress Disorder of Infancy, and Early Childhood Psychosis—a rare disorder that manifests itself in extreme anxiety and a distorted perception of reality. These disorders are characterized by anxiety but also by many other symptoms. Finally, Specific Relationship Disorder of Infancy/Early Childhood is the correct diagnosis if the child's anxiety symptoms

---

[5] Anthony Browne, 2011, *Silly Billy*, published by Walker Books.

are observed only within a specific relational context. Still, it should be emphasized that this diagnosis can co-occur with an anxiety disorder, as shown in the earlier clinical vignette, when some anxiety symptoms occur across all the contexts of the young child's life, whereas other symptoms are only observed in the context of a specific relationship.

Course of Anxiety Disorders From Infancy on

What does the future hold in store for young children with an anxiety disorder? Will they continue to have the disorder in childhood, adolescence, and adulthood? Or will their anxiety retrospectively prove to have been no more than a preliminary expression of other syndromes that they will have developed later in life? An anxiety disorder in infancy, for example, does not predict the appearance of depression in late childhood, whereas an anxiety disorder in childhood does predict the appearance of depression at a later age (Karevold, Roysamb, Ystrom, & Mathiesen, 2009). In their longitudinal study, Karevold et al. (2009) followed the development of 300 boys who had anxiety disorders at 2 years old. On reexamination at 10 years old, only 17% of them still had an anxiety disorder or depression.

Children who had anxiety disorders since infancy tend to be exposed to several risk factors, including an intrusive style of parenting, maternal depression, and problematic familial functioning (Hitchcock, Chavira, & Stein, 2009). This is yet another example of the environment exerting greater influence than genetics at different stages of development and possibly even leading to the persistence or extinction of a disorder appearing in infancy. The existence of a genetic predisposition to a given disorder does not necessarily predict the latter's manifestation in one's lifetime. Moreover, one should keep in mind that whereas most genes become active as life begins—some of them already during pregnancy—others lie dormant for many years. The timing of a gene's manifestation depends on its characteristics and on circumstantial events.

Treatment of Anxiety Disorders in Infancy and Toddlerhood

The professional literature does not provide specific guidelines for treating anxiety disorders in infancy. Treatment is to be conducted as per the general principles for treating early psychopathology (see chapter 17). One must identify parental behaviors that reinforce the child's anxiety, trace them to the source, and try to modify them.

Our clinical experience also indicates the effectiveness of group therapies in treating social anxiety in young children, with parent–infant/toddler groups moderated by one or two therapists. Such treatments have brought down anxiety levels in young children and their parents in a relatively short time. The treatment of choice for specific phobias, however, is behavioral, involving a gradual exposure of the toddler to the frightening stimulus in the presence of the young child's attachment figure. Psychodynamic treatment of severe separation anxiety should also incorporate a behavioral component. Medication for anxiety disorders in infancy and toddlerhood is not recommended other than in exceptional and rare cases in which the child is overwhelmed by anxiety to the point of being unable to function.

Conclusion

Anxiety among young children is widespread and generally a normal developmental phenomenon. However, when its intensity impedes functioning and disrupts everyday life for all members of the family, seeking professional advice might be a good idea to check whether the child has an anxiety disorder requiring treatment. As mentioned, parents often contribute unintentionally to the appearance or persistence of the disorder, which is why the recommendation in most cases is to treat both the parents and the child (dyadic or triadic therapy). Some toddlers continue to have anxiety disorders later in life, mostly when several risk factors—biological, psychological, and environmental—cluster together.

References

Brumariu, L. E., & Kerns, K. A. (2008). Mother–child attachment and social anxiety symptoms in middle childhood. *Journal of Applied Developmental Psychology, 29*, 393–402.

Chess, S., & Thomas, A. (1996). *Temperament.* New York, NY: Brunner-Routledge

Cohan, S. L., & Chavira, D. A. (2008). Refining the classification of children with selective mutism: A latent profile analysis. *Journal of Clinical Child and Adolescent Psychology, 37*, 770–784.

Field, T., Diego, M., & Hernandez-Reif, M. (2006). Prenatal depression effects on the fetus and newborn: A review. *Infant Behavior and Development, 29*, 445–455.

Goldsmith, H. H., & Lemery, K. S. (2000). Linking temperamental fearfulness and anxiety symptoms: A behavior–genetic perspective. *Biological Psychiatry, 48*, 1199–1209.

Hitchcock, C. A., Chavira, D. A., & Stein, M. B. (2009). Recent findings in social phobia among children and adolescents. *Israel Journal of Psychiatry and Related Sciences, 46*, 34–44.

Kagan, J. (1997). Temperament and the reactions to unfamiliarity. *Child Development, 68*, 139–143.

Karevold, K. E., Roysamb, E., Ystrom, E., & Mathiesen, K. S. (2009). Predictors and pathways from infancy to symptoms of anxiety and depression in early adolescence. *Developmental Psychology, 45*, 1051–1060.

Murray, L., de Rosnay, M., Pearson, J., Bergeron, C., Schofield, E., Royal-Lawson, M., & Cooper, P. J. (2008). Intergenerational transmission of social anxiety: The role of social referencing processes in infancy. *Child Development, 79*, 1049–1064.

Nicol-Harper, R., Harvey, A. G., & Stein, A. (2007). Interactions between mothers and infants: Impact of maternal anxiety. *Infant Behavior and Development, 30*, 161–167.

ZERO TO THREE. (2016). DC:0–5™: *Diagnostic classification of mental health and developmental disorders of infancy and early childhood* (DC:0–5). Washington, DC: Author.

Recommended Reading

Beesdo, K., Knappe, S., & Pine, D. S. (2009). Anxiety and anxiety disorders in children and adolescents: Developmental issues and implications for DSM V. *Psychiatry Clinics of North America, 32*, 483–524.

Feng, X., Shaw, D. S., & Silk, J. (2008). Developmental trajectories of anxiety symptoms among boys across early and middle childhood. *Journal of Abnormal Psychology, 117*, 32–47.

CHAPTER 10
I'm Sad

In the book, If My Mom Can't Love Me—Who in the Whole Wide World Ever Can?,[1] *Nurit Zarchi describes a kitten named Petunia whose mother had lost her in the backyard. In the mother's absence, Petunia feels like she has lost her voice and identity, her ability to communicate and call for help, and—hence—her sense of being. Petunia feels that her mother fails to see her and her needs, being always self-absorbed. Worse still, she only sees Petunia's shortcomings: She finds her too big or too small, too silent or too talkative. Moreover, because she is neither seen nor heard, the kitten bursts into tears so bitter that she melts away, turns transparent, and vanishes. It is precisely in this transparent state that she is no longer afraid, because she is invisible, unwanted, unloved, and nonexistent.*

Petunia fades away, and only her tears linger as a silent testimony to her pain. Only after she has disappeared, her mother opens her eyes and sets out to find her. After searching for a long time, the mother finds a tear suspended in midair and licks it with her tongue. Having licked the tear, one of Petunia's eyes appears. Another lick unveils the other eye. Thus, by means of this feline licking, the mother cat makes it possible for Petunia to materialize once again, one step at a time. The instinctive maternal act is what breathes life into the little one, who so craves a mother who can see, watch, and act.

Depression in Infancy: How Is That Possible?

CASE STUDY

Two-year-old H., the youngest of three children, was referred to our unit because of late development of speech, extreme dependence on her mother, and a constantly sad look. During the first session, the mother reported that she was often angry at her girl because she could not stand her "sticky" behavior. She added that the child woke up frequently at night and had no

[1] Nurit Zarchi, 1995, *If My Mom Can't Love Me—Who in the Whole Wide World Ever Can?,* published by Danny Books.

appetite. The mother said she preferred her oldest son to her two other daughters. The father said nothing during the meeting, but he did cooperate.

During the evaluation, H. did not play at all and remained poker-faced; however, she did establish eye contact with the therapist. She gave us the impression of being a highly dependent girl. The more she latched on to her mother, the more the mother tried to fend her off ("I can't stand being touched," she said). Because H. did not talk, it was hard to gauge her level of cognitive development. The diagnosis of severe delay in language develop-ment could not explain why H. stuck so close to her mother, did not play, and kept an unexpressive face.

During the evaluation process, the mother was tense and soon became truly aggressive, manifesting hostility even toward the therapist. "I feel as if I am now in a test, as if you know that I'm going to fail," she said when asked by the therapist to play with the girl and, without even a pause, proceeded to pour out her childhood experiences. She mainly told the therapist about her difficulties learning at school and the rejection she had experienced from her mother. It gradually dawned on us why the mother did not accept her youngest daughter. Indeed, the girl's delayed development reminded her of the failure and rejection she had experienced in her own childhood and made her unconsciously reject her daughter exactly like her mother had rejected her. During that same meeting, the mother confessed to the therapist that she discriminated against H. and often gave her "an educational beating."

Following this revelation concerning the maltreatment of the child, we met with both parents. The father confirmed the mother's maltreatment of their daughter, adding that she maltreated him as well. He further noted that he was also a victim of abuse at home as a child. We reported the family, as required, to the social welfare services. The mother agreed to embark on individual treatment but sometime into therapy had a psychotic-depressive crisis and needed to be hospitalized. The father was left alone with the three kids, and a foster family was appointed to help him take care of them. Paradoxically enough, it was then, with her mother away, that H.'s situation improved. She started to talk (albeit haltingly), play, and display vitality—as if she could be herself for the first time.

This case illustrates how the unique characteristics of a child in a family, in this case a child with significant developmental delays, might arouse feel-ings and behaviors that carry pathological consequences. The awakening of painful unconscious memories in parents might render them seriously dys-functional and cause depression in their offspring. One goal of therapy was, thus, to help the mother free her girl of her pathological projections and to encourage the father to get more involved.

The notion that depression in the first 3 years of life does exist developed many years after researchers had extensive clinical knowledge on depression that appears in childhood and adolescence. Spitz (1946) was the first to write about baby depression. He observed children who grew up in orphanages, having lost their parents to the London Blitz, and described the depression they developed within. He was the first to claim that a baby could die of depression—that depression developed gradually and might lead to absolute wasting away even when a baby was adequately sheltered and fed. Most babies he observed in institutions exhibited indifference, looked sad, did not respond to alternative caregivers, failed to thrive, and had considerable psychomotor retardation. Anaclitic Depression Syndrome, as termed by Spitz, demonstrated that extreme early emotional deprivation negatively affected a baby's emotional and physical development and could even cause death. Interestingly, the same orphanages were also home to several babies who had not developed a depressive state and proved more resilient. For about 30 years, the psychiatric community ignored the existence of depression in infants and young children. Only in 1980 did it start considering the matter. Bowlby (1980) was among the first to describe depression experienced by infants and young children following separation from their parents. Three stages were described: In the first stage, the baby is anxious, protests, cries, and has sleep and eating problems. Next, a full-blown depressive state sets in, and the baby seems to be indifferent to his surroundings and withdrawn. The third stage, named *detachment*, is the child's relinquishment of emotional investment in the lost caregiver and readiness for new attachment relationships. Bowlby described the syndrome precisely, but he too, like Spitz, failed to see depression as anything more than a reactive emotional state brought on by separation from the parent. They did not acknowledge the possibility that depression could appear as a disorder in its own right, independently of separation from the parents.

Kreissler (1985) was one of the first clinicians to think that life-threatening eating disorders in infancy could be an expression of depression. He ran a psychosomatic clinic in Paris and examined babies referred to him by pediatricians who found no physical cause to explain their eating disorders. Kreissler described several cases of psychogenic vomiting that ended up killing infants less than 2 years old. He was the first to introduce the idea of "the baby who does not want to live." Kreissler tried to understand the intrapsychic process that led such a young child to choose death over life. He described it in the spirit of Freudian theory and its distinction between two impulses: *Eros* (the desire to love and live) and *Thanatos* (the desire to die).

Françoise Dolto (1981), a French psychoanalyst, also addressed the issue of "the will to live or die" in young children during the same period. She likewise reported cases of infants and young children who became depressive and even starved themselves to death. Dolto, a Lacanian in her approach, saw the baby as an entity possessing her own free will as early as the fetal stage. She distinguished between babies who "want to come into the world" and those who "do not want to come into the world." According to her, the latter "make" their mother miscarry them. This view did not rely on empirical studies and was never accepted by the scientific community. It is, however, interesting to consider, especially in light of a published study (Pijnenborg, Vercruysse, & Hanssens (2008) on the physiology of birth, which described pregnancy, contrary to conventional wisdom, as a fighting ring pitting the biology of the mother's body against that of the developing fetus's body, a struggle that might endanger the mother's—and sometimes the fetus's—physiological system.

Even though these observations and clinical reports, which attest to the existence of a depressive condition in babies, were already published in the 1980s, too few clinicians are aware of it, even today. Pediatricians faced with babies who show somatic symptoms of depression (e.g., eating problems, sleep problems) often overlook the diagnosis. The possibility that a baby could have depression often does not even occur to them, given their belief that babies cannot "comprehend" that they have cause for sadness and that their level of cognition does not allow this. Many psychoanalysts also share the notion that depression cannot be diagnosed at such an early age for the reason that it reflects a disorder in the formation of the superego, which is not yet developed in the first 3 years of life. This principled objection to the possible existence of a depressive condition in infancy has subsided lately following the publication of studies by Luby and colleagues (Luby, 2009; Luby et al., 2009); they showed that 2½- to 3-year-old children could already present clinical signs of depression. The inclusion of Depression Disorder as a diagnosis in the *Diagnostic Classification of Mental Health and Developmental Disorders of Infancy and Early Childhood, Revised Edition* (DC:0–3R; ZERO TO THREE, 2005) was a substantial step in the process of conceptualizing the clinical cases handled by pediatricians and psychiatrists in numerous countries. Still, and despite the recognition that babies can be depressed, a debate is still ongoing regarding the youngest age at which the term depression can be used to mean the same as it does in adults. According to Guedeney (2007), a depressive state can only be diagnosed beginning at 18 months old, with the appearance of preoperational cognitive ability and the development of the toddler's symbolization ability. Before that age, he suggested using the term "sustained withdrawal."

Michael Ende's The Neverending Story[2] *gives powerful fictional expression to the unconscious presence of depression in children. The book focuses on the personal journey that hero Bastian Balthazar Bux goes through after his mother's sudden unexplained death, which he cannot comes to terms with. His father, a dental technician plunged in grief over his wife's death, withdraws to his work room among the plaster casts of teeth sets, leaving Bastian to face the unresolved loss alone.*

The plot opens with Bastian finding himself in an antique book store face to face with a wondrous book seller, Carl Conrad Coreander. During

---

[2] Michael Ende, 1983, *The Neverending Story*, translated by Ralph Mannheim, published by Doubleday.

this surprise encounter between them, Carl learns that Bastian considers himself a complete failure in all areas of life: He is a pathetic coward, the laughingstock of his friends, a bad student—who repeated a grade—and defenseless against the outside world, which keeps coming at him time and again.

*Yet, despite his impressive list of failures, Carl is able to extract a confession from Bastian about one outstanding talent he had before his mother's death: "I make up stories." Carl then maneuvers Bastian into "lifting" one particular book from his store—*The Neverending Story*—and encourages him to embark on the adventure of reading it. Bastian enters the fictional world of the book to escape reality—the world he cannot figure out. In fact, he steps inside himself, into a world he is not the least bit aware of. The journey into the magical land of Fantastica, where the plot of the book takes place, is thus a journey into the depths of the unconscious. The story begins with a detailed description of "the Nothing," an illness that is constantly spreading throughout the kingdom of Fantastica, reducing to nothing everything it comes into contact with.*

The detailed description of the Nothing's spread in Fantastica reflects what is going on in Bastian's inner world, where depression over his mother's death has taken over his soul. The depiction of the spreading nothingness allows the readers to grasp the harsh nature of the depression and its power and ability to reel in a hopeless child who has lost faith in his ability to live.

At the end of the novel, Bastian leaves Fantastica on his way back to the land of the living. Before taking leave, he jumps into the spring of life, the crystal-clear water; he drinks from the water and scoops up some of it in his hand as a gift for his father. His last wish in the kingdom of Fantastica is to grant his mourning father a present too: water from the spring of life. In the extrafantastical reality, the magical water turns into tears streaming down from the father's eyes when his son returns. Bastian then knows that, despite everything, he has brought his father the Water of Life.

Etiology of Depression in Infancy

The debate surrounding the etiology of depression in infancy is about whether depression at this age can be intrinsic, as in older children, or whether it always comes as a response to external factors. In fact, this question should be raised around any affective or behavioral disorder in a baby. Some researchers have claimed that symptoms in babies are always a response to some serious parental dysfunction and never derive from a primary constitutional disorder. They have argued that it is the negative experiences the baby has had that cause the internalization of problematic interpersonal representations and that lead to changes at the cerebral level. These changes underlie the depressive disorder that will emerge later in life, even if the relationship between the parent and the child improves over time.

The debate still goes on, but the authors of the DC:0–3R and the DC:0–5™: *Diagnostic Classification of Mental Health and Developmental Disorders of Infancy and Early Childhood* (DC:0–5; ZERO TO THREE, 2016) have taken a stand and have determined that depression in babies is to be recorded on Axis I—that is, as a major disorder in babies—even if most cases satisfy the conditions for a comorbid Axis I diagnosis of Relationship Specific Disorder of Infancy/Early Childhood. Let us note that in our 18 years of working with babies, we have never witnessed even one case of a baby having endogenic depression with no external factor to explain it. The main environmental factors responsible for the appearance of a depressive state in babies follow.

Loss of a Parent and Prolonged Grieving

This condition has been named by Spitz (1946) as *anaclitic depression*. Because not every baby who loses his parent develops this extremely severe form of depression, one thought is that those babies who are unable to recover from the loss and reinvest in a new caregiver figure may have a biological—and perhaps even genetic—vulnerability to depression.

Emotional Deprivation and Neglect

An interesting conceptualization of emotional deprivation and neglect was introduced by psychoanalyst André Green (1999). Green coined the term "the Dead Mother" by way of an attempt to describe the clinical condition of psychologically absent mothers. As Green's work shows, the baby identifies with the mother's emptiness to try to stay connected to her. In Green's opinion, this early experience often leads to severe psychopathology of the personality because emptiness becomes a core permanent feature of the person.

Maltreatment

In many studies, researchers have explored the relationship between babies' exposure to maltreatment and domestic violence on the one hand and the appearance of abnormal behaviors as early as infancy on the other hand (see chapter 16). These abnormal behaviors reflect a deep impingement on the baby's basic sense of trust, in both himself and others. This is understandable: The adult, on whom the baby depends so much, had indeed betrayed his trust.

A negative image thus forms in the baby's mind regarding the nature of close interpersonal relations. This manifests itself in various emotional problems, such
as difficulty in forming interpersonal relationships (e.g., aggression toward or
avoidance of other children), poor emotional regulation (e.g., lack of enjoyment
or interest, sudden outbursts of crying or anger), distorted self-development,
poor self-confidence, and lack of vitality. Depression as a result of maltreatment
or neglect takes on various manifestations, such as sadness, disinterest, and
indifference toward the environment as well as aggressive behaviors directed at
oneself or at one's surroundings.

Terminal Medical Illness in the Baby

Golse (2001) studied the depressive behavior of infants hospitalized because
of terminal illness. These babies feel lonely even though their loving parents
are constantly near them, as is currently the practice in all children's hospitals.
Indeed, they sense the despair of the adults—their parents and the staff—who
are preparing for their death (this phenomenon is called anticipated grief).

CASE STUDY

R., a 3½-year-old child, was hospitalized at the pediatric intensive care
unit with a terminal tumor. The pediatrician asked to consult with a child
psychiatrist because R. refused to play and talk even after his physical condition improved somewhat. When the child psychiatrist came to the room, she
saw the child lying motionless in bed. He was staring into space, did not turn
his head to see who was entering the room, and wore a bleak and blank facial expression. He looked like an old man trapped inside a little child's body.
Sitting by his side were both his parents, bleak and disconnected too, each
enveloped in their own mourning, incapable of supporting each other, much
less so their child. Death shrouded them before it even touched the child.
The child psychiatrist tried to talk to the parents and help them process the
ordeal, but to no avail. They found it hard to reconnect with the child only to
lose him for good. The option to treat the child with antidepressants came
up, but he died within a week. The pediatrician was surprised because his
physical condition had been relatively stable. He asked the psychiatrist in
wonder: "Could it be that such a young child felt he had no more chances of
survival?" "Yes," she answered, "he might have seen the abysmal sadness in
the eyes of his parents, who no longer saw him but only the void."

Chronic Physical Pain

Up until 20 years ago, pediatricians took no interest in the effect of chronic
pain on the emotional state of babies, thinking that infants had no memory and
could therefore not remember suffering. Pediatrician Gauvain-Piquard (1993)
painted a picture of the baby's reaction to chronic pain: First, sadness appears,

followed by behavioral withdrawal, and then silence. It is a kind of depressive–autistic state. Following the publication of these observations, most medical centers in Western countries changed their approach to the treatment of pain in babies. It is nowadays customary to administer analgesics to any child, regardless of age, who undergoes a painful medical procedure or who has a chronic illness involving pain.

CASE STUDY

G., a 2½-year-old toddler with terminal renal insufficiency, was referred to us by his nephrologist because of general irritability and refusal to eat. She worried that if he did not put on weight, she would have to postpone the kidney transplant. G.'s schedule revolved around his three weekly dialysis sessions and his even more frequent blood tests. The doctors first thought that he refused food because of his medical condition, but after ruling this out, they suspected an emotional reaction. Indeed, the little boy was afraid of the pain and used to scream each time he was approached by a stranger. His entire universe seemed to boil down to pain and fear. His face was sad and angry. He took no interest in games. Even soap bubbles, a source of delight for almost all children this age, left him indifferent. At times, he would yell, "It hurts, it hurts," even when no one was touching him.

When asked, "Did you try to speak to him about his everyday pain?" the parents answered, "Not at all, he can't possibly understand all these explanations. Plus, he was born into this reality, he's used to it!" The medical team likewise saw no point in speaking to such young children about their illnesses and their constant pain. This attitude changed following G.'s reaction to hearing his pain discussed by the psychiatrist together with the parents and the nephrologist: G. suddenly stopped shouting and turned his head attentively toward the adults. At the end of that meeting, it was agreed that G. would be given analgesics during the dialyses, and after three meetings in which we discussed the illness with the parents and the child, his mood and appetite improved remarkably.

Diagnosing Depression in Infancy

Depression in the first 2 years of life is manifested in a sad facial expression, apathy, psychomotor retardation or agitation, failure to thrive, and lack of responsiveness to the surroundings. In children 3–5 years old, depressive symptoms are similar to those observed in older children with anhedonia (lack of pleasure and interest in activities), dysphoria, irritability, and insomnia as prominent characteristics.

The DC:0–5 provides a clear diagnostic algorithm for diagnosing Depressive Disorder of Early Childhood: Depressed mood or irritability across activities, as well as anhedonia, most hours of the day, most days of the week, for at least 2 weeks are obligatory criteria. In addition, at least two of the following symptoms must be present:

1. Significant change in appetite leading to significant weight gain or loss (5% of body weight within a month).
2. Insomnia or hypersomnia.
3. Psychomotor agitation or sluggishness.
4. Tiredness or lack of energy.
5. Evidence of harboring feelings of low self-esteem or exaggerated guilt feelings, as expressed in play or speech.
6. Diminished ability to think and concentrate, difficulty solving problems, and reduced reactivity to the surroundings.
7. Repeated verbal or behavioral clues suggesting the child's preoccupation with death or suicidal thoughts or, alternatively, attempts by the child to inflict self-damage. This preoccupation with death might find expression in the child's play or in behaviors.

Finally, the criterion of impairment in the child's or family's functioning must be met. Also, caution should be exercised in making the diagnosis in children who are less than 2 years old.

Prevalence of Depression in Infancy

Prevalence rates of depression in 3- to 5-year-old children range from less than 0.5% to 2%. Prevalence rates of depression for children younger than 3 years old are less clear, despite the clear criteria provided by the DC:0–3R. Figures vary quite a bit in different countries and clinical settings. In Portugal, for example, 3% of infants were reported to have depression, compared with only 1.2% in France and 0.5% in our own clinic in Israel. Do these data reflect the true prevalence of the phenomenon? Not necessarily, because frequency of diagnosis often depends on the medical context in which it was established, such as community primary pediatric clinics versus hospital-based clinics specialized in depression.

Differential Diagnosis and Comorbidity

Before diagnosing Depressive Disorder of Early Childhood, one must first rule out medical illnesses such as space-occupying lesions, hypothyroidism, and metabolic disorders. Adjustment Disorder with depressive features needs to be considered if the onset of depression is sudden and follows a specific event. Autism Spectrum Disorder and Posttraumatic Stress Disorder must also be ruled out. Reactive Attachment Disorder should be considered if the child has experienced severe deprivation. Disorder of Dysregulated Anger and

Aggression of Early Childhood should also be looked into, especially if the main symptom is irritability and tantrums. Relationship Specific Disorder of Infancy/Early Childhood may be the diagnosis rather than depression if the symptoms occur only in the context of a specific relationship; however, it may also be a comorbid diagnosis in cases in which the child's depressive symptoms are pervasive across all contexts and the child exhibits additional symptoms only in the context of a specific relationship. Regarding comorbidity, it is quite common among 3- to 5-year-old children with depression to find symptoms of anxiety disorders, Attention Deficit Hyperactivity Disorder, and Disruptive Behavior Disorder.

Course of Depression in Infancy

To the best of our knowledge, there are still no longitudinal studies available that have followed the course of Depressive Disorder of Early Childhood. Still, it seems that in families with a history of Bipolar Disorder, depression at 3 years old could predict the subsequent appearance of an affective disorder (Luby, 2009; Luby et al., 2009).

Treatment of Depression in Infancy

In elaborating the appropriate treatment plan, clinicians need to identify the underlying causes of the depression in the child and aim the intervention accordingly. The indicated treatment is usually dyadic or triadic psychotherapy for both parents and the infant. When one of the risk factors is parental psychopathology, the parent should concurrently undergo individual treatment. When the infant's depression is secondary to parental incompetence, treatment will consist of considering placement outside the home while working with the social welfare authorities. Each case requires a tailored work plan.

Conclusion

In this chapter, we have reviewed the nature of depressive disorders in infancy. We have described how infants and young children can have depression and how their development can be adversely affected by it. We have reviewed issues pertaining to the diagnosis of depression in infancy and presented the DC:0–5 diagnostic criteria. Many questions remain, and all that can be done is to wait for results of long-term studies to come in. Until that time, clinicians can only rely on their experience and on the knowledge built up around depression in older children, adolescents, and adults.

References

Bowlby, J. (1980). *Attachment and loss: Loss, sadness, and depression* (Vol. 3). London, England: Hogarth Press.

Dolto, F. (1981). *Au jeu du désir* (About desire). Paris, France: Editions du Seuil.

Gauvain-Piquard, A. (1993). *La douleur de l'enfant* [The pain of the child]. Paris, France: Calmann-Levy.

Golse, B. (2001). *Du corps a la pensée* [From body to thought]. Paris, France: Presses Universitaires de France.

Green, A. (1999). *The dead mother*. London, England: New Library of Psychoanalysis.

Guedeney, A. (2007). Withdrawal behavior and depression in infancy. *Infant Mental Health Journal, 28,* 393–408.

Kreissler, L. (1985). La clinique psychosomatique du nourrisson [The Psychosomatic Infant Clinic]. In S. Lebovici, R. Diatkine, & M. Soule (Eds.), *Nouveau traite de psychiatrie de l'enfant et l'adolescent* [New treatment of child psychiatry and adolescent] (pp. 1995–2014). Paris, France: Presses Universitaires de France.

Luby, J. (2009). Depression. In C. H. Zeanah, Jr. (Ed.), *Handbook of infant mental health* (3rd ed., pp. 409–420). New York, NY: Guilford Press.

Luby, J., Belden, A., Sullivan, J., Hayen, R., McCadney, A., & Spitznagel, E. (2009). Shame and guilt in preschool depression: Evidence for elevations in self-conscious emotions in depression as early as age 3. *Journal of Child Psychology and Psychiatry, 50,* 1156–1166.

Pijnenborg, R., Vercruysse, L., & Hanssens, M. (2008). Fetal-maternal conflict, trophoblast invasion, preeclampsia, and the red queen. *Hypertension, 27,* 183–196.

Spitz, R. (1946). Anaclitic depression: An inquiry into the genesis of psychiatric conditions in early childhood. *Psychoanalytic Study of the Child, 1,* 47–53.

ZERO TO THREE. (2005). *Diagnostic classification of mental health and developmental disorders of infancy and early childhood* (Rev. ed.). Washington, DC: Author.

ZERO TO THREE. (2016). DC:0–5™: *Diagnostic classification of mental health and developmental disorders of infancy and early childhood* (DC:0–5). Washington, DC: Author.

Recommended Reading

Dollberg, D., Feldman, R., Keren, M., & Guedeney, A. (2006). Sustained withdrawal behavior in clinic-referred and non-referred infants. *Infant Mental Health Journal, 27,* 292–309.

Keren, M., Feldman, R., & Tyano, S. (2003). A five-year Israeli experience with the DC:0–3 classification system. *Infant Mental Health Journal, 24,* 337–348.

Keren, M., & Tyano, S. (2006). Depression in infancy. *Child Adolescent Psychiatric Clinics of North America, 15,* 883–897.

Thompson-Salo, F. (2001). Depression in infants: Research and clinical findings. In F. Thompson-Salo, J. Re, & R. Wraith (Eds.), *Childhood depression: Why is it so hard to understand?* (pp. 26–32). Melbourne, Victoria, Australia: Royal Children's Hospital.

CHAPTER 11
I've Experienced Danger and It's Coming Back to Me

Children's books that touch on trauma are hard to find. Most children's authors avoid writing about the enduring mental pain it causes. However, many stories and poems address physical pain for which an immediate cure is available, such as a kiss from mom, or common developmental fears, such as fear of darkness or a tiger lurking under the bed—fears that can be handled with some parental help. Even books on the trauma of the Holocaust—such as The Island on Bird Street *by Uri Orlev,[1] which describes 5 months spent in solitude by a boy whose mother suddenly "disappears" and who loses his father during a sudden roundup by the Germans—scarcely touch the pain, the anguish, and the enduring depression. We assume that the writers themselves have a hard time facing prolonged mental pain when it comes to children because children are supposed to be well-shielded from the things that adults dread so much.*

Yet, despite the natural reluctance to cause children deep emotional pain, some writers have dared to venture into the realm of pain and to describe a hard emotional experience befalling a child, without offering instant remedy for the pain. Among them is Nurit Zarchi, who deals with hardships that children might be exposed to during their childhood—abandonment, loss, and other pains. Her story, Tinturu: A Tiny Elephant,[2] *is about a 1-week-old female elephant whose mother, Queen Buditza, is captured by poachers in the forest. The grown female elephants around her, all subjects of Queen Buditza, beg Tinturu to join them, but she does not heed their pleas. She stays put, motionless, hoping for the captured mother's return. The female elephants leave without her, and she falls asleep.*

---

[1] Uri Orlev, 1984, *The Island on Bird Street*, translated by Hillel Halkin, published by Houghton Mifflin.

[2] Nurit Zarchi, 1993, *Tinturu: A Tiny Elephant*, published by Hakibbutz Hameuchad.

At dawn, the hunters return, take the tiny elephant, and sell her off to the owners of a famous circus, who jump at the bargain, believing she could bring in substantial profits if only she could stay alive. Tinturu is placed on a rug, and the circus owners offer her a warm bottle of milk, but she is so weak that she is unable to hold on to the bottle's nipple.

This book, like The Neverending Story[3] *discussed in chapter 10, deals extensively with posttraumatic depression: the pain that does not go away, the unbearable loss, the feeling of loneliness and helplessness. Only after the internal world has been described elaborately and very credibly—just like shock is described in medical textbooks—can the slow and winding recovery process begin. Mr. Tenderly, a kind of male version of the mother, pledges to take care of the elephant under two conditions: that he will be her only handler and that she would never again have to perform in the circus. With infinite tenderness, Mr. Tenderly inserts the bottle between the elephant's lips, encourages her to start sucking, and stays by her side all night. At dawn, Tinturu opens her eyes and starts getting back to life.*

Mr. Tenderly sees her through her slow recovery process. He teaches her how to live without her mother, and when he himself gets sick and can no longer tend her, he finds himself a replacement: Milosh, son of the new circus worker, who had acquired his handling education observing Tinturu's slow recovery process.

Milosh, deeply empathetic to the now-recovered elephant, leads her back to the elephant herd. As Tinturu approaches the herd, the elephants make way for her, and all of a sudden she beholds her lost mother.

Nurit Zarchi does not hesitate to describe the little elephant's painful world, yet insists on providing a credible, detailed account of her path toward recovery. Mr. Tenderly and Milosh, who took care of Tinturu in her mother's absence, were able to keep the elephant alive: Love, perseverance, constant physical presence, as well as reliable and repeated treatment by a caregiving figure are all ingredients conducive to the "happy ending" that envelops the readers, protects them, and allays their anxieties. Although the story of the trauma ends in full recovery and rehabilitation, it allows the reader throughout to be steeped in the pain and to identify with it.

---

[3] Michael Ende, 1983, *The Neverending Story*, translated by Ralph Mannheim, published by Doubleday.

Introduction: Babies Remember Traumatic Events

This chapter is devoted to infants' and young children's reactions to stressful situations. This is yet another phenomenon, like depression in infancy, that the professional community is taking a long time to acknowledge. It is still widely held that infants do not remember traumatic experiences and cannot comprehend the notion of danger, and therefore, they cannot develop symptoms of Posttraumatic Stress Disorder (PTSD) because these appear only when the individual realizes the extent of the danger he had been through. Indeed, just 3 decades ago, this disorder was still only diagnosed in adolescents and adults. The first-ever description of possible PTSD symptoms in a young child appeared in 1977, in the case of a 4-year-old child. Following Terr's works (e.g., Terr, 1981, 1988), in which she looked at large samples of children who had lived through natural disasters or man-made accidents and conceptualized the diagnosis of PTSD in early childhood, this subject gained academic acceptance and acknowledgment. In Terr's (1988) study, she described the traumatic recollections of 20 young children who had experienced psychological trauma before 5 years old. This study led her to an understanding that traumatic experiences were quite accurately and reliably inscribed in memory at every age. She then went on to a longitudinal study of children and adolescents who had been through life-threatening events (Terr, 1991). Terr identified two types of PTSD: Type I, characterized by the appearance of symptoms in the aftermath of an isolated traumatic event and by full and detailed recollection of the event, and Type II, characterized by the appearance of symptoms following repeated traumas, including denial, indifference, detachment, and unexplained bursts of anger. N.'s case, described later in this chapter, illustrates Type II PTSD.

Drell, Siegel, and Gaensbauer (1993) looked at a population of youngsters who had experienced trauma in early childhood. Their study suggested that young children mainly remembered traumatic events in their implicit memory. They also showed that the clinical presentations of the disorder in a child depended on the stage of development she was in when the traumatic event hit.

Not all traumatic events necessarily trigger the development of PTSD. Moreover, many years will sometimes elapse before symptoms of anxiety, depression, or serious behavior disorders show up. It is important to note that infants who experience trauma will have a hard time dealing with future traumatic events, even if those are not necessarily related to the first trauma. Furthermore, they are much more at risk for developing PTSD in response to a subsequent traumatic event compared with children confronted with the same adverse event who had not lived through an earlier trauma.

Treating adults has revealed that traumas in infancy are a hefty risk factor for the development of Borderline Personality Disorder, especially if the attachment figure was the one responsible for the trauma. When this happens, the trauma is twofold; the infant not only experiences a significant threat but loses trust in adults, including his parents, who have hurt him instead of protecting him.

Pynoos and his team (e.g., Stuber, Nader, Yasuda, Pynoos, & Cohen, 1991) defined what constitutes a traumatic event for infants and young children: any direct exposure to or witnessing of an event that posed a threat to the physical or emotional integrity of the child or parent. This definition remains acceptable to this day, after Pynoos showed that the foremost risk factor for the appearance of posttrauma was not an event targeting the baby's own body, or one that endangered her life, but the baby's presence in an event threatening her attachment figure. Observations by Scheeringa (2009) of 41 children younger than 2 years old who suffered from PTSD made it possible to describe the range of symptoms that might appear after a traumatic event, going from Acute Stress Disorder to full-blown PTSD. As for the link between the age of the child and the appearance of the symptoms, it was found that toddlers who were 18 months or older at the time of the traumatic event developed posttraumatic symptoms more often than toddlers younger than that age.

Alongside the growing psychological understanding gained regarding the effect of trauma on the emotional development of infants and young children, neurobiological studies using brain imaging have also been conducted. The first works published on the subject showed that exposure to stressful experiences or trauma during the development of the brain might "scar" it in a way that impairs it functionally. Schore (2002) examined in detail the sequence of neurobiological and hormonal events that occur following stress. It is these changes inscribed in the neurobiological systems in the brain that create vulnerability to stressful situations. In other words, it is these changes that will entail an excessive emotional response and the appearance of posttraumatic symptoms if and when the child is exposed at an older age to a new stressogenic situation.

CASE STUDY

N. was referred to our clinic when he was 2 years and 3 months old, the only child of a young divorced mother. He was a restless child who was highly aggressive to everyone. He was also in the habit of spitting on people, saying, "Idiot, idiot" (an unusual phrase at this age, all the more so given his language retardation). He had a hard time separating from his mother in the mornings when she dropped him off at day care. He would not play with his peers, would keep his backpack on all day long in day care, eat little, wake up frequently at night, and refuse to sleep alone in bed. N. also threw many tantrums, which were difficult to calm. During the initial evaluation at our clinic, the mother said that, 5 months earlier, N. had returned from a visit to his dad's house with second-degree burns on his hands. Since then, he had become very agitated, repeatedly saying, "Ouch, ouch" and avoiding the use of his hands and screaming each time he had to be put in the bathtub. These behaviors disappeared after about a month, only to be replaced by the symptoms described earlier. The circumstances of the traumatic event were hazy. The father was suspected of maltreating his son and consequently lost his visitation rights for an indefinite period. As a result, N.'s relationship with him was practically cut off except for a few telephone calls.

During our second session at the clinic, the mother provided the following information: N. was born following a desired pregnancy and normal delivery. He was an accommodating baby, who ate from the breast and had no trouble sleeping. His psychomotor development was within the norm, but his language development was very behind. At 2 years and 3 months old, he pronounced only several words. He never had a transitional object and constantly needed his mother's physical presence to settle down. He stayed at home with his mother up to 2 years old, and he started going to day care 2 months after the incident with the burns. The mother told us how the violent streak in her husband, a suspecting and impulsive man, had already reared its head when she was pregnant. Then, about a month after the birth, when she was about to leave the house with N. in her arms, her husband tried to strangle her. She lost consciousness, and the baby dropped to the ground, losing consciousness for hours. The police arrived, and a complaint was filed against the father. The mother decided to divorce him and return to her parents' home with N. The father was approved for visitation rights and would sometimes take the child. Arguments accompanied by yelling between the parents were routine. At 6 months old, N. saw his father slap his mother and spit on her.

On examination, N. looked normal for his age. He sat on his mother's knees but showed no interest in toys or in exploring his surroundings. He moved his hands freely, and there were no visible scars. N. looked sad and anxious. He established eye contact with the clinician, yet refused to talk or play with her. He kept repeating the words, "Don't want, don't want" while kicking his mother's knees. Suddenly, for no apparent reason, he slapped his mother's face. She responded feebly, "N., that's not nice, I'm angry with you," looking anxious and helpless. N. started screaming, went back to hitting his mother, and threw his bottle, saying, "Idiot, idiot." When the therapist mentioned the father's name, the mother's eyes took on a frightened look and her voice dropped, whereas N. immediately fell asleep. He switched off.

During the next three meetings, N. continued to switch off when hearing his father's name mentioned. What impressed us during these sessions was his restricted play, his sadness and suspicion of those around him, his short attention span, his hypervigilance, his dependence on his mother mixed with his anger at her, and his lack of playfulness and inquisitiveness. The clinical picture was thus rich in symptoms, including the dissociative symptom manifested by N.'s immediate disconnect when hearing his father's name. We also noted the young mother's insecurity and low self-esteem.

The trauma in N.'s case was probably twofold: his exposure over time to the father's physical and verbal aggression toward the mother as well as the real threat to his own bodily integrity. After all, he fell as an infant from his mother's arms when she herself was in danger, and he suffered from burns apparently caused by the father, whether intentionally or by mistake.

The *DC:0-5™: Diagnostic Classification of Mental Health and Developmental Disorders of Infancy and Early Childhood* (DC:0-5; ZERO TO THREE, 2016) diagnoses for N. would be as follows:

- Axis I: Clinical Disorders
  » Posttraumatic Stress Disorder of Infancy
  » Relationship Specific Disorder of Infancy/Early Childhood
  » Neurodevelopmental Disorder—Developmental Language Disorder

- Axis II: Relational Context
  » Level 2—Strained to Concerning relationship with mother
  » Level 4—Disordered to Dangerous relationship with father

- Axis III: Medical Condition
  » Second-degree burns on both hands

- Axis IV: Psychosocial Stressors
  » Direct and indirect exposure to domestic violence
  » Mother's PTSD

- Axis V: Developmental Competence
  » Competencies are inconsistently present in all domains

This case is a relatively common combination of mother and child who both suffer from PTSD. It was evident right from the first meeting that both feared the father. Indeed, whenever his name came up, the mother would fall silent and tighten her hold around N., who, for his part, would immediately fall asleep. Psychotherapy for both mother and child lasted about 1 year. N. remained a vulnerable, tense kid with few friends, although his general functioning improved.

The way in which PTSD will manifest itself in young children depends on how far advanced their competencies are in the following areas:

- *The ability to feel danger through the senses.* This is an innate capability. The baby hears, touches, smells, and sees. Despite being nearsighted at birth, his sight develops to become optimal by 6 months old.

- *The ability to recall the traumatic event.* As mentioned, a baby possesses an implicit memory from birth, even from her fetal stage. One example of this kind of memory in N.'s case is the slap he gave his mother. This slap, replicating the one his father had given his mother in his presence at 6 months old, goes to show that N. had probably internalized the incident, even though he was young. This is an essentially unconscious memory that is registered via the senses and differs from explicit memory, the conscious memory, which first appears at around 18 months old and mature at 3 years old. Terr (1988) found that a young child's memory was behavioral in nature—often recalling the behaviors of those present during the traumatic event better than the event itself.

- *The ability to express emotions.* A baby can express sadness at 3 months old, concern at 4 months old, anger and surprise at 6 months old, and fear at 9 months old. Furthermore, a baby reads his parents' facial expressions and distinguishes between them. What this means is that their fearful facial expression often exacerbates his own fear more than the traumatic incident itself (in N.'s case, the mother's anxiety at the mention of the father's name greatly compounded the toddler's anxiety, which prevented her from offering him the sense of security that he needed so much in those moments).

- *The verbal ability to express emotions.* In Terr's experience (e.g., Terr, 1981, 1988), a toddler is unable to provide a coherent verbal account of a traumatic experience before 28–36 months old.

In sum, the developmental capabilities needed to express the whole gamut of posttraumatic stress symptoms are not present before 9 months old. With that said, these components are not required for an event to be experienced as traumatic or be etched as such into the infant's implicit memory even before she is 9 months old. Tension-filled experiences, stressful situations, and traumatic injury can leave an emotional mark very early, perhaps even as early as the fetal stage.

Incidence of PTSD in Infancy

To the best of our knowledge, no study to date has been published on the prevalence of this syndrome among infants and toddlers. This might be due to clinicians being relatively unaware of the possibility that children that young can be affected by traumatic events.

Diagnosis of PTSD in Infancy

Aggression, irritability, and reduced positive expression of emotions are the most common symptomatic behaviors displayed by young children who have experienced stressors, trauma, loss, or deprivation. These are all nonspecific symptoms and so tracing them back to their etiology is essential for proper diagnosis. It is also important to note that not all infants and young children exposed to trauma, stressors, or deprivation will eventually develop a full-blown disorder. For instance, new fears and fearfulness, the onset of new aggressive and angry behaviors, oppositional behavior, separation anxiety, and developmental regression are all common symptoms brought on by exposure to trauma. It is therefore important to check when each symptom appeared, at what frequency, for how long and with what intensity, and the extent to which it affected the child's functioning. When it comes to infants and young children, this is a particularly challenging task because most of the information comes from the child's parents or other adult caregivers. What makes this difficult is that the caregivers had often experienced the trauma themselves and might therefore, for various reasons, magnify or play down the importance of the symptoms. At times, moreover, they themselves have perpetrated the trauma, which gives them cause to conceal or deny it.

The diagnosis of PTSD in infancy always requires direct or indirect (through witnessing or hearing about) exposure to a terrifying event or series of events, such as abuse, domestic violence, natural disasters, armed conflict, car accidents, as well as painful and frightening medical procedures. The DC:0–5 provides a precise diagnostic algorithm for the diagnosis of PTSD in infancy: The infant must show evidence of re-experiencing the traumatic event(s), persistently attempt to avoid reminders of the trauma, experience a dampening of positive emotional responsiveness, and show signs of increased arousal. Impaired functioning is an obligatory criterion, and the symptoms must be present for at least 1 month following the event(s).

The main difference between PTSD in infancy and in older ages for diagnostic purposes is the emphasis placed on how symptoms are expressed behaviorally in young children as opposed to greater reliance on verbal reports of inner feelings and experiences later on. During our first evaluation of a child and his caregivers, we naturally observe the child's behavior and responses to what is being said and done in the room. This, however, is generally insufficient because most PTSD symptoms appear only when reminders of the trauma trigger distress. Many researchers have deliberated which technique to use to extract memories of a traumatic event from infants and toddlers as well as which technique would elicit the most significant symptoms for diagnosing the disorder, if those exist. Scheeringa, Peebles, Cook, and Zeanah (2001) watched video footage of 15 toddlers who had experienced serious trauma. They examined each video using five different techniques. It was demonstrated that the most effective way to gather diagnostic information for PTSD between 18 months and 3 years was the combination of free play with the parent (or adult caregiver) and trauma-focused play directed by the clinician. Still, it is important to note that optimal procedures for diagnosing PTSD in infants and young children have yet to be officially determined.

In regard to the content of the clinical examination, clinicians must pay attention to the following points:

- *The parents' mental resources and, especially, how they reacted to the child's traumatic experience.* The presence of posttraumatic symptoms in the parent has been proven to increase the risk of PTSD appearing in the infant or young child and has led to the concept of relational trauma. Three types of parental reaction to a traumatic event have been described: (a) withdrawal and avoidance of any type of reminder of the traumatic event, (b) intrusive thoughts, or (c) unconscious replaying of the trauma through dangerous acts.

- *The child's developmental–emotional state, currently and before the traumatic event.*

- *The presence of symptoms of hyperarousal or dissociation.* A variety of dissociative states can be displayed by the child (as well as by the parent), ranging from daydreaming and depersonalization (subjective feeling of estrangement from the self and the environment) to fainting and stupor (shock). The younger the child, the higher her likelihood of responding to a traumatic experience by disconnecting rather than by hyperarousal. Selma Fraiberg (Fraiberg, Adelson, & Shapiro, 1975) described two types of reactions to traumatic situations in babies: At 3 months old, a baby's response is complete avoidance of any threatening environmental stimulus, whereas at 5 months old, he will tend to freeze and remain transfixed when confronted with threatening stimuli.

Differential Diagnosis of PTSD in Infancy

The main diagnoses to rule out include Acute Stress Disorder, anxiety disorders, depression, and Autism Spectrum Disorder. The main determining criterion for diagnosing PTSD rather than other conditions is the presence of a clear traumatic event. It is important to note that when the trauma has been caused by a caregiver, PTSD and Relationship Specific Disorder of Infancy/Early Childhood (or Reactive Attachment Disorder) are noted as comorbid diagnoses.

Risk Factors and Protective Factors for the Development of PTSD Following a Stressful Event

To deepen the understanding of how PTSD develops in infancy, we turn to Sameroff's (2009) developmental model. In this model, the number of risk factors and protective factors in the development of any psychiatric disorder are considered. Hence, in the case of PTSD, the greater the number of risk factors, the higher the chances of a child developing a disorder in the presence of a traumatic event. Conversely, the greater the number of protective factors, the smaller the likelihood of a disorder developing. Thus, the nature of the event is not the only factor that determines whether the disorder will develop. Two children can be exposed to the same event, with only one of them developing PTSD. The risk factors that can set them apart are presented next.

Genetic Make-Up

One of the methods commonly used in medical genetic studies to determine the relative weight of heredity and environment in the appearance of a disorder is to see how prevalent the disorder is in twins. Studies of twins have shown a genetic predisposition to develop PTSD. This hereditary tendency has been found to contribute 30% to the appearance of the symptoms, in particular the neurophysiological ones (Scheeringa, 2009).

The Parents' Response to the Event

As mentioned earlier, Scheeringa (2009) introduced the term of Relational PTSD and proposed a model based on the understanding that PTSD develops within the context of the relationship between the infant or toddler and the parent. This model describes three ways in which this relationship affects the appearance and severity of the symptoms:

- *Moderating parental influence.* Sensitive, containing parents can mitigate the posttraumatic symptoms and even prevent them altogether.

- *Indirect and negative parental influence.* When a parent who had experienced a traumatic event in the child's absence develops posttraumatic stress, her emotional state will particularly impair her parental functioning.

- *Complex parental influence.* When parent and child go through the same trauma, they amplify each other's symptoms. This also happens when the child's posttraumatic symptoms reawaken memories of traumatic experiences from the parent's own past.

N.'s case, presented earlier in this chapter, illustrates how a multiplicity of risk factors (i.e., domestic violence, physical abuse perpetrated by the father, the absence of the protecting parent during the traumatic distressing event, low self-esteem in the mother who suffers herself from PTSD) led to serious symptoms with an overall detrimental effect on the child's development and functioning.

Some protective factors that may prevent the development of PTSD despite a child's exposure to a traumatic event include the following:

- *The child's physical proximity to the parent at the time of the trauma* (proximity to the attachment figure, in accordance with the attachment theory).

- *Family, community, and social support for the family.*

- *Adequate familial functioning.* A close link was found to exist between familial dysfunction and the appearance of severe symptoms in young children who had been through trauma. The dysfunction may be due to the presence of PTSD in the parents themselves. The impact of parental PTSD on the young child depends on whether the sick parent is the father or the mother. In paternal PTSD, the symptom that affects the child the most is depression, often accompanied by bursts of anger and violence, whereas the impact of maternal PTSD is mediated by the mother's low self-esteem as a protective figure for her child. Finally, the family's socioeconomic status has been shown to be an additional risk factor for the development of PTSD following a traumatic event.

- *Gender.* Girls are reported to be more susceptible than boys to developing PTSD, and their PTSD lasts longer. One example illustrating this is the collapse of the Buffalo Creek dam, a national disaster that occurred in the United States in 1972. Of 207 minors examined following the event, 32% were found to suffer from PTSD. Seventeen years later, 100 of the sample's children were reexamined, and only 7% of them still had the disorder—all of them women. There is no sure explanation for this difference between the sexes in their reaction to stressful situations. One hypothesis put forward suggests a structural and functional difference in the brain and the endocrine system.

The following case illustrates how different protective factors prevent the development of PTSD in infancy.

CASE STUDY

P., a 2½-year-old toddler, was seriously injured in her abdomen during a suicide bombing. The mother, who was pregnant at the time of the attack, was also badly hurt, in her arm, but was not separated from her daughter following the blast. The girl did not lose consciousness, but she was also unaware of all that was going on around her or the injuries sustained by her mother and others. The mother did not panic, took the girl in her arms, and ran to the ambulance. They arrived together at the emergency room. The mother never left her side for a second.

P. was a healthy toddler. Her development was normative, and relationships within the family were stable. Although she was a bit "spoiled" at home, her functioning in day care was perfectly normal.

The girl was addressed to our clinic to have her mental health status evaluated at the request of the hospital medical team shortly after the operation she underwent. The evaluation showed up symptoms of Acute Stress Reaction (agitation, startle response on hearing ambulance sirens, and separation anxiety), but these disappeared within a month of the injury. P. did not develop PTSD. In a follow-up consultation 3 months later, it turned out that the mother had developed delayed PTSD after giving birth. P. had not developed the disorder, but she did display symptoms of anxiety and anger, by way of an expected reaction to her mother's disturbed emotional state and the birth of her brother.

Some protective factors present around the traumatic event can account for P.'s relatively good emotional state. First, there is the fact that the mother had immediately grabbed the child and removed her from the scene. Second, the family had normative functioning before the event. Finally, the family received significant communal support after the event and had the beneficial presence of the father. These protective factors were so significant as to outweigh the risk factors (the mother's incapacitated arm and the PTSD she developed several months after giving birth to her second child).

The specific response of each child will thus depend on many factors. The presence of PTSD in one of the parents may often be more harmful than the infant's or young child's actual exposure to the traumatic event. This explains why most infants and young children involved or injured in accidents or terrorist attacks develop posttraumatic symptoms only when their parents reacted likewise.

Long-Term Consequences of Stressful Events in Infancy

In regard to the long-term consequences of the disorder, a distinction should be made between the impact of an isolated stressful event and that of continuous and severe stress. Studies on adults who had experienced a one-time stressful event in childhood showed that even though some of them developed symptoms years after the fact, they fared better than adults who had experienced chronic abuse or neglect in childhood.

Principles of Treatment of PTSD in Infancy

Parent–infant psychotherapy is the most recommended and common course of action when it comes to psychopathology in infancy, particularly in the case of PTSD, given its relational aspects described earlier. Only a few controlled studies have been published on the effectiveness of different parent–infant therapeutic approaches for treating PTSD in infancy. Lieberman and Van Horn (2008) developed a unique therapeutic method for young children who had lived through one or more traumatic events, called trauma-focused Child–Parent Psychotherapy. The core principle behind this method is the necessity to talk about everything that had happened in clear terms in the presence of both the young child and his parents, and to establish the connection between his symptoms and the traumatic experience.

The therapist's empowerment of the parent is critical in reducing the parent's feelings of helplessness with respect to the situation. One example of this is

N.'s case, described earlier in the chapter. As long as the mother was unable to deal with the anxiety that each mention of the father aroused in her, the toddler too continued to respond with repeated dissociative spells. The more she managed to calm down and gradually become a more containing figure, the child's symptoms became less frequent until they disappeared outright.

Along the therapeutic process, therapists strive to combine stress-soothing methods for both parents and child, together with desensitization methods targeting situations reminiscent of the traumatic experience. The therapist and the parents recreate the experience of the traumatic event through play, and while so doing, alternative, more positive scenarios are offered to the child to open a gateway to recovery and hope. For example, a game that reenacts a deadly accident will end well with the passengers being saved and gradually restored to normal function. This technique helps not only the toddler but her parents too. Also, one has to keep in mind that young children do not have the cognitive ability to place the traumatic event in time or understand that the images that come back to them belong in the past. They experience them as if they were taking place here and now. Therapy helps the child to differentiate between what happened in the past and what she is experiencing in the present. An article by Terr (1981) provides an example of such a treatment, involving a 2-year-old girl who had witnessed her parents murder her baby sister. Therapy continued until she was 14. This article describes how the adoptive mother learned to play with the girl. Playing together built a relationship of trust between them, which allowed them to deal with difficult events from the past.

Schechter et al. (2006) developed a treatment method specifically designed for mothers who suffer from PTSD following violence directed at them by their husbands. Among other things, these mothers find it difficult to tolerate their baby's crying, which serves as an unconscious reminder of their own traumatic experiences. Their past gets mixed up with the present reality. Consequently, these mothers may perceive their baby as "persecutory" and lose their reflective ability. They feel threatened and only want to ignore the crying or leave the room. They sometimes experience the baby as the most significant stressor in their lives. The treatment approach proposed by Schechter et al. is called Clinical Assisted Videofeedback Exposure Session. This is a targeted, short-term treatment aimed at changing the mother's persecutory perception of her child and developing "reflective functioning." During the first session, the mother–infant interaction is videotaped. They start off with free play between them, after which the mother leaves the room, then returns, and finally they tidy up. After the session, the therapist selects four segments from the film: one that records a positive moment (a moment of joy, joint attention, spontaneity, reciprocation), one that records the moment of separation, one that records the moment of reunification, and one where the mother has a hard time self-regulating. Mother and therapist watch these segments together, and the mother is asked to answer questions relating to empathic insightfulness and reflective functioning, such as the following: What do you think happened here? What do you think your child was thinking at this precise moment? What did he feel? What were you thinking at this point? What are you feeling now when watching the recording? Why do you think I chose to screen this particular segment?

Watching the recording exposes the posttraumatic mother to both the moments in which the child experienced distress—such as the moments of separation—and the good moments shared between them. The mother learns to listen to the baby, to interpret her crying correctly in times of distress, and to understand her and the unique language in which she communicates with her, and their situation slowly improves.

> It sometimes takes a long time, almost a lifetime, until the repressed stuff of trauma resurfaces into consciousness. Writers who experienced trauma early on in life struggle mightily to process it and deal with it in their work. Amos Oz, for example, was able to describe the suicide committed by his mother, Fania, during his childhood only when he was 60 years old. Even though his earlier books indirectly and implicitly describe how the mother's desertion affects a child (e.g., his story The Hill of Evil Counsel[4]), he avoided a head-on confrontation with the great pain he experienced in his childhood.

> It was only in 2002 that Amos Oz published his autobiographic novel, A Tale of Love and Darkness, with his mother's figure at its center. In it, he describes the lengths to which he would have gone to prevent his mother's suicide if only he had been there with her in the room. He would have tried to reason with her, and if that failed, he would have shamelessly attempted to make her take pity on him by crying, pleading, and hurting himself. He might even have pounced on her to physically neutralize her and destroy all those pills and tablets that might serve her in the act.[5]

> The boy, however, was not there when she committed suicide, and he was not even allowed to attend the funeral, all of which seems to have only magnified the trauma he experienced. The pain remained blocked and locked away inside him in all its intensity.

---

[4] Amos Oz, 1978, *The Hill of Evil Counsel*, translated by Nicholas de Lange, published by Harcourt Brace Jovanovich.

[5] Amos Oz, 2005, *A Tale of Love and Darkness*, translated by Nicholas de Lange, p. 516, published by Vintage Books.

Conclusion

Even today, there is still not enough awareness that PTSD can appear in the first 3 years of life. This lack of awareness is visible in the scientific domain as well as in the world of books for children. In this chapter, we tried to show that infants and young children can actually be affected in their functioning by various events threatening their own bodily or emotional integrity or that of their caregivers. We have emphasized the crucial role of the parent–child relationship in the emergence of PTSD. We also established the importance of the child's stage of development and showed the extent to which it influences not only the emergence of PTSD but its expression as well. We listed the risk factors and protective factors at play in the development of the disorder, and we pointed out the adverse effects that trauma might have in the long run—in both psychological and neurobiological terms. We hope that following the exposure to these data, public health early childhood practitioners and pediatricians might become more sensitive to the existence of PTSD in infancy and to the great importance of its early detection and treatment.

References

Drell, M. J., Siegel, C. H., & Gaensbauer, T. J. (1993). Posttraumatic stress disorder. In C. H. Zeanah, Jr. (Ed.), *Handbook of infant mental health* (pp. 291–304). New York, NY: Guilford Press.

Fraiberg, S., Adelson, E., & Shapiro, V. (1975). Ghosts in the nursery: A psychoanalytic approach to the problem of impaired infant–mother relationships. *Journal of the American Academy of Child Psychiatry, 14,* 387–422.

Lieberman, A. F., & Van Horn, P. (2008). *Psychotherapy with infants and young children—Repairing the effects of stress and trauma on early attachment.* New York, NY: Guilford Press.

Sameroff, A. J. (2009). *The transactional model of development.* Washington, DC: American Psychology Association.

Schechter, D. S., Myers, M. M., Brunelli, S. A., Coates, S. W., Zeanah, C. H., Jr., Davies, M., . . . Liebowitz, M. R. (2006). Traumatized mothers can change their minds about their toddlers: Understanding how a novel use of videofeedback supports positive change of maternal attributions. *Infant Mental Health Journal, 7,* 429–448.

Scheeringa, M. S. (2009). Posttraumatic stress disorder. In C. H. Zeanah, Jr. (Ed.), *Handbook of infant mental health* (3rd ed., pp. 345–361). New York, NY: Guilford Press.

Scheeringa, M. S., Peebles, C. D., Cook, C. A., & Zeanah, C. H., Jr. (2001). Towards establishing procedural, criterion, and discriminant validity for PTSD in early childhood. *Journal of the American Academy of Child and Adolescent Psychiatry, 40,* 52–60.

Schore, A. N. (2002). Dysregulation of the right brain: A fundamental mechanism of traumatic attachment and the psychogenesis of posttraumatic stress disorder. *Australian and New Zealand Journal of Psychiatry, 36,* 9–30.

Stuber, M. L., Nader, K., Yasuda, P., Pynoos, R. S., & Cohen, S. (1991). Stress responses after pediatric bone marrow transplantation: Preliminary results of a prospective longitudinal study. *Journal of the American Academy of Child and Adolescent Psychiatry, 30,* 952–957.

Terr, L. C. (1981). "Forbidden games": Posttraumatic child's play. *Journal of the American Academy of Child and Adolescent Psychiatry, 27,* 96–104.

Terr, L. C. (1988). What happens to early memories of trauma? A study of 20 children under age five at the time of documented traumatic events. *Journal of the American Academy of Child and Adolescent Psychiatry, 27,* 96–104.

Terr, L. C. (1991). Childhood traumas: An outline and overview. *American Journal of Psychiatry, 148,* 10–20.

ZERO TO THREE. (2016). *DC:0–5™: Diagnostic classification of mental health and developmental disorders of infancy and early childhood* (DC:0–5). Washington, DC: Author.

Recommended Reading

Azarnow, J., Glynn, S., Pynoos, R. S., Nahum, J., Guthrie, D., Kantwell, D. P., & Franklin, B. (1999). When the earth stops shaking. *Journal of the American Academy of Child and Adolescent Psychiatry, 38,* 1016–1023.

Green, B. L., Lindy, J. D., Grace, M. C., & Winget, C. (1990). Buffalo Creek survivors in the second decade. *American Journal of Orthopsychiatry, 60,* 43–54.

Keren, M., & Tyano, S. (2009). A developmental approach: Looking at the specificity of reactions to trauma in infancy. In D. Brom, R. Patt-Horenczyk, & J. D. Ford (Eds.), *Treating traumatized children: Risk, resilience and recovery* (pp. 85–101). East Sussex, England: Routledge Press.

Laor, N., Wolmer, L., Mayes, L. C., & Gershon, A. (1997). Israeli preschool children under Scuds: A 30-month follow-up. *Journal of the American Academy of Child and Adolescent Psychiatry, 36,* 349–356.

Lieberman, A. F., Compton, N. C., Van Horn, P., & Ghosh Ippen, C. (2003). *Losing a parent to death in the early years: Guidelines for the treatment of traumatic bereavement in infancy and early childhood.* Washington, DC: ZERO TO THREE.

Lieberman, A. F., Van Horn, P., & Ghosh Ippen, C. (2005). Towards evidence-based treatment: Child–parent psychotherapy with preschoolers exposed to marital violence. *Journal of the American Academy of Child and Adolescent Psychiatry, 44*, 1241–1248.

Osofsky, J. D. (2004). *Young children and trauma: Intervention and treatment.* New York, NY: Guilford Press.

Schechter, D. S. (2004). How post-traumatic stress affects mothers' perception of their babies: A brief video feedback intervention makes a difference. *ZERO TO THREE Journal, 24*(3), 43–49.

Scheeringa, M. S., & Zeanah, C. H., Jr. (2008). Reconsideration of harm's way: Onsets and comorbidity patterns in preschool children and their caregivers following Hurricane Katrina. *Journal of Clinical Child and Adolescent Psychology, 37*, 508–518.

Scheeringa, M. S., Zeanah, C. H., Jr., Myers, L., & Putnam, F. W. (2004). Heart period and variability findings in preschool children with posttraumatic stress symptoms. *Biological Psychiatry, 55*, 685–691.

CHAPTER 12
I Pull My Hair Out

An Infant/Toddler Pulls His Hair Out, Really?

CASE STUDY

R., a 1-year and 8-month-old toddler, was referred to our clinic with both his parents because of sleep difficulties and self-hair-pulling, which caused some bald spots on his scalp. His parents never saw him in the act, but they would find lumps of hair on his pillow in the morning.

R., the couple's only child, was born following a planned, desirable pregnancy. His birth, however, was experienced as a traumatic event for his parents. His mother fell ill immediately following the delivery, and she had to be hospitalized during his first months of life. Her mother-in-law took care of the baby. The mother felt anxious, desperate, and even angry with her husband and mother-in-law for "tearing the baby away from her." She felt they had spoiled her initial bonding with him. Considerable tension built up between the mother and her in-law around the best care for the baby, and the father was caught in the crossfire.

During the evaluation session, R.'s "slow-to-warm-up" temperament was the only finding. No difficulty in sensory processing was observed. The mother's parenting behaviors were based on her wish "to always be there for him, to make it up to him for her absence at the dawn of his life." Still, the mother–infant relationship did not meet the criteria for being diagnosed as disordered. The father, very much involved in R.'s upbringing, seemed far less anxious than his wife but also less inclined to show emotions. The mother said she had grown up in a "loving and stifling" family, whereas the father said that his was a family "with formal relationships, where emotions were not discussed too much."

The triadic therapy (father–mother–child) spanned five sessions, during which it transpired that the mother still held a grudge against her husband for the paternalistic attitude he had taken with her when he decided what was good and what was bad for her. In fact, the spouses had never discussed these hard feelings between them. They had adopted a pattern of "not talking about negative emotions." Following the therapy sessions, the tension between them dissipated, following which R. stopped pulling his hair and could give direct verbal expression to his frustrations and angers.

The *DC:0-5™: Diagnostic Classification of Mental Health and Developmental Disorders of Infancy and Early Childhood* (DC:0-5; ZERO TO THREE, 2016) diagnoses for R. would be as follows:

- Axis I: Clinical Disorder
  » Trichotillomania

- Axis II: Relational Context
  » Level 2—Strained to Concerning mother–infant relationship
  » Level 2—Strained to Concerning caregiving environment

- Axis III: Medical Condition
  » Alopecia areata

- Axis IV: Psychosocial Stressor
  » Posttraumatic delivery

- Axis V: Developmental Competence
  » Functions at age-appropriate level in all domains

Trichotillomania, or the impulse to pull out hairs from one's head and sometimes eyebrows, was first described in 1889 by French dermatologist Hallopeau. It appears to be a more common disorder in boys up until 6 years old, then becoming more prevalent in girls (2.5 times more). It usually starts in childhood and adolescence and is much less frequently seen in adulthood. More recently, this phenomenon is also being witnessed in children younger than 3 years old.

Our clinical experience, spanning some 50 cases we have handled to date, has taught us that hair-pulling in infancy is often a complex phenomenon requiring intensive psychological treatment rather than a self-limited habit as it is often perceived by pediatricians and pediatric dermatologists.

The Symbolic Meaning of Hair in Human Civilization

Hair-pulling in infants and young children is surely an intriguing symptom, which leads one to wonder whether it has symbolic meaning. First, hair has a social value, which varies across cultures. For example, its length, arrangement, and care usually serve to differentiate men and women. Each culture and period has its own codes related to gender. Hair has also been a sign of rebellion against parents and bourgeois society, like the one carried out by the hippie generation.

At the individual level, a woman's hair is part of sexuality. Some religions require that women cover their head to tone down their sexual attraction and the temptation that men cannot resist.

An avatar of the religious conception can be found in the Brothers Grimm's Rapunzel. *The tale describes the fatal encounter between the young*

Rapunzel and the prince, a story that starts with erotic hair and ends in the matrimonial bed.

Rapunzel is locked away in a high tower by a witch to keep her forever in her exclusive custody. Only the witch can reach her by scaling the girl's golden hairs. A prince who passes by is enchanted by Rapunzel's singing. He imitates the witch's voice, upon which the girl unfurls her hair to let the "witch" up. The prince then climbs the golden "ladder" to her room. Their encounter culminates in a marriage proposal on his part, which she instantly accepts.

Religion also has a say about the male hair: A man in mourning is not allowed to shave—as a symbol of preoccupation with the loss—and rabbis are not allowed to shave out of awe before God. The biblical story about Samson states, "and no razor shall come on his head, for the child shall be a Nazarite unto God from the womb" (Judges 13:5). Samson breaks his commitment to God because he succumbs to his desire for Delilah. He has lost his spiritual potential to his corporeal need for intimacy and love for a woman. In fact, Samson's hair also symbolizes his supernatural power: "If I be shaven, then my strength will go from me, and I shall become weak, and be like any other man" (Judges 16:17).

Finally, from a medical perspective, hair reflects growth and health. Indeed, the baby's hair is transformed into a good head of hair during his first years of life. Serious physical illnesses, medications, and lack of vitamins have a detrimental effect on the hair.

Causes of Trichotillomania in Infancy

The few studies concerned with the etiology of trichotillomania have distinguished between the disorder's early and later appearance. Several theoretical approaches have tried to explain the reasons underlying the disorder regardless of the age when it appears.

According to the psychodynamic approach, hair-pulling comes from auto-erotic self-soothing impulses or aggressive impulses toward the parent. Under this theoretical conception, trichotillomania is a behavioral manifestation of a primary disorder in a mother–child relationship characterized by ambivalence and aggression, reflecting a conflict between the mother's narcissistic needs and the child's needs for closeness. The term "hair-pulling symbiosis" appears in the literature regarding mothers and daughters whose pathological relationship is characterized by nonseparation and ambivalence or by love–hate relations. The anxiety that goes along with this dynamic pushes the girl to calm herself through auto-erotic behavior—that is, tearing her hair, the object that she has in common with her mother. This explanation, however, is not necessarily relevant to all cases of trichotillomania. In 1978, Aleksandrowicz and Mares reported the case of a 2½-year-old girl who used to pull out her hair and swallow it to the point of having a trichobezoar—a ball of hair in her stomach. The child, desired and loved by her parents, had started to rip her hair when she was 1 year old. Her parents seemed to function normally, and the relationship between them was apparently good. The hair-pulling started when the mother became pregnant for a second time. The authors of the article explained the trichotillomania as the girl's reaction to her narcissistic injury occasioned by the loss of her exclusive relationship with her mom. Her omnipotence fantasies were thus shattered all at once during the pregnancy of her little brother. These explanations, however, do not answer the question why the girl "chose" the hair-pulling symptom of all things. After all, she could have expressed her angers in other ways, such as refusing to eat or refusing to be toilet-trained.

Another approach regarding the etiology of trichotillomania is based on the theory of learning, according to which trichotillomania reduces the intensity of the tension felt, whatever its source. Initially, a child will often automatically go through the motion of pulling her hair out while sucking on her finger or drinking from a bottle. This habit is liable to turn into a symptom when she finds herself in a state of anxiety, discomfort, or anger. Hair-pulling will then become her first go-to means of relaxation.

A third approach, the neurobiological one, sees trichotillomania as a form of Obsessive Compulsive Disorder or motor tic. This approach has been adopted by the DC:0–5 and the *Diagnostic and Statistical Manual of Mental Disorders* (5th ed.; DSM–5; American Psychiatric Association, 2013), which classify trichotillomania under the category of Obsessive Compulsive and Related Disorders.

Our clinical experience has taught us that, sometimes, babies play with their mother's hair during breastfeeding, and then, when weaned off the breast, they express their anger at being "torn away" from it by tearing out their hair.

It seems difficult to come up with a single explanation for all cases of trichotillomania in infancy. Our suggestion is, therefore, to try to understand the causes of each individual case and offer treatment accordingly. In our clinical experience, the quality of the relationship between the parent and the young child appears to play an important, if not decisive, role in many cases of trichotillomania. This still does not explain why the child should choose to express the difficulty in his relationship with his parents with such peculiar behavior such as hair-pulling. Why not express his aggression openly?

In our clinical work over the years with these cases, we have observed that most cases of trichotillomania involved a significant difficulty in talking about negative emotions as a family, coupled with an environmental stressogenic factor such as marital tension, relocation, the birth of a brother or sister, or unresolved losses in the parents' past. For example, in the vignette in the beginning of this chapter, the parents preferred not to express their true feelings to "keep the peace within the family." This, in turn, had taught the child not to aggravate his parents. Indeed, his hair-pulling diminished the more he allowed himself to express direct aggression.

It would thus seem that trichotillomania in young children might express a combination of several factors: neurophysiological factors, aggressive impulses toward the parents because of difficulties in the parent–child relationship, and parental oversensitivity to manifestations of aggression. Clearly, a controlled study must be undertaken to validate or refute this hypothesis.

Diagnosing Trichotillomania

Trichotillomania in adults was listed as a disorder under the heading of Anxiety Disorders in the *Diagnostic and Statistical Manual of Mental Disorders* (4th ed., text rev.; DSM–IV–TR; American Psychiatric Association, 2000). Now, in the DSM–5, as well as in the DC:0–5, it appears under Obsessive Compulsive and Related Disorders.

At the clinical level, two types of trichotillomania have been described: the focused type and the automatic type. Children classified under the former appear tense before and relieved after having pulled their hair out. They are often angry and particularly more so when prevented from doing the act. The automatic type of hair-pulling is more prevalent than the first. It usually takes place when the child is lying in bed, watching television, or sucking her thumb. It is an involuntary activity, which means that the child's attention can be distracted away from it by offering her another activity or by paying her positive attention.

The diagnostic process for trichotillomania should include the following components:

- Characterization of the parent–child relationship and the family's communication patterns.

- Identification of stressogenic factors that may have triggered the development of the symptom.

- Identification of the situations in which the symptom manifests itself—such as in front of television, lying in bed, or sucking a thumb—and whether it is the focused or the automatic type.

- Identification of the symptom's influence on the different aspects of the family's life.

Treatment Methods

There are three principal approaches to treating trichotillomania in infancy: the psychodynamic approach (dyadic, triadic, or family psychotherapy, depending on the dynamics of each individual case), the behavioral approach (which tries to prevent the act or to modify the habit), and a "hybrid" approach combining psychodynamic and behavioral components. There are still no comparative studies on these three types of treatment. It would seem, though, that behavioral treatment is effective when no major familial psychopathology is present; these are the cases usually treated by pediatricians or dermatologists. By contrast, most cases that come to us usually require recourse to psychodynamic therapy focused on the parent–child relationship.

Regarding the common question of whether to focus on the disorder in the parent–child relationship or on the symptom itself, we recommend adopting a bidimensional approach to treat both the problem in the parent–child relationship and the actual trichotillomania, paying particular attention to the difficulties both parents and child have directly expressing their negative feelings.

Of the two types, the automatic type of trichotillomania is easier to treat, and behavioral treatment is often the most effective. The focused type is often more complex and harder to treat, and it usually requires a combination of dynamic psychotherapy and behavioral guidance. The following case illustrates the complexity of treating trichotillomania during infancy.

CASE STUDY

G., a 1-year and 11-month-old toddler, was referred to our clinic because of hair-pulling that started about a month and a half earlier. At the start of the session, the parents were unable to recall any discernible factor that had preceded the symptomatic behavior, but as we went deeper, it turned out that the hair-pulling started at a time when her father was preoccupied with his parents' divorce. G.'s parents noticed that she stuck too much to her mother, but they never associated this with the hair-pulling. Before the development of the trichotillomania, G. exhibited no inclination to play with her or other people's hair. The parents told us that the hair-pulling mainly occurred when she was sucking her thumb or lying down to rest or sleep (the automatic type of trichotillomania). G. also started pulling her dolls' hair out, and hair was also found in her feces, indicating a habit of swallowing it.

G., the third of three children, was born after a planned, normal pregnancy. Delivery was spontaneous and uncomplicated. Her mother said that she had felt nervous after the birth because she found herself home alone with her three children. Her husband was at work most of the time. She wanted to breastfeed G. all through the first year, but she was forced to stop after 4 months because of milk shortage. She described G. as "too good a

baby," who ate well and did not cry one bit, even when hungry. G.'s development was normative, except for slight retardation in language development.
The mother expressed worry only over the quality of her sleep. G. never
slept through the night. She would fall asleep on her own, but she would often wake up, drink milk, and stay in her parents' bed until morning. Notably,
G. never had a transitional object, and the mother's explanation for this
surprised us: She did not want G. "to become attached to an object because
she might lose it." Instead of a transitional object, the mother used milk bottles to calm her. G. spent her first year of life at home with her mother, her
exclusive caregiving figure.

The name given to the girl conjured up "the ghosts in the nursery"
(i.e., those hard experiences from a parent's past that continue to affect her
perception of her infant into the present). During her pregnancy, the mother
had a nightmare in which G. was choking, and she, her mother, rushed to
save her. When she got to G.'s bed in her dream, the mother discovered her
grandmother lying in it, dead, with her face covered. She interpreted the
dream as a sign that she needed to name her daughter after the late grandmother. Nevertheless, the parents decided on a neutral name for their girl.
They felt that the parents' families on both sides had a difficult history of
illnesses, losses, and tough separations, and they hoped to lift the "curse" in
this way.

G.'s father grew up in an overly protective family atmosphere. He remembered being his parents' favorite, but at the same time he described how his
parents always pretended that all was well in their life. Thus, for example,
they never discussed difficulties he had at school together, and he never told
them about his feelings of loneliness. The "happy" façade and the feeling
that "all is hunky-dory" started to disintegrate when he himself was married.
His parents divorced, and it was around that time that G.'s trichotillomania
began. G.'s father took on the role of mediator in his parents' divorce. He
was too much invested in the life of his family of origin at the expense of his
involvement in his nuclear family and their needs. His wife was angry with
him, but she did not dare express it openly. She too had a hard childhood.
Her parents died when she was a little girl, after which she moved in with her
aunt. The aunt had three children of her own, and hers was a loving family,
but not one given to expressing emotions. G.'s mother secretly developed
feelings of inferiority and jealousy toward the aunt's children, and she
privately grieved her parents' death every night. In fact, the grieving never
ended, and to this day she sometimes experiences serious crying bouts,
accompanied by a need to be alone.

During the first evaluation at our clinic, G. appeared to be age-appropriately
developed. Initially, she stayed close to her mother, checked out the therapist
and the room, and smiled from afar. After taking a good while to "warm
up," she set out to explore the toys in the room and hesitantly approached
the therapist. While her parents were busy describing their families and
personal difficulties, G. demonstratively ignored her father (who did not
lend her any attention either) and drew near her mother. She tried to grab
her attention, with little success. G. was incredibly attentive to the mother's

facial expressions, and when the mother started crying, G. too showed signs of distress. She handed her mother a tissue and sat close to her. No less astounding was to see the parents' lack of involvement with G. She sat down alone and played joyfully with a doll. During the second session, the mother was instructed to play with the girl as she usually does, and 10 minutes of that play were videotaped. The mother looked sad during the game, distanced at times and intrusive at others. There was no mutual enjoyment observed or physical closeness between the two. The mother did not join in G.'s symbolic play. A long silence invaded the room, up to the point where G. threw her head back as if looking to get away from this hard, complex situation. Despite the considerable tension between mother and daughter, no overt signs of aggression were observed on either side.

Considering the information available to us, we saw G.'s trichotillomania as a sign of significant emotional distress. We assumed that she was feeling angry at her distant father and depressive mother. The parents seemed completely oblivious to the possible connection between G.'s dependent behavior and her hair-pulling. Both were still too deeply absorbed in their own attachment figures and the losses they had known. Neither one of them had positive models of emotional, interpersonal communication. As a result, G. too remained lonely—alone with the fears, the anger, and the sadness— exactly like each of her parents.

Still, we wondered why it was G., the youngest of the family's three children, who ended up developing the disorder. Did the mother identify with G., of all her children, because she herself had been the youngest in her family? The mother brought up two matters that helped us better understand things. The first was her fear of loss, reflected in her depriving G. of a transitional object ("I cannot bear the thought that it might get lost") and in her dream about her dead grandmother. The second matter was the solitude she felt as the sole parent involved in the upbringing of her three children, given the physical and psychological absence of her husband from home. The insecure attachment that characterized the relationship between the mother and her mother was now patently evident in her relationship with her daughter. The reversal of roles that took place between the mother and the daughter when the latter tried to comfort her sad mother is an expression of this style of attachment.

With the father engulfed in his parents' divorce, the mother's loneliness and depression worsened, and no emotional communication could take place between the parents. G. also felt alone, and her hair-pulling may be construed as self-soothing behavior.

G.'s DC:0–5 diagnoses would be as follows:

- Axis I: Clinical Disorders
  » Trichotillomania
  » Relationship Specific Disorder of Infancy/Early Childhood (with mother and father)

- Axis II: Relational Context
  » Level 3—Compromised to Disturbed parent-child relationship
  » Level 3—Compromised to Disturbed caregiving environment

- Axis III: Medical Condition
  - » Alopecia areata
- Axis IV: Psychosocial Stressor
  - » Maternal depression
- Axis V: Developmental Competence
  - » Functions at age-appropriate level except in the emotional domain

On completing our diagnosis, we recommended a triadic psychodynamic therapy with three objectives in mind: to encourage the creation of a renewed relation between the spouses that would alleviate the mother's feeling of loneliness; to allow the development of a secure and satisfying triadic relationship within a fun, joyful atmosphere that would allow the expression of emotions; and to raise the parents' awareness of the girl's emotional state and the internal processes they are going through as parents.

During the first triadic session, the mother talked about her loneliness and the absence of "anyone who will listen" to her. Surprisingly, the father was able to do just that. Thanks to this, he was able to be more attentive to G.'s feelings throughout the meeting. He explained to G. that although her mother was indeed sad, she would soon calm down, and he assured her that she was not sad because of her. This three-way meeting was special for all three members of the family. For the first time in her life, G. witnessed her parents in an emotional exchange. Moreover, the parents shared with her what was going on. A new "schema-of-being-with-dad-and-mom," to use Stern's formulation (1985), was thus created in G.'s representational world.

In the following session, the father was much more involved, at both the behavioral and emotional levels, and there was a predominant atmosphere of being a threesome. The mother said that she was afraid of being overtaken by negative emotions and feelings of loss in her relationship with her daughter. The therapist helped her see how her fear of loss was related to G.'s ambivalent style of attachment. The therapist also pointed out to the mother her paradoxical attitude when, during their game, she called her girl back while declaring her wish for the girl to be more independent.

With these insights starting to sink in, G.'s need for a transitional object came up in the next session. G. went for a doll. The mother found it hard to grant her the freedom to go with the doll that she wanted because the doll's hair was "dirty and unkempt." She told G. to clean the doll and to cut its hair(!). At this point, the therapist helped G. stand her ground and demand that the doll be accepted as is.

As G.'s language skills developed, she also started expressing aggression during play. Gradually, her doodles became bolder. In one of the sessions, she threw the dolls and made scary faces. She thus gave ever greater expression to her aggression and anxiety directly through play. Three sessions later, the mother reported that the hair-pulling had stopped entirely. Therapy ended after 16 sessions because all the symptoms were gone. Three and a half years later, we followed up on G. over the phone. The parents told us that G., now 5 years old, was developing normatively, was well-integrated into kindergarten, and would soon go into first grade. In parallel, the mother had been in individual psychotherapy.

It is important to note the prominent role played by the motif of fear during this parent–child psychotherapy. In her fear of losing her mother, G. did not dare express her resistance and anger, whereas the mother too was afraid of losing her beloved daughter. Thus, for example, after G.'s sleep improved, the mother signaled a regression; G. started waking up again at night and switched to the parents' bed, as she had done when treatment began. The therapist helped the parents make sense of this behavior. As it turned out, in fact, G.'s return to the parents' bed was the mother's initiative, owing to her difficulty to stand G.'s crying at night, which she interpreted as a sign of solitude and grief. In fact, she projected onto her daughter her own solitude along with the unresolved grief she had carried inside from childhood.

Conclusion

Contrary to common opinion, trichotillomania is not a rare phenomenon in infancy. It does not necessarily reflect severe emotional deprivation or depression, as the professional literature often says. Nevertheless, the disorder must not be taken lightly or seen as "nothing more than a habit that will pass with time." It is a disorder that probably has a multifactorial etiology, including the quality of the parent–child relationship, the child's biological profile, and family antecedents of unresolved intergenerational problems. It seems that trichotillomania breaks out at a time of crisis, expressing a lack of familial communication around negative emotions, such as frustration, fear, and anger. The clinical cases we have presented illustrate the place of the parent–baby relationship in the formation of the symptoms in the child. To our knowledge, no specific psychotherapy exists for trichotillomania in infants and young children. Each case must be examined individually. As far as we know, no longitudinal studies have followed children who suffered from trichotillomania in infancy. The question of whether trichotillomania has any specific psychopathological meaning at this age as opposed to its meaning in adolescence and adulthood still stands.

References

Aleksandrowicz, M. K., & Mares, A. J. (1978). Trichotillomania and trichobezoar in an infant. *Journal of the American Academy of Child and Adolescent Psychiatry, 17*, 433–539.

American Psychiatric Association. (2000). *Diagnostic and statistical manual of mental disorders* (4th ed., text rev.). Washington, DC: Author.

American Psychiatric Association. (2013). *Diagnostic and statistical manual of mental disorders* (5th ed.). Washington, DC: Author.

Hallopeau, M. (1889). Alopecie par grattage [Alopecia by scratching]. *Annals of Dermatology and Syphiligraphy, 10,* 440–441.

Stern, D. N. (1985). *The interpersonal world of the infant.* London, England: Karnac Books.

ZERO TO THREE. (2016). *DC:0–5™: Diagnostic classification of mental health and developmental disorders of infancy and early childhood* (DC:0–5). Washington, DC: Author.

Recommended Reading

Bloch, M. H. (2009). Trichotillomania across the life span. *Journal of the American Academy of Child and Adolescent Psychiatry, 48,* 879–883.

Bloch, M. H., Landeros-Weisenberger, A., Dombrowski, P., Kelmendi, B., Nudel, J., Pittenger, C., . . . Coric, V. (2007). Systematic review: Pharmacological and behavioral treatment for trichotillomania. *Biological Psychiatry, 62,* 839–846.

Bruce, T. O., Barwick, L. W., & Wright, H. H. (2005). Diagnosis and management of trichotillomania in children and adolescents. *Pediatric Drugs, 7,* 365–376.

Grant, J. E., Odlaug, B. L., & Kim, S. W. (2009). N-acetylcyteine, a glutamate modulator, in the treatment of trichotillomania: A double-blind, placebo-controlled study. *Archives of General Psychiatry, 66,* 756–763.

Keren, M., Ron-Mayara, A., Feldman, R., & Tyano, S. (2006). Some reflections on infancy-onset trichotillomania. *The Psychoanalytical Study of the Child, 61,* 254–272.

King, R. A., Scaihill, L., Vitulano, L. A., Swabston, M., Tercyak, K. P., & Riddle, M. A. (1995). Childhood trichotillomania: Clinical phenomenology, comorbidity, and family genetics. *Journal of the American Academy of Child and Adolescent Psychiatry, 34,* 1451–1459.

Oranje, A. P., Peereboom-Wynia, J. D. R., & de Raeymaeckir, D. M. J. (1986). Trichotillomania in childhood. *Journal of the American Academy of Dermatology, 15,* 614–619.

O'Sullivan, R. L., Mansuetto, C. S., Lerner, E. A., & Miguel, E. C. (2000). Characterization of trichotillomania: A phenomenological model with clinical relevance to obsessive compulsive spectrum disorders. *Psychiatric Clinics of North America, 23,* 587–605.

Sweedo, S. E., & Leonard, H. L. (1992). Trichotillomania: An obsessive compulsive disorder? *Psychiatric Clinics of North America, 15,* 777–790.

Zalsman, G., & Shoval, G. (2002). Nonpharmacological therapies for trichotillomania. *Expert Review Neurotherapy, 2,* 212–216.

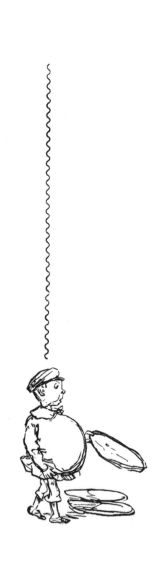

CHAPTER 13
I Process the World Differently

CASE STUDY

N., a toddler 2 years and 10 months old, whose two parents are successful academics, was referred to our unit because she refused to eat solid food and stuck to soft textures. During the evaluation, particularly when eating, she was noticeably avoiding eye contact with the adults. She did not form sentences (only stringing two words together occasionally), referred to herself in the third person instead of the first, spoke in a monotonous tone, and often repeated the words of the adults (echolalia). She clearly seemed to prefer playing with toys over interpersonal interaction. Before coming to our clinic, the parents thought nothing much of these difficulties, and they only consulted their pediatrician about the eating problem. During the first session, they described themselves as not very sociable people, and the father added that he too was the odd child out among his peers in childhood.

Introduction

Autism is an innate neurodevelopmental disorder characterized by severe impairments in social interaction and communication and the presence of restrictive and repetitive behaviors, which manifests itself in the course of the first 4 years of life. The etiology of the disorder is still unknown.

Since the first description of a case of autism by Kanner (1943), the diagnostic range has been enlarged to what is now termed Autism Spectrum Disorder (ASD). Once considered rare, ASD is now being diagnosed in 1:68 children. Boys are approximately 4 times more likely to be affected than girls: The estimated prevalence is 1 in 42 for boys and 1 in 189 for girls. Global Developmental Delay is common in children with ASD. The genetic component of ASD is significant: The younger sibling of a child diagnosed with ASD has a risk of about 19% to have the disorder as well.

Autism is perceived as a strange and frightening disorder, mostly because of the helplessness felt when confronted with these children's noncommunicability. These are toddlers who seem normative, but when they are addressed, it turns out that they perceive and process the world differently.

In phenomenological terms, autism is a pervasive deficit in reading social signals—for example, in identifying the emotional meaning of facial expressions or tones of voice, and in interpersonal verbal and nonverbal communicative skills (e.g., a child with ASD shows a preference for interacting with objects rather than people). It seems that ASD stems from a fundamental deficit in the development of theory of mind, which is a core component of social understanding. Contrary to the once-prevailing opinion, children with ASD do show the capacity to form secure attachments to their parents, as long as they do not have profound intellectual disability (formerly known as mental retardation).

Etiology of ASD

It was once thought that autism was mostly due to an abnormal parent–baby relationship. Today, this view is much less widespread. Tustin (1991) described a subgroup of infants who react with "autistic defenses" to common daily-life changes such as weaning off breastfeeding or their mother's going to work, which are experienced as traumatic. According to Tustin, these children respond positively to long, psychoanalytic psychotherapy.

The current understanding is that ASD is the result of several impaired genes. It is still not clear whether every single gene is responsible for clinically manifesting a single symptom or whether some interaction between all defective genes produces the range of the symptoms associated with the disorder. Of all cases of ASD, 1%–2% are due to specific genetic diseases, such as Fragile X syndrome (with around 50% of its carriers having autistic symptoms) and tuberous sclerosis (with around 30% of its carriers having autistic symptoms).

Many hypotheses have been put forward regarding the role played by environmental factors in bringing on ASD. For instance, no causal correlation has been found between vaccines and ASD, despite the common claim from parents that autistic symptoms appeared after their baby's vaccination. In contrast, viral infections during pregnancy and hypoxia at birth have been thought to influence the appearance of the disease in children born with dormant genetic material who would not have otherwise developed the disorder.

Diagnosis of ASD in Infancy

Under the *Diagnostic and Statistical Manual of Mental Disorders* (5th ed.; DSM–5; American Psychiatric Association, 2013) and the *DC:0–5™: Diagnostic Classification of Mental Health and Developmental Disorders of Infancy and Early Childhood* (DC:0–5; ZERO TO THREE, 2016) classification systems, ASD is diagnosed given a severe impairment in social interaction and communication, and the presence of restrictive and repetitive behaviors.

The impairment in social interaction and communication must be manifested by three symptoms: limited or atypical social attention and reciprocity, deficits in nonverbal social communication behaviors, and peer-interaction difficulties. Major sensory deficit, such as vision or hearing problems, excludes the diagnosis of ASD.

At least two of the following four restrictive and repetitive behaviors must be present: stereotyped babbling or speech, motor movements, or manipulation of toys and objects; rigid routines and resistance to change; unusual interests; and atypical responsivity to sensory stimuli.

The common practice in the past was not to diagnose autism before 3 years old, with the understanding that the criteria needed for a diagnosis were strongly related to the development of social cognition. This approach has changed since the publication of several studies of home video recordings taken by parents of 1-year-old infants who were later diagnosed with ASD. These showed that, compared with babies who evolved typically, these babies showed less interest in human faces as early as their first year of life. Furthermore, they did not establish eye contact with others, and their faces expressed no emotions. It is important to note that these characteristics were not observed in babies with intellectual disability.

Today, given the knowledge on the plasticity of the brain and the effect of early interventions on its development, the minimal age for diagnosing ASD has dropped to 18 months. This approach also has its drawbacks, of course. It might induce erroneous diagnosis whereby a child is wrongly labeled. Therefore, the DC:0–5 has added a new diagnostic category, called Early Atypical Autism Spectrum Disorder (EAASD), for infants between 9 and 36 months old who only partly meet the diagnostic criteria for ASD. The diagnostic threshold for EAASD requires only two of the three social communication symptoms and only one of the four restrictive and repetitive symptoms.

Infants showing early red flags that warrant close follow-up and eventually diagnosis of EAASD are those with the following:

- *A relatively low level of interpersonal communication compared with babies their age, with less interest in others and less smiling directed at those around them.* For the sake of caution, one should remember that a 1-year-old infant's lack of response to being called by name may be due to intellectual disability and not necessarily autism.

- *Atypical eye contact.* Eye contact is an essential element in interpersonal, face-to-face, and nonverbal communication from the beginning of life. Brief, fleeting eye contact appears in some toddlers with autism but without focus on people or objects.

- *A reduced or limited ability to initiate joint attention, meaning an interest or emotion shared between the infant and his caregiver.* To establish joint attention, the infant must be aware of the other person's presence and interest in the same object. A persistent lack of interest in the peekaboo game is also a red flag because it is a common turn-taking activity observed in babies as young as 9 months old.

- *Poor social referencing.* This is indicative of a deficit in the infant's capacity for identifying and understanding the emotional meaning of facial expressions. Healthy babies are capable of this by the time they are 9 months old. It is unclear whether a link exists between the difficulty establishing eye contact and lack of social referencing: Indeed, avoidance of eye contact may stem from failure to understand that looking at another person's facial expression can provide important contextual information. This is probably linked to the nondevelopment of the theory of mind, a core deficit in ASD.

- *A restricted range of facial expressions and nonverbal gestures.*

In 2010, Barbaro and Dissanayake published a study that followed the communicative and social behavior of more than 20,000 infants. The infants were examined when they were 8, 12, 18, and 24 months old. The examination included the following components: peekaboo, interest in voices, eye contact, the infant's reaction to being called by name, use of language, spoken-language comprehension, imitation, social smile, enjoying affection, pointing to a person or object, behaviors of a communicative nature, joint attention, pretend play, interpersonal communication, and parallel play (children sitting side by side without paying attention to each other). Two hundred and sixteen infants from this sample failed on some of these developmental tasks. They scored particularly poorly on eye contact, pointing, communicative behaviors, and pretend play. This group was referred for more in-depth examination by a group of experts, who put them through more specific tests. It was found that 110 of them had symptoms that raised suspicions of impending ASD. When these children were 10 years old, they were given additional checks to diagnose autism, which included an interview with their parents (Autism Diagnostic Interview; Lord, Rutter, & Le Couteur, 1994) and a structured observation test (Autism Diagnostic Observation Schedule; Lord et al., 1989). These tests showed that 89 of them had ASD. The other 20 children were diagnosed with Global Developmental Delay, including late language development. This study has two important applications. First, it means that health professionals in the community can spot toddlers with signs that raise suspicions of ASD or EAASD and can refer them to a specialist for more in-depth evaluation. Second, it underscores the need to carry out repeat evaluations every few months because a child's young age increases the risk of getting the diagnosis wrong on the basis of a one-off examination.

Differential Diagnosis of ASD or EAASD

ASD symptoms are sometimes similar to those of other psychiatric disorders, including the following:

- *Primary Language Development Disorder.* Young children with ASD and children with a primary language development disorder both struggle with communication. What makes the difference between the two disorders is the presence of repetitive and restrictive behaviors in children with ASD or EAASD. In addition, the receptive ability (the ability to understand spoken language) of toddlers with ASD or EAASD is significantly inferior to that of children with Primary Language Development Disorder.

- *Global Developmental Delay.* One of the distinguishing features between toddlers with Global Developmental Delay and those with ASD or EAASD is the ability to manifest shared pleasure when playing with others and the absence of repetitive and restrictive behaviors among the former.

- *Reactive Attachment Disorder.* When babies grow up with no attachment figure or in a highly emotionally deprived environment, cognitive and socioemotional development are severely impaired. Some infants show autistic behaviors, such as repetitive self-soothing behaviors, flat affect, lack of interest in toys, and lack of play. The condition of these babies is so reminiscent of an autistic disorder that some clinicians use the term "reactive autism" to characterize them.

- *Major sensory deficit (audition, vision).* It is nowadays common practice to carry out a hearing test for every toddler suspected of having ASD or EAASD.

The differential diagnosis is vital if infants and young children who do not have ASD or EAASD are to be oriented to the right kind of therapy befitting their diagnosis. Unfortunately, in recent years, there has been a tendency by clinicians from different disciplines to diagnose children with ASD when their symptoms are not sufficiently clear-cut.

Therapeutic Approaches

Addressing the Parents' Emotional Distress

Parents who learn that their child has ASD or EAASD are swamped by hard feelings of helplessness and panic, as illustrated in the poem "Rice Pudding":

What is the matter with Mary Jane?
She's perfectly well, and she hasn't a pain;
But, look at her, now she's beginning again!—
What is the matter with Mary Jane?

What is the matter with Mary Jane?
I've promised her sweets and a ride in the train,
And I've begged her to stop for a bit and explain—
What is the matter with Mary Jane?

What is the matter with Mary Jane?
She's perfectly well, and she hasn't a pain,
And it's lovely rice pudding for dinner again!—
What is the matter with Mary Jane?[1]

The speaker in the poem is the parent who cannot figure out why her beloved daughter Mary Jane is distressed and is, thus, unable to find her a remedy. The parent feels unworthy of her parental status because of her failure to fulfill the role of the potent parent, in charge of her offspring's happiness.

The parent reports her failed attempts to stop the crying using the experience that multiple generations have made available to her: food (not just any food, but rice pudding!), sweets that girls cannot but rejoice in, and promises of a glittering future—such as a ride in the train.

When all the usual means have failed, the parent—in her despair— looks for the ultimate cause of her distress: illness or abuse ("What is the matter with Mary Jane?/She's perfectly well, and she hasn't a pain"), the only ones that, according to the wisdom of many generations, might account for the incessant, unfathomable crying. These reasons are brought up and ruled out on the spot, and the parent faces her impotence stark naked: "What is the matter with Mary Jane?"

The experience described in this poem is one known to all parents who face the incomprehensibility of their baby's language, who stand defeated at the gates of their child's world, which they behold but cannot enter. In the absence of the word, in the absence of a common language, the parent is exposed to the threatening otherness of the "other."

Parents of children with autism, then, experience a frustrating relationship with their children. Parents of typical toddlers or toddlers with only minor developmental problems quickly learn to adapt to their child's special rhythm; the perplexing moments gradually change into moments of partial understanding, and before long a harmonic dialogue is established between the toddler and his parents. By contrast, when a toddler has ASD, the enigma never entirely goes away. Providing support, guidance, and hope to the parents thus becomes a critical component of the treatment program.

The goal of parental guidance is to help parents find ways to achieve some understanding of the child's abnormal behaviors and often unclear emotions. Parenting a child with autism does require considerable material and psychological resources. Parents need to cope not only with their child's needs but also with the "maelstrom" of feelings that each of them harbors toward the child. They also need to leave room for their own needs and those of their other children. Sometimes, the family becomes divided when one of the parents makes the treatment of the child with autism the household's "exclusive mission," at the expense of everybody else's emotional needs.

Addressing the Infant's or Toddler's Needs

There are two guiding principles for treating toddlers who have ASD or EAASD: (a) educating for socialization—including speech therapy, occupational therapy, and behavioral therapy—and (b) empathic support achieved by setting up a unique environment "tailored" to the child's strengths and weaknesses.

In regard to behavioral treatment, there are several known approaches, ranging from the highly structured and strict Applied Behavior Analysis method to the Floortime method developed by Greenspan and Wieder (2006), which addresses the behavioral components of the disorder without ignoring the sensory and emotional components.

There is also a vast literature on recommended dietary supplements for treating ASD, but no empirical proof of their efficacy has been found so far. As for medications, no drug has yet been found to treat autism. However, drugs can sometimes be used to alleviate the various symptoms of the disease, including short attention span, psychomotor agitation, and aggressive behaviors (see the section devoted to pharmacotherapy in chapter 17).

In 2001, the American Academy of Pediatrics (2001) spublished treatment guidelines for ASD. The recommendation is to start the therapeutic intervention program after the diagnosis has been established, and this should include the following elements:

- Encourage the toddler to engage in structured activity during most hours of the day and most days of the week, within the context of her natural environment.

- Use short repetitive learning sequences based on the child's profile and capabilities.

- Supervise most of the toddler's activities and provide parental guidance.

Choice of Educational Framework

There are no universal guidelines on the type of educational framework appropriate for infants and young children with ASD or EAASD, especially when their level of functioning is moderate to high or when the ASD diagnosis is still inconclusive. The quantitative ratio of staff to children, availability of paramedical therapies (e.g., speech, occupational, and music therapies), and training level of the adults in charge are all important parameters.

Prognosis of EAASD and ASD Over the Years

In toddlers and preschool children, the best predictor of functioning at an older age is the level of language, cognitive, and joint-attention skills. There is evidence to suggest that regardless of whether infants presented all ASD symptoms prior to or after 2 years old, they are indistinguishable by 3 years old. Social communication deficits are the domain where the impact of early intervention is most evident.

Multiple Complex Developmental Disorder (MCDD): Between Autism and Psychosis

The MCDD syndrome was described by Towbin, Dykens, Pearson, and Cohen (1993), and, despite not being included in either the DC:0–5 or DSM–5, we encounter these children in our everyday clinical work. They described a cluster of symptoms of fluctuating frequency and intensity, whereby a child may appear almost normative at times and totally abnormal at others (incidentally, these children were once diagnosed under the heading "Borderline"). MCDD is a disorder that includes a deficit in social communication (like ASD), a distorted perception of reality (like psychosis), extreme anxiety, and compulsive behaviors. Children with these symptoms do not follow a uniform course of development. The disorder is thought to lie somewhere in between autism and psychosis. It is close to psychosis owing to the presence of poor affect regulation, abnormal thought process, unrealistic anxiety, and compulsive symptoms. Although they have difficulty with interpersonal relations and communication, these children have better communication skills than those who have ASD, as well as a larger range of facial expressions. They also handle changes better, enjoy periods of quasi-normative functioning, and do not exhibit the odd speech and repetitive and restrictive behaviors typical of children with ASD or EAASD.

Even the physiological apparatus of these children differs from that of children with ASD, supporting Towbin et al.'s (1993) idea that MCDD is a distinct disorder. A few years back, studies were published showing that toddlers with MCDD responded to stressful situations with little secretion of cortisol compared with typical children and children with autism. They also displayed higher nerve conduction velocity than children with autism. Compared with children with Early Childhood-Onset Schizophrenia, toddlers with MCDD present symptoms at a younger age, have a different course of illness, show no evidence of delusions or hallucinations, and can calm down with the help of an adult.

The etiology of MCDD is unknown. All that is known is that organic defects are common in these cases, as is an abnormal family atmosphere resulting from complex conflicts, whether overt or hidden.

Because MCDD has not been included in either the DSM–5 or DC:0–5 classification systems, no follow-up research has been done on these children. On the basis of previous studies by Towbin et al. (1993) and van der Gaag, Kaplan, van Engeland, Loman, and Buitelar (2005), it seems that some children will develop along the psychotic path and later be diagnosed with Early Childhood-Onset Schizophrenia, some will become socially withdrawn and later be diagnosed with ASD, whereas others will greatly improve following family-based therapeutic intervention. This is why it is so important to spot these toddlers at a young age, diagnose them, and treat them. They are usually offered family therapy in addition to occupational therapy and sometimes even low-dosage antipsychotic medication, mainly meant to relieve the anxiety, impulsiveness, and attention symptoms. An example of this is shown in the following case study.

CASE STUDY

D., a 2½-year-old toddler, was referred for professional evaluation by his pediatrician because of an inexplicable fear of television sets, poor peer relationships, use of sophisticated language in a screechy voice, a highly unstable mood, sharp transitions from anxiety and anger to joy without any obvious external stimulus, and a low frustration threshold alongside the ability to calm down with help from his parents. At times, D. seemed absorbed in his inner world, whereas at other times, he displayed hypersensitivity to his environment and a burning need for proximity and warmth. His anxiety from television sets was so extreme that he could not stay in a room that had one. His sensory sensitivity threshold was unusually high.

During the evaluation, D. played a symbolic game with a dollhouse and established eye contact, but his attention span was short. He talked to us in a way that conveyed both connection and distance. An associative thought process was also conspicuous. He did not display repetitive behaviors or movements, but he tended to walk on tiptoes. The parents' history-taking revealed several significant family biological and psychological risk factors. In addition, D. had undergone a traumatic urological surgery when he was 18 months old. The father–child relationship seemed quasi-symbiotic, as opposed to the mother–child relationship, which seemed distant, given that he and his mother rarely addressed each other.

Because MCDD is not a valid diagnosis in the existing classification, the DC:0–5 diagnosis we would give him is EAASD. A follow-up session at 11 years old revealed that D. had not changed. He remained odd, sensitive, and easily anxious; had no close friends but did not mind it; preferred to stay home; and was able to carry on a conversation, albeit in a superficial kind of way. He had no psychotic symptoms. His final diagnosis was ASD.

Social Communication Disorder

This new diagnostic category replaces the diagnosis of Asperger syndrome in the DSM–5. Because these children develop typically during their first 3 years, the diagnosis has not been included in the DC:0–5. It is only at the start of kindergarten or first grade that the disorder shows its first signs: poor social judgment, patterns of reduced interest, and a tendency to focus on irrelevant details. These children usually develop typically in cognitive terms. They are primarily characterized by difficulty to communicate spontaneously and emotionally with others (despite normative cognitive and verbal capabilities) and difficulty to describe and explain their own as well as other people's emotions and intentions. These children can carry on a long one-sided conversation without realizing that their interlocutor has already disengaged from them. Their nonverbal communication is also often lacking—their facial expressions are strange and their look insufficiently clear. In most cases, they are also socially secluded. They feel no need for company and do not initiate contact. However, they do not shun the presence of other children. Attention Deficit Hyperactivity Disorder as a comorbid diagnosis is prevalent among children who have this disorder.

In a study on drawings (Lim & Slaughter, 2008), children with Social Communication Disorder were asked to draw a house, a tree, and a human figure. These drawings were then compared with those produced by a group of typical children. The results showed that both groups drew the house and the tree in the same way, but they significantly differed in how they drew the human figure: The children with Social Communication Disorder did not start to draw from the head but instead from other parts of the body, and no clear emotion was displayed on the face.

Treatment for children with Social Communication Disorder should be adapted to the unique characteristics of each child and his family. Social-skills group therapy has been developed for these children. They are usually integrated in a typical class with the assistance of an auxiliary teacher.

> *The hero of Mark Haddon's* The Curious Incident of the Dog in the Night-Time[2] *is Christopher Boone, a child who probably has Asperger syndrome. Christopher is also the narrator telling his story in the first person. The author thus offers the reader a look inside the special world of those who have this syndrome, or at least Christopher's world, which features many of the syndrome's characteristics.*

> *From the outset, the reader of the book is acquainted with the different way in which Christopher perceives the world when he describes a dog lying on the neighbor's lawn, speared by a garden fork.*

> *The horrific sight of the speared dog is related by Christopher as a factual report—cold, alienated, and distanced. There is not a single word in the whole passage to indicate feelings of shock, horror, pain, or sorrow. The emotional distance, the scientific precision, and the detailed account of each of the elements found in the crime scene are the characteristic features of Christopher's way of looking at the world.*

> *The book subsequently reveals various dimensions of the syndrome—for example, the noticeable absence of words expressing emotion, Christopher's inability to communicate with people in his closest environment, his obsessive preoccupation with the things that interest him, the compulsive rituals he adopts, and his inability to deal with too many stimuli around him.*

Conclusion

The past decade has seen impressive strides made in detecting, understanding, and diagnosing ASD in children less than 3 years old. The new diagnostic category of EAASD has been introduced for those infants and young children who present some but not all the symptoms of ASD but do need early intervention. Treatment methods have also improved greatly. Nevertheless, the etiology of ASD and EAASD remains unclear. Also, the relative efficacy of the different therapeutic approaches has not yet been clearly determined.

With that said, clinicians agree on the need to adapt the treatment program to the characteristics of the infant or toddler and her family. It is important to help the parents better understand how their child perceives and reacts to the world differently compared with other children her age. Family therapy should help the parents plan the distribution of emotional and material resources between all members of the family, to the extent possible. The therapeutic

---

[2] Mark Haddon, 2003, *The Curious Incident of the Dog in the Night-Time*, published by Jonathan Cape.

message is that early intervention improves things for most children, even if it does not cure the disorder.

References

American Academy of Pediatrics. (2001). The pediatrician's role in the diagnosis and management of autism spectrum disorder in children. *Pediatrics, 107,* 1221–1226.

American Psychiatric Association. (2013). *Diagnostic and statistical manual of mental disorders* (5th ed.). Washington, DC: Author.

Barbaro, J., & Dissanayake, C. (2010). Prospective identification of autism spectrum disorders in infancy and toddlerhood using developmental surveillance: The social attention and communication study. *Journal of Developmental and Behavioral Pediatrics, 31,* 376–385.

Greenspan, S. I., & Wieder, S. (2006). *Engaging autism: Using the Floortime Approach to help children relate, communicate, and think.* Cambridge, MA: Da Capo Press.

Kanner, L. (1943). Autistic disturbances of affective contact. *Nervous Child, 2,* 217–250.

Lim, H. K., & Slaughter, V. (2008). Brief report: Human figure drawings by children with Asperger's syndrome. *Journal of Autism and Developmental Disorders, 38,* 988–994.

Lord, C., Rutter, M., Goode, S., Heemsbergen, J., Jordan, H., Mawhood, L., & Schopler, E. (1989). Autism Diagnostic Observation Schedule: A standardized observation of communicative and social behavior. *Journal of Autism and Developmental Disorders. 19,* 185–212.

Lord, C., Rutter, M., & Le Couteur, A. (1994). Autism Diagnostic Interview-Revised: A revised version of a diagnostic interview for caregivers of individuals with possible pervasive developmental disorders. *Journal of Autism and Developmental Disorders, 24,* 659–685.

Towbin, K. E., Dykens, E. M., Pearson, G. S., & Cohen, D. J. (1993). Conceptualizing "Borderline Syndrome of Childhood" and "Childhood Schizophrenia" as a developmental disorder. *Journal of the American Academy of Child and Adolescent Psychiatry, 32,* 775–782.

Tustin, F. (1991). Revised understandings of psychogenic autism. *International Journal of Psychoanalysis, 72,* 585–591.

van der Gaag, R. G., Kaplan, R., van Engeland, H., Loman, F., & Buitelar, J. K. (2005). A controlled study of formal thought disorder in children with autism and multiple complex developmental disorders. *Journal of Child and Adolescent Psychopharmacology, 15,* 465–476.

ZERO TO THREE. (2016). *DC:0–5*™: *Diagnostic classification of mental health and developmental disorders of infancy and early childhood* (DC:0–5). Washington, DC: Author.

Recommended Reading

Callahan, K., Schukla-Mehta, S., Magee, S., & Vee, M. (2010). ABA versus TEACH: The case for defining and validating comprehensive treatment models in autism. *Journal of Autism and Developmental Disorders, 40,* 74–88.

Carr, T., & Lord, C. (2009). Autism spectrum disorders. In C. H. Zeanah, Jr. (Ed.), *Handbook of infant mental health* (3rd ed., pp. 301–317). New York, NY: Guilford Press.

Courchesne, E., Carper, R., & Akshoomoff, N. (2003). Evidence of brain overgrowth in the first year of life in autism. *Journal of the American Medical Association, 290,* 337–344.

De Bruin, E. I., de Nijs, P. F., Verheij, F., Hartman, C. A., & Ferdinand, R. F. (2007). Multiple Complex Developmental Disorder delineated from PDDNOS. *Journal of Autism and Developmental Disorders, 37,* 1181–1191.

Gardener, H., Spiegelman, D., & Buka, S. L. (2011). Perinatal and neonatal risk factors for autism: A comprehensive meta-analysis. *Pediatrics, 128,* 344–355.

Levy, S. E., & Hyman, S. L. (2005). Novel treatments for autistic spectrum disorders. *Mental Retardation and Developmental Disabilities Research Reviews, 11,* 131–142.

Maestro, S., Muratori, F., Cesari, A., Cavallaro, M. C., Paziente, A., Pecini, C., . . . Sommario, C. (2005). Course of autism signs in the first year of life. *Psychopathology, 38,* 26–31.

McConachie, H., Le Couteur, A., & Honey, E. (2005). Can a diagnosis of Asperger syndrome be made in very young children with suspected autism spectrum disorder? *Journal of Autism and Developmental Disorders, 35,* 167–176.

Molloy, C. A., Murray, D. S., Akers, R., Mitchell, T., & Manning-Courtney, P. (2011). Use of the Autism Diagnostic Observation Schedule (ADOS) in a clinical setting. *Autism, 15,* 143–162.

Schnur, J. (2005). Asperger syndrome in children. *Clinical Practice, 17,* 302–308.

CHAPTER 14
My Body Doesn't Work Well

Among the first songs that infants and toddlers listen to, many deal with body parts. "I have, I have these two hands"; "These 10 fingers that I have can do almost everything"; and "Raise your hands up, on your head" might be the best known children's songs in Israel. These songs describe parts of the baby's anatomy, their functions, and their location in the body, enhancing the pleasure that comes from identifying and using body parts. A classic example of this idea can be found in the song "I Have Two Hands" by Amos Barzel (music and lyrics) mentioned earlier. Not only do the hands do everything (e.g., wash the face, brush the teeth), but using them is a sign of competence and mastery: "Let's see who can, let's see who can."

What do young children and their parents feel when the body fails to live up to its role? How does this affect a young child's development of self? Sara Shilo's novel, The Falafel King Is Dead, *tells the story of a family that experiences the birth of a child with congenital deformation of the upper and lower limbs (arthrogryposis). The story gives expression to the mental damage caused to the child who is disabled and the difficulties facing a family that is forced to deal with a child who is physically distorted.*

Here is how the child narrates his own story when he turns 13 years old:

"Since I was small, I've thought about what God was thinking when he stopped my hands and feet growing inside Mum…. No one could help Mum see what he was doing to the babies inside her. She had no choice. She just had to put herself in God's hands…. When I was little I used to lie on the floor a lot… I'd try to do things the other children at nursery would do, but nothing worked. When this happened, I'd lie on the floor quietly, shut my eyes, and imagine I was back inside Mum's belly, listening to God decide about each of my fingers, when to stop it growing. I'd see God walking by silently, each week pointing at a different finger, and the angel flying with him writing down on my notes what God had ordered. I'd

see the picture of my feet and hands on the note in the angel's hand, and that he'd written to stop the fingers that had begun to sprout. Then I'd feel my heart exploding with pain, and I'd go beserk. I'd head-butt the floor – buf-buf-buf… until my body hurt more than my head… When my sweat cooled, I'd get up and start trying to be like all the other kids again…. At first I used to hate God for making me this way for his own fun…. When did I get my new idea? Four months ago, when I turned thirteen without a bar mitzvah or anything…. I used to think God… just wanted to invent a new type of person altogether…. He chose me when I was in Mum's belly: Me, Itzik Dadon, the first boy of a new kind of people."[1]

In another passage, the mother talks to her late husband, reminding him of his reaction to Itzik's birth:

"For a year you wouldn't say kiddush [Jewish wine benediction] at home. You wouldn't look at the baby and say kiddush on Sabbath. I dressed him in big shirts, the sleeves covering his hands so you didn't have to look at them. Nothing helped. You'd look at him then turn away. Quickly, very quickly, I got pregnant with Dudi… to bring the colour back to your face."[2]

Thirteen-year-old Itzik has a negative self-image. He trusts neither himself nor others, and he has a hard time connecting with other kids. Dudi, his brother, describes him as follows:

"Itzik's big hat sits above his ears like a helmet. He never takes it off. He even sleeps in it….He never looks at himself in a mirror. He walks around like he's invisible. Itzik and people don't go well together….He thinks everyone and everything is a traitor."[3]

Itzik is very apprehensive about showing his feelings: His tears linger, as if finding it hard to come out, and when they do, he erases them with his fists. Itzik's parents failed to see the child beyond his deformity. Itzik's father's sudden death (from a bee sting), the mother's struggle for survival as a young widow, and life in the shadow of terrorist attacks in the north of the country were all risk factors that brought about the sense of rejection felt by Itzik at home and outside of home, his distrust of others, as well as his existential anxiety and loneliness.

As illustrated in this story, illness or disability thus influences the development of the child's self-image already in the first years of life.

---

[1] The Falafel King Is Dead, copyright © 2012 by Sara Shilo. Reprinted with permission of Portobello Books.
[2] Ibid.
[3] Ibid.

Introduction: Development of the Baby's Self-Image

Daniel Stern, psychoanalyst and researcher, extensively studied the development of the self from birth on, on the basis of direct observation of healthy babies with their parents (Stern, 1985). For Stern, body and soul are two inseparable facets of human functioning. Furthermore, Stern suggested that babies came into the world equipped with a biological apparatus serving to organize their primary sensations. He saw the development of the baby's self as a build-up of parallel layers rather than a sequence of stages in which each stage is more advanced than the preceding one. These layers thus continue to develop side by side, each at its own pace and independently of the other.

Stern called the first layer in the development of self the emergent self. In his first months in life, the baby organizes his sensory and physical sensations with the help of the adults around him. The second layer, the core self, develops from the end of the second month on: The baby then organizes his own activity more coherently thanks to his ability to better distinguish himself from the environment. He starts to experience the continuity between his body and his environment. For example, the satiety he feels after receiving food from a familiar figure makes him feel secure in the presence of that figure. This is the start of the baby's subjective perception of others, the sense of being separate from his mother. The third layer, which develops at 7–18 months old, was termed the body self. At this stage, the baby explores his human and material environment using the cognitive and motor skills already at his disposal. For example, when a 9-month-old baby deliberately drops a spoon from his high chair expecting the nearby adult to pick it up, he feels not only that his body is separate from that of the other person but that he, the baby, controls the adult. At this stage, it is very important for the caregiver to exhibit affect attunement— that is, understand what the baby expects. This parental attunement and empathy, conveyed to the baby, forms the ground on which the baby's empathy develops from his first year of life. From the 18th month, the verbal self layer starts to develop—namely, the toddler's ability to express feelings and desires through language.

So far, we have described normative behavior. How illness and physical disability could disrupt it is well illustrated in the poem described next.

Hayim Nahman Bialik's poem, "In the Vegetable Garden,"[4] describes just another ordinary weekday in the garden flowerbed, a day when the cabbage suddenly feels like dancing around the barrel, for no reason, and having the cauliflower join it. All vegetables in the garden get carried away in the happy dance, and the cabbage and cauliflower are enthusiastically joined by a beetroot and tomato; a chubby turnip and a carrot; a watermelon

[4] Hayim Nahman Bialik, 1933, "In the Vegetable Garden," appears in *Poems and Short Songs for Children*, published by Dvir. Reprinted with permission.

and a pumpkin; a corn and a sunflower; and even the pauper potato, the
onion, and the garlic, who are surprised to see themselves admitted into the
vibrant skipping bunch despite their smelly reputation. Standing by oppo-
site them is a pea pod, leaning on its stick, mortified: "Only Pod, the poor
lad/Stood by looking on . . . How could I be dancing/And with joy explode/
With my sprouts all fallen/And my still empty pod." Only the pea pod—
the cripple leaning on his stick—does not partake in the merrymaking. The
pea pod experiences itself as an impotent creature with an "empty pod."
The other vegetables are prancing together full of joie de vivre, *whereas*
the pea pod, "the poor lad," stands there helpless, enclosed in its sterile
loneliness. The pea pod (cripple) is doomed, perhaps dooming itself, to a
life devoid of joy and movement, feeling that it will never again be able to
take an active part in the happy lives of those who are of sound body.

"Speaking the Disability or the Disease"

It is quite astounding to see how little time physicians, researchers, and parents actually devote to speaking about the emotional burden that attaches to physical disabilities compared with the time devoted to their physical treatment. As we were told by the parents of a toddler who was hard of hearing, "We are constantly occupied with our son's deafness itself, but not with its impact on our emotional life or his. In fact, we have no idea how he perceives himself as a deaf child."

We suggest using some of the basic concepts developed by Françoise Dolto (1984) following her many years of working with paralyzed and blind children in a pediatric hospital in Paris. Dolto conceptualized two dimensions of the way in which people relate to their own body: body schema and body image. Body schema is the way in which individuals perceive their concrete body, where it starts and where it ends, how it moves in space. This is a mostly conscious dimension. The second dimension, body image, includes a person's thoughts and emotions about her body, about its beauty and attractiveness, the way she thinks others see it. This dimension, largely unconscious, comes very close to what the analytic literature terms primary narcissism. Dolto diagnosed children's body schema and body image through their drawings. She used not only the drawings themselves—that is, the way in which children drew themselves and their families—but also what the children told her about their drawings.

Children with psychiatric disorders usually have a healthy body schema and a negative body image. However, children who are physically disabled have a negative body schema by definition, but they can develop a normative body image. For this to happen, according to Dolto, one has "to speak the disability/ disease"—that is, explain the nature of the disability to the child at a young age, using clear, practical, and concrete language. One example would be "Your right hand is weaker than the left, but it can help the left do so and so." It is important to talk to the child about her fantasies, about what she would have done as a completely healthy child. For example, a child who is paralyzed should be encouraged to engage in imaginary play with her parents, jumping and running with them, even though everybody knows this will never happen under the current circumstances. This way, the child gets to experience true emotional communication with others, feeling worthy of their true, positive attention. The parents also need encouragement to start talking with their child about the disability or the chronic disease at a young age, immediately after the pediatrician has made the diagnosis and they have understood its implications for the child's future.

The therapeutic team assisting the family of the child who is disabled also plays a major role in helping the child develop a healthy self-image. That team must be alert to parental responses that curtail the development of a sound body image. One should not forget that children who are disabled can accomplish a lot despite their limitations. A child born with one hand can hold objects and function almost typically in many areas. However, when parents do not artic-ulate the child's existing capacities beyond the disability (e.g., avoid exposing the child to tasks that involve the use of both hands, such as eating on his own), they increase his dependence, prevent him from discovering his inner strengths, and even deprive him quite often of opportunities to communicate directly with his environment. As a result, the young child often develops a negative self-image, encounters interpersonal difficulties, and withdraws or acts out of chronic anger and frustration (like Itzik in the story). Some children become clinically depressed.

The difficulty that caregivers have when helping their child who is dis-abled or chronically ill may stem from their own psychological reactions. For instance, they may be stuck grieving the loss of the healthy baby they had expected or they may be overwhelmed with feelings of pity, guilt, resentment, and even rejection. Parents of an infant or a young child who is disabled or chronically ill often feel they owe the child compensation for her suffering. As a result, they avoid frustrating the child by not setting the limits so vital for her normative development. In all these situations, caregivers thus greatly need support and professional help.

Regrettably, in many clinical settings (mainly rehabilitation and devel-opment centers) where these children are taken care of, the physical needs of the young child who is disabled are more readily addressed than the emotional ones.

The folk tale Tom Thumb *describes a destitute couple who crave a child of their own; a child would fill their lives with joy and turn their poor house into a home "like all others." The desire for a child brings the mother to pray for even a tiny child, no bigger than a thumb. Her prayers are answered, and a child is soon born, whose growth is stemmed. The parents call him Tom Thumb, love him, and nurture him, and he grows up to be an intelligent, clever, and agile boy.*

One day, the boy overhears his father, the poor woodcutter, say to himself how easier his life would be if a carter were on hand to transport the load of wood he hews. Tom volunteers for the task and asks to help his father with this chore. The father, initially skeptic about the boy's ability ("but you are small"), ends up acquiescing and allows him to give it a try. From this point on, a complex chain of events ensues: Tom falls into the hands of two scoundrels, who ask for the father's permission to exhibit the tiny boy in a circus, hoping to make a fortune. The adventure-thirsty boy asks his father to agree to the deal, promising to return home to his parents in one piece. Indeed, he manages to outwit the two crooks, as well as other shady characters that cross his path, returning home to his parents in the end. The tale ends with the boy's emotional reunion with his parents, who are delighted that he could get back home on his own. The boy decides to stay with his beloved parents, who swear that they will never again sell him off. This tale expresses the parents' difficulty to trust their child who is disabled and let him experience things, choose, and discover his powers in confronting an environment that harasses him and throws him curve balls.

Chronic Diseases and Common Disabilities in Infancy

CASE STUDY

D., a 1½-year-old toddler born with moderate cerebral palsy, was referred to our unit because of extremely frequent (10–12 times a day) breath-holding spells (crying bouts accompanied by apnea), occurring mainly around physiotherapy sessions and mealtimes.

D. was born following a physically and emotionally complicated pregnancy for the mother, who suffered from Type 1 diabetes, bulimia, and anorexia. Delivery was also complicated and traumatic: It did not proceed as expected and resulted in a fractured clavicle for the baby. More seriously, the baby had to be operated on because of a potentially lethal hiatal hernia immediately after birth. For a long time, his condition remained unstable, and the doctors were not too optimistic about his chances of survival. Contrary to the gloomy prognosis, the baby's condition improved, and he was released to go home at 4 months old, with a diagnosis of mild to moderate cerebral palsy. During hospitalization, the parents were not able to benefit from much psychological support from the team at the neonatal intensive care unit (NICU). Returning home was difficult, and the parents were left alone to deal with the baby's eating problems and slow development.

Physiotherapy treatments became more of an issue with each passing day, mainly because D. resisted them. His opposition translated into more frequent breath-holding spells during physiotherapy. However, his mother refused to give up, "or else," she claimed, "he will suffer the same fate as mine . . . my parents left me alone to cope with my diabetes. He will get better treatment than I did, even if I have to foist it on him." The father supported his wife but did not dare help her take care of the child: "The doctors said after the birth that the baby might die; I was scared to take him home. Since we got back home, I decided that only my wife could take care of him; these breath-holding spells are so scary that I can't take it anymore!"

During our evaluation, we tried to better understand the complexity of the mother–child relationship. The mother, who also suffered from a chronic medical condition, identified with her son while projecting onto him undesirable parts of herself, including her body image and conflictual issues relating to food and eating. She perceived herself as an intelligent woman with high expectations of herself who did not achieve much owing to her emotional problems. She interpreted D.'s eating pattern as rebellious behavior directed at her, just like the food-refusal behavior that she had displayed toward her parents since adolescence. She perceived her baby's cerebral palsy as a cynical continuation of "my bad luck, just like I got diabetes at age 6." Her ambivalent projections onto the child paved the way for an angry parental behavioral pattern, bordering on hostile, which markedly emerged at meal-times and during the physiotherapy sessions. The breath-holding spells had the effect of ending the angry interactions between mother and child, and they consequently increased in frequency over time. It should be noted that, in kindergarten, none of these appeared and D. ate and played normatively.

The *DC:0-5™: Diagnostic Classification of Mental Health and Developmental Disorders of Infancy and Early Childhood* (DC:0-5; ZERO TO THREE, 2016) diagnosis would be as follows:

- Axis I: Clinical Disorders
  - » Neurodevelopmental Disorder: Cerebral palsy with left hemiplegia and language delay
  - » Relationship Specific Disorder of Infancy/Early Childhood (with mother)
- Axis II: Relational Context
  - » Level 3—Compromised to Disturbed mother–child relationship
  - » Level 2—Strained to Concerning father–child relationship
  - » Level 2—Strained to Concerning caregiving environment
- Axis III: Medical Condition
  - » History of medical procedures
- Axis IV: Psychosocial Stressor
  - » Maternal anorexia/bulimia nervosa and diabetes mellitus

- Axis V: Developmental Competence
  » Competencies inconsistently present

The triadic parents–child psychotherapy focused on the mother's ambivalent and often angry projections on D. and the father's fear of being left alone in the company of his child, as well as on "speaking D.'s physical disability." For example, when D. was reluctant to use his weak hand, the therapist said to him, "Let's play ball with two hands; you'll see that your left arm does not work as well as your right one, but it can help the right one throw the ball stronger." The parents were amazed at the direct mentioning of the cerebral palsy; they did not think that D. was aware of it and was frustrated. Until then, they had not made the link between his chronic frustration at his own body and the breath-holding spells. Therapy lasted about 10 months, and the child's breath-holding and food refusal at home disappeared.

We now review some common medical conditions that have long-term effects on baby development and the parent–baby relationship.

Prematurity

One in 10 babies is born before the 37th week. Of these babies, 1%–2% weigh less than 1,000 grams at birth. Life expectancy for premature babies depends on weight at birth. Some 80%–85% of preemies born weighing 1,000–1,500 grams survive, as opposed to only 50%–60% born lighter than 1,000 grams. Premature births are considerably more prevalent among young mothers without means and families from a low socioeconomic background.

The lower the weight of a preemie, the more likely he is to develop medical complications. The most common complications include intraventricular hemorrhage, chronic lung disease (bronchopulmonary dysplasia), necrotizing enterocolitis, and retinopathy of prematurity. These complications greatly prolong the preemie's hospitalization while increasing the parents' sense of uncertainty about the baby's future. As a result, many parents have a hard time bonding emotionally with the baby; some wait for "the fog to lift" before naming the preemie. They sometimes hold on to their mourning for the healthy baby they had hoped for, sadly wondering about the reason for the premature delivery. It is therefore no surprise that parents who do not benefit from support from their environment or those who lack the psychological resources required to cope with this kind of situation sometimes end up hitting a crisis as a couple. In addition, the long hospitalization period of 2–3 months might affect the development of the premature baby, exposed as he is to many stressful stimuli (monitor alarms, neon lights, repeated blood drawing, painful procedures). Indeed, some premature babies struggle with self-regulation later on. During these protracted hospitalizations, parents feel helpless in handling such a fragile little baby, leaving the baby's care to the highly competent nurses. This makes them more passive compared with parents of premature babies hospitalized for shorter periods. The situation becomes problematic when the parents withdraw, hardly come to visit their baby at the NICU, and seldom touch him. When this happens, professional intervention is required to prevent the development of a serious disorder in the parent–baby relationship because these behavioral patterns often persist even after the baby had been released home.

Discharge from the hospital does not necessarily alleviate the parents' anxieties because they know that preterm birth has been linked with subsequent medical, neurodevelopmental, and behavioral problems. These concerns are somewhat mitigated when they learn that their premature baby can catch up in the course of her first 4 years in life. When carrying out periodical developmental follow-up, the point of reference is the child's "corrected" age, meaning the age adjusted to the originally expected date of birth. Some close the gap, and some do not. A greater number of neurological problems is associated with a higher risk for the appearance of learning and behavioral problems. As for the relationship between the mother and the baby, some children who were preemies tend to cling to their mother, at the expense of their inquisitiveness. Mothers, on their part, often tend to be highly protective. They may find it difficult to hand the baby over to the care of a nanny or sometimes even the father. In general, it is quite often seen how much a premature birth throws family life off balance, forcing each of the parents to reorganize emotionally. The birth of a preemie, especially when first-born, greatly influences the intrapsychic process involved in entering parenthood (that which Stern, 1995, named "motherhood constellation").

Considering all of the above and the broad scientific knowledge that has built up over the years on prematurity and the important role of the environment in the development of preemies, most NICUs try to pay attention to the emotional aspects of prematurity as it affects both parents and baby. To this end, the medical team usually encourages parents to visit the NICU on a daily basis and take part in the care: Parents are instructed to hold their baby close to their body (the skin-to-skin, or "kangaroo," procedure) and to massage him and talk to him, as far as his physical condition allows, of course. These parental interventions have been found to have a clear positive effect on the preemie's physiological parameters and ability to self-regulate. It has also been found that support groups for parents held within the framework of the NICU contribute to reducing their anxiety and tension and that this positive influence lingers even after the parents go back home. These group sessions are beneficial for parents because they boost their confidence in their parental competence, which will, in turn, later influence the way in which they encourage their child to explore and be independent.

As part of our consulting work for one of the NICUs, we introduced a semi-structured interview—the Clinical Interview for High-Risk Parents of Premature Infants (Keren, Feldman, Eidelman, Sirota, & Lester, 2003)—which was originally developed by Lester and Meyer at the Rhode Island Women and Infants Hospital in the United States. We conducted it with parents toward the end of the hospitalization, and we asked them to relate their experiences following the unexpected premature birth and the long hospitalization. The idea behind the interview is to detect those parents who had experienced their baby's premature birth as a trauma and who are still in a state of emotional shock. Doing so is important because without therapeutic intervention, they might struggle with the attachment process, to the detriment of the baby's emotional development. A significant correlation between the quality of the experience at the NICU (as brought out in the interview) and the quality of the interaction between the mother and her premature baby was shown (Keren et al., 2003). This tool is now used in some NICUs to identify, already during hospitalization, those families that will also need psychological accompaniment after their return home.

Asthma

Asthma is one of the most common chronic pediatric illnesses. In the United States, around 10% of children less than 6 years old have it. Because it is so widespread, many of its aspects have been studied. Our focus here is mainly with its emotional component and the role of the parents and the treating team in accompanying the toddler with asthma. First, and maybe most important, the way in which parents deal with the illness will largely determine, as in other chronic illnesses, how the infant or toddler will internalize her own body and illness. Studies on families in which one of the children was asthmatic showed that the family's cohesion level and the level of internal parental coherence predicted their ability to cope healthily with the child's illness. "Internal sense of coherence" is a concept coined by Israeli sociologist Antonovsky (1979) relating to the parents' inner sense of confidence in their ability to deal with negative events. Some parents of toddlers with asthma find treating asthma attacks challenging. Although asthma medications do prevent attacks, they might also cause various side effects, including behavioral disorders. This is why parental guidance should include an explanation about the relationship between the drugs and the appearance of behavioral disorders as well as encouragement to parents to set the child clear boundaries of conduct. This parental attitude might prevent the child from internalizing the "sick person's role."

Kalia, the heroine of Nurit Zarchi's Solitude Games,[5] had suffered from asthma attacks in childhood. Whenever she had attacks at night, Kalia would sit facing her father's back as he toiled away at his translation work.

---

[5] Nurit Zarchi, 1999, *Solitude Games*, published by Yedioth Aharonot.

*She narrates how the father's presence during the attack allows the girl
to breathe—that is, be herself and feel real. Kalia experienced her father
as a container shielding her from the terrifying illness, and it is this oft-
recurring childhood experience of hers that promoted the development of
a competent self capable of ending her attack by her own means. In other
words, the presence of a father who asks for nothing allows Kalia to feel
omnipotent and make the transition from a passive state of being to an
active role in which she is her own savior.*

Severe Skin Diseases and External Congenital Malformations

From the moment a baby emerges into the world, his parents embrace and
touch him empathically. This skin-to-skin contact will help the baby define
the boundaries of the body and, by extension, of his self. The parent helps the
baby differentiate between his own body and that of others as well as the world
outside him, between the "me" and the "non-me." Anzieu (1989) coined the
term "skin ego," serving to emphasize how deeply significant parental touch is
in the development of the baby's personality. Bick (1968) delved deeper into
the subject and described the development of personality as a corollary of skin
development, which draws the line separating the baby's body from his environment. Being held in the caregiver's arms to be soothed is what will allow
the baby to acquire the ability to regulate sensations of tension and negative
emotions that sweep over him.

When a toddler suffers from a skin disease, soothing through touch becomes harder for the parents because she will often recoil from their touch and
sometimes even reject it outright. Such rejection might leave the parent feeling
frustrated, scared, and even angry. Skin diseases in infancy may impair the
quality of the initial bond between the baby and her parents and, consequently,
her long-term emotional development.

For example, allergic inflammatory skin disease (atopic dermatitis)
sometimes appears in severe form in the first year of life, typically causing a
prolonged, hard itch (pruritus). Parents find it very hard to bear the suffering
of the baby who scratches and injures himself and to soothe him. Nighttime
is particularly challenging for both baby and parents. The whole experience
threatens to perturb the family's functioning and cause emotional responses in
the other children.

Skin diseases affect a child's outward appearance to one degree or another,
depending on severity. External, disfiguring diseases are harder to cope with
than other illnesses that are just as bad yet invisible. Parents are ashamed to
show their babies, isolate themselves, and often even stay away from social

gatherings to avoid other people's expressions of disgust, fear, or pity. Some parents, deep down, even reject their child. Some couples, unable to withstand the stress, separate. The medical team plays an important role in helping parents adapt to this difficult situation. In fact, parents cope better when the physician and the medical team give them straight answers and recognize their individual needs.

CASE STUDY

A., an 18-month-old single child of healthy parents, was referred to our unit because of a suspected autistic disorder. On first evaluation, he did seem locked up in a world of his own. He did not talk, cried a lot, did not play, and did not seek his parents' proximity.

His parents explained that his persistent crying was caused by a chronic itching pain that was due to severe atopic dermatitis that he had since birth. They painfully described how A. had always rejected being touched because "everything hurt him" and how he had learned to self-soothe. They felt helpless and guilty, and they identified with his pain. Crawling, for example, was hard for A. because it aggravated the abrasion on his knees. Going to the sea and rolling in the sand, which is a positive experience for most children his age, was hell for him. Watching television was his only pain-free activity. Furthermore, A. was behind in the language department in terms of development and understanding.

We decided to put the autistic diagnosis on hold and to start therapy, which included triadic sessions and movement therapy. Therapy focused on "speaking the painful and frustrating body." Gradually, A. opened up more and was more willing to experience his parents' physical contact. At the same time, his speech also started to come along, and his ability to communicate with his day care peers improved. Two years later, it was clear that A. did not have autism but had an emotional reaction to the chronic and severe skin disease. His final DC:0–5 diagnosis would be as follows:

- Axis I: Clinical Disorder
  - » Adjustment Disorder (with depressive symptoms)

- Axis II: Relational Context
  - » Level 2—Strained to Concerning dyadic relationships and caregiving environment

- Axis III: Medical Condition
  - » Severe atopic dermatitis

- Axis IV: Psychosocial Stressor
  - » None

- Axis V: Developmental Competence
  - » Competencies inconsistently present

Kidney Diseases

Another group of serious chronic diseases among children is kidney diseases. The emotional burden shouldered by the parents is heavy and may hinder their relationship with the baby. Because of the cumulative impact of painful medical procedures, side effects of medications, and burdens on parental functioning, infants and young children with kidney disease are at higher risk for developing cognitive, behavioral, and emotional difficulties—just like those who suffer from any other chronic medical diseases. Kidney failure requiring dialysis causes disruption to the child's and the parents' everyday life. The child cannot go to day care on a regular basis, and one of the parents must often stay at home.

In all these cases, the family's functioning—particularly in terms of mutual support and emotional communication—also determines the emotional and developmental state of these children. The fewer the conflicts between family members, and the more the child is encouraged to express feelings directly, the better will her development be.

Cancer

Cancer is not rare in the first 3 years of life and naturally has an earth-shattering effect on family life. The threat to the baby's life is very real, yet inconceivable for the parents, most of them young couples. Even though most pediatric oncology wards offer parents psychological support, some still develop posttraumatic reactions to their baby's disease, which often persist even after the child has recovered. The child with cancer also often adopts abnormal patterns of behavior, such as demanding behavior and clinginess. On top of these difficulties, there are developmental delays because of the secondary effects of chemotherapy and radiation therapy.

CASE STUDY

B. was referred to an infancy mental health unit at 3 years old because she refused to get toilet-trained and displayed unusual withdrawal behavior. Her brother was born several weeks before her arrival at the center. Her parents kicked off the first session declaring that "B. got cancer when she was 10 months old." The little girl sat close to her mother throughout the first hour. She spoke on occasion, but in such a baby-like, weak voice that it was impossible to understand her. At this initial point in the evaluation, she seemed to have serious developmental delay.

Despite B.'s physical recovery, the parents continued to avoid frustrating her, on the pretext that "she had suffered enough," and they did not encourage her to become autonomous. They continued to treat her like a miserable, sick baby. Therefore, on the one hand, they expected her to show emotional independence by demanding that she drop the nappies, whereas their behavior, on the other hand, conveyed to her their perception of her as being little, weak, and miserable. Moreover, the birth of the new baby encouraged B. to persist in her refusal to be toilet-trained and grow up. Communication at the family level was tense.

Her DC:0–5 diagnoses would be as follows:

- Axis I: Clinical Disorders
  » Relationship Specific Disorder of Infancy/Early Childhood (with mother and father)
  » Adjustment Disorder

- Axis II: Relational Context
  » Level 3—Compromised to Disturbed dyadic relationships
  » Level 3—Compromised to Disturbed caregiving environment

- Axis III: Medical Condition
  » History of cancer and medical procedures

- Axis IV: Psychosocial Stressor
  » Birth of sibling

- Axis V: Developmental Competence
  » Inconsistently present competencies

The triadic-psychotherapeutic treatment process agreed on was long and hard. On the one hand, the parents struggled to start viewing their daughter as a healthy, independent girl, and on the other hand, the child had already assimilated their perception of her and thus expected to be constantly protected by adults.

Integrative Body–Mind Therapeutic Model

The Phase of the Announcement: Telling the Parents About Their Infant's Chronic Disease or Disability

Parents always remember the day they received the news of the disease (or disability) as a traumatic turning point in their life. In the case of a prenatal diagnosis, parents must decide whether to carry out an abortion. The doctors make recommendations, but it is up to the parents to decide.

Postnatal diagnoses are not always clear or definitive. Members of the medical team often disagree on the diagnosis and the baby's likely development path. These differences cause anxiety and often undermine the parents' trust in the medical establishment. Who is the optimal person to announce the bad news? Should it be the pediatrician or rather the family doctor who has known the parents for much longer? Or perhaps the hospital doctor, who is a stranger to the parents but more familiar with the types of congenital disabilities and their implications? We tend to think that the better choice would be the family doctor who knows the family and who will assumedly also be coordinating the care for the child and the family in the years to come. Still, the reality is that the hospital doctor is usually the one to divulge the diagnosis. In some wards, the physician informing the parents is accompanied by a social worker, who is supposed to provide support and information.

The hero of the fairy tale Hans My Hedgehog *is a child born to parents who were ashamed of their sterility and desired a child, any child, "even a hedgehog." Their wish is, in fact, fulfilled to the letter. Although they thought they were ready to accept any child as long as they had an offspring, their first encounter with Hans—half child and half hedgehog—causes them much grief. Hans is not beloved by his parents. From his moment of birth, they experience him as a "problem" child, and no one agrees to be his godfather. They lay the baby on a stack of hay behind the oven, where he lies for 8 years. Then, one day, the father travels to a fair in a neighboring town and buys presents for Hans and his mother, each according to their wish. Hans gets bagpipes and a cockerel. Now he can leave his home and never return.*

This, the only gift he had so far received in life, allows him to set out on the cockerel's back. On his way, he comes across a herd of pigs and a donkey and becomes their shepherd. Thus, mounted on the cockerel and playing his bagpipes, he is able to grow a large herd and, after many an adventure, marry the king's daughter. On their wedding night, he promises his bride never to hurt her with his pointy spines. Indeed, he later loses his spines and turns into a handsome prince (just like the famous frog from another tale).

At the end of the story, Hans and his wife meet his parents. His father denies the possibility that he had had a real boy born to him, insisting that he had fathered no more than a spiny hedgehog–son. Hans does not give up. He shows him distinctive marks, and the father ends up acknowledging Hans and joining him and his wife.

The shame and disappointment felt by Hans's parents eventually make way for acceptance. The hedgehog turns out to be a complete human being who, despite being deprived of love at home, was able to find a woman and insisted on making his parents recognize him. In this tale, as in the previous one, the child who is disabled creates real change, this time not thanks to his parents—through dialogue with them and based on their love and acceptance—but through the realization that he has inner strengths despite his deformity. Hans discovers his musical talent and finds an easy, alternative mode of transportation (mounted on the cockerel); he is the one who believes in his ability to make it through life in his own way, and he is able to work, earn money, and get himself a bride. It is Hans's ability to find strengths in himself and his trust in his powers that allow him to find his human virtues within, which lend credibility to the physical metamorphosis in this tale.

The role of the treating staff is to evaluate the resilience of the family dealing with the child's chronic medical condition. Resilience in these cases is the family's ability to get past the initial shock and overcome the disappointment and the anxiety about the future. Only then can the parents recognize the scope of the problem and mobilize the resources to cope with it. After they renounce the obsessive quest for the origins of the disease or disability, their eyes open up to see the child as he is—disabled, yes, but also capable in many respects.

Sometimes, the medical team sees early signs of parental vulnerability and of a difficulty to adapt to the baby's particular situation. As previously noted, this difficulty often arises from a biased perception of their baby, focused on the lacks and weaknesses to the exclusion of everything else. This attitude might lead parents to do everything in the child's stead and thus deprive her of the chance to develop compensatory and adaptation mechanisms. The constant attempt to get to the bottom of the medical problem and to imagine incessantly how life would have turned out if the child had been born healthy does nothing to help the child's emotional development. Parents who have trouble coming to terms with the child's disability sometimes exhibit confusion and disorganized thinking, similar to people who suffer from posttraumatic stress disorder.

Parental Coping Patterns

Individual parents respond differently to their child's disease or disability in a way that often resembles their response to difficult life events. The most common dysfunctional emotional reactions are grief, depression, and guilt. These may, in turn, impinge on their parenting behaviors toward the child with the disability or illness and his siblings as well as on their marital relationship. Instead of supporting each other, parents sometimes drift apart as a result of negative feelings such as disappointment and resentment. Some of them blame fate or the other parent for the disability or project their frustration on the medical team. Often, in this state of mutual distancing, one parent takes total charge of the child's care, whereas the other withdraws.

CASE STUDY

A., a 2-year-old toddler, was referred to our clinic by a nurse in the community because of refusal to wean off the breast as well as slow motor and speech development. The first session was solely attended by the toddler and her father. A. sat, but neither crawled nor walked during the evaluation, and she did not reach out for toys. The first sentence that came out of the father's mouth when we asked her to come closer and take a toy was, "She can't do this alone, her muscles are weak." During the conversation, it turned out that the father was anxious about illnesses because he experienced previous losses in his family of origin, and he interpreted his daughter's hypotonicity and motor difficulties as a severe handicap. He was, in fact, in a state of mourning the healthy girl who was supposed to be born.

Since his daughter's birth, the father had spent all his energy seeking physiotherapy treatments for her. He had decided "to do everything for her." His wife was angry at his behavior, and their relationship as a couple was deteriorating. As a reaction to her husband's overinvolvement with their daughter, she withdrew from her. This is also why the mother did not attend our first meeting—an unusual response that reflected how deep the couple's crisis ran. She joined us for the second session, and, together, we defined two main objectives for intervention: first, to help the father adopt a more realistic perception of his child's motor difficulties and, thus, make for a more even distribution of his attention between his daughter and wife; second, to change the child's self-perception as a "girl who is incapable of anything" and finally help the mother reinvest in her relationship with her daughter.

The DC:0–5 diagnoses would be as follows:

- Axis I: Clinical Disorders
  » Neurodevelopmental Disorder (motor delay due to mild hypotonia)
  » Relationship Specific Disorder of Infancy/Early Childhood (with mother and father)

- Axis II: Relational Context
  » Level 3—Compromised to Disturbed relationship with each parent
  » Level 3—Compromised to Disturbed caregiving environment

- Axis III: Medical Condition
  » None

- Axis IV: Psychosocial Stressor
  » Parental conflict

- Axis V: Developmental Competence
  » Inconsistently present competencies in all domains

Theirs was a slow therapeutic process because, on the one hand, the father was not easily persuaded of his daughter's capabilities and, on the other hand, the mother had a hard time letting go of her resentment toward her partner. Gradually, the parents moved forward, and the child went into kindergarten (initially, the father would hide behind a tree to make sure that his daughter really fit in); she adapted well there and greatly improved in her motor and linguistic capabilities, well beyond the parents' expectations.

In other cases, the parents' coping pattern is characterized by focusing on the actual child, seeing her upbringing as a challenge and investing boundless resources in her—sometimes beyond their means and at the expense of their own needs. The extended family can also respond in a variety of ways, being either supportive or distant. When the extended family shuns the parents and the new baby, it deprives the parents of the environmental support they need so much precisely at this point in time.

The Impact of the Infant's Characteristics

So far, we have described the important role of the emotional response of the child's environment to his chronic disease or disability. Not less important are the young child's own characteristics. Sometimes, it is the baby himself who helps his parents and family overcome their initial rejection and attach to him by manifesting surprising coping skills and creativity. It is important to bear in mind that unlike the adults—who compare the baby with healthy, intact babies—the infant's reality is the body he knows with its limited capabilities, and he meets life's challenges to the best of his abilities within the means available to him.

The baby's astounding coping skills often trigger a change in the parents' perception, promoting the bonding process between them and the baby. Koester, Karkowski, and Tracey (1998)—for example—showed a decade ago that babies with an auditory deficiency fixed their gaze intensely at their mothers' faces, thus eliciting a strong response from them. Similarly, Preisler (1994) showed that toddlers with visual impairment were particularly attentive to voices, amazing their parents with their abilities to "see with their ears." Even toddlers with no upper limbs make up for their deficiency by using their feet to move nearby objects. These surprising capabilities strengthen the parents, who are preoccupied with those things that the child is unable to do. The child, for her part, is busy developing compensatory skills and seeks her parents' positive feedback.

To sum up, evaluating the infant's or young child's physical disability is not enough. One must also evaluate the child's emotional state, temperament, ability to play and self-regulate, and level of cognitive development. Observing a toddler engaged in imaginary play can reveal a lot about his view of the world, his self-image, and the way in which he solves problems.

Quality of Attachment

The question of the impact of the infant's chronic illness or disability on security of attachment has been a topic of research. For instance, Howe (2006) found that the percentage of babies with a secure style of attachment was lower in the group with disabilities (50% compared with 65% in the general baby population), given more parental risk factors. Howe also showed that children with disabilities were more likely to suffer from neglect and abuse from their parents when they had a childhood history of abuse and loss of attachment figures. It has also been demonstrated that neurological disabilities have the most negative effect on attachment security vis-à-vis the mother. Parents have an erroneous tendency to equate any neurological impairment with intellectual disability (formerly known as mental retardation), and they consequently find it hard to establish secure attachment. The prevalence of insecure attachment between healthy parents and babies who are blind or deaf has been found to be higher than in the general population. However, when the parent is also deaf, the rate of secure attachment among babies who are deaf is the same as it is in the general population (Preisler, 1993).

In light of these findings, when observing the interaction between a child who is disabled and her parents—during mealtimes, diaper change, bathing, and play—it is important to pay particular attention to the quality of the physical contact between them. If mutual avoidance is observed, it is important to find out its source. For example, is the parent's touch avoidant because of fear of hurting the baby or disgust? If the child seems to be avoiding physical contact, is it for fear of her parent? It is indeed important to dwell on touch because studies have shown that bodily contact between the child who is disabled and her parents helps her deal with stress; reduces her muscular tension; improves her range of motion; improves the quality of her sleep, eating, and bowel movements; and even allows her to benefit more from physiotherapy.

The Effect of a Toddler's Disability or Disease on Siblings

In a study involving 122 families in which one child was sick or disabled and the other siblings were healthy, Kao, Plante, and Lobato (2009) found that the latter were more likely to display symptoms of emotional and behavioral disorders as the place accorded to the former's disability (or illness) within the family's life grew. The special attention devoted by the parents to the child who is sick or disabled often gives rise to considerable jealousy in that child's siblings. Thus, for example, the twin brother of a child born deaf said to his parents, "I want to be like him, only without being deaf."

The Public Health Care System and Children Who Are Disabled or Chronically Ill

The public health care system should recognize that the optimal care to offer the infant who is disabled or chronically ill involves integrating both the physical and emotional components, and care should be organized accordingly. Medical and physical care must be accompanied by psychological therapy to

help the child and his family speak the disability or the disease and to overcome their negative emotions. Hence, the team providing care to babies who
suffer from a chronic disease or disability should be multidisciplinary, including a pediatric rehabilitation physician, a child psychiatrist, a social worker, a
developmental psychologist, an occupational therapist, a speech therapist, a
physiotherapist, and a special education teacher.

Moreover, families need information about the disability criteria and
their infant's rights. Each country has its own system, with more or less well-
integrated care. For example, in Israel, three official committees have attempted
to define the needs of the child who is disabled or chronically ill—the National
Council for Rehabilitative Medicine, the National Council for Mental Health,
and the Head of the Child Development Department at the Ministry of Health.
Each of them approached the subject from its own perspective and published
a document with guidelines on treating children who are disabled. Their
work was not coordinated. Furthermore, the National Insurance Institute, the
Ministry of Education, and the Ministry of Social Affairs each classify children
who are disabled according to their own criteria.

Sociocultural Aspects of Disability or Chronic Illness in Infancy

Immigration formed societies, such as Israel's, are highly diversified. They
are made up of ethnic groups that differ in religion, culture, origin, and language. In Israel, for instance, the Arab population comprises Muslim Arabs,
Christian Arabs, Druses, and Bedouins, and each of these groups has beliefs,
value systems, and worldviews of its own. The Jewish population likewise
encompasses different ethnic groups, each forming a "mini society" with its
own values and norms. It is no surprise, then, that children who are disabled
or chronically ill are perceived and cared for differently within each group. In
some sectors, for example, the family is expected to hide the child's disease or
disability to ensure that her other siblings remain eligible for marriage. This
negative label might push the self-image of the child who is disabled even lower
than it already is. The treating team needs to be aware of these differences of
perceptions and tailor the intervention plan for each child in accordance with
her social group.

Conclusion

In this chapter, we addressed the emotional aspects of disabilities and
chronic diseases in infancy. We looked at the impact that disability has on
the baby and his family as well as the ways in which the disability affects the
parent–child relationship and the family's functioning. We showed that the way

in which the child is treated by his environment largely determines how he will integrate into and function in society, whereas the physical disability itself and its severity weigh much less. We also noted the importance of the psychological processes that parents who have a child with a disability go through from the moment they are given the diagnosis to the start of the rehabilitation work. We further pointed out the prominence accorded to the physical aspect of disability at the expense of the emotional component as well as the medical team's preoccupation with bodily function while omitting talk about the disability itself. Disability or chronic illness in an infant or young child can arouse highly intense feelings among his caregivers and the treating team. For the members of the team providing the physical treatment to be able to help the child and his parents speak the disability, they must be aware of themselves and their emotional world. They must be able to sense, for example, when they are acting out of overidentification with the child or the parents. This self-reflective stance on the part of professionals is not self-evident and is far from simple, and it is made easier through team discussions of difficult cases and mutual support.

References

Antonovsky, A. (1979). *Health, stress, and coping.* San Francisco, CA: Jossey Bass.

Anzieu, D. (1989). *The skin ego.* New Haven, CT: Yale University Press.

Bick, E. (1968). The experience of the skin in early object relations. *International Journal of Psychoanalysis, 49,* 484–486.

Dolto, F. (1984). *L'image inconsciente du corps* [The unconscious body image]. Paris, France: Editions du Seuil.

Howe, D. (2006). Disabled children, maltreatment and attachment. *British Journal of Social Work, 36,* 743–760.

Kao, B., Plante, W., & Lobato, D. (2009). The use of the Impact on Sibling Scale with families of children with chronic illness and developmental disability. *Child: Care, Health and Development, 35,* 505–509.

Keren, M., Feldman, R., Eidelman, A., Sirota, L., & Lester, B. M. (2003). Clinical Interview for High-Risk Parents of Premature Infants (CLIP) as a predictor of early disruptions in the mother–infant relationship at the nursery. *Infant Mental Health Journal, 24,* 93–110.

Koester, L. S., Karkowski, A. M., & Tracey, M. A. (1998). How do deaf and hearing mothers regain eye contact when their infants look away? *American Annals of the Deaf, 143,* 5–13.

Preisler, G. M. (1993). A descriptive study of blind children in nurseries with sighted children. *Child: Care, Health and Development, 19,* 295–315.

Preisler, G. M. (1994). Early patterns of interaction between blind infants and their sighted mothers. *Psychiatrie de l'Enfant, 37,* 81–113.

Stern, D. N. (1985). *The interpersonal world of the infant: A view from psychoanalysis and developmental psychology.* New York, NY: Basic Books

Stern, D. N. (1995). *The motherhood constellation: A unified view of parent-infant psychotherapy.* New York, NY: Basic Books.

ZERO TO THREE. (2016). *DC:0–5™: Diagnostic classification of mental health and developmental disorders of infancy and early childhood* (DC:0–5). Washington, DC: Author.

Recommended Reading

Als, H., Duffy, F. H., McAnultry, G. B., Rivkin, M., Vajapeyam, S., Mulkern, R. V., . . . Eichenwald, E. C. (2004). Early experience alters brain function and structure. *Pediatrics, 113,* 846–857.

Barker, D. H., Quittner, A. L., Fink, N. E., Eisenberg, L. S., Tobey, E. A., & Niparko, J. K.; CDaCI Investigative Team. (2009). Predicting behavior problems in deaf and hearing children: The influences of language, attention, and parent–child communication. *Developmental Psychopathology, 21,* 373–392.

Barrera, M. E., & Vella, D. M. (1987). Disabled and nondisabled infants' interactions with their mothers. *American Journal of Occupational Therapy, 41,* 168–172.

Hadadian, A., & Rose, S. (1991). An investigation of parents' attitudes and the communication skills of their deaf children. *American Annals of the Deaf, 136,* 273–277.

Holdith-Davis, D., Docherty, S., Miles, M. S., & Burchinal, M. (2001). Developmental outcomes of infants with bronchopulmonary dysplasia: Comparison with other medically fragile infants. *Research in Nursing & Health, 24,* 181–193.

Keren, M. (2011). An infant who was born with a life-threatening skin disease: Various aspects of triadic psychotherapy. *Infant Mental Health Journal, 32,* 617–627.

Koblenzer, C. S. (2005). The emotional impact of chronic and disabling skin disease: A psychoanalytic perspective. *Dermatology Clinics, 23,* 619–627.

Madden, S. J., Ledermann, S. E., Guerrero-Blanco, M., Bruce, M., & Trompeter, R. S. (2003). Cognitive and psychosocial outcome of infants dialyzed in infancy. *Child: Care, Health and Development, 29,* 55–61.

Mayes, L. C. (2003). Child mental health consultation with families of medically compromised infants. *Child Adolescent Psychiatric Clinic of North America, 12,* 401–421.

Melamed, B. G. (2010). Parenting the chronically ill infant. In S. Tyano, M. Keren, H. Herrman, & J. Cox (Eds.), *Parenthood and mental health: A bridge between infant and adult psychiatry* (pp. 277–288). London, England: Wiley-Blackwell.

Minde, K. (2000). Prematurity and serious medical conditions in infancy: Implications for development, behavior, and intervention. In C. H. Zeanah, Jr. (Ed.), *Handbook of infant mental health* (2nd ed., pp. 176–194). New York, NY: Guilford Press.

Müller Nix, C., & Ansermet, F. (2009). Prematurity, risk factors, and protective factors. In C. H. Zeanah, Jr. (Ed.), *Handbook of infant mental health* (3rd ed., pp. 180–196). New York, NY: Guilford Press.

Rahi, J. S., Manaras, I., Tuomainen, H., & Hundt, G. L. (2004). Meeting the needs of parents around the time of diagnosis of disability among their children: Evaluation of a novel program for information, support, and liaison by key workers. *Pediatrics, 114*, 477–482.

Semple, C. J., & McCance, T. (2010). Parents' experience of cancer who have young children. *Cancer Nursing, 33*, 110–118.

Soliday, E., Kool, E., & Lande, M. B. (2001). Family environment, child behavior, and medical indicators in children with kidney disease. *Child Psychiatry and Human Development, 31*, 279–295.

Spittle, A. J., Treyvaud, K., Doyle, L. W., Roberts, G., Lee, K. J., Inder, T. E., . . . Anderson, P. J. (2009). Early emergence of behavior and social–emotional problems in very preterm infants. *Journal of the American Academy of Child and Adolescent Psychiatry, 48*, 909–918.

Sullivan, P. M., & Knutson, J. F. (2000). Maltreatment and disabilities: A population-based epidemiological study. *Child Abuse and Neglect, 24*, 1257–1273.

Svavarsdottir, E. K., McCubbin, M. A., & Kane, J. H. (2000). Well-being of parents of young children with asthma. *Research in Nursing & Health, 23*, 346–358.

Vaccari, C., & Marschark, M. (1997). Communication between parents and deaf children: Implications for social–emotional development. *Journal of Child Psychology and Psychiatry, 38*, 793–801.

CHAPTER 15
My Parents Are Ill

The Bear Is Ill

The bear is ill, not feeling good,
Must've been something in the food,
Now he is lying oh so sad,
And moaning, groaning really bad . . .
Around him everyone's astir,
With good advice to offer Bear:
Perhaps a little iodine?
It always seems to work just fine.
. . .

And each piece of advice is tops—
But still his crying never stops.
. . .

Then Mr. Rabbit saved the day,
A clever chap, what can we say.
"Thermometer!" he claimed, so sure,
"This is the one and only cure."
. . .

Five minutes later, not one more—
And Bear was dancing on the floor.[1]

What does it mean for a child to have a parent who is sick? How is this illness treated, and by whom? Moreover, how is the child to relate to the parent who is sick? Illnesses involving prolonged and uncertain recovery are hardly a theme of choice in children's literature. Miriam Yalan-Shteklis's poem describes the bear's illness: What caused it? ("Must've been something in the food"); how does it affect the patient's mental state ("sad . . . and moaning, groaning") and the mental state of those around him? Friends try to help the bear with their best advice, only to discover to their

---

[1] Miriam Yalan-Shteklis, "The Bear Is Ill," appears in *I Gave Nurit a Flower*, pp. 10–11, published by Kinneret Zmora-Bitan. Reprinted with permission.

regret that despite their eagerness and identification with his pain and wretchedness, they cannot make things easier for him, let alone cure him. Rabbit's brilliant solution saves the day in the nick of time, restoring the bear to joy—the kind of joy that comes from physical health. However, what happens when everyone around the person with an illness is at a loss to come up with a cure? What happens when, despite the deep identification of all those around, despite the medications and the doctors, the much-loved patient continues to suffer? In this chapter, we address exactly this—namely, what happens to the sick bear's children when there is no rabbit jumping out of the hat.

Introduction

A parent's illness, either physical or mental, affects the infant's emotional development, all the more so when it brings in its wake changes in parenting behaviors. In our experience, medical staff treating adults are insufficiently aware of this. In fact, treatment for a parent who is sick takes up most of the household's attention and worry, and the young children are addressed to us, if at all, only when their distress takes on visible symptoms. Moreover, even when the parents do seek counseling, they often fail to associate between the parent's illness and the young child's behavior, repeatedly claiming that "the child is too little to understand." However, utterances by young children prove how wrong they are. For example, a toddler only 2½ years old, whose mother was ill and who had developed provocative and anxious behavior, declared that "Mommy is sad!" on entering the consultation room. The mother was confused, surprised that he was aware of her state of mind.

Physical or mental illness in a parent is often accompanied by a change in the quality of his relationship with the child. Young children sense disease, and they somehow understand the situation and worry about what might happen to the parent. This concern sometimes has the effect of making a child negatively disposed toward her parent, who will mistakenly respond by being critical, impatient, or insensitive. Hence, the parent's disease might affect the child's development and mental health, mainly when the environment is not supportive enough and the financial situation is bad. It is therefore important to support the family and explain to the child, however young, that the parent who is sick loves her, and that no one—certainly not the child—is to blame for the appearance of the disease. Explanations of this type will promote the child's continued typical development and allow her to cope with the complex situation.

Nurit Zarchi had to wait many years before she was able to give direct expression to her childhood trauma in her book Solitude Games.[2] *Her*

---

[2] Nurit Zarchi, 1999, *Solitude Games*, published by Yedioth Aharonoth.

father, Yisrael Zarchi, a writer and translator, who had always protected her, fell ill.

The father dies shortly after contracting the disease, when Kalia, the heroine of the book, is about 5 years old. The sudden, premature loss robs her not only of a chance to know her father but—being part of him—to know herself, to get down to who she is. Thus, throughout her life, the initial traumatic loss remains inscribed in her soul, which cannot detach from the father who had detached himself from her all at once. The mental infrastructure underlying Kalia's entire adult existence will forever be steeped, until her death, in the inescapable darkness of the eternal shadow cast by the giant figure of the missing father.

From Kalia's point of view, her blessed literary talent is another result of the absent-father curse. Indeed, after his death, she finds herself time and again descending into the dark recesses of the underworld, where he disappeared, and there she meets Cerberus, the guardian dog at its gates. To pacify the monstrous dog with the three drooling heads, she becomes acquainted with the power of poetry, the only power from which the intimidating dog recoils. Like Orpheus who went down into the underworld to retrieve Eurydice, she uses her poetic skills to appease the dog of the underworld. The narrator's early loss has prevented her not only from knowing herself and being who she was for many years but also from seeing the great talent she was endowed with as an avenue for dealing with the existential anxiety she was exposed to in childhood.

A Parent Who Has a Psychiatric Disorder

Many poets and writers have written about their childhood in the shadow of a parent with mental illness, but the scientific interest brought to the subject is relatively recent.

In his novel A Tale of Love and Darkness, *Amos Oz portrays the figure of the narrator's mother as an educated, beautiful, and dreamy woman—a lonely, introverted woman who is mostly cooped up in her room steeped in ever-growing depression, which probably led her to suicide.*

As he sees it, she was caught in a twilight zone between a sublime, dream world on the one hand and agonizing loneliness on the other hand. This, along with lifelong delusions of yearning, lured her unto death until she finally heeded its call in 1952, when she was 39 and he was 12½ years old.[3]

---

[3] Amos Oz, 2005, A Tale of Love and Darkness, translated by Nicholas de Lange, p. 203, published by Vintage Books.

In one of the chapters of the book, the narrator further tries to figure out what caused the depression his mother suffered from until her suicide. Her life's dreams and promises, he thinks, may have been contaminated—already in youth—by a poisonous romantic notion associating death with the muses. Then, as life failed to deliver on any of these promises, death was seen as a seductive, ultimate lover promising to heal her lonely heart.

The culprit, then, is death, the old murderer as the narrator calls him, a serial killer of broken-hearted, disappointed souls who assumes alluring youthful appearances and a tempting voice and uses various other cunning devices to draw them into his murderous grasp.[4]

The narrator's long search for the "old murderer" and his ability to provide such a meticulous description of him attest to his profound familiarity with Thanatos (the death instinct), who, disguised as Eros (the life instinct), lured his mother into death.

The child described in the novel is intelligent, sensitive, and vulnerable. Like his mother, he is a lonely individual who has only his extended family as a beneficial and protective factor. He basks in their admiration of him and every word he utters, a sign for them of his incredible intelligence, his originality, sensitivity, and artistic penchant. At the age of 4 or 5, he thus became an arrogant little boy, confirmed in his arrogance by the adults around him.[5]

Despite the ironic look taken by the writer at the cocky boy that he was, evidently the environment that reveled in his talents was for him a supportive environment that allowed him to go on developing, playing, and creating. This is indeed a tale of love and darkness, but the title beautifully puts love before darkness.

It is known today that parental psychopathology greatly affects the quality of the relationship with the baby and his subsequent development, but the underlying mechanism is still not sufficiently clear. Deeper investigation into the matter only uncovers a more complex, multivariate picture. Factors pertaining to the baby's constitution, including his temperament, sex, and genetic vulnerability, will determine, to a certain extent, the impact of the mother's or father's mental disorder on him. This also explains why, in many cases, one child in the family is more strongly affected by the parent's illness than his siblings, although all seem to have grown up in the same environmental conditions. Let us take,

---

[4] Amos Oz, 2005, *A Tale of Love and Darkness*, translated by Nicholas de Lange, p. 209, published by Vintage Books.

[5] Amos Oz, 2005, *A Tale of Love and Darkness*, translated by Nicholas de Lange, published by Vintage Books.

for example, the interplay between a baby born with a difficult temperament and his depressive mother. Such a mother tends to show negative emotions more than she expresses positive ones and will therefore have a hard time regulating her baby's moods. This might reinforce the temperamental baby's inclination to express negative emotions and put him at further risk. Inversely, the depressive mother's encounter with her baby's difficult temperament could also have an adverse impact on her, reinforcing her sense of failure and sinking her self-image even lower than it already is.

Gender, yet another constitutional factor, plays an important role in the interplay between the parent who is sick and the child. Tronick (2007) followed children's response to their parents' distresses and showed that boys and girls significantly differed in their response to maternal depression. He found, for example, that the more the mother's depression was chronic and profound, girls were more given than boys to symptoms of depression and delinquency.

Support from a well-functioning family can be a protective factor because the parent who is sick is well embraced. In contrast, a dysfunctional family is a significant risk factor for the young child of a parent with mental illness. A single-parent family situation with no social support can make things worse for both the mother who is ill and the baby.

As we show later, mental illness in a parent is not necessarily a liability to the child's development, barring other risk factors. Moreover, protective factors, such as good functioning of the healthy parent or the child's secure attachment to one of the parents, can mitigate the effect of the illness.

It is important to note that the specific psychiatric diagnosis is less important for the child than the way in which the illness affects parenting behaviors. For example, self-harming behaviors, suicide threats, detachment, and total lack of vitality are parental behaviors that have been shown to be detrimental to the child's development and functioning, regardless of whether these are due to parental Borderline Personality Disorder or Major Depressive Disorder. We now review several parental psychiatric disorders and their potential effects on a baby's development.

Parents Who Have Depression

Depression as such, provided it does not last too long and is not associated with other risk factors such as parental psychopathology or environmental stressors, will not necessarily produce emotional distress in a baby. Prolonged maternal depression, however, affects the baby in different ways, depending on her characteristics and on contextual factors. Generally speaking, babies of mothers with prolonged depression can be said to be at high risk for the appearance of emotional regulation difficulties, for the development of inse- cure attachment to their mother, and for even lower than average motor and cognitive development. This might be linked to the fact that mothers with depression are often less sensitive to their baby's needs, that their facial expressions are mostly negative, and that they look at and speak to the baby less than healthy mothers. They often have a hard time being flexible and adapting their behavior to the baby's emotional needs. Others have an angry and intrusive pattern of interaction, which is also detrimental to the young child.

Deeper and longer depression translates into a larger number of adaptation problems observed in infants and toddlers, especially girls. An empirical study (Goodman & Brand, 2009) showed that, from their fourth month of life, babies responded to their mother's depression with withdrawal and sadness. Stern (1995) showed that sometimes, in identifying with her mother, a baby will imitate her sadness, loss of vitality, and disinterest in others. These babies are at risk of becoming children and adolescents with social difficulties, low academic achievements, and low response thresholds to stressful situations. In adolescence, they often have anxiety, depression, and behavioral disorders as well.

The stressful impact of depression is also reflected in the baby's physiological indicators, such as cortisol, secreted by the hypothalamic axis. Indeed, a direct correlation has been found between maternal depression and the level of cortisol in these mothers' 1-year-old children. These hormonal changes are linked to the lower ability to regulate emotions observed in children of mothers with chronic depression.

So far, we have focused on maternal depression and its effect on the young child. The impact of paternal depression on the young child has been less extensively studied, even though the past 15 years have seen tremendous strides made in understanding the father's place in the development of children and the importance of his direct involvement, daily attachment, and care-based routines. Furthermore, the father plays a highly important role when the mother is ill: A child's secure attachment to his father becomes a protective factor against the corrosive effects of his mother's illness (Seifer, Sameroff, Dickstein, Keitner, & Miller, 1996). Indeed, a study (Vakrat, Aper-Levy, & Feldman, 2017) that monitored the development of babies whose mothers had suffered from postpartum depression but whose attachment to the father was secure showed that the babies had internalized a positive image of the father figure and had adapted better at school age, despite the negative image they had of the mother figure.

Sometimes, the father fails to understand his wife's sluggish behavior following birth, her avoidance of—and even indifference toward—the newborn. He will often even quarrel with her and blame her for being dysfunctional. The existence of prolonged marital strife might compound the effects of maternal depression on the baby's development. Indeed, it was shown (Owen & Cox, 1997) that babies reacted strongly to these situations of parental conflict, and more particularly to the father's aggression and hostility toward the mother.

Some researchers have even argued that this factor affects the baby more than the maternal depression.

Parental depression used to be treated with medication and individual psychotherapy without, however, considering the parent–baby relationship. Ever since awareness was gained of the detrimental, prolonged effects of parental depression on the young child, dyadic and triadic parents–baby therapy is strongly recommended, coupled with individual therapy for the parent.

Parents Who Have Schizophrenia

CASE STUDY

A 6-year-old boy described how he perceived his mother, who had paranoid schizophrenia:

"My mother thought I was a hedgehog when I was inside her belly. When I was born, she named me after a scary animal. My mom was afraid of me. I could tell by the way she looked at me, and I was scared to look at her, so I would turn my head sideways. I heard my mother say: 'You see, he doesn't like me,' and I wanted to cry out that I did, but I was simply terrified of her look and her face, which never smiles at me, and never moves at all. Yes, I prefer being taken care of by my grandma, my mother's mom, but don't get me wrong, I notice what's happening to my mom, and I know that she is my mom."

Schizophrenia is among the most severe mental illnesses, mostly because it appears at a relatively early age and is accompanied by a gradual and irreversible deterioration of cognitive, affective, and social skills. Among others, this illness manifests itself in hallucinations and delusions distorting the perception of reality.

A longitudinal study (Seeman, 2002) on the socioemotional outcomes of offspring whose mothers were schizophrenic showed that those who were exposed to their mother's illness during their first 5 years of life were highly at risk for developing psychopathology at an older age. The study showed that mothers with schizophrenia demonstrated negative emotions toward their babies and that their psychological investment and sensitivity were lower than those of healthy mothers. They also conveyed a lesser sense of protection and stability, did not spontaneously play with the baby, and did not offer their baby sensory stimulation. These behaviors have a lot in common with those of mothers with severe depression, but the chronic nature of schizophrenia and its accumulative negative impact on parental behaviors explain its deep and pervasive influence on the child's overall development. Given these circumstances, these children are sometimes forced to grow up prematurely and assume a parental role. This "pseudo" maturation, solely functional, brings their childhood to an end and has long-term implications for their functioning.

The difficulty experienced by mothers with schizophrenia to fill their parental role requires cooperation between the adult psychiatrist, the child psychiatrist, and the social welfare services. Sometimes, treatment fails and there is no choice but to take the child away from her parents. Such a hard decision will only be taken, of course, after making sure that the other parent's parental competence is also lacking. In some cases, the extended family takes over and cares for the baby, more or less officially.

Parents Who Have Anxiety Disorder

Anxiety disorders are one of the most prevalent disorders among adults, affecting 13% of the general population. There are many types of anxiety disorders: panic attack, agoraphobia, social phobia, specific phobias, Obsessive Compulsive Disorder (OCD), Generalized Anxiety Disorder (GAD), and Posttraumatic Stress Disorder (PTSD). Relatively fewer studies have examined the specific influence of maternal anxiety disorders on babies compared with the number of studies that have analyzed the impact of depression on parenting behaviors and children's outcomes. Parental anxiety disorders can be transmitted to the offspring genetically as well as through anxious parental behaviors.

Generalized Anxiety Disorder

Again, the main question is how this disorder affects parental behavior. For example, observations of mothers with GAD have shown that they tended to hit the panic button if everyday occurrences in the baby's life were slightly out of the ordinary, that they were intrusive, that they often felt guilty toward the baby for no apparent reason, and that they did not leave the baby enough leeway. Also, a mother with GAD will often not allow anyone, including the father, to take care of the baby, fearing some catastrophe. Generally speaking, their babies tend to assimilate a representation of the outside world as a dangerous place, often become dependent on their mother, barely explore their immediate surroundings for fear of getting too far away from the mother, and manifest separation anxiety. These behaviors on the child's part drive the mother, in turn, not to let other adults be involved on the pretext that the baby only calms down with her. It is therefore hardly surprising to find a very high rate (80%) of insecure attachment among these children.

CASE STUDY

B., an 18-month-old toddler, was referred to our unit at her parents' initiative because of difficulties falling asleep "since forever," multiple tantrums at home, and a tendency to cling to her mother. Her functioning at day care was normative except for separation difficulties. During our first session, the mother described herself as a "perfectionist," as someone who cannot allow herself to function at an average level and is always afraid of failing and disappointing those around her. She added that she had a hard time bearing her girl's dissatisfaction and tantrums: "I give her everything, how can she not be satisfied?" The parents also reported that the toddler was their first daughter and that her pregnancy was preceded by a stillbirth—a traumatic event for both of them.

During the evaluation, the toddler stayed glued to her mother, without playing, and both looked somewhere between anxious and sad. The father sat next to them, but he made no attempt to draw his daughter toward him. All three kept silent. The atmosphere was "heavy" and frozen.

"Actually, what's your concern?" asked the therapist.

"Everything . . . since the incident."

"You mean the miscarriage?"

"Yes. It's been clear to me since then that bad stuff can happen to us. I lost my innocent outlook on life. Everything seems scary and threatening to me; it is as if, since then, anything bad can happen to us."

"Before the miscarriage, were you an anxious type by nature?"

"Yes, it runs in our family . . . But up until the miscarriage, I was able to convince myself that nothing bad would happen, because up until that point things were going well for me in life."

According to the mother, her second pregnancy was shrouded in anxieties ("I wasn't able to enjoy it"), and the period after the birth was tense ("I let no one take care of the baby, constantly fearing that something might happen to her"). The baby's difficulties to fall asleep appeared very early on, probably because of the difficulty the mother had to leave her daughter alone in bed. The baby also exhibited excessive stranger anxiety, separation difficulties, and exaggerated dependence on the mother. To this the mother responded with frustration and anger. An anxious and ambivalent relationship formed between the two. The mother was constantly wary of "making mistakes and hurting the girl," which prevented her from setting her clear, consistent boundaries. The father, for his part, was apprehensive about hurting his wife, and therefore did not insist on his right to take his place within the triad and set age-appropriate limits for the child.

The *DC:0-5™: Diagnostic Classification of Mental Health and Developmental Disorders of Infancy and Early Childhood* (DC:0-5; ZERO TO THREE, 2016) diagnoses would be as follows:

- Axis I: Clinical Disorders
  - » Sleep Onset Disorder
  - » Relationship Specific Disorder of Infancy/Early Childhood (with mother)

- Axis II: Relational Context
  - » Level 3—Compromised to Disturbed relationship with mother
  - » Level 2—Strained to Concerning caregiving environment

- Axis III: Medical Condition
  - » None
- Axis IV: Psychosocial Stressor
  - » Marital tension
- Axis V: Developmental Competence
  - » Functions at age-appropriate level

We recommended triadic psychotherapy as well as having the mother work on her GAD with an adult psychiatrist. The triadic therapy lasted about 8 months. The girl's symptoms disappeared, except for the falling asleep difficulties that sometimes returned, especially when things got tense between the parents. The girl integrated well into day care, yet remained shy in character.

Obsessive Compulsive Disorder

OCD is a relatively common disorder that runs in families. It is chronic in nature and may seriously disrupt parental functioning. It is a disorder characterized by recurrent, intrusive thoughts or images that trigger anxiety and rituals meant to extinguish the anxiety (such as endless checks, putting things in order, counting, cleaning, and washing). Additional characteristics of the disorder are constant doubt and uncertainty. Many continue to suffer from this disorder at some level or another, despite medication and behavioral therapy.

Children whose parents suffer from OCD are at risk for developing the same disorder or some other psychopathology, depending on their genetic heritage and the impact the disorder has on parental behaviors. Only a few longitudinal studies have examined how OCD affected parenthood. Some (Challacombe & Salkovskis, 2009) pointed out the tendency of mothers who have this disorder to be more intrusive and judgmental than healthy mothers or mothers who have a different kind of anxiety disorder. A higher rate of interpersonal problems and introversion was found in children 7 years old and up whose mothers had this disorder.

CASE STUDY

T., a 2½-year-old boy, was referred to our unit by his pediatrician because he used to run away from his parents when they came to pick him up from day care. He also exhibited severe delay in language development and hyperactivity, poor eating, poor sleep, and lack of joy. He had previously been diagnosed by a child neurologist as having Autism Spectrum Disorder and Attention Deficit Hyperactivity Disorder.

During the initial evaluation, the parents described him as "a stupid and nervous boy"; they did not believe that he would ever be able to speak. They added that they could not attribute any emotional meaning to his behaviors because he was not at all capable of understanding his environment. They thought that the child was not attached to them: "He doesn't care about us."

During the meeting, they expressed anger and deep disappointment. We noticed the little boy's untidy appearance, his sad or indifferent expression—it was hard to tell which—and the absence of attachment behaviors toward his parents. He did not initiate any game, but he responded to the therapist's invitation to play with a car. During the session, he scarcely talked, yet he pronounced the words "mine" and "I" several times. When he encountered a problem, he did not seek his parents' help but rather the clinician's, a stranger figure though she was.

The mother suffered from OCD since she was 12 years old. She was never treated. The family's genetic heritage was heavy, including an extremely anxious mother, a brother who had schizophrenia, and a sister with Trichotillomania.

T.'s pregnancy and birth were normal. The mother breastfed him but derived no pleasure from it. When he was 6 months old, she was overtaken by bouts of anger against the baby because the care he required kept her away from her compulsive washing of clothes and walls. Fearing contamination and disease, she imposed severe limitations on the baby: He was not allowed to crawl and touch things around the house. He spent long hours during the day in the playpen so as not to get dirty. The toys too were set aside for the same reasons. The baby grew increasingly irritable. The parents attributed this behavior to his "innate bad temperament." At 8 months old, T. started attending day care. His behavior improved. When he was not home, he was calmer. When he turned 2 years old, he started resisting returning home from day care. He would also cry every day during bath time and diaper change. It turned out during the session that the mother washed him endlessly, fearing dirt and contamination.

The child's DC:0–5 diagnoses would include the following:

- Axis I: Clinical Disorders
  - » Deprivation Disorder (rather than autism)
  - » Relationship Specific Disorder of Infancy/Early Childhood (with mother)

- Axis II: Relational Context
  - » Level 4—Disordered to Dangerous relationship with mother
  - » Level 3—Compromised to Disturbed caregiving environment

- Axis III: Medical Condition
  - » None

- Axis IV: Psychosocial Stressors
  - » Maternal OCD
  - » Marital tension

- Axis V: Developmental Competence
  - » Inconsistently present competencies

We embarked on triadic psychotherapy with a view to change his parents' perception of him and improve the mother–toddler relationship. Toilet training was particularly hard for the mother, who could not stand soiling and initially refused to let her son wean from diapers at his own pace. The father agreed to take charge of this.

The child's general condition greatly improved after 1 year of therapy. He did not develop OCD and formed a good relationship with the father, but his relationship with the mother remained tense. When discussing T.'s prognosis, we weighed the risk factors and protective factors. The risk factors we came up with for developing a psychiatric disease in general and OCD in particular were the following: heredity, male gender, exposure to negative parental perception of the child, the mother's negative behavior and negative emotional attitude, the conjugal tension due to the mother's illness, and general familial dysfunction. Counteracting these risk factors were two major protective factors: the mother's newfound motivation to treat her illness on becoming a mother, and the mental health of the father, who was very much involved in the child's daily care.

The Impact of PTSD on Parenting

What is known about children's responses to their parents' PTSD? Researchers and clinicians have shown that symptoms are more likely to appear in young children when the father is the one with PTSD. In a study conducted in the United States, Hoven, Duarte, and Mandell (2003) examined the responses of children whose parents had been injured in the 9/11 terrorist attacks on the World Trade Center. They found that when the parent had comorbid PTSD and depression, 50% of the children developed emotional problems compared with 10% of children in the general population. The children in this study presented with aggressive behavior (40% compared with 5% in the general population), anxiety or depression (32% vs. 8%), somatic symptoms (25% vs. 3%), social withdrawal (20% vs. 8%), and attention problems (17% vs. 7%). In terms of gender difference, the symptoms were generally more prevalent in boys than in girls. Boys also tended to respond with aggression, whereas girls displayed symptoms of anxiety and depression.

Eating Disorders in Parents

In this section, we discuss eating disorders in mothers and their effects on babies because this disorder mainly afflicts women. Are infants and young children whose mothers suffer from an eating disorder more prone to develop one in infancy/early childhood themselves? How does the mother's eating disorder affect her parental behavior and the quality of her relationship with her child?

Of all known eating disorders, the most common is bulimia nervosa. Few women who have severe mental anorexia become mothers because one consequence of this illness is the absence of ovulation and diminished likelihood of conception. To illustrate this, a woman with anorexia will conceive on average 29 months after deciding to do so, compared with 6 months in a healthy woman. A study conducted in Scandinavia (Micali, Simonoff, & Treasure, 2009) showed that 17% of children born to women with anorexia had eating problems until at least 5 years old, and they became preoccupied with their body and diets by 10 years old.

The effect of a maternal eating disorder on the baby's eating patterns

In a longitudinal study (Wright, Parkinson, & Drewett, 2006), mothers with eating disorders were regularly assessed. Children whose mothers had an eating disorder were more prone than others to show eating problems. In another study, Reba-Harrelson et al. (2010) compared babies of mothers with bulimia to those of mothers with anorexia. Babies of mothers with bulimia tended to be overweight because of overfeeding, whereas babies of mothers with anorexia tended to be underweight because of food refusal and exhibited withdrawal behaviors during meals.

The effect of a maternal eating disorder on parenting behavior

Becoming a parent is no easy task for anyone, much less so for mothers with eating disorders. A study comparing the attitudes of new mothers who had eating disorders with new healthy mothers showed that 92% of the former considered the transition into motherhood difficult compared with only 13% of the healthy mothers (Saarilehto, Keskinene, Lapinleimu, Helenius, & Simell, 2001). There were even extreme cases of mothers with anorexia starving their babies for fear of fatness. A maternal eating disorder often breeds conflict between mother and baby, especially around food and eating. In conflict situations, these women tend to be rigid—unable to find a compromise that respects the child's needs for independence and differentiation. A core characteristic of women with an eating disorder is a constant need to be in control. The power struggle between mother and infant occurs during mealtimes, especially when the child wants to eat solo, makes a mess all around, or refuses to eat at the appointed time. During meals, mothers with anorexia dominate the baby, both verbally and physically, and present a negative attitude. In these conflictual situations, the baby will often have a hard time putting on adequate weight. Still, some mothers with eating disorders read their baby's independence-seeking signals and manage to overcome their food aversion and their difficulty to put up with the way their child eats.

Treating mothers with an eating disorder usually requires addressing their personal difficulties alongside therapeutic work on the parent–child relationship. Our experience has also taught us that targeted therapy focused on videotaped footage of the eating interaction itself adds to the effectiveness of treatment. The videotaped meal is viewed together with the mother, followed by a therapeutic discussion with her. These discussions gradually improve the ability of a mother with an eating disorder to see her baby's signals—to understand that he wants to experiment with food, get dirty, and eat independently. This method considerably reduces the friction between mother and baby, resulting in weight gain for the baby and improved emotional state for both. At the same time, mothers must take care of their own eating disorder as well.

Parental Personality Disorders

Personality disorders manifest themselves in a set of rigid behavior patterns and significant difficulties in close interpersonal relations, reflecting a basic problem of self-identity and trust in others. The impact of Borderline Personality Disorder on parenting has started to be studied. The findings so far are that specific parental behaviors—such as affect lability, bursts of uncontrolled anger accompanied by rejection of the infant's need for closeness, verbal abuse, self-harm behaviors, and suicide threats—are particularly detrimental to the child's emotional development. Moreover, a parent who has Borderline or Narcissistic Personality Disorder is also a highly likely candidate for depression, which raises the risk for complex and problematic parenting.

Antisocial Personality Disorder

Antisocial Personality Disorder has emotional, social, and moral aspects. Individuals with this disorder are for the most part violent, impulsive, and destructive in behavior. These are people who have failed to internalize social norms, and who do not therefore believe that these norms should be respected. They lack empathy and sensitivity to others, including their children. They are the opposite pole of the "good-enough parent." When the father is the one who has Antisocial Personality Disorder, the mother often has a weak, submissive personality and cannot protect her children from his violence or counteract his negative influence. The child is then at a high risk to develop a behavior disorder that will transmute into an antisocial disorder in adolescence, often associated with drug addiction. These children exhibit signs of abnormal violence and of sadness from infancy, as described in chapter 8.

Indeed, Antisocial Personality Disorder is often passed on from parents to their children, and this intergenerational transmission involves genetic–biological and environmental factors. The environmental factors include authoritarian, coercive, and inconsistent disciplinary practices toward the child; lack of empathy and warmth; and aggressive interpersonal communication that the child imitates. Genetic studies have pinpointed a genetic callous–unemotional trait that might be present in people with psychopathy (Hawes, Brennan, & Dadds, 2009; Waller et al., 2016). Psychopathy is the extreme end of Antisocial Personality Disorder. It is characterized by total lack of empathy and by instrumental aggression that may lead to cruel criminal acts and cold murders with no regard to the penalty.

Parents with Antisocial Personality Disorder do not realize how problematic their parental behavior is and do not seek counseling. Furthermore, they blame all their problems on society. When they are forced to consult with clinicians, they put up a lot of resistance and change little in terms of parental behaviors.

Borderline Personality Disorder

Borderline Personality Disorder is more common among women. It is characterized by difficulty in regulating emotions and controlling impulses, self-identity problems, fear of loneliness, separation anxiety, and difficulties in close interpersonal relations. A strong link has been demonstrated between early experiences of neglect, abuse, and traumatic losses in infancy and the appearance of Borderline Personality Disorder in adulthood; there is also a strong tendency to reproduce the problematic parenting patterns experienced in childhood.

Despite the relatively high prevalence of Borderline Personality Disorder among young women, researchers have only recently begun to study its impact on parenting behaviors and on the outcome of their offspring. Typically, these mothers have a hard time dealing with the toddler's need for both autonomy and dependency. These mothers sometimes find it hard to play with the child; some of them get bored and yawn with disinterest, whereas others are jealous of the child ("No one ever did this for me."). Their behavior is inconsistent— intrusive at times and uninvolved at others, sensitive at times and rejecting at others. This emotional lability frightens infants and young children and often creates insecure resistant/ambivalent attachment, or even disorganized attachment when maltreatment is involved. Later on in life, these children will often have relational problems with others as well as adaptation difficulties. Separation anxiety is conspicuous in these mothers, as is their high intolerance to solitude. Some commit "demonstrative" suicidal gestures (e.g., vein slicing, ingestion of medication). Maternal self-harming behaviors are especially detrimental to the child because they are perceived by the child as a problem-solving strategy. Sometimes, a mother with Borderline Personality Disorder sees her young child as an adult who fails to understand her and her needs sufficiently well, and she feels toward her both hostility and dependence. In addition to the problematic relationship that the child has with her mother, she is also exposed to the instability of her mother's other interpersonal relations— for example, with her intimate partners. Such a mother might hang on to a drug-addicted or violent partner just because she is afraid of being alone. In some cases, especially when the mother has experienced sexual abuse and trauma in her own childhood, her reactions endanger the well-being of the infant, and child protection services must be informed.

CASE STUDY

An 18-month-old toddler approaches his mother with his right hand slightly raised. The mother recoils, with fear on her face. The little one is startled by the look on her face and starts to cry. The mother says, "I thought he was about to hit me. Suddenly he appeared to be a man; I forgot he was a little boy who couldn't do me any harm." This short incident illustrates the "frightening–frightened" relationship between mother and child. The mother had suffered from abuse all her life—by her father in her childhood and later by her partners, two violent men with Antisocial Personality Disorder.

Narcissistic Personality Disorder

Narcissistic Personality Disorder is characterized by a self-centered constant need to obtain positive reinforcements from the environment. Others are either idealized or devalued according to their reaction to the person with Narcissistic Personality Disorder. These individuals experience intense anger when they—wrongly—feel rejected ("narcissistic rage"). To the best of our knowledge, no studies have been published on how Narcissistic Personality Disorder affects parenting and the development of young children. From our experience, this type of personality disorder should be seen as a risk factor because the parent might reject and even neglect the child when he believes that the child does not reward him and does not affirm his success as a parent. In other words, parents with Narcissistic Personality Disorder can be easily offended ("narcissistic injury") when their child disappoints their expectations and can react harshly.

CASE STUDY

A Well-Baby nurse asked for our opinion on the relationship between a mother and her 3-month-old baby. The nurse noticed that the mother did not talk much to her baby and kept her at arm's length. She suspected postpartum depression. The therapist happened to overhear a previous exchange between the clinic's secretary and the mother. When the secretary asked the mother for her girl's name, she hesitated for a while, then gave what was actually a boy's name. The mother was a pretty blonde woman, well groomed, who looked more irritated than depressive. The baby girl—dark skinned, with her head slightly leaning sideways because of torticollis (contracted neck muscles)—was very quiet. Her mother held her in her arms but facing away from her.

In our first session, the mother said she had experienced an emotionally difficult birth. On the physical side, everything went well. The mother had decided before the birth that she would not breastfeed, fearing that breastfeeding would mess up her cosmetic breast surgery. The pregnancy was planned and desirable; however, during this period, the couple lost a very close friend, who was killed in an accident. The couple decided to name their daughter after him, although she was a girl. "I was sure I would give birth to a blonde girl like me, and look what came out—a black curly girl!" (she actually had her father's skin and hair color), the mother blurted out suddenly, with a taint of anger and disappointment in her voice. This utterance afforded a glimpse into the great importance she attached to external appearance. She had trouble seeing the baby's needs and was narcissistically hurt by the baby's dissimilarity to her.

The mother's difficulty to bond with her baby was not due to postpartum depression but to her narcissistic injury. At the end of that session, the mother admitted her difficulty to love her girl. She agreed to go into mother–baby psychotherapy to help her see her baby as a whole and not through the prism of her lack of resemblance to her. Indeed, her daughter's qualities stood out increasingly more as she developed, and the mother accepted her more. Still, thinking that this little girl was at risk for developing a "false self" (Winnicott, 1956) meant to satisfy the needs and expectations of the mother, we advised the mother to undertake psychotherapy for herself. She agreed, understanding that she was otherwise prone to re-create with her daughter the difficult relationship she had experienced with her own mother (whom she described as "cold and self-absorbed"). We did not give the baby any diagnoses because she had no symptoms.

Treating the parent–child relationship when one of the parents has a personality disorder

When a parent suffers from any type of personality disorder, and Borderline Personality Disorder in particular, one of the most effective modalities of treatment is the "Watch, Wait, and Wonder" parent–child therapy (see chapter 17).

Along the therapeutic process, the therapist needs to be aware of the complexity of the difficult experiences that the parent has often had in the past to contain the parent's anxiety and distress while still paying attention to the baby, and to avoid showing either rejection or dismissal. The goal of therapy is to develop the parents' ability to understand the child's inner world through her behaviors and, thus, facilitate the building of trust and bolster the child's self-confidence. Sometimes, babies of this type of parent form a better relationship with the therapist than they do with the parent, which could spark envy in the parent. The therapist must not fall into the countertransference trap by identifying with the child's distress and criticizing the parent for her lack of reflective skills.

Parents Who Have a Chronic Physical Illness or Disability

Little scientific literature has been published on the parenting of individuals who are sick or physically disabled. In the United States, the right of an individual with a disability to become a parent was only anchored in law in 1942, after many court cases became precedents. Disabilities vary in nature, but they all have social stigma in common. Worse still, women with a disability are often discriminated against compared with men who have the same disability;

it is harder for them to find employment, marry, and perceive themselves as mothers. Legally speaking, too, the right of women who are physically disabled to become mothers has not always been self-evident.

Partial and full deafness are two of the most common disabilities (86 cases per 1,000 inhabitants are reported in the United States). The number of people who are visually impaired and blind from birth is, however, much lower. According to data published in the United States, 56% of adults who are congenitally disabled marry, but only 27% of those with orthopedic disabilities and 39% of those with hearing or visual disabilities have children. Ninety percent of people who are deaf pick a partner who is also deaf, and in most cases (nine out of 10), they give birth to a hearing baby.

Any type of disability poses a challenge for parents. How will a parent who is deaf–mute respond to a baby who is not immediately within sight? How can a baby whose parent is blind safely explore his environment? How can parents who are bound to a wheelchair physically take care of their children? The difficulty is huge and often requires creative coping strategies to support the parent–child relationship and meet the child's needs.

Babies of Parents Who Are Deaf

Does having a disability influence the personality of the person who is disabled? Apparently not. Disability does not prompt the development of a particular kind of personality. It does, however, seem that individuals with disabilities in general and individuals who are deaf in particular often have low self-esteem, especially those whose caregivers did not know how to deal with their disability in childhood. Obviously, those who are able to find a partner have a better self-image and self-esteem—a crucial element when it comes to parenting.

Many deaf parents hope for a baby who is also deaf: "who would be like us, one of us; after all, our life is good despite the deafness." However, there are also parents who desire the opposite. These different attitudes are, in all likelihood, related to the self-esteem that each parent has built up in life. The main difficulty for parents who are deaf and who have a hearing child is not communication between them, which is usually normative (Koester & Lahti-Harper, 2010), but their ability to teach the baby the spoken language and regulate her behavior from a distance (Barker et al., 2009). Indeed, most hearing children born to parents who are deaf start out somewhat behind in terms of language and speech acquisition, but most of them eventually catch up. Besides this difficulty, children of individuals who are deaf present the same rate of secure attachment as children of hearing parents. This finding is not surprising because mothers who are deaf are highly sensitive to their babies and touch them a lot. As far as family functioning goes, a hearing child seems to be harder on parents who are deaf than a child who is deaf like them. Most children of parents who are deaf do not consider their parents' hearing impairment a "disability," and they tend to speak fondly and lovingly of their parents. When they hit adolescence, they report a sense of constant responsibility for their parents, a need to mediate between them and society, as well as a need to protect them. Still, the situation is sometimes more complex—for example, when the child takes upon himself the role of parent and actually controls his parents, or when the child avoids them. Here is what a hearing mother, born to parents who were deaf–mute, told us: "I had no communication problem with them, but we only communicated on a very basic and instrumental level. It was hard talking to them about complicated stuff, and so I did not really share my problems with them. I learned to trust myself more than I did others." Without being aware of it, she herself talked little to her daughter, and the daughter was on her way to developing oppositional behavior.

Thus, when evaluating an infant or young child whose parent (or parents) is disabled, we pay special attention to their interpersonal communication, to their degree of collaboration, and to their ability to show warmth together with assertiveness while setting adequate limits for the child.

Babies of Parents Who Are Blind

Fewer women who are blind than women who are deaf marry and become mothers. Most women who are blind live with a seeing man. Few studies have examined relationships between parents who are blind and their children, and most of the literature on the subject is based on clinical experience. It would seem that mothers who are blind have a harder time responding optimally to their baby than do mothers who are deaf. Moreover, seeing babies of mothers who are blind differ in their responses from babies of mothers who are deaf: The former tend to divert their gaze from the mother's face, responding to her face as if it were a negative stimulus. Mothers who are blind must use verbal communication and touch to offset the negative effect of their unseeing eyes.

In an Israeli study that examined the interaction within eight families between parents who are blind and their seeing children (Deshen & Deshen, 1989), the whole range of responses were observed in the children: from a sense of pride to a feeling of shame, from social involvement to avoidance and withdrawal, and from helping the parent to avoidance and distancing.

Furthermore, for a parent who is blind, daily baby-care tasks—such as changing diapers, feeding, and toilet training—are quite challenging. Significant variability is observed among parents who are blind in their ability to raise their baby, depending on social facilities and support.

Babies of Parents With Motor Disabilities

Cerebral palsy is the most common congenital motor disability (1–2 cases per 1,000 births), accounting for 50% of cases of motor disability. Multiple sclerosis is the second most prevalent motor disability. These make things particularly difficult because they cause chronic fatigue, personality changes, and considerable uncertainty regarding the future.

The difficulties of parenting are particularly felt in the child's first 5 years in life, in which care is physically intensive. Parenting behavior is influenced by the parent's ability to deal with her disability and "speak it" clearly to the young child. In some cases, a pathological relationship comes about between the parent who is disabled and the child.

CASE STUDY

A mother with cerebral palsy had twins: G. and S. The family came in for a diagnosis at our clinic when the children were 2½ years old because of late language development and social difficulties. The twins were born at 36 weeks of gestation, 8 years into the marriage. Initially, the mother did not want kids. She preferred to pursue her professional career, which in her mind symbolized her triumph over the disability. Apart from that, she feared that she would give birth to a defective child, especially in view of the fact that her brother had been born with intellectual disability (formerly known as mental retardation).

Despite all this, her husband badly wanted children, and she finally agreed to get pregnant. When she found out that she was carrying a pair of twins, she asked for reduction, feeling that she "would be capable of raising only one child." Her husband objected to the reduction, and the twins were born. After the birth, an au pair came to live in with the family and to help the mother with the physical handling of the twins. In reality, the au pair became the children's main attachment figure even though it was clear to both parents that she was not providing them with sufficient stimulation. A week before they came to us for an evaluation, the children started going to day care.

The meeting brought out the mother's underinvolvement in the children's daily life. One of the twins was constantly trying to grab her attention, whereas the other never approached her.

The DC:0-5 diagnoses for both children would be as follows:

- Axis I: Clinical Disorder
    - » Relationship Specific Disorder of Infancy/Early Childhood (with mother)

- Axis II: Relational Context
    - » Level 3—Compromised to Disturbed relationship with mother
    - » Level 3—Compromised to Disturbed caregiving environment

- Axis III: Medical Condition
  - » None
- Axis IV: Psychosocial Stressor
  - » Mother's cerebral palsy
- Axis V: Developmental Competence
  - » Inconsistent capacities

The children's language delay was not due to a neurodevelopmental disorder but to the lack of verbal stimulation. We offered triadic parents–child psychotherapy for each twin, with the aim of speaking the mother's physical limitations and enhancing each parent's reflective capacity. Treatment lasted approximately 6 months and led to a general improvement for both mother and twins.

Babies of Parents With a Life-Threatening Physical Disease

Most studies on the outcome of babies born to parents with a life-threatening disease were conducted in the United States. Approximately 24% of all adults who suffer from cancer have children who are less than 18 years old. Cancerous tumors in the skin, the head, and the neck, as well as lymphoma, are common between 20 and 44 years old. A third of breast cancer cases are detected in mothers of young children.

When the parent who is sick is no longer able to provide the "usual" care for the children and is forced to ask for their help, the feeling is one of not being a good-enough parent any more. Akram and Hollins (2009) found that girls tended to stay away from their mother, whereas boys tended to draw closer. Parents who have a life-threatening disease are greatly preoccupied with how and what to tell their children. In fact, it is absolutely vital to speak about the disease with the children, regardless of their young age, in understandable terms for their age and level of development. One has to talk frankly about the disease while expressing some optimism, without going into too much detail. Parents need to explain its nature and emphasize that it prevents them from functioning as usual, not because they do not want to but because they are unable to. It is important to emphasize to the toddler that he is not responsible for the appearance of the disease. In the event of an incurable disease, the explanation to give the toddler is that the body stopped working properly and that the doctors tried but were unable to fix it. Continuous support is the key to allowing all family members—the parent with the disease, the healthy parent, and the child—to deal with the tragic situation in a healthy way. Lieberman, Compton, Van Horn, and Ghosh Ippen (2000) wrote an eloquent book about losing a parent through death in the early years of life. Naturally, a child's reaction depends on his ability to understand—that is, his cognitive maturity. An infant or young child will be affected mainly by the change in his care routine; an older child will also grasp the meaning and the implications of the loss hovering over the family. The most important thing is to talk with the child and explain the changes taking place at home in his daily life.

Conclusion

In this chapter, we have shown that a parent's mental or physical illness affects the baby by changing parental behaviors. We noted that, regardless of the actual illness diagnosed, what matters is the way in which it influences parental behavior on a daily basis. The mental health of the other parent and the support received by the family are two major protective factors. In this domain, as in all others, the relationship between risk factors and protective factors is dynamic and complex. Studies on young parents who grew up in the shadow of a parent with an illness have revealed that a physical disease can affect a child's development just as much as mental illness. Loss-related anxieties, a tendency to avoid asking for help, and precocious self-reliance characterize many children who grow up with a parent who is physically or mentally ill. Early interventions with both parents and the infant or young child are meant to forestall the appearance of these defense mechanisms and the danger they pose for the subsequent development of the child's personality.

References

Akram, A., & Hollins, S. (2009). Being a parent with a disability. In S. Tyano, M. Keren, H. Herrman, & J. Cox (Eds.), *Parenthood and mental health: A bridge between infant and adult psychiatry* (pp. 311–324). London, England: Wiley-Blackwell.

Barker, D. H., Quittner, A. L., Fink, N. E., Eisenberg, L. S., Tobey, E. A., & Niparko, J. K.; CDaCI Investigative Team. (2009). Predicting behavior problems in deaf and hearing children: The influences of language, attention, and parent–child communication. *Developmental Psychopathology, 21*, 373–392.

Challacombe, F., & Salkovskis, P. (2009). A preliminary investigation of the impact of maternal obsessive compulsive disorder and panic disorder on parenting and children. *Journal of Anxiety Disorders, 23*, 848–857.

Deshen, S., & Deshen, H. (1989). Managing at home: Relationships between blind parents and sighted children. *Human Organization, 48*, 262–267.

Goodman, S. H., & Brand, S. R. (2009). Infants of depressed mothers: Vulnerabilities, risk factors, and protective factors for the later development of psychopathology. In C. H. Zeanah, Jr. (Ed.), *Handbook of infant mental health* (3rd ed., pp. 153–170). New York, NY: Guilford Press.

Hawes, D. J., Brennan, J., & Dadds, M. R. (2009). Cortisol, callous-unemotional traits, and pathways to antisocial behavior. *Current Opinions in Psychiatry, 22*, 357–362.

Hoven, C. W., Duarte, C. S., & Mandell, D. J. (2003). Children's mental health after disasters: The impact of the World Trade Center attack. *Current Psychiatry Reports, 5*, 101–107.

Koester, L. S., & Lahti-Harper, E. (2010). Mother–infant hearing status and intuitive parenting behaviors during the first eighteen months. *American Annals of the Deaf, 155*, 5–18.

Lieberman, A. F, Compton, N. C., Van Horn, P., & Ghosh Ippen, C. (2000). *Losing a parent to death in the early years: Guidelines for the treatment of traumatic bereavement in infancy and early childhood.* Washington, DC: ZERO TO THREE.

Micali, N., Simonoff, E., & Treasure, J. (2009). Infant feeding and weight in the first year of life in babies of women with eating disorders. *Journal of Pediatrics, 154*, 55–60.

Owen, M. T., & Cox, M. J. (1997). Marital conflict and the development of infant-parent attachment relationships. *Journal of Family Psychology, 11*, 152–164.

Reba-Harrelson, L., Von Holle, A., Hamer, R. M., Torgersen, L., Reichborn-Kjennerud, T., & Bulick, C. M. (2010). Patterns of maternal feeding and child eating associated with eating disorders in the Norwegian Mother and Child Cohort Study (MoBa). *Eating Behavior, 11*, 54–61.

Saarilehto, S., Keskinene, S., Lapinleimu, H., Helenius, H., & Simell, O. (2001). Connections between parental eating attitudes and children's meager eating: Questionnaire findings. *Acta Paediatrica, 90*, 333–338.

Seeman, M. (2002). Women with schizophrenia as parents. *Primary Psychiatry, 9*, 39–42.

Seifer, R., Sameroff, A. J., Dickstein, Keitner, G., & Miller, I. (1996). Parental psychopathology, multiple contextual risks, and one-year outcomes in children. *Journal of Clinical Child Psychology, 25*, 423–435.

Stern, D. N. (1995). *The motherhood constellation: A unified view of parent-infant psychotherapy.* New York, NY: Basic Books.

Tronick, E. Z. (2007). The impact of maternal psychiatric illness on infant development. In E. Tronick (Ed.), *The neurobehavioral and social–emotional development of infants and children* (pp. 305–318). New York, NY: Norton.

Vakrat, A., Aper-Levy, Y., & Feldman, R. (2017). Fathering moderates the effects of maternal depression on the family process. *Development and Psychopathology.*

Waller, R., Trentacosta C. J., Shaw, D. S., Neiderhiser, J. M., Ganiban J. M., Reiss, D., Leve, L. D., & Hyde, L. W. (2016). Heritable temperament pathways to early callous-unemotional behaviour. *British Journal of Psychiatry, 209,* 475—82

Winnicott, D. (1956). Primary maternal preoccupation. In *Through paediatrics to psychoanalysis* (pp. 300–305). London, England: Hogarth

Wright, C. M., Parkinson, K. N., & Drewett, R. F. (2006). How does maternal and child feeding behavior relate to weight gain and failure to thrive? Data from a prospective birth cohort. *Pediatrics, 117,* 1262–1269.

ZERO TO THREE. (2016). *DC:0–5™: Diagnostic classification of mental health and developmental disorders of infancy and early childhood* (DC:0–5). Washington, DC: Author.

Recommended Reading

Bagner, D. M., Pettit, J. W., Lewinsohn, P. M., & Seeley, J. R. (2010). Effect of maternal depression on child behavior: A sensitive period? *Journal of the American Academy of Child and Adolescent Psychiatry, 49,* 699–707.

Barnow, S., Spitzer, C., Grabe, H. J., Kessler, C., & Freyberger, H. J. (2006). Individual characteristics, family experience, and psychopathology in children of mothers with borderline personality disorders. *Journal of the American Academy of Child and Adolescent Psychiatry, 45,* 965–972.

Cox, J., & Barton, J. (2010). Maternal postnatal mental disorder: How does it affect the young child? In S. Tyano, M. Keren, H. Herrman, & J. Cox (Eds.), *Parenthood and mental health: A bridge between infant and adult psychiatry* (pp. 217–230). London, England: Wiley-Blackwell.

Dietz, L. J., Jennings, K. D., Kelley, S. A., & Marshal, M. (2009). Maternal depression, paternal psychopathology, and toddlers' behavior problems. *Journal of Clinical Child and Adolescent Psychology, 38,* 48–61.

Field, T., Diego, M., & Hernandez-Reif, M. (2006). Prenatal depression effects on the fetus and newborn: A review. *Infant Behavior & Development, 29,* 445–455.

King, S., & Laplante, D. (2005). The effects of prenatal maternal stress on children's cognitive development: Project Ice Storm. *Stress, 8,* 35–45.

Malhotra, S., & Kaur, R. P. (1997). Temperament study on children of mentally ill parents. *Hong Kong Journal of Psychiatry, 7,* 39–45.

Murray, L., Halligan, S. L., Goodyer, I., & Herbert, J. (2010). Disturbances in early parenting of depressed mothers and cortisol secretion in offspring: A preliminary study. *Journal of Affective Disorders, 122,* 218–223.

Newman, L., & Stevenson, C. (2008). Issues in infant–parent psychotherapy for mothers with borderline personality disorder. *Clinical Child Psychology and Psychiatry, 13,* 505–514.

O'Hara, M. W., & Fisher, S. D. (2010). Psychopathological states in the father and their impact on parenting. In S. Tyano, M. Keren, H. Herrman, & J. Cox (Eds.), *Parenthood and mental health: A bridge between infant and adult psychiatry* (pp. 231–240). London, England: Wiley-Blackwell.

Sherkow, S., Kamens, S. R., Megyes, M., & Loewenthal, L. (2009). A clinical study of the intergenerational transmission of eating disorders from mothers to daughters. *Psychoanalytic Study of the Child, 64*, 153–189.

Snellen, M., Mack, K., & Trauer, T. (1999). Schizophrenia, mental state, and mother–infant interaction: Examining the relationship. *Australian and New Zealand Journal of Psychiatry, 33*, 902–911.

Stein, A., Woolley, H., Murray, L., Cooper, P., Cooper, S., Noble, F., . . . Fairburn, C. G. (2001). Influence of psychiatric disorder on the controlling behavior of mothers with 1-year-old infants. *British Journal of Psychiatry, 179*, 157–162.

Stein, A., Woolley, H., Senior, R., Hertzmann, L., Lovel, M., Lee, J., . . . Fairburn, C. G. (2006). Treating disturbances in the relationship between mothers with bulimic eating disorders and their infants: A randomized, controlled trial of video feedback. *American Journal of Psychiatry, 163*, 899–906.

Thompson-Salo, F. (2001). The trauma of depression in infants: A link with attention deficit hyperactivity disorder? In F. Thompson-Salo, J. Re, & R. Wraith (Eds.), *Childhood depression: Why is it so hard to understand?* Melbourne, Victoria, Australia: Royal Children's Hospital.

Wan, M. W., Moulton, S., & Abel, K. M. (2008). A review of mother–child relational interventions and their usefulness for mothers with schizophrenia. *Archives of Women's Mental Health, 11*, 171–179.

Woolgar, M., & Murray, L. (2010). The representation of fathers by children of depressed mothers: Refining the meaning of parentification in high risk samples. *Journal of Child Psychology and Psychiatry, 51*, 621–629.

CHAPTER 16
Who Will Raise Me?

Moses, Oedipus, and twin brothers Romulus and Remus are some of the mythological figures who were adopted by compassionate families and who survived despite the dangers that lay in wait for them early on in life. From their moment of birth, death loomed over them: Moses because of Pharaoh's decrees; Oedipus because his parents, fearing the Oracle's prophecy, wanted him dead; and Romulus and Remus because the ruler condemned them to death by drowning. All were saved by strangers: Moses was saved by Pharaoh's daughter, who took pity on him; Oedipus by a shepherd who was passing by and who handed him over to the queen and king of Corinth; Romulus and Remus thanks to a servant who took pity on them and let them float on the Tiber, to the god of the river who watched over them, to the she-wolf who suckled them, and to a shepherd and his wife who raised them until they were young men. In all three myths, adoption saved the babies from certain death, the adopters were all endowed with human compassion and generosity, and the adopted children grew up to become illustrious leaders.

In the second half of the 19th century and the start of the 20th century, many stories of adoption were written for adolescent and adult target audiences. Some of the famous ones include the following: David Copperfield *by Charles Dickens (1848–1850),* Adventures of Huckleberry Finn *by Mark Twain (1885),* The Jungle Book *by Rudyard Kipling (1894),* Anne of Green Gables *by Lucy Maud Montgomery (1908), and the* Tarzan *series by Edgar Rice Burroughs (1912–1940).*

In these novels, the motif of danger to the life of the forsaken child is re-encountered, as in the ancient myths: a father who treats his stepson cruelly and causes the mother's death (David Copperfield); *a drunken father who turns his back on his son* (Huckleberry Finn); *the adoption of a child left by himself, after the death of his parents, by a brave family of wolves in the Indian jungle* (The Jungle Book); *an orphan girl who finds herself in an orphanage after her parents' death and is later adopted by a brother and sister who actually wanted a boy (Anne of Green Gables); and an English child adopted and raised as a son by a brave ape family after his parents are killed by apes in Africa at the end of the 19th century (Tarzan). In these novels, as in the myths mentioned earlier, most adoptive families are characterized by compassion, empathy, and at times even extraordinary courage (the apes and wolves) as well as acceptance of the adoptees.*

Alongside the similarity between the early stories and those of the 19th century, differences can also be found, especially in the way in which the adoptees—and even some of the adopters—are portrayed. The adopted children are described as wonderfully adaptive, ingenious, morally immaculate, and strongly driven to find out the identity of their biological parents. Their early lives—prior to adoption, and sometimes after—are hardly serene: David Copperfield is sent to study at a boarding school run by a ruthless headmaster; after his mother's death, he is forced to leave school and is sent to work for a wine merchant. David flees to his aunt Betsey, who agrees to raise him to prevent his stepfather's harassments. Huckleberry Finn is also adopted by a rigid, puritanical widow who imposes on him normative behavior not in keeping with his character. The adopters of Anne Shirley the orphan, who had actually hoped to adopt a boy to serve as a farm hand, agree to take her only because of her special character and temperament, and they end up happy with their choice.

Introduction

In this chapter, we discuss the development of infants and young children who are raised by adults other than their biological parents. The most common reasons for removing a baby or toddler from his parents' custody are abandonment at birth (for various reasons, including adolescent mothers, drug use, prostitution, or the birth of a child with severe congenital malformation), parental incompetence, neglect, and abuse. We close the chapter with a broad discussion on the rare but dramatic phenomenon of parental filicide.

A baby taken from her parents is entrusted to an institutional baby home, a foster care family, or an adoptive family on the basis of numerous considerations that we elaborate on later in this chapter. Some babies are handed over voluntarily by their parents, who have no wish or ability to raise them. Others are taken away from the parents because of serious parental dysfunction. In any case of out-of-home placement, the family court and the social welfare system are naturally involved. Mental health professionals are often called to offer their professional opinion as to parental competence. We address this issue as well as divorce between parents of infants and issues related to custody later in this chapter.

The reasons for taking a baby away from his parents are varied and require careful consideration with an eye to the child's best interest first and foremost. In these situations, two basic rights are at odds: the parents' right to be the guardians of their children and the child's right to grow up in a good-enough environment that meets his developmental, emotional, and social needs. Even though parental competence is defined in law, real life gives rise to many in-between cases, and the tendency in some countries (such as Israel) is to give parents who failed to live up to their role a second chance at raising their child, provided they take psychological treatment. Whereas in some cases, treatment helps significantly, in other cases the change is insufficient, and the child will have lost precious time in the meantime.

This is the place to introduce the concept of "Child Time." Albert Solnit developed the idea that time has a very different meaning for children compared with adults because their brain goes on developing very fast during the first 3 years of life and is shaped especially by the quality of attachment experiences (Solnit, Schowalter, & Nordhaus, 1995). For example, a young child placed in a foster care family for a limited period defined by the court, during which time the biological parents are supposed to try to improve their parental skills, will attach to the foster family. If the court then orders her return to her biological parents, the child will need to cope with the new loss of attachment figures and the need to adapt to a new environment again. All these adverse experiences are potentially damaging to brain development. By the same token, Child Time is to be taken into account when considering whether a child should continue to grow up with her highly dysfunctional parents. Neglect and maltreatment in infancy have been proved to cause considerable, sometimes irreversible, brain damage.

Studies by Zeanah et al. (2009) pointed to 2 years old as the watershed moment concerning the negative effects that severe emotional and environ-mental deprivation have on the brain. Having examined children who grew up in an institution under difficult conditions, they showed that those who stayed there after 2 years old suffered from more subsequent emotional and behavioral problems than those who left before this age. Their adoption after 2 years old only partially corrected their situation. It is important to note that this research was conducted in an orphanage in which the care dispensed to the children was poor in quality. Since the publication of the findings, these institutions have changed their policy on the care provided to babies under their charge.

The so-called "best interest of the child" is the core value that guides the family court in its decision to remove a child from home (Goldstein, Freud, Solnit, & Goldstein, 1986) This means choosing an environment for the child that can provide for his every physical, material, and emotional need. In the event of divorce, for example, the child's best interest would be to have his lifestyle from before his parents' separation maintained as much as possible, as well as his relations with both parents (as long as these do not harm him). This principle is also highly relevant to foster care situations in which the young child and the biological parent remain in touch. Obviously, in cases of parental neglect or maltreatment, the child's best interest conflicts with the parents' interest.

CASE STUDY

A mother addicted to drugs had a baby, struggled to provide for him, and handed him over voluntarily to a short-term foster care family. She promised to abstain and asked for him to be returned to her at the end of her detoxification treatment. She began the process, but she was unable to persevere. She appealed to the family court to be given a second chance and to have the child stay with the foster care family a few more months. From her perspective of time, this was not much to ask. From the baby's time perspective, his best interest was to have his final placement decided at this point so that he could either strengthen his attachment to the foster care family or renew his attachment to the biological mother. However, it is also important to give the biological mother a chance to raise her child.

The final decision lies with a judge but will largely be influenced by the expert opinion of child psychiatrists and psychologists. The expert report is usually complex because it requires integrating (a) observations of interactions between the biological parent and the baby as well as the infant's attachment to the foster care family and (b) information from the welfare services about the parent's psychiatric and social background as well as parental behaviors that led to the baby's placement out of home. The case is discussed in light of the scientific knowledge relevant to the specific situation. Ideally, the principle of Child Time should mean a short judicial process; in reality, it usually takes months, especially when there is more than one expert opinion, because each can attribute different weights to the various parameters of the case.

Parental abuse in the first years of life has long-term consequences for the child's development. Typically, in fact, in her first years, a child learns through trial and error, takes initiatives, tries new things, and takes pleasure in repeating successes over and over. At other times, the child will fail, avoid the frustrating activity for a while, then try it again with better chances of success thanks to new skills that will have developed in the meantime. In this way, she develops her cognitive and motivational system. A violent parent impinges on this developmental process by misreading the child's behaviors as "bad behaviors." Let us take the example of a child who, trying to eat or drink without help, dirties things around her and herself; this might elicit a violent response from the parent in interpreting the baby's behavior as one intentionally directed against him. A parental reaction of this kind will inhibit the baby's desire to explore and will discourage her initiatives. Initiation and exploration are building blocks in the formation of personality. When the parent's aggressive impulses are not regulated, the infant or young child also has trouble regulating her own impulses, fears, and anger. The clinical manifestations include an angry mood, aggression, fears, attention problems, agitation, learning difficulties, social inhibition, low self-esteem, behavior disorders, and later personality disorders. Moreover, in some cases, the child's clinical picture shows Posttraumatic Stress Disorder with dissociative states. At the interpersonal level, the capacity for empathy in children who have been maltreated is often greatly impaired. Parental abuse affects not only the psychological system but also the physiological one, especially the stress-related hypothalamic–pituitary–adrenal (HPA) system and the hormonal system. Also observed is increased prevalence of psychosomatic symptoms in those who had suffered from neglect or abuse in their childhood.

It is therefore not surprising that adults who had suffered from abuse in their past usually suffer from personality disorders accompanied by depression; anxiety; self-harming behaviors; antisocial behavior; drug use; and tempestuous, unstable, and often violent interpersonal relationships. Without treatment, these individuals end up reproducing the abusive relationship and directing their aggression toward their partners and children.

> *In Leah Goldberg's book,* Apartment for Rent,[1] *another kind of mother is described. Contrary to the mother whose dignity comes from within, who stays at home to raise her children, the cuckoo bird prefers wandering outside and paying short visits to her children that others painstakingly raise. The use of the word "visits" to characterize her relationship with her children reflects the cultural critique leveled at mothers who do not toil hard to raise their own children. Furthermore, the prospective tenant in the apartment house accuses the cuckoo not only of hedonistic behavior but of abandoning her children in strangers' nests.*

Abuse and Neglect in Infancy: Definitions

There are five types of child abuse: physical abuse, sexual abuse, emotional abuse, neglect, and social exploitation.

The definition of physical abuse includes beating, shaking, throwing, poisoning, burning, cigarette extinguishing, drowning, strangling, or any other physical damage that an adult causes a child. This definition includes those cases in which the parent deliberately "creates" physical symptoms in the child (Munchausen by proxy syndrome). This particular type of abuse is usually

---

[1] Leah Goldberg, 1970, *Apartment for Rent*, published by Sifriat Hapoalim.

suspected by pediatricians in the absence of any plausible medical explanation for the symptoms described by the parents. Confirming this diagnosis often requires secret surveillance during hospitalization in a pediatric ward.

CASE STUDY

R., a 4-month-old baby, was brought by his mother to the emergency room on several occasions because of convulsions. The mother's relative indifference when describing the dramatic symptoms was inconsistent with what one would expect of a concerned mother. An electroencephalogram showed nothing, and after numerous tests, the doctors started to suspect that the mother was behind these mysterious convulsions, without, however, being able to prove it. It was only later that the baby's older brother came forward and told his father that the mother strangled his little brother in secret. The mother, of course, was incarcerated, and the father became the only parent in charge of the children. Long-term family psychotherapy was required.

Sexual abuse is defined as an act of forcing someone to take part in any kind of adult sexual activity.

Emotional abuse in infancy is defined as actively ignoring the child's attachment needs, keeping him away from the rest of the family or secluded from the company of his peers.

Neglect is defined as failure to meet the basic physical and emotional needs of the child to the point of harming her cognitive, physical, or emotional development. This form of abuse is the hardest to detect and prove despite being the most common.

Social exploitation is defined as the use of child labor (not applicable to infants or toddlers).

Sixty percent of cases of domestic violence take place between the parents. This influences the child at any age, even if he is only witnessing it. The aggressive parent frightens the child, who feels that the parent who is the victim is incapable of self-defense and hence of protecting him. One also should keep in mind that children less than 2 years old might get incidentally hit by their simple presence on the "battlefield." Infants' or young children's reactions to parental violent behaviors are reflected in emotional and behavioral symptoms, mainly depression, anxiety, and violence toward themselves or other children. In addition, depending on the gravity of the violence they witness, these children are at risk for developing Posttraumatic Stress Disorder of Infancy. The following two descriptions illustrate the type of traumatic event that infants or young children can be exposed to.

CASE STUDY

A 1-year and 10-month-old infant was in his mother's arms when her husband shot her dead with a pistol. This happened as she was leaving the police station in which she had just filed a complaint against the father for threatening her with murder. The toddler sat by his mother's body until a police car arrived.

A 2-year-old toddler witnessed a violent fight between her two parents. When the father pointed a gun at his wife, the child hung on to her, thus preventing a potentially lethal injury. The mother was hit in the head but survived. When she came to us for an evaluation, the toddler said, "Daddy boom-boom mom."

Abuse and Neglect: Risk Factors

A distinction should be made between risk factors originating in the child herself and risk factors originating in the parents.

Risk Factors Emanating From the Child

Infants with a difficult temperament—as well as children with significant developmental delays, malformations, or chronic diseases—are more at risk to be mistreated, especially when additional risk factors in the parents and life adversities are present.

Risk Factors Emanating From the Parents

Potentially violent parents often have trouble regulating their negative emotions and impulses, are diagnosed with low-functioning personality disorders, and often use addictive substances. Among this at-risk population, many of the pregnancies are neither planned nor wanted, and if, on top of this, the baby is born with one of the risk factors mentioned earlier, he will often be subjected to abuse or neglect.

Abusive or neglecting parents describe their baby with negative attributes, especially if she fails to satisfy their expectations for a disciplined, considerate, easy-to-raise child. They fail to understand that a baby who grows up in a violent setting cannot meet such expectations. It is important to understand that abusive parents had often experienced maltreatment in their own childhood as well and therefore have not been able to assimilate a representation of a "good-enough parent" who is sensitive to the child's needs. It should be noted, however, that not every child who had suffered from abuse in childhood becomes an abusive parent in adulthood—only one third of them do. In fact, additional environmental risk factors probably need to be present for abuse and neglect to take place. These include low socioeconomic status, unemployment, loneliness and isolation from community and family life, as well as life in poor and violent neighborhoods. The more risk factors there are originating in the baby, the parents, or the environment, the greater the risk for neglect and abuse.

The Effects of Neglect on the Bio–Psycho–Social Development of the Baby

The United Nations Children's Fund estimates that about eight million children around the world currently live in institutions—about a million and a half of them in Europe. Hence, a baby landing in an adoptive or foster care family does not come as a "tabula rasa" because the conditions in which he had grown before reaching the safe haven have had physical, developmental, psychological, and cognitive adverse effects, at least in part irreversible. Babies raised in institutions do not usually have the benefit of a permanent attachment figure. Moreover, the physical, emotional, and social interactions between caretakers and babies and between the babies themselves are quite limited. The same goes for the quality of stimulation to which infants in institutions are exposed.

The published data relating to the impact of growing up in an institution on the physical development of infants are impressive: Every 3 months spent in an orphanage sets them back 1 month in terms of development. They are shorter than other children their age and have a smaller head circumference. One explanation would be that these children are subject to numerous stressful situations since birth, which trigger hypersecretion of cortisol (the stress hormone), which, in turn, inhibits secretion of growth hormone. In addition, this negative impact on the hormonal axis responsible for regulating stress (HPA) also explains the difficulty of infants and young children who grow up in institutions to regulate their emotional responses under stress and to adapt to new situations.

Emotional neglect during the first 2 years also affects cortical maturation, as reflected in electroencephalograms. Electroencephalograms in typical babies show a gradual increase, in the first year, of the quantitative ratio between rapid and slow waves. A study on the electric activity of the brain in babies who were institutionalized showed retardation in the process of cerebral maturation, with an inversion of this rapid-to-slow-wave ratio (McLaughlin et al., 2010). Similar results were observed in children who grew up in an impoverished environment. It is thus possible to assume that the absence of environmental stimulation plays a major role in the late maturation of the cortex.

An important longitudinal intervention study carried out in a Bucharest orphanage in Romania by Zeanah et al. (2009) showed that when the stress and the emotional deprivation and the absence of caretaker attention were severe, the HPA axis was more dysfunctional, regardless of the time spent in the orphanage. Also, as the number of foster care families that the child had gone through increased, her HPA system became depleted and did not respond to stress anymore. Also, the clear beneficial effect of a definitive placement in a foster care family was stable over the years on two conditions: that the child had spent less than 2 years in the institution and that the foster family benefited from psychological support from the moment the child joined it. The beneficial impact of a child's early placement was reflected in her electrical brain activity: Shortly after the time of placement in a foster care family at 18 months old, the infant's electrical brain activity patterns remained the same as in those who stayed at the institution; at 6 years old, the brain activity normalized and was the same as that of typical children raised in their biological families. These results are tremendously important because they show that the deep impact, at the level of cerebral function, of therapeutic and systemic interventions takes time to appear. Long-term follow-ups are thus greatly important, and there is room for optimism despite the gravity of the neglect suffered initially in life.

Sensory stimulation is likewise essential to child development. This is the place to recall the work of René Spitz, who followed babies growing up in institutions in the period following World War II. Spitz (Spitz, 1951; Spitz & Wolf, 1946) showed that toddlers who spent a long time in institutions without sensory stimulation developed a state of anaclitic depression, sometimes lethal. On the basis of this knowledge, a sensory intervention was set up in a Korean orphanage: 2-week-old babies were exposed to multisensory stimulation for 4 weeks, 5 days a week, twice a day. The babies were tested at the end of the 4-week period and 6 months later. Six months on, their physical development was identical to that of babies who grew up in their families. Again, this proves the reversibility of at least some deficits occasioned by life in an institution.

Also, imaging studies (Fries, Shirtcliff, & Pollak, 2008; Pollak et al., 2010) have demonstrated that neglect and abuse affected the limbic system, especially the amygdala and hippocampus. The research paradigm was to show the babies several images of different facial expressions and record their physiological and brain responses. Contrary to the typical babies, the babies who were maltreated or neglected failed to recognize facial emotions. This anomaly remained stable for many years (Vorria et al., 2006). The same procedure was then administered to a group of young adults who grew up in institutions. It was found that, in comparison with their peers in the general population, their amygdala overreacted as they perceived facial expressions to convey anger or threat more often than youngsters with a typical childhood. They also had a hard time matching various facial expressions to happy, sad, or frightening social situations. Only when presented with faces that expressed anger or threat did they score as well as the general population. These results point to the role that the amygdala plays in the perception of others—a perception distorted by early experiences of abuse, which becomes a personality trait if no psychotherapeutic intervention takes place. The following case illustrates the impact of neglect and abuse on an infant's development and behavior.

CASE STUDY

L., a 1-year-old infant, was brought to a baby home after being taken by emergency order from the guardianship of his biological parents on grounds of extreme neglect. His parents used to leave him in bed for hours on end in a dark room—awake, wet, and soiled—while they took drugs in the adjacent room.

At the baby home, we saw an angel-faced baby who looked with big wonder-filled eyes at everyone entering the institution, a baby waving his little arms and smiling indiscriminately at every stranger. However, every time people got close, his face would take on a scared expression, and he would break out in tears. At night, L. was unable to fall asleep without swaying back and forth for a whole hour at least. This also happened every time he woke up at night.

Believing that this auto-stimulating behavior was a consequence of the serious parental neglect that L. had experienced, the team at the institution decided to give the baby more individual attention. Within several months, L.'s need for self-stimulation almost disappeared, only reappearing in moments of frustration. It is as if his outward behavior had improved but the type of response to stress remained engraved deep in his brain.

L.'s case illustrates these auto-stimulatory behaviors that have been observed in babies who grew up in institutions, as well as abrupt transitions between emotional indifference and bursts of aggression. These young children are often observed to have hyperactivity, difficulties concentrating, indiscriminate sociability and friendliness to strangers, and poor capacity for closeness and intimacy. In one study, Stams, Juffer, Rispens, and Hoksbergen (2000) followed 90 children who had been adopted, some immediately after birth and others after spending 6 months at an institution. The latter exhibited significant signs of emotional regulation disorder—including a tendency to confuse reality and imagination in situations of stress—hyperactivity, and inattention; they also displayed poor language and repetitive symbolic play.

Winnicott (1964) noted the relationship between severe emotional deprivation and delinquency when he looked after children placed in an institution. Controlled studies carried out later confirmed this observation. When a child who spent his first 2 years in an institution is adopted by a family, his physical and cognitive condition greatly improve, but some emotional and peer-relationship problems tend to persist because children who had been deprived of affection and empathy in their early years have difficulties identifying other people's emotional state correctly and regulating their behavior within the framework of interpersonal relations.

Lessons to Draw for Baby Homes

As part of the Bucharest Project conducted in a Romanian orphanage, Zeanah et al. (2009) were able to induce major changes in the local personnel's caregiving behaviors and knowledge about development in the early years of life. They demonstrated the beneficial impact of these changes on the emotional and developmental status of the infants and toddlers. Moreover, the changes observed among the caretakers took root and stuck with them for many years. Despite the researchers' concern that intervention by external professionals would create tensions within the local team, the personnel actually reported less burnout thanks to the new atmosphere at work. A similar change was reported when we implemented an intervention of this kind in an Israeli baby home. These results are encouraging, and efforts should be made to bring them about in all baby homes.

Evaluation of Parental Competence

When neglect or child abuse is suspected, parental competence must be tested and reported to the court. Parental competence is a juridical–social concept, defined as the parent's ability to meet the child's physical and emotional needs. One thing to bear in mind is the relative nature of this concept—parental competence is often measured against accepted norms in a given society.

Parental competence should be viewed as a multidimensional construct with behavioral, emotional, and cognitive aspects. To be considered competent, parents are expected to have the following basic aptitudes and abilities:

- Capability to provide physical care to the child.

- Capacity for individuation—that is, the ability to separate between their own needs and those of the child. (A mother who came to our clinic used to bathe her baby several times each day. When asked why she did it, she answered, "It simply gives me great pleasure to bathe her.")

- The ability to identify and contain distressing and conflictual situations in the child and deal with them effectively.

- The ability to provide the child with age-appropriate stimulation.

- The ability to build and maintain a daily routine adapted to the age of the child.

- The parent's ability to understand her own limitations and her openness to accept outside help.

Here are the key components of the process of evaluating parental competence:

- *Data collection:* It is necessary to obtain all the medical and psychological tests previously undergone by the parents and the baby as well as reports of treatments and hospitalizations, Well-Baby center follow-up data, reviews by the welfare services, and court decisions.

- *Clinical evaluation:* This covers each of the parents and their respective interaction with the child. The style of attachment is determined as well as the child's socioemotional development.

- *Psychological tests:* These are supposed to reveal the parent's personality structure with its defense mechanisms and ego-strengths. They are especially needed when the parent's credibility comes into question during the clinical evaluation. It is important to note that tests are no more than auxiliary tools in assessing parental competence.

The expert report integrates the background information and the clinical assessments, and the main principle on which the recommendations will be based is that of the child's best interest and Child Time (rather than the parent's). Still, it is up to the judge to decide who will raise the child. The judge may impose a psychotherapeutic intervention on parents before making the final decision to remove the child from their custody.

How to Avoid Out-of-Home Placement

In many societies, a neglecting or maltreating parent may be given a chance to improve his parental competence with the help of parent–child therapy and, if necessary, individual psychiatric treatment before deciding on the child's removal from his custody. The objective of therapy is to improve the parent's empathy toward his child and to understand what drove him to neglect or mistreat the child.

Neglectful and abusive families are characterized by the parents' inability to identify and understand the emotions that underlie their infant's behaviors. Among other things, they are unable to read the distress signals emitted by the baby. Thus, in treating these parents, attention should be paid to three main issues:

- First, these parents should be taught to observe the baby, her behaviors and expression of emotions, while trying to figure out their meanings.

- Second, they must be made aware that the baby's emotional states are greatly influenced by their own behavior, which is, in turn, often linked with adverse childhood experiences in their own past.

- Finally, parents must be helped in building a safe environment for the child that will satisfy his curiosity—his need to investigate the world—while also serving as a shelter where he can vent distress without fearing rejection.

As described in detail in chapter 17, a useful therapeutic tool for handling these difficult situations is video feedback—that is, viewing videotaped parent–infant interactions together with the parent. Home visits also contribute greatly to creating a therapeutic alliance with parents who have a hard time trusting the system. When working as a team, it is important to assign an experienced case manager because these are complex, time- and effort-consuming therapies, considering that most of the parents in question have a hard time trusting others and themselves to achieve any kind of change. The therapeutic intervention needs to be regular and frequent, such as 2 or 3 times a week.

We insist on frequency of treatment because these are situations in which time is of the essence. Parent–infant group therapy, home visits, and parents–infant therapy can be combined in different ways toward a single goal: to improve parental skills around everyday child care tasks, identify pathological parental projections on children, understand their source, and help parents come up with a better response to the child's behaviors. In our clinical experience, the minimal duration for effective treatment in these difficult cases is 6 months. When treatment ends, parental competence needs to be reevaluated. Whenever placement outside the biological family is in question, the pros and cons of tearing a child away from her home must be considered, as explained earlier.

Placing a Child in a Foster Care Family

There are times when intensive therapeutic intervention can do nothing to improve parental functioning, and the family court orders an out-of-home placement for the child. Out-of-home placement is aimed at providing the child with safety and opportunities to build trusting relations with adults (Rushton & Minnis, 2008). Still, the transition from home to a new family is yet another stressful event, added to all the adverse events the child has already experienced. Thus, placement is only the first therapeutic step, and the medico-social system must plan for therapy tailored to the child's specific emotional and developmental needs, including psychological support for the foster parents because the young child may present challenging behaviors in response to everything he has gone through.

Examining the Infant or Young Child on Arrival at the Foster Care Family

The goal is to evaluate the infant's emotional and developmental status and determine her specific needs. The evaluation is best performed at around 1 month after the baby's arrival at the foster care family, with a view to allow her time to adjust to the separation from the biological family or the baby home. Some clinicians recommend follow-up examinations for the child every 6 months in the first 3 years following placement.

The Infant's or Young Child's Adaptation to the Foster Care Family

From the standpoint of foster parents, caring for an infant or young child who has reached their home after experiencing neglect or abuse is no small challenge, which they are not always up to. Those in charge of the foster care system have to identify in the potential foster caregivers risk factors likely to make the foster process fail, such as burnout and ambivalence.

Even when the foster care family is an optimal fit, close professional accompaniment and parent–child therapy have been proven to reduce the number of transitions for children (Price et al., 2008). This help is needed because young children's adaptation to their new family is often a rocky road, strewn with symptoms of anxiety, clinginess, hypervigilance, eating and sleep disturbances, aggressive behaviors toward themselves and others, and severe temper tantrums. Sometimes they are in grief and depressed over their separation from the family of origin or, later on, over separations from short-term foster care families with which they had spent some time. Hence, these children's emotional responses and behaviors can be extremely challenging to the foster care parents. Following are several examples of symptomatic behaviors of toddlers entering a long-term foster care or adoptive family.

The foster parents of K., a 1½-year-old toddler, came to our clinic complaining about her repeated insertion of toys into her vagina, her outbursts whenever men came into the foster care home, and the many sleeping difficulties she suffered from.

G., a 1½-year-old toddler who also grew up in a foster care family, was referred to our clinic because he ate without stopping, stuffing himself ad nauseam and even taking food off other children's plates.

A., a 2-year-old toddler, was adopted after an unusually long stay at the baby home, which earned him privileged treatment there. He was often forgiven his aggressive and demanding behavior toward the staff and other toddlers. The adoptive family consisted of two parents and three biological children who seemingly functioned well until the adoption, which the parents did for altruistic motives. A.'s behavior made it hard for the mother to connect to him. The father, however, identified with him and formed a coalition with him against his wife and two daughters. Following the crisis, the parents were referred to us for a consultation, and family therapy was decided on involving the entire family. The therapeutic process revealed how A.'s behaviors brought up "ghosts" from the family closet that had theretofore been suppressed and may not have otherwise surfaced.

L., a 2-year-old toddler, spent a year with a foster care family after being taken away from his biological parents. The latter were suspected of violence between them and toward him. L. was brought in for evaluation at our clinic to determine whether he could go back to live with his biological mother. She claimed that her life had stabilized and was now organized and calm and that she was able to offer him a good-enough environment. When examined with the foster mother, he exhibited poor language, flat affect, as well as little curiosity and inquisitiveness. L. hung on to his foster mother throughout the examination. We wondered why he did not build a secure attachment with the foster mother during the whole year following his removal from home. It turned out that during that year, L. was taken out twice to foreign families, when the foster care family exercised their right to go on vacation by themselves once in a while. On top of that, the foster care family took in a few more kids that year, whereas others left. These repeated attachment disruptions were the reason why the little boy was still afraid and sad and did not bridge the developmental gap following placement outside the violent environment into which he was born.

The goal of an intervention plan is thus to reduce the risk of the foster placement failing and the child being transferred to another family. Moving between families takes a heavy toll: Monitoring of children placed in foster care families shows that the number of transfers between families is just as significant, if not more, in its long-term impact as the child's psychological state on the day of his initial placement.

Choice of Long-Term Foster Care or Adoptive Family— Is Kinship Always in the Child's Best Interest?

After the necessity has been established of placing a child outside her home, the next step is to decide which placement is optimal—with relatives or a foreign family. A study (Berrick, Barth, & Needell, 1994) that compared baby placement with relatives and with foreign foster care families showed that placement with close family was preferable for two major reasons. First, babies experienced greater stability and had lower chances of continuing to "wander" to other families. Second, they stood better chances of staying with their siblings or keeping in touch with them or even their biological parents. This being said, placement with family members also has its disadvantages, such as advanced age and poor physical health; particularly concerning are the cases in which psychopathology and conflicts run in the family and become exacerbated by the infant's arrival.

CASE STUDY

M. was born to young parents who both had an active psychiatric illness. The pregnancy was planned, and the parents were keenly aware of the significant genetic risk of their daughter developing the same illness in the future. Toward the end of the pregnancy, the mother's mental state deteriorated, and she was hospitalized. Immediately after the birth, her sister informed the welfare services of her willingness to care for the baby until the mother's release from the hospital, and the biological father consented. The welfare services granted her request, in line with the principle that placing the baby with relatives is better than placement in a foreign family. However, as is well known, there are exceptions to every rule. In this case, as it turned out, the relationship between the infant's mother and her sister was for many years complex and fraught with jealousy and competition. One year had passed since M. was taken in by her aunt. The argument that placement with the aunt was "in the child's best interest" seemed doubtful considering the alarming clinical picture that emerged from our evaluation: a sad toddler who talked little and even seemed to have developmental delays. However, removing M. from this setting to a new and foreign family might have harmed her even more. The compromise lay in making M.'s aunt and her husband agree to professional support from the foster care services.

More than half the children placed in foster care switch between at least three families during their first 3 years away from home. Hence, they come across several attachment figures along the way but experience repeated attachment disruptions, leading them to lose trust in adults. The short-term foster parent also faces a similar dilemma—whether to attach to the child or maintain a neutral emotional stance to the point of even minimizing interactions, knowing that the relationship is temporary. It is thus not surprising to see these children have emotional and developmental difficulties in the long run.

Another question concerns the best course of action to follow when siblings are taken out of the biological parents' care together. Is it in their best interest to be placed together in the same family or rather give each one of them more attention in different homes at the price of separating them? Proponents of their placement together argue that siblings support each other, despite the occasional jealousies and disputes that come up, as in any family setting. Blood ties do help in situations of distress, especially when the distress is shared by all the siblings: They all experience separation, lose familiar figures, and face the need to adapt to a new environment. These challenges are easier to cope with when the group of siblings goes through them together. Unfortunately, the welfare services often have a hard time locating a foster care family capable of accommodating all of the siblings.

Making an Adoption Plan for a Baby

The best known story of adoption in Jewish sources is that of Moses. Jochebed placed him in a chest, which she sent afloat on the Nile, hoping with all her heart that an altruistic figure would be found to take the newborn baby into her home, save his life, and ensure his future. This was commonly done in the ancient world when newborn babies were in mortal danger or their mother could not raise them. As was the case of other adopted children in many mythological and historical accounts, Moses too became a hero, social leader, and lawmaker. The story of Moses and the stories at the beginning of this chapter reflect a social perception that views the ability of adopted children to survive after separation from attachment figures and adapt to a new environment an expression of healthy physical and mental resilience.

Adoption of children is a well-known social practice from ancient times. It is mentioned several times in the Bible and forms part of the social code in different cultures. The decision to adopt a child stems from both the natural altruistic tendency to care for a child who was abandoned or rejected by its progenitors and the strong desire of sterile parents to raise a child. The altruistic tendency is not an exclusively human characteristic but one that also exists in other mammals. Observation of chimpanzees in the wild showed that they also had the altruistic tendency, as expressed in their adoption of suckling monkeys who were abandoned by their parents and their seeing to all their existential needs. Similarly, female elephants also adopt every abandoned little elephant. Adoption, then, is not the sole province of human beings (Holland, 2011).

One may often find that the general public and professionals basically see no real difference between adoptive parents and biological parents as far as a child's future is concerned. This view is based on the notion that infants and young children quickly forget the adversities they went through and that they never understood what was happening to them to begin with. The love and proper care of adoptive parents were thought to compensate for all the losses. It is even common practice in some societies to erase a child's past by changing his first name, hiding all the information about his past, and telling him he is adopted only when he reaches school age. With the knowledge currently available on the nature of attachment and babies' abilities to perceive and retain early experiences, this approach is not considered well-founded anymore.

In many countries, a distinction is made between foreign adoption and local adoption. In the past 2 decades, more people seek to adopt children than before. In view of the small number of babies available locally, many parents adopt abroad. Among other things, international adoption raises the issue of intergenerational transmission of cultural and historical values. The professional literature has dubbed this the intercultural paradox of international adoption. As part of the typical process of intergenerational transmission from parents to their biological children, parents tend to equip the child from infancy with a cultural baggage and values that they had received from their own parents. Some recommend preserving the values of the adopted child's culture of origin—that is, exposing her to the culture from which she hails and thus fostering an important element of her self-identity: cultural pride. The final say naturally lies with the adoptive parents and will mainly depend on their cultural tolerance. For clinicians, it is important to know where the adopted baby comes from to understand what she had been through. Babies from Guatemala, for example, stay with their biological or foster care families before being adopted, whereas most babies from East European countries come from baby homes.

Adoption is not self-evidently bound for success, all the more so when the parents adopt a baby who had spent some time in an institution or with a neglecting or abusive biological family. Some adoptive parents, moreover, remain frustrated with their infertility even after deciding on adoption. Others do come to terms with their sterility and give up their dream of bringing a child of their own into the world. As paradoxical as this may sound, adoptive couples may encounter difficulties in making the transition into parenthood. Having spent many long years investing time, emotional energy, and money in fertility treatments, they are often worn out by the time the child arrives. It is not rare for postadoption depression to develop, and it is increasingly recognized by professional practitioners. Contrary to postpartum depression, postadoption depression has yet to gain social recognition and legitimization, and parents who have it are still often looked down upon by their peers and families. Consequently, these parents (mothers and fathers alike) are ashamed to seek treatment. We encounter some of them later on, when they come to consult with us about their adopted child, complaining about symptoms that are in fact related to the early relational problem created as a result of their parental depression.

How likely are toddlers who spent their first—and maybe second—year of life in an institution to take a new developmental and emotional path within the context of their new adoptive family? These toddlers face a formidable task: to deal with the separation from the familiar institution and form a secure attachment with the adoptive parent. In a study conducted in Holland, Stams et al. (2000) looked at 7 year olds, some of them from relatively good orphanages, who had been adopted before 6 months old. These children were compared with a sample of same-age children from the general population. Around 30% of them, mostly boys, were found to have behavioral problems, as opposed to only 10% from the general population. Most of these behavioral disorders manifested themselves at home rather than in school, pointing to a parent–child relationship disorder rather than a conduct disorder.

Clinical Application: Therapeutic Support During the First Year of Adoption

In 2004, we implemented a preventive intervention study for international adoptive parents who received children who were, on average, 15 months old. The intervention consisted of attachment-based interactional guidance provided by a trained developmental psychologist who visited the family home for a year, once a week in the first 6 months, then once a month. After 1 year of this preventive intervention, the parents were compared with a group of parents who had also adopted a child from abroad and who had received the standard accompaniment provided by the adoption agency. The toddlers from both groups improved their developmental score, indicating the positive effect of adoption as such. However, the parents who had benefited from our intervention showed a significantly higher level of reflective functioning—that is, a higher ability to attribute emotional motives to their children's behaviors—compared with the control group. In addition to this, we compared single mothers and mothers with partners, and we found that the former were more vulnerable but also benefited more from the intervention.

CASE STUDY

A. was adopted from abroad when he was 18 months old. The parents agreed to take part in the study mentioned in the previous paragraph, and they ended up in the control (nonintervention) group. This came as a relief for them because, as they explained, "We are not too keen on psychological stuff." When the child was 2½ years old, they came to our clinic because A. was having socialization difficulties in day care, accompanied by physical violence toward his peers. During the evaluation, we observed a handsome little boy who displayed some language delay and excessive separation anxiety. A.'s behavior was not that of a child who rebels against the rules but one who is testing the strength of his relationship with his parents. His mother looked angry and frustrated, and his father looked sad and helpless. Both expressed frustration about the behavioral problems their son had despite their considerable investment in him. They even voiced their concern that A. might be carrying some "bad genetic heritage."

We asked the parents to tell us about the adoption process from Day 1. They answered that they would gladly discuss it, that they had already brought the subject up with A., and they even proposed to bring his photo album in for the next session—an album that he was very fond of browsing through, according to them. A. played with two dollhouses during the whole duration of that next session. The therapist called the parents' attention to a possible connection between the topic of the conversation and the content of their son's symbolic play. The parents looked at the therapist, perplexed, and asked, "What are you trying to tell us . . . that A. understands what we are saying here?"

"Not only does he understand, but he also responds to what he hears, and he hears that we are talking about the adoption," answered the therapist.

"And you think there is a connection between his playing with the two houses and his transition from the children's institution to our house?"

"There might very well be a link . . . I see that this thought comes as a big surprise to you."

"So you mean to tell us that he remembers things from back there?" asked the father, his eyes tearing up.

"Yes, because babies possess implicit memory from before verbal memory develops. And besides, you told me that A. liked going through his photo album."

"That's right," answered the mother, "but this only has happy photos, and you seem to be implying that he might also remember bad moments."

At this point in the conversation, the child asked for the photo album, and we suggested that he bring it in for the next meeting as well.

During the next session, we browsed through the album, paying particular attention to the child's sad facial expression at the orphanage. The father said, "Yes, but look how fast he became joyful!"

This session brought up the difficulty experienced by the parents talking about the emotions surrounding the adoption process—about the mother's unresolved sterility (it turned out that she had miscarried a spontaneous pregnancy during the exact same period of their consultation with us), about A.'s poor developmental and emotional state when they took him in, about their fears around the child's psychiatric genetic heritage, and mainly about their difficulty to accept the idea that A. remembered his past—at least implicitly.

The *DC:0-5™: Diagnostic Classification of Mental Health and Developmental Disorders of Infancy and Early Childhood* (DC:0-5; ZERO TO THREE, 2016) diagnoses would be as follows:

- Axis I: Clinical Disorders
  - » Adjustment Disorder
  - » Relationship Specific Disorder of Infancy/Early Childhood (with mother and father)

- Axis II: Relational Context
  - » Level 2—Strained to Concerning dyadic relationships
  - » Level 2—Strained to Concerning caregiving environment

- Axis III: Medical Condition
  - » None

- Axis IV: Psychosocial Stressor
  - » Adoption

- Axis V: Developmental Competence
  - » Competencies are inconsistently present

Triadic therapy was set up, lasting approximately 6 months, following which A.'s aggressive behavior in day care completely stopped. His language also came along nicely. After a brief pause, the parents wished to consult us again because of A.'s difficulty getting toilet-trained—a stage symbolizing the end of infancy. A year after finishing the second treatment round, A. asked his parents to come to the clinic "to talk about the adoption"!

Child Custody of Divorced Parents

Divorce has become a very widespread phenomenon almost everywhere in the world. Many of the children involved are less than 3 years old. The divorce process is tough on both parents and children. Professionals have long debated the question of what is best for the children: whether they are better off if their parents stick together and they continue to grow within a conflictual setting, or whether they are better off if their parents divorce and they grow up in a calmer atmosphere, while losing the representation of a stable marital relationship. One of the most common issues in divorce trials, in particular when the children are young, is the father's custody. Mothers often argue that damage might be caused to the baby should he be allowed to sleep at his father's home. Various studies have refuted this argument. Furthermore, studies published in the last 10 years have shown that the infant's security of attachment is one and the same vis-à-vis his father and his mother (Grossmann, Grossmann, & Waters, 2005). The clearest recommendation emerging from contemporary professional literature (Lamb & Kelly, 2009) is to base custody decisions on the principle of maintaining continuous relationships with the attachment figures.

The Inconceivable: Filicide

We have chosen to broach this difficult subject because, unfortunately, the phenomenon of parents murdering their children is not as rare as one might imagine. After each case of filicide, psychiatrists are always asked how such a thing might be possible and whether it could have been avoided. Here are a few cases reported by the press.

A 4-year-old girl who had gone missing for 2 months was found dead inside a suitcase at the bottom of a river. Her mother's husband confessed to the murder, and her mother was suspected of having asked him to do it.

A 4-year-old boy was drowned by his single mother. He had been the whole world to her until then. She planned on committing suicide but did not go through with it.

A 2-year-old toddler was murdered and hidden in the woods by her father. The parents were divorced. "I knew this would be the solution to all of my problems," the father said.

The prohibition on filicide is still not legally and morally anchored in all societies. Abraham was the first to have almost murdered his child, the first father to have agreed to sacrifice his son on the altar of religion as absolute proof of his unconditional devotion to God. However, God did not let it happen. The message is clear. No law, certainly no man-made law, can sanction such an act.

In most Western cultures, the thought of a parent killing her own child arouses a deep sense of horror and rage. It is inconceivable for a parent to betray the trust put in her by her own child. The fundamental premise that all human beings love their children, the fruit of their loins, their successors, lies at the core of culture, which is why this kind of murder is considered a crime committed by "madmen." People cannot conceive of a situation in which a parent would commit such an act without being labeled as abnormal. The very possibility of the act is a threat to the foundations of society, and yet these murders still occur.

A look at the history books shows that infanticide was practiced in many societies in the past, including in Greece, China, Japan, India, Brazil, England, Italy, and France. Infanticide immediately following birth was the most common form of population control.

Even at the dawn of the 21st century, economic motives and considerations often override ethical ones and lend legitimization to infanticide. In northern India, for example, the family's welfare trumps the survival of one child or another. Beside these economic considerations, babies are sometimes murdered for cultural reasons. A custom in Bolivia, for example, is to kill "bewitched" babies whose souls have been trapped by bad spirits.

Prevalence of Filicide in Western Society

A review (West, 2007) showed that murder was the fourth most common cause of death in children 5–14 years old and the third most common cause of death in children 1–5 years old. The first year of life is the most dangerous. According to the survey, 61% of children murdered by 5 years old were killed by their parents, half of those (30%) by their mothers and half (31%) by their fathers. This finding shatters the myth that most filicides are perpetrated by mothers. A study (Bourget & Gagné, 2005) that retrospectively looked at 60 cases of filicide committed by fathers showed that 23% of the victims were younger than 1 year old, 26% were 1–5 years old, 22% were 6–10 years old, and 29% were more than 10 years old. In 23% of cases, other siblings were murdered along with the child. In 60% of the murders committed by the father, the latter committed suicide, after sometimes killing more than one child.

The most common means of murder were firearms (34%) and beatings (22%). The use of knives was much less frequent, as was, in descending order, the use of blunt objects, strangling, and poisoning. These data reveal two important things: Filicide is common enough to be taken seriously, and the first 3 years in life are critical for the early detection of at-risk infants.

A semantic distinction is commonly made between murder committed within 24 hours after birth (neonaticide), murder committed in the first year of the child's life (infanticide), and murder of children 1 year old and up (filicide). Neonaticide is mostly perpetrated by young, poor single mothers who got no treatment and support before birth. Many of them denied or hid their pregnancy (even though most still lived with their parents). Murder is sometimes committed by mothers who suffer from psychosis and who do not benefit from social support.

What Drives Parents to Murder Their Children?

Parents kill their children for various reasons. In this respect, they can be crudely divided into two groups: those afflicted by mental illnesses, such as depression or psychosis, and those who do not have a psychiatric disorder. It is harder to understand, and accept, the motives of those parents belonging to the second group. People often ask themselves whether a parent who murders his child can be mentally sane at all. The answer, as it turns out, is yes, at least by psychiatric–juridical standards, whereby a sane person is defined as someone who is able to distinguish between reality and imagination, between good and bad.

Among mothers who killed their babies and were diagnosed as mentally ill, depression, and sometimes abuse and violence in childhood, are the most common backgrounds found. Many of them try to kill themselves after the murder. Some filicidal mothers perceive murder as an altruistic act meant "to save the child from a cruel world," and they also try to commit suicide.

Among the filicidal parents who do not suffer from a psychiatric disorder are also those who murder out of revenge against a partner and those who harbor hard feelings of rejection toward the child. Finally, there are those who abuse the child chronically, causing her death by accident (e.g., the "shaken baby" syndrome). In some cases, socioeconomic factors also come into play.

Murderers: Mothers Versus Fathers

As mentioned, 61% of children murdered before 5 years old in the United States were murdered by their parents—half of them by their fathers and half by their mothers. However, it turns out that there are substantial differences between fathers who kill their children and mothers who do so. The number of fathers who commit suicide after the fact is double that of the mothers.

The sex of the crime perpetrator is also linked to the age of the victims. In an epidemiological study carried out in Canada, Bourget, Grace, and Whitehurst (2007) found that mothers tended more to commit neonaticide, whereas fathers were more prone to filicide of children more than 3 years old. Interestingly, more studies were conducted on mothers than fathers who had murdered their children, despite the equal frequency of the phenomenon. This is one of the reasons why more is known about the dynamic characterizing the murder of children by their mothers. As concerns fathers, in 60% of cases, fathers had severe psychopathology as follows: depression, schizophrenia and other forms of psychosis, as well as toxicomania. Abusive and murdering fathers often suffered from abuse in their childhood, and they also had a personality disorder, which could explain their tendency to commit suicide following the vengeful act against the mother. Among mothers, however, vengeance is a much rarer motive in cases of divorce.

Mental Structures of the Filicidal Parent

Psychiatric disorder in itself cannot explain the phenomenon of filicide. After all, most parents who have a psychiatric illness and environmental pressures to deal with do not end up murdering their children. Even parents who had experienced abuse and neglect in childhood and have poor parental competencies do not murder their children. This same goes for divorced parents.

It follows that clinicians and researchers are faced with a complex phenomenon, in which an understanding of its characteristics and risk factors can help prevent its occurrence but not necessarily explain it. Papapietro and Barbo (2005) tried to get to the bottom of the phenomenon through interviews with many parents over time. They distinguished two levels of personality organization among filicidal parents: psychopathy and psychosis.

Psychopathic individuals react with rage and a need for vengeance when they feel injured in their narcissism. Filicide then takes on sadistic motives. For many of them, the child was never wished for to start with, and the murder occurs either intentionally with the desire to exact revenge on the partner or by accident following serious abuse. These parents, being nonpsychotic, will be convicted of voluntary homicide and sent to prison.

Psychotic parents, by contrast, are driven to their murderous act by a totally different dynamic. According to Papapietro and Barbo (2005), the act, however radical, is meant to protect them or their child from a delusional threat. Two types of psychosis are mentioned:

- *Disorganized psychotic disorder*: This is an extreme disintegration of personality, caused by an amalgam of a chronic psychiatric illness and extremely adverse past events (e.g., neglect, maltreatment, sexual abuse, traumatic losses). Filicide in this case is the result of a strange dynamic in which the baby is not perceived as a human being but rather as an inanimate object onto which the parent projects undesirable and threatening parts of his disintegrated self.

- *Organized psychotic disorder*: This disorder afflicts individuals who had functioned well in terms of work and interpersonal relations, who had had a relatively stable childhood, and who suddenly undergo a serious but temporary crisis when transitioning into parenthood. The logic behind the filicide in this case is easier to follow: These parents aspire to use the child as a tool for changing their internal structure, that which Bollas (1989) called a "self-mending tool." The murderous act takes place at a moment of crisis, when stressful events (e.g., conjugal tension, separation, financial hardships, solitude) come in interplay with the mother's psychic vulnerability. The feeling of being alienated from her surroundings and the unbearable anxiety turn into psychotic depression with annihilation fantasies in which the child—seen by the mother as undifferentiated from her—is included. In this kind of mental state, an action plan begins to hatch in the mother's mind. The words of a filicidal mother during psychotherapy, as cited by Kunst (2002), provide a clear illustration of this destructive dynamic: "I didn't kill my son, I killed myself."

This distinction between different dynamics underlying the murderous act of parents with mental illness is important for a better understanding of the phenomenon of filicide. Furthermore, this distinction can eventually help with devising therapeutic interventions for filicidal parents. Indeed, women in the organized-psychotic-disorder group can sometimes benefit from psychotherapy, capable as they are of understanding the delusions that led them to commit the crime.

Which Children Are at Risk for Being Killed by Their Parents?

Studying the characteristics of the filicidal parent must also be accompanied by studying those of the murdered children. It would seem that children who are at risk for filicide, like those at risk for abuse and maltreatment, are children who are undesired or disabled. There is also some correlation between the sex of the filicidal parent and that of the child victim: Fathers tend to murder boys, and mothers girls.

Prevention and Intervention

The knowledge presented earlier makes it necessary for the health care and child protection systems to invest efforts and resources in early detection of parents who might murder their children. For example, a mother who is psychotic or who has depression should be identified whenever additional risk factors are present (e.g., single parenthood, low IQ level, solitude, drug use). These women especially need social and psychiatric support in the months following birth. Similarly, isolated and poor teenagers who become mothers also need considerable support, in particular around their first child. Furthermore, the possibility that fathers might kill their children tends to be ignored, despite the statistics mentioned earlier. This blind spot stems from a traditional social conception that views mothers as the symbol of parenthood. It is, therefore, important to regularly assess the probability of fathers with depression murdering their children, especially when their depression is accompanied by suicidal thoughts or a shaky relationship with the other parent. These recommendations are mainly directed at health professionals because half the women and men who murdered their children had some form of contact with medical practitioners in the weeks preceding the act, yet slipped under the radar.

In the United States and other Western countries, preventive programs are available designed for at-risk families—for example, families with a high level of violence. Trained nurses make home visits during the pregnancy and in the 2 years following birth, and they are often able to intervene and prevent neglect and even abuse, especially in cases of the first-born children of unmarried teenage mothers coming from a low socioeconomic background.

We believe that it is important to put in place such programs. Moreover, we support the initiative of the World Association for Infant Mental Health to compose a Declaration of Infants' Rights. This declaration will raise awareness of the baby's right to live, from birth on, as an entity with rights of her own alongside and despite her existential dependence on her parents.

To conclude this difficult issue of filicide, we might say that the relative reluctance shown by the scientific community to explore this phenomenon in greater depth possibly lies in a truism so well put by Henri Bergson, French philosopher and Nobel Prize laureate in literature for 1927: "The eye sees only what the mind is prepared to comprehend."

Conclusion

Infants and young children who have been removed from their parents' guardianship owing to parental failure constitute an at-risk population for several reasons: First, they are seen by their foster or adoptive parents as carriers of unknown genetic baggage. Second, some of them do "come bundled" with symptoms resulting from neglect or abuse. Babies placed with foster care families sometimes continue to experience insecurity in their attachment relationships. Those who are adopted often encounter parents who have been painfully let down by their own infertility, parents who carry within them anxieties about the child's future on the one hand and high expectations of him on the other hand. Removing a baby from an environment that endangers his developmental future is, without a doubt, a positive and necessary intervention but one that cannot in itself guarantee a future devoid of affective or behavioral problems. This is why we believe that the hosting family should be offered guidance by a mental health professional, to help it deal with the challenges involved in foster care and adoption. Infant mental health professionals have many roles, one of which is to provide their opinion on parental competence. They are expected to represent the child's best interests, and they often find themselves in conflict with the adult psychiatrists treating the parents and their legal representatives.

Also, we deem it important for a professional not to be in a position of double loyalty. Indeed, for ethical and therapeutic reasons, the clinician treating the baby and her family should not draft an expert opinion on parental competence but can, of course, recommend a third party to evaluate the parents. Conversely, the person evaluating parental competence should not be in a therapeutic relationship with the family.

References

Berrick, J. D., Barth R., & Needell, B. (1994). A comparison of kinship foster homes and foster family homes: Implications for kinship foster care as family preservation. *Children and Youth Services Review, 16*, 33–64.

Bollas, C. (1989). *Forces of destiny: Psychoanalysis and the human idiom.* London, England: Karnac Books.

Bourget, D., & Gagné. P. (2005). Paternal filicide in Quebec. *Journal of the American Academy of Psychiatry and the Law, 33*, 354–360.

Bourget, D., Grace, J., & Whitehurst, L. (2007). A review of maternal and paternal filicide. *Journal of the American Academy of Psychiatry and the Law, 35*, 74–82.

Fries, A. B., Shirtcliff, E. A., & Pollak, S. D. (2008). Neuroendocrine dysregulation following early social deprivation in children. *Developmental Psychobiology, 50*, 588–599.

Goldstein, J., Freud, A., Solnit, A. J., & Goldstein, S. (1986). *In the best interests of the child.* New York, NY: Free Press.

Grossmann, K. E., Grossmann, K., & Waters, E. (2005). *Attachment from infancy to adulthood.* New York, NY: Guilford Press.

Holland, J. S. (2011). *Unlikely friendships: 47 remarkable stories from the animal kingdom.* New York, NY: Workman Publishing.

Kunst, J. L. (2002). Fraught with the utmost danger: The object relations of mothers who kill their children. *Bulletin of the Menninger Clinic, 66*, 19–38.

Lamb, M. E., & Kelly, J. B. (2009). Improving the quality of parent–child contact in separating families with infants and young children: Empirical research foundations. In R. M. Galatzer-Levy, J. Kraus, & J. Galatzer-Levy (Eds.), *The scientific basis of child custody decisions* (2nd ed., pp. 187–214). Hoboken, NJ: Wiley.

McLaughlin, K. A., Fox, N. A., Zeanah, C. H., Jr., Sheridan, M. A., Marshall, P., & Nelson, C. A. (2010). Delayed maturation in brain electrical activity partially explains the association between early environmental deprivation and symptoms of attention deficit/hyperactivity disorder. *Biological Psychiatry, 68*, 329–336.

Papapietro, D. J., & Barbo, E. (2005). Commentary: Toward a psychodynamic understanding of filicide — Beyond psychosis and into the heart of darkness. *Journal of the American Academy of Psychiatry and Law, 33*, 505–508.

Pollak, S. D., Nelson, C. A., Schlaak, M. F., Roeber, B. J., Wewerka, S. S., Wiik, K. L., . . . Gunnar, M. R. (2010). Neurodevelopmental effects of early deprivation in postinstitutionalized children. *Child Development, 81*, 224–236.

Price, J. M., Chamberlain, P., Landsverk, J., Reid, J., Leve, L., & Laurent, H. (2008). Effects of a foster parent training intervention on placement changes of children in foster care. *Child Maltreatment, 13*, 64–75.

Rushton, A., & Minnis, H. (2008). Residential and foster family care. In M. Rutter (Ed.), *Rutter's child and adolescent psychiatry* (5th ed., pp. 487–501). Malden, MA: Blackwell.

Solnit, A. J., Schowalter, J. E., & Nordhaus, B. F. (1995). Best interests of the child in the family and community. *Pediatric Clinics of North America, 42*, 181–191.

Spitz, R. A. (1951). The psychogenic diseases in infancy: An attempt at their etiologic classification. *The Psychoanalytic Study of the Child, 6*, 255–275.

Spitz, R. A., & Wolf, K. M. (1946). Anaclitic depression: An inquiry into the genesis of psychiatric conditions in early childhood, II. *The Psychoanalytic Study of the Child, 2*, 313–342.

Stams, G. J., Juffer, F., Rispens, J., & Hoksbergen, R. A. (2000). The development and adjustment of 7-year-old children adopted in infancy. *Journal of Child Psychology and Psychiatry, 414*, 1025–1037.

Vorria, P., Papaligoura, Z., Sarafidou, J., Kopakaki, M., Dunn, J., van IJzendoorn, M. H., & Kontopoulou, A. (2006). The development of adopted children after institutional care: A follow-up study. *Journal of Child Psychology and Psychiatry, 47*, 1246–1253.

West, S. G. (2007). An overview of filicide. *Psychiatry (Edgmont), 4*, 48–57.

Winnicott, D. W. (1964). *The child, the family and the outside world.* Hammondsworth, England: Penguin Books.

Zeanah, C. H., Jr., Egger, H. L., Smyke, A. T., Nelson, C. A., Fox, N. A., Marshall, P. J., & Guthrie, D. (2009). Institutional rearing and psychiatric disorders in Romanian preschool children. *American Journal of Psychiatry, 166*, 777–785.

ZERO TO THREE. (2016). *DC:0–5™: Diagnostic classification of mental health and developmental disorders of infancy and early childhood* (DC:0–5). Washington, DC: Author.

Recommended Reading

Boesch, C., Bole, C., Eckhardt, N., & Boesch, H. (2010). Altruism in forest chimpanzees: The case of adoption. *PLOS One, 5*, 1–6.

Brisch, K. H. (1999). *Treating attachment disorders: From theory to therapy.* New York, NY: Guilford Press.

Fisher, P. A., Kim, H. K., & Pears, K. C. (2009). Effects of Multidimensional Treatment Foster Care for Preschoolers (MTFC-P) on reducing permanent placement failures among children with placement instability. *Child Youth Services Review, 31*, 541–546.

Hawk, B., & McCall, R. B. (2010). CBCL behavior problems of post-institutionalized international adoptees. *Clinical Child and Family Review, 13*, 1–36.

Juffer, R., Hoksbergen, R. A., Riksen-Walraven, J. M., & Kohnstamm, G. A. (1997). Early intervention in adoptive families: Supporting maternal sensitive responsiveness, infant–mother attachment, and infant competence. *Journal of Child Psychology and Psychiatry, 38*, 1039–1050.

Kaufman, J., & Ziegler, E. (2010). Do abused children become abusive parents? *American Journal of Orthopsychiatry, 57*, 186–192.

Keren, M., Dollberg, D., & Feldman, R. (2017). *A controlled outcome study of attachment-based intervention among new adoptive parents.* Manuscript in preparation.

Lee, R. M. (2003). The transracial adoption paradox: History, research, and counseling implications of cultural socialization. *Consulting Psychologist, 31*, 711–744.

Leslie, L. K., Gordon, J. N., Meneken, L., Premji, K., & Michelmore, K. L. (2005). The physical, developmental, and mental health needs of young children in child welfare by initial placement type. *Journal of Development and Behavioral Pediatrics, 26*, 177–185.

Maheu, F. S., Dozier, M., Guyer, A. E., Mandell, D., Peloso, E., Poeth, K., . . . Ernst, M. (2010). A preliminary study of medial temporal lobe function in youths with a history of caregiver deprivation and emotional neglect. *Cognitive, Affective & Behavioral Neuroscience, 10*, 34–49.

Rubin, D. M., Downes, K. J., O'Reilly, A. L. R., Mekonnen, R., Luan, X., & Localio, R. (2008). The impact of kinship care on behavioral well-being for children in out-of-home care. *Archives of Pediatric and Adolescent Medicine, 162*, 550–556.

St. Petersburg–USA Orphanage Research Team. (2008). The effects of early social–emotional and relationship experience on the development of young orphanage children. *Monographs of the Society for Research in Child Development, 73*, vii–viii, 1–262, 294–295.

Tarabulsy, G. M., Pascuzzo, K., Moss, E., St. Laurent, D., Bernier, A., Cyr, C., & Dubois-Comtois, K. (2008). Attachment-based intervention for maltreating families. *American Journal of Orthopsychiatry, 78*, 322–332.

Tyano, S., & Cox, J. (2010). Filicide: Parents who murder their child. In S. Tyano, M. Keren, H. Herrman, & J. Cox (Eds.), *Parenthood and mental health: A bridge between infant and adult psychiatry* (pp. 207–214). London, England: Wiley-Blackwell.

Vorria, P., Papaligoura, Z., Dunn, J., van IJzendoorn, M. H., Steele, H., Kontopoulou, A., & Sarafidou, Y. (2003). Early experiences and attachment relationships of Greek infants raised in residential group care. *Journal of Child Psychology and Psychiatry, 44*, 1–13.

CHAPTER 17
Treating Me and My Parents

Introduction

This chapter covers the psychotherapeutic methods commonly used to treat infants with their parents, and the use of medications in rare situations. We first describe the principles of treatment in infancy. Next, we review preventive intervention programs meant to forestall later psychopathology. We end with a description of the various treatment methods. Their common goals are mainly to identify the distortion in the parent's perception of his child, to identify the traits that earn the young child the parent's negative attributions and narcissistic projections, and to interpret the child's symptoms in light of these insights. In this chapter, we show how we implement the principles of parent–child psychotherapy in different combinations (dyadic, triadic, or group) and different settings (the clinic or the patient's home). It is important to differentiate between preventive and therapeutic interventions, even if both often use the same methods.

Psychotherapy in Infancy: Basic Concepts

Empathic Parental Reflectivity

Most treatment methods are geared toward improving parental reflective functioning as a cornerstone in the development of a normal relationship between parent and child. This term refers to the parent's ability to attribute emotional intentionality to both her own behavior and her baby's. Oppenheim and Koren-Karie developed the Insightfulness Assessment tool, a procedure that measures the parent's ability to see things from the baby's standpoint (e.g., Koren-Karie, Oppenheim, Dolev, Sher, & Etzion-Carasso, 2002). The procedure involves asking the parent to play with the child for about 15 minutes in three different game modes: a structured game chosen by the parent, free play by the parent and the child, and a brief moment where the child is left to play alone. These three play modes are meant to elicit different behaviors in the child. The play is videotaped, and the parent is later invited, without the child, to view the video together with the clinician and to answer several specific questions relating to each of the three play segments: What do you think the child was thinking about? What did he feel? Is this behavior typical of your child? Does his response characterize his personality? What are you feeling when watching the video? Is there something you see that surprises, worries you, or gives you pleasure? On the basis of the answers given by the parent, the clinician classifies her level of empathic reflectivity. A parent with an adaptive empathic reflectivity has a multidimensional and balanced view of the child, perceiving him as an entity with strengths and weaknesses. By contrast, parents who lack empathic reflectivity take a unidimensional view of their child. They hold prejudiced and set opinions of their child, regardless of his behaviors. Their perspective is unbalanced, and they often consider the toddler's behavior as either positive or negative, black or white, with no shades in between. After they have determined their attitude toward the child, they will not change it. Assessing a parent's level of empathic reflectivity is useful in clinical work—in evaluation, in treatment planning, and in monitoring the change brought about by the intervention.

The Role of Play in Parent-Infant Therapy

As the nonverbal language "spoken" by the infant or young child, play is a natural projective therapeutic tool. Play, especially creative play, allows a child to step off the beaten paths and create new experiences for herself, hence its importance especially in the early childhood years, when the brain is still very malleable. For clinicians, a child's play, however young, is a window into her emotional state and cognitive capabilities. Indeed, with game-playing expressing emotion and cognition, as well as thought and creativity, it is no surprise that toddlers who have emotional and cognitive disorders find it hard to play games of imagination. The presence or absence of spontaneous play is a sensitive gauge of a child's mental health.

The ability to play is also one of the indicators predicting how successful psychotherapy might turn out. Factors conducive to the development of pretend play in toddlers include secure attachment to the parent, the parent's playfulness and creativity, and his patience to read stories out loud on a daily basis. We have observed a negative relationship between the capability for symbolization in pretend play and the level of social aggression. Children who do not conform to social norms at 4 years old exhibit, at 6 years old, poor empathy, low linguistic and ludic competencies, and preference for violent games, compared with children who conform at 4 years old.

Many parents who come to our clinic are limited in their ability to play with their children. This is particularly evident in parents who had suffered from some emotional deprivation in their own childhood—parents whose own parents did not attach any importance to play activities. Improving the parent's playing skills is one of the goals of parent–toddler therapy.

In the course of parent–child psychotherapy, we use toys adapted to the child's age to encourage curiosity and creativity in both the child and the parent. This usually involves dolls wearing different clothes, large and small toy animals that are soft to the touch, blocks, big and small cars, soft balls, pillows, kitchen tools, pretend food, a doctor's kit, and illustrated books.

CASE STUDY

K., a 2-year-old toddler, was referred to our unit because she did not speak at all, hung on to her mother everywhere, including at home, and seemed apathetic. The mother used to express toward her feelings of frustration and anger ("Go play, don't stick to me.") and could not bear the physical contact with her. The parents had an older son and older daughter, and the mother clearly preferred her firstborn son. K.'s sister had adopted the behavior of the "good, obedient girl" to gain her mother's love. Their father worked hard and did not talk much about emotions, but he was aware of the tension-fraught relationship between the mother and K. and the mother's rejection of her daughter. The mother's only concern was that K. did not talk.

This maternal concern paved the way for a mother–child therapy, with the goal of understanding why the mother rejected her daughter. At the same time, sessions were also held with K. and her father to get him more involved.

Paying attention to microevents in the interaction between the two allowed us to understand that the mother could not stand her daughter because she saw herself in her. Indeed, in her own childhood, she had been a little girl with learning difficulties at school, and she was quite less of a success than her two brothers. She described herself as the "black sheep" of the family. These feelings resurfaced when the therapist sat with both of them on the carpet and suggested that the mother encourage her daughter to hook rings onto pegs. The mother perceived this request as a deliberate wish to make her (not her daughter) fail: "You did this to me exactly like my mother!" she said. She was overwhelmed by feelings of persecution, which she transferred to the therapist (negative transfer) and her daughter: She believed that both of them were out to "make her fail her maternal role on purpose."

During therapy, the mother recalled incidents of physical and emotional maltreatment by her own mother. This allowed her to realize that she was re-creating this abusive relationship pattern with K. (and with K. more than the others because her delay in terms of language development reminded her of her own learning difficulties). Thanks to this new insight, the relationship between K. and her mother improved, but the mother concurrently became depressive and highly aggressive (including physically toward her husband). She agreed to undergo psychiatric treatment for herself and was hospitalized. Back home, the father had trouble functioning as a single parent and working at the same time. The three children were placed with foster daytime families and only slept in their father's home. K. went into therapeutic nursery day care and continued to develop despite her mother's absence. The foster family was beneficial for the three children and the father.

The Place of Body Language in Parent–Infant Psychotherapy

A baby's ability to identify the communicative signification of adult bodily configurations and facial expressions was well-studied by Tronick and Cohn (1989) as well as by Beebe and Lachmann (2002). Taking this further, Fivaz-Depeursinge and Corboz-Warnery (1999) were the first to show that babies were in fact able to read not just one significant person but two simultaneously. The ability to identify and understand the signification of nonverbal messages, such as bodily configurations and movements, is an essential element in psychodynamic psychotherapy because it allows a glimpse into unconscious emotions and perceptions.

Body language is conveyed in the way in which people stand, walk, and sit. When treating babies, our therapeutic space is the carpet. We begin the session sitting on it, and we invite the parents to sit where they like. At times, they sit on the carpet and lay the baby between us, and at other times they sit on two high chairs and lay the baby on the carpet. There are of course other possible combinations. For example, one parent might sit on the carpet with the baby, whereas the other will sit on a high chair at a distance. The parents' choice of seating arrangement might take on meaning as the session progresses. The body language of an infant or young child is also reflected in her postures and the movements she makes while we converse with her parents. The therapist should try to attribute meaning to the body language of young children, in contrast to some parents who attach no significance to it.

The Use of Video as a Therapeutic Tool

McDonough (2000) was the first to underscore the importance of filming the parent–child interaction during the therapeutic session. Joint viewing of the video together with the parents makes it possible to identify positive and problematic moments in the parent–child interaction. This method of interactive guidance videofeedback was originally developed by McDonough to treat multirisk families who were difficult to bring into therapy. Therapy focuses on the "here and now" interactions between the parent and the infant. The therapist emphasizes those moments where the interaction was positive, without however ignoring the less pleasant ones. The intervention rests on two principles, "modeling" and encouragement, while avoiding any kind of psychological interpretation. This type of therapy can span 10–12 weekly sessions, and it allows the parent to take a close look, with the therapist's guidance, at the baby's behaviors and at his response to them. It is a powerful tool that makes it possible to speed up emotional and behavioral processes. One can use this method for dyads, triads, as well as for parent–infant groups.

Also, the introduction of video into the therapeutic space allows the therapist to bring the footage into her own supervision sessions. Videofeedback implies self-exposure, which is, in itself, not an easy task for either the parent or the therapist. Indeed, watching what goes on inside the therapeutic session remains taboo for many psychotherapists, even today. Apart from the clinical value of this method, it also contributes considerably to teaching and research, provided of course that ethical rules are maintained and that the parents' consent to be videotaped is obtained.

Videofeedback is used as a therapeutic tool in different clinical situations. Some examples include the following:

- *Attachment-focused therapy.* Here, the parent is taught to identify his child's exploratory and attachment (proximity-seeking) behaviors and to resolve their conflicts in nonintrusive or coercive ways. The parent learns to give his child positive reinforcements, praise her on positive behaviors, and ignore attention-seeking behaviors. The therapist explains to the parent how important it is to respond immediately and appropriately to the child's distress signals, emphasizing various moments—moments where the toddler sends out a signal and the parent responds with sensitivity or sets appropriate limits—and pointing out the child's reactions.

- *Psychodynamic-based therapy.* The sequence of interactive microevents, whether verbal or nonverbal, is used for a thorough analysis of the parent's mental representations and projections, which often originate in his own childhood.

- *Triadic psychotherapy.* This therapy is based on the Lausanne triadic paradigm and is discussed both in chapter 3 and later in this chapter.

Primary Preventions in Infancy

In the previous chapters, we mentioned the risk factors and protective factors and showed how they affected a baby's development. To promote the normative development of the baby and to prevent psychopathology, one must try to reduce the risk factors and to strengthen the protective factors. In this chapter, we review the findings of several studies indicating the effectiveness of various actions aimed at preventing the development of psychopathology.

Van den Boom (1995), for example, focused on two risk factors that play a major role in the development of an insecure style of attachment: a baby's difficult temperament and the precarious financial situation of mothers. He identified a group of 6-month-old babies born with a difficult temperament whose mothers come from a weak socioeconomic background, and he constructed a preventive intervention program based on weekly home visits by community nurses; the goal was to increase the mother's sensitivity to her infant and her understanding of her child's behaviors and to have her adapt her own reactions to her little one's difficult temperament. Van den Boom reexamined these children 3 years later and found that 68% of them had developed a secure style of attachment to their mother, as opposed to only 28% in the control group, who had not benefited from any intervention process.

Another preventive intervention program was conducted by Olds et al. (1998, 2002). Olds et al. focused on several risk factors associated with maltreatment at a young age, especially when combined together. These risk factors included single teenage mothers from a low socioeconomic background who had suffered from serious emotional deprivation in childhood. This intervention program was carried out with the participation of public health nurses, who regularly visited the mothers at home throughout their pregnancy and the first year following birth. Olds et al. followed these children over time, and they examined them again in childhood, adolescence, and adulthood. They found that the intervention group presented less frequent child abuse, better birth planning, and less juvenile delinquency compared with the control group of mothers (who had the same risk factors but did not participate in the intervention program).

Another researcher, Reynolds (2003), developed a preventive intervention program based on group therapy for high-risk dyads of parents and babies. The goal of this therapy was to awaken the parents' empathic insightfulness toward their babies. Indeed, the security of attachment of the babies in the intervention group was higher than that of the control group, and it remained so into adulthood.

Ports of Entry Into the Therapeutic Process

When treating infants and parents, access may be gained into their psychological world through one of several doors: the child's behavior, the parents' behavior, the parents' inner representations of the child, or the marital relationship. This largely depends on the diagnosis and on family dynamics. We might talk to the parent about a behavior or a statement we had noticed, whether his own or the baby's—for example, a parent who does not at all respond when his infant approaches the window, a mother who says that her baby "is stubborn like his dad," a parent who describes himself as "the worst parent," a toddler who plays with a baby doll that says "you don't love me" when it is beaten by an "adult doll," a father who is mad at his wife for spoiling the baby, or a mother who blames the father for not paying sufficient attention to the baby.

For Stern (1995), whatever the port of entry into treatment, it will always lead to positive changes in the parent–baby relationship.

Different Approaches to Treating Parents and Their Babies

The Psychodynamic Approach

The psychodynamic therapeutic approach applied to infants and their parents assumes that the goal of therapy is to change the parents' representations of their baby. This change often takes place when the parent understands her relationship with her own parents and siblings. Parental representations are the port of entry into psychodynamic parent–infant therapy. The experience of parenthood and the baby's characteristics activate the parents' representations of their own attachment figures, and these greatly affect the relationship with their baby (and the relationship with the therapist via the transference process). Under the psychodynamic approach, treatment is supposed to improve the parents' empathic insightfulness and their ability to distinguish between the baby's needs and their own. It is supposed to allow parents to see their baby more objectively and satisfy his needs in the most appropriate way. In this way, clinicians help the parent get rid of the "ghosts in the nursery," which mask the real baby.

In the course of the therapy session, clinicians should pay considerable attention to nonverbal interactions between those present: baby–parent, parent–therapist, and baby–therapist. Among others, we note the following elements:

- *The bodily configurations of parents.* The parents' body movements often reveal their internal emotional stance regarding the therapeutic situation. For example, parents who feel reticent about the therapist may express their reservations by choosing to sit far away from her. The therapist, for her part, should notice this nonverbal expression of parental reluctance and open the subject for discussion, with a view to form a therapeutic alliance with them ultimately.

- *On–off visual contact.* There are moments during therapy where the baby takes his eyes off his parent, the therapist, or both. When this happens, the therapist should explain to the parents that the baby wants to "'rest," to withdraw into his personal space. Without this explanation, the parents might interpret the baby's behavior as rejection, whereas it is in fact normative.

- *Emotionally loaded moments.* These are situations during therapy in which new insights provoke strong feelings in the parent, either positive or negative. The therapist must see to it that they do not lead to dangerous emotional turmoil.

The Interactive Behavioral Approach

Unlike the psychodynamic approach, which looks at the past, the behavioral approach focuses on behaviors that come up during therapy, in the moment. This approach is adapted to parents who are either not too psychologically minded or who have learned from past adverse situations not to trust the system. The therapist using this approach does not go into the parents' internal representations but tries to identify moments where the parent and the child enjoy each other's company. This is far from being self-evident because parents often have a hard time enjoying their baby or sensing when she is happy around them. Further down the line, after the atmosphere has turned positive, the therapist can call the parents' attention to their functional failures and suggest more effective and healthy behaviors without setting off their resistance.

The "Watch, Wait, and Wonder" (WWW) Approach

The so-called WWW treatment modality combines the psychodynamic and behavioral approaches. In the first half of the session, the parent is invited to sit down on the carpet and to observe the infant's behavior, which allows the baby to take the initiative. In this way, the parent develops availability, the capability to contain the child, and empathic insightfulness—that is, attunement to the baby's emotional and developmental needs. The baby feels her parent treat and see her in a different way and responds accordingly. In the second half of the session, the therapist talks to the parents and asks how they felt when they were asked to let the baby take the initiative and lead the way. By contrast to the behavioral approach, here the therapist neither interferes in whatever unfolds nor offers concrete advice. He only provides a secure, supportive environment that allows the parents to express thoughts, emotions, and insights about their infant. Therapist and parent try to figure out together the infant's difficulties as well as the parent's (e.g., the difficulty to allow the child freedom and to be led by her). Through play and talk, both parent and young child are supposed to gradually change the way in which each of them experiences and understands the other. This type of therapy is also an opportunity for the parents to find out with the therapist how intergenerational transmission influences their relationship with the young child. This therapeutic approach is particularly advised for parents whose personality makes it hard for them to separate between their own needs and those of their children, and who have a strong tendency to feel rejected when the therapist is highly attentive to the baby.

The Therapy Setting

The Participants

The therapist chooses the type of treatment configuration suited to each family, and the options are either dyadic (parent–child), triadic (both parents and the baby), or family therapy, a parent–infant group or individual play therapy for the toddler. In any of these treatment configurations, each of the approaches presented above can be applied (psychodynamic, behavioral interactive guidance, WWW).

Dyadic Setting

This setting is recommended when each one of the parents has a conflictual relationship with the baby or when the parents' couple relationship is too conflictual to allow them to concentrate on their relationship with the baby. Following is a detailed example of dyadic treatment and the use of video, which was meant to develop the mother's empathic insightfulness and strengthen the infant's ability to regulate emotions.

CASE STUDY

A. and his mother were addressed to our unit by a social worker when he was 11 months old. He was defined "at risk" because his dad committed suicide during the pregnancy, and his mother was in a state of mourning and depression ever since. A few months before killing himself, the husband quit his job with a view to find something else, "to change things." The mother described theirs as a "symbiotic" relationship (in her terms): They lived voluntarily isolated from society and their family. "We needed no one, we had each other." The couple did not feel a need for a child. When she was 36, after 8 years of marriage and following a routine checkup at the gynecologist's, the mother was told that the clock was ticking ("for me, not for my husband," she emphasized bitterly). They decided it was time to have a child. She got pregnant, with mixed feelings.

The husband's suicide was preceded by a dispute between them, which started out, according to her, around "some trifling matter" and then turned into a fit of rage during which she struck her husband. "I was aggressive, even violent." The dispute took place in the bedroom. When she turned around to leave the room, her husband shot himself. Following the event, the mother experienced severe feelings of guilt and suicidal thoughts, but she never actually attempted to do the deed. These feelings of guilt underlay her pathological grief; her refusal to resume a normal, active life (work, family, and social connections); and her anger at others who had gone on with their lives. She decided to go on with the pregnancy "because everyone promised to help me." Truly enough, the family did see to all her basic needs and continued to assist her on a daily basis ("They have to, because I can't do everything alone, and they did promise to help me.").

The baby was actually raised by five figures: his four grandparents and mother. His main caregiver was his maternal grandmother, whereas the others "took turns," mostly afternoons. The child spent all his weekends at his maternal grandparents' place, "so that I can have some time for myself," said the mother, "even though I sometimes feel that he is like a package being moved around."

Parental projections of the narcissistic type (understanding the child through her own needs) were evident in the way the mother described her everyday life with A. For example, she combined breastfeeding with bottle feeding for 6 months and explained that A. adapted himself to her needs, as if he was making things easier for her. When it came to sleep, the mother reported that A. slept whole nights from an early age, with the added comment that "He adapted himself to me, or maybe he is just like me. I too need many hours of sleep. He is an accommodating baby, who does not wake up his mommy in the morning. When I wake up, he is usually awake already; I hear him mumbling to himself. He does not cry until I show up, unless he is very hungry or bored. Sometimes it's 9:30 in the morning, even 10:00." As far as play was concerned, the mother said that "A. can occupy himself alone." However, she also made negative and persecutory comments about the baby, such as "Sometimes I get the feeling that he is happy to be rid of me . . . that deep down he is tricking me."

During the evaluation, the mother's personality traits slowly came to light. For instance, she functioned as "her internal time" dictated: She was constantly late and talked slowly with no regard for the allotted session time. She had always had few social contacts and avoided crowds. She was angry at how her family had behaved following the birth: "On the one hand, they prepared everything at home for me, including a nanny; they organized everything for me to be ready on time, but they all went back to life: My mother-in-law even went to the hairdresser's a week after the funeral." Her father-in-law, according to her complaint, was unreliable: "He comes whenever it suits him, not when I need him."

The mother felt guilty around her husband's suicide, on account of the dispute that had preceded it, and held on to the image of her symbiotic relationship with her spouse. She refused to accept her new status of mother and widow (she did not change her marital status on her identity card). She similarly refused to use the word "mother" when she referred to herself.

During the evaluation, the 11-month-old baby turned out to be well-developed, interactive, and full of vitality. His exploratory behavior was, however, excessive and came at the expense of seeking his mother's proximity. His attachment was of the avoidant type, as evidenced during the session when the mother went out to the toilet without saying a word to A., who continued to play with the therapist (a stranger to him) without showing any sign of distress and did not turn his head to look at the door when she came back in. During their interactions, the mother did not encourage the child's attachment behaviors toward her, thinking that "A. might be better off growing up in another, normal family, without becoming attached to me. And besides, in this way he will not suffer if I commit suicide."

It was patently evident that the mother and infant were working apart without converging: The mother had trouble engaging in spontaneous play with the child ("What am I supposed to do?"), talked about him more than to him, made little emotional contact with him, and talked a lot about herself.

The *DC:0-5™: Diagnostic Classification of Mental Health and Developmental Disorders of Infancy and Early Childhood* (DC:0-5; ZERO TO THREE, 2016) diagnoses would be as follows:

- Axis I: Clinical Disorder
  - » Relationship Specific Disorder of Infancy/Early Childhood (with mother)
- Axis II: Relational Context
  - » Level 3—Compromised to Disturbed relationship
- Axis III: Medical Condition
  - » None
- Axis IV: Psychosocial Stressor
  - » Suicide of father during pregnancy
- Axis V: Developmental Competence
  - » Functions at age-appropriate level

The chosen mode of therapy for mother and infant was attachment-based interactive guidance. The mother was followed by an adult psychiatrist, who was in touch with our treating team. The psychiatrist diagnosed her with Borderline Personality Disorder and Dysthymia (which did not warrant prescription of medication). During the interview with the psychiatrist, the mother denied any suicidal intention or intention to hurt her son. A. also entered day care.

When treatment started, the mother would regularly come in late (by at least 15 minutes). The therapist felt that "she was walking on eggs" for fear that the mother "would commit suicide or stop coming with her son." She would not answer her phone but left messages on the unit's answering machine at 11:00 p.m. Progressively, the therapeutic relationship changed: The mother became cooperative, arrived on time, and returned phone calls.

When viewing a videotaped session together, the therapist asked "What do you think the child felt and thought in this segment?"—to which the mother replied, "He is stubborn, and he's playing me, but it's also a good thing, because it means that he is a smart kid, not some puppet . . . I just can't figure him out; I'm worried about those quick transitions from enjoyment and happiness to anger and impatience. The two of us are walking parallel paths, each doing what he thinks. I want an egalitarian relationship:

'I'll do things for you, and you will be considerate toward me'; me and him, we're like a couple."

A turning point in therapy came when the mother wondered why her boy was mad at her. She hypothesized that the anger had something to do with what was going on between them: "Perhaps he feels that I am abandoning him; maybe he remembers his first months of life, when I wasn't there for him." This was the first indicator of the ability to attribute emotional motives to her son's behavior (what we call "parental reflective functioning"). By the end of 3 full years of treatment, the mother–child relationship greatly improved, and the child was asymptomatic.

Triadic Setting

In the past, the mother–child dyad was more commonly treated than the mother–baby–father triad for several reasons. First, mothers were supposedly more regularly available for treatment, whereas fathers were not expected to attend on the pretext of having to work. Second, and more important, the child's primary relationship with his mother was long considered primordial for his development. More recently, the father's importance in the child's normative development has become evident. For the father to also attend treatment is therefore highly valuable. Our experience has taught us that when clinicians are convinced how important it is for the father to come to the clinic, the father commits to the task and makes the time required.

The triadic setting allows clinicians to work on coparenting—that is, the extent to which parents work or not as an effective team, with mutual respect and solidarity. Parents with effective coparenting are capable of recognizing that their child's optimal development occurs in the context of a good relationship with each of them, whereas one parent's denigration of the other harms the child. The emotional bond between parents and their mutual respect matter more for the baby's emotional development than the distribution of daily chores at home. Two concepts must be differentiated: coparenting and the conjugal relationship. In fact, parents who have just separated may well maintain good coparenting that is also effective for the baby. However, continuous disruption of coparenting, with each parent imparting to the child different, even contradictory, rules, and norms of behavior with relation to everyday activities (eating, sleeping, playing) makes it hard for the child to achieve inner equilibrium and to self-regulate. Thus, behavioral disorders can appear even if the child has a relatively good dyadic relationship with each of his parents. Research (McHale & Rasmussen, 1998) has shown a direct relationship between children's behavioral problems and the quality of coparenting. The latter can be assessed using the McHale Coparenting Interview (McHale, 2007) using the following questions:

- What are the most significant differences of opinion between you on how your child should be raised?

- Do you think these differences affect your child?
- Are there certain situations in which you find it difficult to trust in your partner when it comes to caring for your child?
- Do you often criticize your partner's parental behavior?
- Do you sometimes feel that your partner does not support you?
- When you try to bring up these differences between you, to what extent can such a conversation lead to agreement between you?
- How often do you complain about your partner to your child?

We have added two questions to this interview:

- Do you remember how your own parents worked together at raising you?
- Do you think it has any bearing on your way of being a parent?

The goal of triadic treatment is thus to work together with the parents to identify foci of coparenting difficulties, explore their source with them, and ultimately improve their child's schema of being with mom and dad.

CASE STUDY

P., a 4-month-old baby girl was addressed to our unit for refusing to eat when awake. P., the only child of a young couple, ate well during her first 2 weeks in her grandmother's arms. Her mother had been hospitalized after birth because of a fever. When the mother came back home, the little girl refused to eat from a bottle, and the parents fed her mainly in her sleep. She gradually developed a sleeping disorder. During the first session, even though they all sat together on the carpet, there was little exchange and lack of mutual pleasure. We proposed to the parents to set up "a family game" based on the Lausanne Triadic Play paradigm (see chapter 3) and videotape it. Viewing the video of the session together with the parents allowed them to identify the competitive nature of their interpersonal communication. The therapist pointed out the link between their behavior, of the competitive-anxious type, and the internal representations they had of their own parents (on the basis of information that each of them had provided during the first meeting).

A decisive moment occurred when each of the parents understood, with the therapist's help, just how much the other parent lacked self-confidence as a parent. By the end of five sessions of parents–baby psychotherapy, their baby girl ate while awake and slept uninterrupted, whereas the parents felt far more competent as parents, both together and individually.

Parent–Infant Group Therapy

This relatively frequent type of treatment makes it possible to create a therapeutic space that facilitates multiaxial communication among parents, babies, and group therapists. It encourages inquisitiveness on both the parent's and the child's side. In group therapy, the participants' emotional experiences are discussed reflectively, giving parents (father or mother) a chance to deepen their understanding of the link between emotions and behaviors. In structural terms, these are usually 90-minute sessions involving four to six parent–baby dyads, two co-therapists, and an observer who documents the session in writing or on film. A session usually opens with a common activity such as passing a ball around, or a children's song, and then moves on to free play between parents and babies. The therapists first observe what happens in the group, and then it is time for reflecting (similar to the WWW method described previously). The group functions as a receptacle for the participants' emotions. Each session ends on a common activity such as a song or a game, whose goal is to ensure continuity of the shared positive emotional experience.

Individual Treatment of Toddlers

In those rare cases in which a parent's presence is extremely obstructive to treatment because of extremely pathological projections onto the child, individual treatment needs to be considered for the toddler. The parents in question generally suffer from psychiatric disorders and a highly symbiotic relationship with the toddler. It is important to note that this type of treatment is rarely used for children less than 3 years old.

Pharmacotherapy in Infancy

Rarely do clinicians offer medication-based treatment in infancy when it comes to babies or toddlers with serious emotional problems that cause suffering and disrupt functioning. In the last decade, there has been a sharp increase in the use of medication to treat young children, in particular the use of stimulants to manage Attention Deficit Hyperactivity Disorder and of antipsychotic drugs to treat severe anxieties and behavioral problems. Not knowing as yet how exactly these medications affect the evolving brain, we recommend drugs only as a last resort and only in situations that jeopardize the toddler. One must keep in mind that side effects are more common the younger the child is, which is why a minimal dosage should be initially administered. It is important to explain to parents that medications are just one side of the overall treatment and are in no way an alternative for psychotherapy. Some parents see medications as a panacea, and some even pressure the physician into prescribing them. Others see the administration of medication confirmation that their child is ill, and they object to its use.

L., a 2-year and 10-month-old toddler, underwent surgery for a tumor in her brain. Following the operation, the girl started demanding food all the time, day and night. She would scream for hours throughout the night. The parents were exhausted and at a loss. The biological cause of constant hunger was damage to the satiety locus in the brain, which lay close to the tumor. However, it was also clear that there was a behavioral component involved because the child would sometimes declare she was not hungry during the day. It was also clear that the parents were unable to set her boundaries (which they had no trouble doing with their first two children) because they pitied her. It is also possible that L.'s multiple nighttime arousals were caused by nightmares relating to painful treatments that she received to treat her cancer.

The DC:0–5 diagnoses would be as follows:

- Axis I: Clinical Disorder
  - » Overeating Disorder

- Axis II: Relational Context
  - » Level 2—Strained to Concerning dyadic relationships
  - » Level 2—Strained to Concerning caregiving environment

- Axis III: Medical Condition
  - » Brain tumor

- Axis IV: Psychosocial Stressor
  - » None

- Axis V: Developmental Competence
  - » Competencies are inconsistently present or emerging

An interactional guidance therapy was set up, in addition to a sedative prescribed to reduce the little girl's nocturnal agitation. The guidance provided to the parents around their difficulty to set the child clear and consistent boundaries during the day, combined with the soothing effect of the medication, greatly decreased her demands to be fed.

The Therapeutic Environment

The location where therapy takes place directly influences the therapeutic dynamic. It can take place at a community-based clinic, the family's home, a pediatric hospital ward, or perhaps even the institution in which the child is staying.

Therapy at Home

Selma Fraiberg (1980), a social worker and psychoanalyst by training, emphasized the need for flexibility and degrees of freedom in methods used to treat families not naturally inclined to seek psychotherapy. These are parents who have largely lost their faith in the establishment in general, and in mental health services in particular, mostly because of negative past experiences in this area. The therapist's readiness to make time and leave the clinic, a symbol of her status, conveys respect and gives the parent a sense of control. Indeed, the basic distrust that characterizes these families makes it necessary, at the initial stage of therapy, to establish a positive and reliable relationship between parent and therapist. The home environment is conducive to a relationship of this sort: The therapist is no longer a patronizing figure but more of a consultant serving the baby's physical and emotional needs. The therapist "nurtures" the parent by providing support and practical help in taking care of the infant. That being said, the clinician must preserve the therapeutic character of home sessions, maintain the accepted boundaries, and thus prevent the session from becoming a social encounter.

CASE STUDY

The mother of G., a 1-year and 8-month-old boy, was addressed to us by her psychiatrist because of her poor relationship with her child. G. was born in the 32nd week of pregnancy weighing 1,500 grams, and he remained in neonatal intensive care for 5 weeks. When G. was 8 months old, his mother was hospitalized with psychotic depression for several months. His paternal grandmother took care of him since he was 2 months old, with the consent of both parents and the welfare services. G. slept in that part of the house where his grandfather and grandmother lived. He had no trouble separating from his grandmother every morning when he went to day care.

The mother first became ill at around 15 years old with anorexia and bulimia nervosa. At 22 years old, she was hospitalized for the first time in a psychiatric ward and was diagnosed with schizophrenia. She married at 25 years old, giving birth to G. a year later.

G.'s father was adopted when he was 1 month old. The paternal grandmother described him as a quiet, solitary boy who had had learning difficulties throughout his school years and who found permanent work as a driver. He met his wife through a local newspaper ad. He was diligent and persevering in his work, leaving the house at 5 in the morning and returning at 7 in the evening. He manifested a lot of tenderness toward G. yet was incapable of caring for him on his own.

The first session was held at our unit. The father entered the room carrying G.—then 1 year and 10 months old—in his arms. The mother marched behind them, slightly hunched over. They heeded the therapist's invitation to sit down on the carpet. G. examined the toys and seemed to take particular interest in two of them. He pulled away from his father and made his way toward the hooking rings. During the next half hour, the toddler never turned even once to his father or mother. He looked bigger than his age. He wore glasses, which made him look "serious" even though he occasionally laughed.

The DC:0–5 diagnoses would be as follows:

- Axis I: Clinical Disorder
    - » Relationship Specific Disorder of Infancy/Early Childhood (with mother and father)
- Axis II: Relational Context
    - » Level 4—Disordered to Dangerous mother–child relationship
    - » Level 3—Compromised to Disturbed father–child relationship
    - » Level 4—Disordered to Dangerous caregiving environment
- Axis III: Medical Condition
    - » Post-prematurity vision problem
- Axis IV: Psychosocial Stressors
    - » Maternal mental illness
    - » Paternal poor intellectual capacities
- Axis V: Developmental Competence
    - » Functions at age-appropriate level

This diagnosis served as the basis for constructing the treatment program. First, home-based treatment was decided. In fact, right from the first session, which was cancelled three times and therefore only took place 2 months after the initial referral, we understood that the family would not be able to attend regular visits to the clinic. The parents accepted our suggestion. The following objectives were set:

- In regard to the toddler: reinforce his relationship with his mother as well as help him understand that his mother "can take care of him a little," that his grandma "can take care of him a lot but also knows how to leave room for mommy," and that his father "can also take care of him but has to work."
- In regard to the mother: reduce her fear of being alone with her son, teach her basics in child development, reinforce her self-confidence within the triad including her mother-in-law and her husband, and work on her feelings of jealousy toward her mother-in-law.
- In regard to the father: increase his involvement with the child.
- In regard to the grandmother: make space for the mother and give more responsibilities to the father in the child's daily care.

This is how the first home session transpired: The mother opened the door to her living quarters. The grandmother, holding G. in her arms, emerged from the grandparents' quarters. We assembled in the central room of the house, explained to those present the principles of the therapy, and discussed what the parents expected of therapy and what the therapists expected of the parents (the process of establishing the therapeutic alliance). Our first therapeutic decision was to start the treatment in the room built for G. in the parents' quarters (one he never slept in). The grandmother was asked to leave the room. The mother looked helpless and nervous, and she had a hard time getting organized even when the therapist guided her. She hesitated about where to sit and what to start with, but then she slowly settled down. She then took out toys from the basket near the bed and was absorbed in finding a game that G. would like. She asked him what he would like to play, without, however, looking at him to see his reaction. The therapist addressed G., saying, "Today, mommy is feeling better and wants to play with G.; show mommy how you like to play with this." The mother responded to this with sadness: "He really never plays with me. Sometimes he wants to, but I can't." Throughout the session, there was no physical contact between the mother and the toddler, and little eye contact seemed to take place. Still, G. never stopped trying to let his mother in on the games.

After a year of treatment, the mother's ability to be near her son, to talk to him, and to touch him markedly improved. The father became much more involved, and the grandmother started trusting him more. The mother's chronic mental illness persisted, which led to yet another hospitalization. Consequently, custody of the child was officially given to the grandmother. G. did not develop any new behavioral or emotional symptoms and continued to function well thanks to the prolonged therapeutic embrace and the grandmother's unusual competency.

Treatment Within the Pediatric Ward in a General Hospital

Pediatrics and child psychiatry are not only distinct disciplines but two different ports of entry into the child's being. The pediatrician's every therapeutic effort is aimed at eradicating a symptom that the child has. For the psychiatrist, each symptom contains a message that needs to be deciphered. The pediatrician feels more comfortable relying on "objective" examinations and lab findings, whereas the psychiatrist prefers addressing the emotional component as she experiences it. It is important that psychiatrists and pediatricians acknowledge these different approaches and pull together. The pediatrician strives to eradicate the pain, whereas the psychiatrist seeks to prevent its emotional consequences.

Among other things, the role of mental health professionals within the general pediatric ward is to explain to the toddler in words what goes on around him and inside his body, to encourage him, to play with him, and to help him express his emotions. In regard to the parents, the clinicians' role is to present to them the needs of the baby who is ill, to support them, to explain to them that their parental role continues even during hospitalization, and to encourage them to go on educating and setting boundaries for their child. Vis- à-vis the medical team, the role of the child psychiatrist is to call their attention to the emotional experience and reactions of the child who is hospitalized. At times, clinicians serve as mediators between the parents and the treating team. The parents and the medical staff are often oblivious to the child's emotional and developmental needs, masked as they are by his frightening chronic illness. A case that illustrates this is presented next.

CASE STUDY

J., an only child, was referred when he was 1 year and 9 months old, with a view to wean him off his gastrostomy tube. He was born after multiple fertility treatments. On the fourth day of his life, serious vomiting appeared, and he was diagnosed with a severe congenital liver disease, along with a heart defect and renal insufficiency. J. spent a whole year in the hospital because of a fever of undetected origin. The parents were afraid to bring him home. For some unknown reason, he stopped eating at 10 months, and a gastrostomy tube had to be inserted. J. also developed breath-holding spells, and the parents started to avoid frustrating him for fear of his crying. Thus, during the first consultation with the parents and the child, J. could even walk over his mother's foot without her objecting: "What difference does it make. I'm not even sure how much longer he will live . . . why insist on boundaries with him anyway?" the mother answered the child psychiatrist, who was surprised at her reticence to set J. limits.

Consequently, J. conducted himself like a little tyrant, and both his parents were relegated to the position of exhausted, angry, and anxious valets. The severity of his medical condition obfuscated the child's developmental needs in the eyes of the parents and the hospital staff. The idea of putting him in day care, for example, was rejected outright, even though everyone clearly understood that spending whole days at home with his mother had a deleterious effect on his emotional development. In addition, the parents' coparenting was poor, and their own marital relationship was unstable and stormy.

The DC:0–5 diagnoses would be as follows:

- Axis I: Clinical Disorders
  - » Adjustment Disorder
  - » Relationship Specific Disorder of Infancy/Early Childhood (with mother)
- Axis II: Relational Context
  - » Level 3—Compromised to Disturbed mother–child relationship
  - » Level 3—Compromised to Disturbed caregiving environment
- Axis III: Medical Conditions
  - » Severe congenital liver and kidney disease
  - » Gastrostomy tube
- Axis IV: Psychosocial Stressor
  - » Parental and marital severe discord
- Axis V: Developmental Competence
  - » Functions at age-appropriate level

The family was offered triadic treatment that would encourage a clear, straightforward discourse around the disease; try to improve coparenting; and help J. wean off the gastrostomy. Therapy started off with "speaking the illness" together with the child. We viewed the refusal to eat and the breath-holding spells as somatic manifestations of the child's emotional distress linked both to his illness and to the family relationships. The parents and the medical staff responded with amazement to the idea of speaking the illness: "What's the point of talking to him about it? He's not even 2!" We chose to talk about the liver disease in the simplest and most concrete terms: "the disease of being very, very yellow." J. was very much able to relate to this metaphor.

Two months into treatment, J. went into day care with no separation difficulties (the mother was even offended by his ease of separation, and she needed to be reminded of the positive meaning of this behavior). J. began to express anger directly at his parents, and as he did so, the breath-holding spells all but disappeared. The emotional improvement was accompanied by a relapse in his physical condition, and we had to prepare him emotionally for a liver transplant. Talking about the body became even more pertinent, and it is only then that the parents began to realize that J. too, like any child of his age, was busy developing a physical self-image and a sexual identity. The notion of physical privacy was theretofore nonexistent in the house. At one point, the mother allowed herself to detach herself from her son and leave for a few days with her sister. J. stayed with his father and started tasting food. "I want to eat with my mouth," he said. Unfortunately, the process of weaning off the gastrostomy tube was interrupted with the sudden deterioration in the liver functioning and the need to prepare him for surgery.

At 3 years old, J. went abroad with his mother to "make the yellow disappear for good." The transplant and subsequent treatment lasted an entire year. J.'s mother was by his side throughout that year. The therapeutic relationship continued by e-mail, giving the mother a sense of security. The child got off the tube and the diapers. Six months later, he had a transient vascular brain event that required arteriography under full anesthesia. This time around, he could express his feelings with words: "I don't want the anesthesia, I'm afraid I might not wake up . . . I'm afraid of dying." He said this to his sister, feeling that his parents would have a hard time hearing him talk like this. Despite everything, J. made it through the procedure, continued to be followed up at the hospital, and is now a functioning—although quite timid—adolescent in good health.

Conclusion

In this chapter, we discussed the principles of treating infants and young children and their parents. We looked at different therapy methods in different contexts, showing that they were all based on the infant's presence, whatever her age, in the therapy room with one or both parents, and the use of nonverbal as well as verbal communication among the child, the parents, and the therapist. The attempt to understand the child and her relationships with the environment and to facilitate parental empathy always takes center stage. Finally, as we have shown, there is little room for medications in the treatment of infants because they are rarely necessary and their potential effect on the developing brain is unclear.

References

Beebe, B., & Lachmann, F. (2002). *Infant research and adult treatment: Co-constructing interactions*. Hillsdale, NJ: The Analytic Press.

Fivaz-Depeursinge, E., & Corboz-Warnery, A. (1999). *The primary triangle*. New York, NY: Basic Behavioral Science.

Fraiberg, S. (1980). *Clinical studies in infant mental health: The first year of life*. New York, NY: Basic Books.

Koren-Karie, N., Oppenheim, D., Dolev, S., Sher, E., & Etzion-Carasso, A. (2002). Mother's empathic understanding of their infants' internal experience: Relations with maternal sensitivity and infant attachment. *Developmental Psychology, 38*, 534–542.

McDonough, S. (2000). Interactive guidance: An approach for difficult-to-engage families. In C. H. Zeanah, Jr. (Ed.), *Handbook of infant mental health* (2nd ed., pp. 485–493). New York, NY: Guilford Press.

McHale, J. P. (1997). Overt and covert coparenting processes in the family. *Family Process, 36*,183–201.

McHale, J. P. (2007). *Charting the bumpy road of coparenthood: Understanding the challenges of family life*. Washington, DC: ZERO TO THREE.

McHale, J. P., & Rasmussen, J. L.(1998). Coparental and family group-level dynamics during infancy: Early family precursors of child and family functioning during preschool. *Development and Psychopathology, 10*, 39–59.

Olds, D., Henderson, C. H., Cole, R., Eckenrode, J., Kitzman, H., Luckey, D., . . . Poweers, J. (1998). Long-term effects of nurse home visitation on children's criminal and antisocial behavior: 15-year follow-up of a randomized controlled trial. *JAMA, 280*, 1238–1244.

Olds, D. L., Robinson, J., O'Brien, R., Luckey, D. W., Pettitt, L. M., Henderson, C. R., Jr., . . . Talmi, A. (2002). Home visiting by paraprofessionals and by nurses: A randomized, controlled trial. *Pediatrics, 110*, 486–496.

Reynolds, D. (2003). Mindful parenting: A group approach to enhancing reflective capacity in parents and infants. *Journal of Child Psychotherapy, 29*, 357–374.

Stern, D. N. (1995). *The motherhood constellation: A unified view of parent-infant psychotherapy*. New York, NY: Basic Books.

Tronick, E. Z., & Cohn, J. F. (1989). Infant–mother face-to-face interaction: Age and gender differences in coordination and the occurrence of miscoordination. *Child Development, 60,* 85–92.

Van den Boom, D. C. (1995). Do first year intervention effects endure? Follow-up study. *Child Development, 66,* 1798–1816.

ZERO TO THREE. (2016). *DC:0–5™: Diagnostic classification of mental health and developmental disorders of infancy and early childhood* (DC:0–5). Washington, DC: Author.

Recommended Reading

Cohen, N. J., Muir, E., Lojkasek, M., Muir, R., Parker, C. J., Barwick, M., & Brown, M. (1999). Watch, Wait, and Wonder: Testing the effectiveness of a new approach to mother–infant psychotherapy. *Infant Mental Health Journal, 20,* 429–451.

Favez, N., Frascarolo, F., Keren, M., & Fivaz-Depeursinge, E. (2009). Principles of family therapy in infancy. In C. H. Zeanah, Jr. (Ed.), *Handbook of infant mental health* (3rd ed., pp. 468–484). New York, NY: Guilford Press.

Lieberman, A. F., & Van Horn, P. (2009). Child–parent psychotherapy: A developmental approach to mental health treatment in infancy and early childhood. In C. H. Zeanah, Jr. (Ed.), *Handbook of infant mental health* (3rd ed., pp. 439–449), New York, NY: Guilford Press.

Marvin, R., Cooper, G., Hoffman, K., & Powell, B. (2002). The Circle of Security project: Attachment-based intervention with caregiver–preschool child dyads. *Attachment and Human Development, 1,* 107–124.

Oppenheim, D., & Goldsmith, D. F. (2007). *Attachment theory in clinical work with children.* New York, NY: Guilford Press.

Rusconi-Serpa, S., Rossignol, A. S., & McDonough, S. C. (2009). Video feedback in parent–infant treatments. *Child and Adolescent Psychiatric Clinics of North America, 18,* 735–751.

Sameroff, A. J., McDonough, S. C., & Rosenblum, K. L. (2004). *Treating parent–infant relationship problems: Strategies for intervention.* New York, NY: Guilford Press.

Solnit, A. J., Cohen, D. J., & Neubauer, P. B. (1993). *The many meanings of play—A psychoanalytic perspective.* New Haven, CT: Yale University Press.

Tortora, S. (2010). Ways of seeing: An early childhood integrated therapeutic approach for parents and babies. *Clinical Social Work Journal, 38,* 37–50.

Tuters, E., & Gauthier, Y. (Eds.). (2011). The practice of clinical infant mental health [Special issue]. *Infant Mental Health Journal, 32*(6).

EPILOGUE

Clinical work with infants and young children and their parents is enriching, diverse, and fascinating. Each encounter teaches us something about children's capabilities. In each session, we are surprised to discover the extent to which they are capable of understanding what goes on around them and adapting accordingly. However, the changes required for their normative development also depend on their parents—on their ability to understand and change. We must keep on researching and understanding the capabilities with which babies come into the world, the processes that take place inside their brains, and all the factors that influence the nature of their behavior. This is a never-ending quest.

In this book, we described the known factors responsible for the emergence of various problems in the baby's socioemotional development. We particularly tried to show the importance of seeking treatment immediately after detecting symptoms of distress to prevent problems from deteriorating or becoming permanently fixed in place.

Our ability to treat babies and toddlers has increased over the years. We believe that we have been able to help many babies and toddlers and their parents and quite often to head off the emergence of a more difficult disorder.

We hope that we have been able to convince you that . . . time does not heal all.

ACKNOWLEDGMENTS

We thank Professor Yoram Yovell, Nitza Brenner, Dina and Yehuda Ilan, Shula Modan, and Tammy Burstein for contributing their time and many skills in reading drafts of this book. Thank you for the proofreading, the constructive comments, and the original ideas you have contributed to us along the writing process.

—Miri, Doreet, and Sam

ABOUT THE AUTHORS

Dr. Miri Keren, a psychiatrist with extensive clinical experience, marries a medico-biological approach with a psychological-emotional understanding of things from a social and cultural perspective. She was formerly president of the World Association for Infant Mental Health.

Dr. Doreet Hopp, a literary scholar with a keen eye for the psychological, lays out an array of literary heroes through which she looks at the interpersonal relationship that toddlers have with themselves and their family.

Prof. Sam Tyano is a psychiatrist highly experienced in working with all age groups, from infancy to adulthood. He is honorary president of the Israel Child and Adolescent Psychiatric Association.

REPRINT PERMISSIONS